SECURING COMPLIANCE

Bargaining, negotiation and civil penalty sanctions together constitute central techniques used by regulators in securing compliance with the law. This book is a timely exploration of these practices, constructing a principled framework for evaluating their legitimacy and thereby drawing into sharper focus the importance of the constitutional principles in regulatory compliance. Although Australian competition law provides the focal point of the book, its analysis and critique is equally applicable to other competition law regimes and to other areas of business regulation. While there are numerous empirical studies of regulatory enforcement, this book introduces a normative dimension to the debate by seeking to identify whether there are certain principled and ethical limits that inform and circumscribe the limits of legitimate enforcement practice. It is likely to be of interest to scholars in the fields of public law, criminology, economics, and regulation, and may also be of considerable assistance to legal practitioners in providing a principled, legal foundation from which to draw in their dealings with regulators.

Securing Compliance
A Principled Approach

KAREN YEUNG
St Anne's College, Oxford

·HART·
PUBLISHING

OXFORD AND PORTLAND, OREGON
2004

Hart Publishing
Oxford and Portland, Oregon

Published in North America (US and Canada) by
Hart Publishing c/o
International Specialized Book Services
5804 NE Hassalo Street
Portland, Oregon
97213-3644
USA

Hart Publishing is a specialist legal publisher based in Oxford, England.
To order further copies of this book or to request a list of other
publications please write to:

Hart Publishing, Salter's Boatyard, Folly Bridge,
Abingdon Road, Oxford OX1 4LB
Telephone: +44 (0)1865 245533 or Fax: +44 (0)1865 794882
e-mail: mail@hartpub.co.uk
WEBSITE: http//www.hartpub.co.uk

British Library Cataloguing in Publication Data
Data Available
ISBN 1–84113–377–9 (hardback)

Typeset by Hope Services (Abingdon) Ltd.

www.bloomsbury.com

Contents

Part II

Part III

Preface

This book originated from discussions with Allan Fels, a former Chairman of the Australian Competition and Consumer Commission, Australia's competition regulator, concerning several aspects of the Commission's enforcement practice that had generated low-level mutterings of discontent within the Australian legal and business communities. Those discussions led me to undertake a more thorough investigation for the Commission into several of the sanctions and strategies that it had employed in securing compliance with competition law. Although my report, which was largely reproduced in published form by the Commission as a policy monograph in 2001, entitled The Public Enforcement of Australian Competition Law, documented most of the findings of that investigation, I was left with a nagging sense of curiosity. Like a child who has just discovered the existence of a treasure chest hidden at the bottom of the garden, I wished to excavate further and deeper, to discover whether I could unlock the mysteries which my initial policy-level inquiry had unearthed. The opportunity to embark upon this deeper, scholarly investigation came in the form of a doctoral thesis, undertaken through the Oxford University Law Faculty where I had already been teaching and researching for several years, and it is my doctoral thesis that provides the foundational material and analysis upon which this book has been crafted and constructed.

One of my animating justifications in writing this book is to provide a normative framework of principles, drawn from public law norms, against which regulatory enforcement and implementation processes may be evaluated. In the course of my attempts to identify why certain aspects of the Commission's enforcement processes and practices had generated controversy, I was struck by the absence of a set of principled and rigorously developed guidelines for informing and shaping the scope and limits of legitimate regulatory enforcement practice. While there is a rich and fertile body of scholarship documenting the findings of a number of ethnographic studies seeking to understand the behaviour of regulatory enforcement officials in seeking to secure compliance, and a well-developed literature exploring rather abstract notions of regulatory legitimacy, there is a relative paucity of normative analysis occupying the interstices between these two bodies of literature. Although a distinct body of regulatory writing is specifically oriented towards regulatory techniques and instruments, it has been largely concerned with selecting legal forms which can most effectively achieve the instrumental goals of collective choice, tending to view regulatory processes and strategies as essentially technocratic in orientation. By adopting a public law approach, my exploration of regulatory enforcement processes is explicitly value-laden, setting out to understand and assess regulatory enforcement practices by reference to 'constitutional values', values rooted in foundational principles of public law and drawing from both administrative law and criminal law norms. In writing this book, I hope not only to illustrate that an evaluation of regulatory instruments and techniques cannot be wholly divorced from normative values, but also to stimulate further debate and reflection about the kinds of values that ought to underpin and infuse regulatory processes.

This book may be understood at several different levels. At its thinnest, it may be understood as an examination of the legality of specific aspects of the public enforcement of Australian competition law. But it may also be understood in a deeper, richer sense. Although the public enforcement of competition law forms the focus point of my inquiry, my concern is with the public enforcement of regulatory law more generally—and competition law serves as a valuable context for identifying the scope and content of legitimate regulatory enforcement practice. Likewise, the notion of 'legality' which I adopt throughout this book entails both 'thin' or technical legality, denoting conformity with specific legal rules and doctrine, and 'thick' legality, referring to the extent to which a specific enforcement practice or activity gives expression to constitutional values. Finally, although I draw primarily (although not exclusively) from the Australian experience of public competition law enforcement, this is used merely to illustrate in more concrete terms the somewhat abstract analytical claims that form the basis of my argument, rather than to suggest that the Australian experience is particularly unusual or idiosyncratic. On the contrary, the challenges and difficulties faced by the Australian Competition and Consumer Commission in seeking to secure compliance with competition law are in many respects rather typical of those confronted not merely by competition regulators in other jurisdictions, but by regulatory enforcement agencies and officials more generally, so that the Australian context serves more general illustrative purposes.

The debt which I owe to those who provided me with assistance, encouragement and stimulus is a large one. Many friends and colleagues have encouraged and supported me in the preparation of this book, and the doctoral thesis upon which it is based, without whom the process of its writing would have been a considerably more arduous task. They are too numerous to name, but this should not detract from my gratitude for them. Special acknowledgment is due, however, to Liora Lazarus, not only for inspiring me to embark on the doctoral thesis in the first place, but also for her loyalty, integrity and good humour as both a trusted friend and colleague. I am also indebted to Allan Fels, for initiating the research that provided the original foundations of this book, and I have benefited enormously from his thoughtful insights and his continual encouragement. I am also indebted to the Australian Competition and Consumer Commission, for providing me access to source material that is not publicly available, and for the helpfulness and enthusiasm of several members of the Commission who assisted me with my inquiries. Thanks are also due to St Anne's College, in providing a stimulating and supportive environment in which to work, and also for generous financial assistance in supporting my underlying doctoral studies. Sections of this book were critically scrutinised by Simon Halliday, Timothy Endicott and Euan Graham, and I am particularly grateful to Bronwen Morgan who bravely read the entire manuscript and provided constructive and insightful comments. Special thanks are also due to my research assistant, Okeoghene Odudu, whose steadfast refusal to accept any of my arguments without searching and scrupulous justification kept me on my toes throughout the course of writing up the manuscript, and he provided much needed objectivity in identifying sections of the work which required further clarification, elaboration and reorganisation. My primary expression of gratitude and appreciation lies, however, with my doctoral supervisors, Andrew Ashworth and Denis Galligan. They were rigorous and unforgiving in their scrutiny of my work, whilst never tiring in the warmth and generosity of their encouragement. Without their guidance, this book would have remained little more than a rather undisciplined collection of related ideas rather than what is, I hope, a scholarly accomplishment. Finally, thanks are due to my parents—for cultivating my belief in the value of academic endeavour, and for continually encouraging me to have the faith and confidence to rise to any challenge I may happen to encounter.

The law is as stated at 31 July 2003.

St Anne's College, Oxford
3 December 2003

Abbreviations and Terminology

Act	Trade Practices Act 1974
ADJR Act	Administrative Decisions (Judicial Review) Act 1977
ADR	Alternative Dispute Resolution
Anglian	Shorthand description of the legal tradition underpinning the English, Australian and North American legal systems
ASIC	Australian Securities and Investment Commission
Commission	Australian Competition and Consumer Commission
Dawson Inquiry	Review of the Competition Provisions of the Trade Practices Act
Dawson Report	Report of the Trade Practices Act Review Committee, January 2003
DoJ	US Department of Justice
DPP	Director of Public Prosecutions
ECHR	European Convention on Human Rights
EU	European Union
FTC	Federal Trade Commission
Hilmer Report	Report of the Independent Committee of Inquiry (1993)
HSR Act	Hart-Scott-Rodino Antitrust Improvement Act 1976
Merger Guideline	ACCC Merger Guidelines (1999)
MMC	Monopolies and Mergers Commission
NPM	New Public Management
NPR	National Performance Review
OECD	Organisation for Economic Co-operation and Development
OFT	Office of Fair Trading
OSHA	Occupational Health and Safety Authority
Policy Guideline	ACCC, *Section 87B of the Trade Practices Act*, Procedural Guide Series, August 1999
TPC	Trade Practices Commission
Tribunal	Australian Competition Tribunal
Tunney Act	Antitrust Procedures and Penalties Act 1974
WTO	World Trade Organisation

Table of Cases

Australia

United Kingdom

European Court of Human Rights Cases

European Court of Justice

Table of Legislation

STATUTES

Australia

United Kingdom

United States of America

REGULATIONS AND STATUTORY INSTRUMENTS

Australia

TREATIES AND EUROPEAN LEGISLATIVE INSTRUMENTS

EC Legislative Instruments

International Treaties

Part I

1

Introduction

A. COMPETITION, COMPETITION REGULATION AND ENFORCEMENT

COMPETITIVE MARKETS ARE claimed to be vital to the success of any industrialised economy. According to economic orthodoxy, competitive markets enable society's limited resources to be produced and allocated efficiently, thereby promoting economic prosperity. The global push for 'deregulation' and 'microeconomic reform' is underpinned by a widely-held belief in the benefits of competition in generating appropriate incentives for both the private and public sector to carry out their activities in a manner that will promote the community's welfare. But if left to their own devices, markets are unlikely to operate competitively because firms are able to reap greater private profits by engaging in anti-competitive conduct. Competition law is therefore required to regulate business activity that tends to impair the competitive functioning of the market and, for this reason, 66 countries throughout Europe, the Middle East, Asia, Africa, North American, Central and South America and Australasia have adopted some system of competition regulation.[1] Yet this vision of a flourishing, competitive market economy will remain nothing more than an aspiration, however, if competition law is not effectively enforced. As one commentator has observed, the 'life blood' of a scheme of competition regulation is its enforcement, for without it, regulation becomes 'somewhat pointless'.[2]

This book is concerned not with substantive competition law, but with its enforcement. Its central concern is therefore of direct importance to both those interested in competition law and regulatory scholars more generally, for success in achieving the collective goals underpinning any regulatory regime relies critically on the effectiveness of its enforcement regime. It is through the enforcement process that a set of legal standards designed to influence human and institutional behaviour is translated into social reality. Accordingly, this

[1] By 2003, the following countries had established some formal scheme of competition regulation: Argentina, Armenia, Australia, Austria, Belgium, Belize, Brazil, Bulgaria, Canada, Chile, Colombia, Costa Rica, Croatia, Czech Republic, Denmark, Estonia, Finland, France, Germany, Guatemala, Hungary, Iceland, India, Indonesia, Ireland, Italy, Japan, Kenya, Korea, Latvia, Lithuania, Macedonia, Malawi, Malta, Mauritius, Mexico, Moldova, Netherlands, New Zealand, Nicaragua, Norway, Pakistan, Panama, Peru, Philippines, Poland, Portugal, Romania, Russia, Singapore, Slovakia, Slovenia, South Africa, Spain, Sweden, Switzerland, Taiwan, Tajikistan, Thailand, Turkey, Ukraine, United Kingdom, United States of America, Uzbekistan, Venezuela, Zambia.

[2] Pengilley (1984), 19.

book may be interpreted at two levels: as an analysis of various mechanisms for enforcing competition law, and also as an analysis of regulatory enforcement more generally. It focuses specifically on the enforcement of regulatory standards by a public enforcement official, adopting what may be described as a 'public law' perspective. In so doing, it seeks to understand regulatory enforcement activities by examining and evaluating whether, and to what extent, such activities conform with constitutional values, drawing from two sets of well-established public law principles: administrative law and criminal law. Although these two bodies of law are generally classified as forms of public law, they tend to be analysed as separate, independent bodies of law. By adopting regulatory enforcement as the focal point of this inquiry, it serves as an illuminating bridge, linking the two bodies of law by reference to their common constitutional foundations.

In order to highlight the value of a public law perspective, instead of presenting a sweeping and generalised review of the full range of enforcement activities that a regulator might engage in, three specific issues are singled out for in-depth examination: penalty quantification, 'plea bargains' or negotiated penalty settlements and the use of administrative settlements. When viewed contiguously, these three issues not only illuminate the intersection between administrative and criminal law, but also demonstrate how various enforcement practices may place several constitutional values under strain. These three enforcement activities also display differing degrees of formality and severity: the imposition of financial penalties for regulatory contraventions constitutes a formal, essentially punitive, mechanism for securing compliance and thus stands in sharp contrast to the use of informal, non-punitive 'administrative settlements' as a means for responding to suspected contraventions. To the extent that punitive and persuasive techniques of regulatory enforcement form the focal point of this inquiry, it covers well-trodden ground. There is a well-established and extensive literature documenting the findings of a rich and diverse array of ethnographic studies of the behaviour of regulatory enforcement officials, demonstrating their extensive reliance on informal, persuasive techniques, invoking formal punitive mechanisms only as a 'last resort' when informal approaches have failed.[3] A burgeoning normative literature has built upon these empirical findings, seeking to construct models prescribing the 'optimal' mix of punishment and persuasion for securing regulatory compliance.[4] By adopting a public law perspective, my approach may be distinguished from both these strands of scholarship, by seeking to identify a set of constitutional values that ought to shape, inform and constrain the techniques and strategies used by regulators when implementing regulatory programmes. While existing scholarship tends to assume that regulatory implementation, including enforcement, is a largely technocratic enterprise, my approach seeks to demonstrate that these issues cannot be

[3] Below, ch 5, Part B (3).
[4] Below, ch 6, Part B (1) and (2).

divorced from broader, deeper questions about the values that ought to inform regulatory processes.

Before we can embark on our analysis, however, we must first give flesh to the location, context and history of these enforcement practices. Part I of this book is thus divided into three chapters. The remainder of this introductory chapter briefly explores the contested nature of regulation and the process of regulatory implementation, setting out the parameters of my inquiry and the central assumptions upon which my analysis is grounded. Chapter two moves away from the conceptual plane, and is largely descriptive in nature, outlining the justification for modern competition regulation, briefly explaining the economic theory upon which it is based and describes the historical and political context in which it operates. In order to make more concrete the largely abstract and theoretical discussion that constitutes the backbone of this inquiry, throughout this book I have drawn from the Australian experience of enforcing competition law. An overview of Australian competition regulation is therefore provided, setting out the general institutional context within which Australian competition law is publicly enforced. Chapter three then returns to a more abstract and conceptual plane, by constructing the normative framework adopted in this book as the basis for evaluating and analysing regulatory implementation, before finally mapping the direction and content of the subsequent chapters and foreshadowing several key themes that emerge from the ensuing discussion.

B. REGULATION AND REGULATORY COMPLIANCE

1. Understanding Regulation

(a) What is Regulation?

Although the term 'regulation' has been used to encompass a variety of different conceptions,[5] I have adopted the following definition because it comfortably accommodates a wide range of regulatory regimes (including competition regulation) and provides a useful frame for analysing the enforcement activities of a public competition regulator. Regulation is thus conceived as the sustained and focused attempt by the state to alter behaviour thought to be of value to the community.[6] A number of aspects of this conception of regulation require elaboration. First, this conception focuses on purposive[7] attempts by the state to

[5] See Moran (2002); Baldwin *et al* (1998), 1–4.

[6] This definition draws from an amalgam of ideas, strongly influenced (but not identical to) the definitions adopted in the following: Ogus (1994); Selznick (1985); Vincent-Jones (2002); Black (2003).

[7] Vincent Jones emphasises regulation as 'systematic control', thereby not only embracing rules restrictive of behaviour but also includes commands and mechanisms for monitoring and compliance, taxes, subsidies, licensing and inspection: *ibid*.

intervene in economic and social activities and therefore excludes non-state actors from its remit.[8] By focusing on the state as purposeful actor, this does not in any way seek to deny the significance of private actors and civil society more generally in the regulatory process,[9] but their role does not fall within the remit of this inquiry given that my primary concern is to examine the role of a public regulator in enforcing regulatory standards. Secondly, the behaviour that is the subject of regulation is thought to be of value to the community—the primary aim of regulation being to modify that behaviour[10] rather than to punish or censure those engaging in the regulated activity.[11] In this way, conduct sanctioned by the traditional criminal law is excluded because one of its principal purposes is to censure conduct considered to be anti-social or otherwise morally reprehensible.[12] Finally, regulation is purposive in orientation: it seeks to implement particular collective goals, that is, goals which are considered by the community to be socially valuable and worthy of pursuit but which would not otherwise be achieved (or at least, not likely to be achieved) in the absence of regulation.[13] The particular collective goal or goals of any regulatory scheme will vary, depending on the scheme in question, and may be economic (such as the promotion of efficient resource allocation), social (such as the elimination of racial discrimination) or both.[14]

(b) Conceptualising the Regulatory Process: Public and Private Interest Theories

Not only is the concept of regulation itself contested, but so too are the ways in which scholars have understood and analysed the regulatory process, with pro-

[8] Some commentators have sought to confine regulation to intervention in markets, thereby focusing exclusively on intervention in economic activity, eg Prosser (1997), Foster (1992), 186. This conception is, however, unnecessarily narrow. Even if the focus is on modifying behaviour for the purpose of implementing economic objectives, this need not be confined to intervention in economic activity. For example, society may wish to regulate divorce in order to ensure that both parties to the divorce have adequate financial provision. In such a case, one purpose of regulation may be economic, but the institution and dissolution of marriage is not primarily regarded as an economic activity: eg Eekelaar (1991).

[9] Eg Yeung (1998); Scott (2000); Moran (2002); Black (2003).

[10] Black claims that the 'real heart' of the regulatory function is 'how to alter behaviour so that people act in a way that they would not otherwise do, and in such a way as to ensure that regulatory objectives are met': Black (2003), 69.

[11] Baldwin (1998); Ogus (1994) *cf* Black (2003).

[12] Below ch 4, Part 2 (a).

[13] Daintith (1998): Vincent Jones observes that in regulating economic and social activity, the state is a 'purposeful actor' pursuing economic and social objectives through linking state law with power resources of instruments, force, wealth, information and persuasion: Vincent Jones (2002). But at its broadest, regulation can refer to all mechanisms of social control, including unintentional and non-state processes: Baldwin *et al* (1998), 4.

[14] Some commentators have drawn a further distinction between economic and social regulation, the former being concerned to facilitate economic objectives such as economic efficiency, and the latter with the achievement of socially desirable non-economic goals, such as the anti-discrimination laws, environmental regulation and so forth: Foster (1992), 186; Ogus (1994), 4–5.

found implications for conceptualising, evaluating and formulating solutions to regulatory problems. Thus in order to understand this book's analytical approach, it is necessary to locate it within the range of existing theoretical approaches. While a plethora of different theoretical perspectives have been employed by scholars in exploring regulation and its multiple and varied facets, they can be broadly divided into two kinds: public interest and private interest theories. Public interest theories of regulation attribute to legislators and others responsible for the design and implementation of regulation a desire to pursue collective goals with the aim of promoting the general welfare of the community.[15] Such theories are generally normative in orientation, typically concerned to evaluate (often from an explicitly economic or political viewpoint) whether, and to what extent, a regulatory scheme fulfils its collective goals. Private interest theories, by contrast, are sceptical of the so-called 'public interestedness' of legislators and policy-makers, recognising that regulation often benefits particular groups in society, and not always those it was ostensibly intended to benefit. Thus, private interest theories conceive of regulation as a contest between selfish 'rent-seeking' participants in the regulatory 'game', analysing the way in which political and law-making processes can be used by these participants to secure regulatory benefits for themselves.[16] Private interest theories are largely positive in nature, concerned with explaining how and why regulation emerges, and why regulatory processes and outcomes take a particular shape and form. Some private interest theories may also seek normatively to assess whether the resulting outcomes are economically efficient, typically observing that resources devoted to winning the regulation game often result in economic waste and are therefore socially unproductive.[17]

2. Values and the Regulatory Process

The analytical approach adopted in this book is explicitly 'public interest' in its theoretical orientation. One of the key enterprises animating my examination of competition law enforcement is to identify and make explicit the multiple and sometimes conflicting values that infuse regulatory processes and practices. It is clear from the preceding account of public and private theories of regulation that the latter are largely uninterested in debating the values that ought to inform regulatory processes. Rather, private interest theories simply assume that those involved or affected by regulation are rational self-interested actors: it makes little sense to ask whether or not this is a desirable motivation for human behaviour—it simply reflects social reality. In contrast, the normative orientation of public interest theories of regulation necessitates a consideration

[15] Ogus (1994), 3.
[16] *Ibid*, 4.
[17] *Ibid*, 71–74.

of the values to which the regulatory process should aspire and reflect. But how are these values to be identified? Ultimately, the chosen set of values will reflect both a particular understanding of regulation and a particular set of political beliefs and ideals. Yet, even within public interest approaches to regulation, one of the distinctive features of existing scholarship is the apparent bifurcation between literature that is broadly concerned with regulatory legitimacy and literature focusing on regulatory implementation.

Scholars concerned with seeking to explore and understand the legitimacy of governmental processes, tend to view regulation as a *form of governance*, wrestling with the intractable difficulties faced by a community in devising legitimate democratic procedures for identifying the collective goals it wishes to pursue, and to ensure that those goals reflect the constantly evolving views of the community. By conceiving regulation as a form of governance (involving both state and non-state actors), debate and discussion about the values that ought to underpin processes of governance to ensure its legitimacy tend to arise explicitly. In this respect, literature concerned with regulatory implementation, which I have already briefly alluded to, may be sharply differentiated. One strand of this scholarship is rooted in numerous and varied ethnographic studies exploring the behaviour of regulatory enforcement officials in responding to suspected contraventions. By identifying the sources of variance in agency behaviour,[18] these studies throw into high relief the discretionary nature of the enforcement process, emphasising regulation as a *site for human interaction*. Viewed in this light, the process of regulatory implementation allows considerable room for human manipulation that can significantly influence the shape of regulatory outcomes. Because the underlying aim of these ethnographic studies is to describe and understand regulatory enforcement, rather than evaluate and prescribe, scholars engaged in this enterprise tend to work from the premise that the function of the regulatory agency is to facilitate and promote compliance with regulatory standards. The predominant value underpinning the enforcement process is, although rarely stated explicitly, the quest for effective outcomes. But in undertaking this task, empirical studies demonstrate that regulatory agencies do not pursue a simple straightforward strategy. Rather, their approach is shown to be contingent on a plurality of features, including the existence or creation of trust and co-operation between the agency and regulated community, institutional capacity, the moral content of regulatory prohibitions and the specificity of the standards which the agency is required to enforce. A second strand of literature concerning regulatory implementation has grown out of these empirical findings, yet is explicitly normative in outlook, seeking to prescribe the 'optimal' strategy for securing policy outcomes.[19] By

[18] Kagan divides the sources of variance arising from these studies into two broad categories: 'legal/task environment' including technical, economic and legal problems shaping official action; and 'political environment' including interest group attempts to control agency leadership: Kagan (1994).

[19] Below, ch 6, Part B (2).

setting out to identify how regulatory standards, techniques and enforcement strategies can best be designed, this literature emphasises the nature of regulation as a *mechanism of social control*. Viewed in this light, regulatory implementation is seen as a largely technocratic enterprise aimed solely at securing policy outcomes effectively and efficiently[20] although this is again typically implicit rather than explicitly stated.

3. A Public Law Approach

Rather than adopting any one of the theoretical approaches identified above, this book adopts what may be described as a public law perspective in seeking to analyse and evaluate regulatory enforcement. My principal concern is to identify, examine and critique the nature and scope of legal constraints that inform and shape the enforcement activities of a regulatory agency. In the Australian context, a former Chairman of the Australian Competition and Consumer Commission (the 'Commission') acknowledged the importance of the Commission's adherence to the law in carrying out its enforcement activities, stating that:

> Although the Commission is committed to the vigorous enforcement of the Trade Practices Act, it is equally committed to following lawful processes. It is always careful to stay within the law in its own behaviour . . . In short, the law should be applied without fear or favour in the way Parliament clearly intended.[21]

But in assessing whether regulators stay 'within the law', several different legal sources must be considered. The primary source of legal constraints stems from the provisions of the legislation establishing the agency's powers and from which its enforcement discretion is primarily derived.[22] A second source of legal constraints derives from administrative law, a considerable component of which is concerned with the exercise of discretionary powers by state authorities. So for example, Anglian administrative law requires that public authorities exercise their powers lawfully, in accordance with the requirements of procedural fairness, and on rational grounds.[23] But although these requirements may be simple to state, identifying their specific content and application to particular circumstances is often a complex task.[24] A third source of legal constraints arises from the criminal law, which may be of particular relevance when the state seeks to impose punitive sanctions on those who violate regulatory standards.[25] Yet

[20] Eg. Parker describes the approach of many contemporary regulation scholars as 'pragmatic in the sense that they use empirical evidence about what is likely to work, rather than being guided purely by ideological concerns about what form of regulation is most desirable.' Parker (1999), 8.

[21] Fels (1998).

[22] Below, ch 3, Part B (2) (a).

[23] *Council of Civil Service Unions v Minister for the Civil Service* [1985] AC 374. I use the term 'Anglian' to describe the legal tradition underpinning the English, Australian and North American legal systems.

[24] Craig (1999); Harlow (1999).

[25] Below, ch 4.

another source of legal (or quasi-legal) constraints on the exercise of discretionary powers of enforcement officials can also be identified, perhaps more accurately described as ethical rather than legal constraints. By ethical constraints, I mean those deeper values and principles reflecting the 'ethos' or 'shared culture' of the community that may not be expressly reflected in legal rules.[26] In many areas where public authorities are required to exercise discretionary powers in carrying out their duties and functions, legal rules may provide little if any guidance and there may be no obviously 'correct' way to proceed. In such cases, these ethical principles or values inform and constrain the official's course of action. Because the role of a regulatory enforcement agency is somewhat akin to the role of a criminal prosecutor, it may also be confronted with many of the well-known ethical dilemmas faced by a criminal prosecutor. It may therefore be appropriate for regulators to take guidance from similar ethical principles in exercising their enforcement discretion, depending on the extent to which the analogy with a criminal prosecutor is considered apposite.

By adopting a public law approach to the examination of enforcement, this book is concerned with each of these four sources of legality.[27] But in so doing, my analysis takes place at two levels. At one level, it is concerned with 'thin' legality, in seeking to evaluate whether the specific aspects of enforcement activity forming the focus of this inquiry conforms to the requirements of the law.[28] But at another level, it is concerned with 'thick' legality—setting out to identify whether, and to what extent, certain 'constitutional values', drawn from a largely formal conception of the rule of law as it applies in a liberal democracy, are preserved and promoted in the practice of regulatory enforcement. It is through this notion of 'thick legality' that my exploration of regulatory enforcement seeks to combine aspects of each of the three theoretical perspectives referred to above. By emphasising the role of constitutional values in shaping and informing the process of regulatory implementation, regulation is thus conceived concurrently as a form of governance, a site for human interaction, and a mechanism of social control. In this way, I set out both to demonstrate and challenge the (typically unstated) assumptions underpinning much of the existing compliance literature in which regulatory implementation is conceptualised

[26] Crispin (1995). Below, ch 5, Part D (2).

[27] It is acknowledged that there is a range of different analytical perspectives that could be adopted in seeking to examine and evaluate issues concerning competition law enforcement. For example, an economic analysis of competition law enforcement might seek to quantify the costs and benefits of enforcement, in order to evaluate whether enforcement activity is efficient: eg Grant (1994); Round *et al* (1996). A sociological analysis might seek to identify the behavioural dynamic between the public enforcement authority and the regulated parties, in order to identify whether the enforcement strategies adopted by the regulator are effective in modifying the behaviour of the latter: Grabosky and Braithwaite (1985). A political analysis might seek to identify how different political values and interests interact in the regulatory process in generating certain outcomes: Fels (1982); Hopkins (1983).

[28] The specific legal requirements will, of course, vary from jurisdiction to jurisdiction. By drawing primarily upon Australian competition law to illustrate my analytical claims, this book will focus specifically on Australian law: see ch 2, Part C.

as a technocratic enterprise concerned with effectiveness and efficiency in securing policy outcomes. My approach thus draws from both the literature concerning regulatory legitimacy and accountability and the literature concerning regulatory design, techniques and enforcement, in the hope of blending together, rather than bifurcating, these two rich and fertile sources of scholarship. Before we can proceed to our analysis, it is important to clarify what we mean when discussing the regulator's role in 'securing compliance'.

4. What Does it Mean to 'Secure Compliance'?

Throughout the literature concerned with regulatory enforcement, it is typically claimed, rather ambiguously, that the purpose of regulatory enforcement is to 'secure compliance'. But with what must compliance be secured? Regulatory theorists appear to use the phrase not only by reference to compliance with the *collective goals* underpinning a regulatory scheme, but also by reference to compliance with *regulatory standards*. The lack of clarity is exacerbated by the tendency of some theorists to use the term interchangeably and inconsistently, sometimes referring to compliance with regulatory standards, but on other occasions referring to compliance with collective goals.[29] The issue is not merely a linguistic, terminological difficulty, for the two reference points, collective goals and regulatory standards, may not necessarily be consistent. So for example, the phenomenon of 'creative compliance', whereby technical compliance with rules may be achieved yet the underlying spirit and purpose of those rules might be simultaneously undermined, is well known.[30] If regulatory standards have been poorly designed, they may fail to influence behaviour in the manner intended, with the result that compliance with regulatory standards may not promote compliance with the scheme's collective goals. And even if standards are well-designed, it is possible to envisage circumstances in which insistence on compliance with standards in situations involving technical or trivial violations could be counter-productive, undermining a general culture of commitment on the part of the regulated community towards the scheme's collective goals. In short, it is possible to distinguish between 'rule compliance' on the one hand and 'substantive compliance' with collective goals on the other, and the two may not always be coextensive.[31]

In order to avoid terminological confusion, I shall define regulatory *implementation* to refer to any action taken with the aim of securing compliance with

[29] Parker defines regulatory compliance as 'obedience by a target population with regulatory rules or with government policy objectives': Parker (1999), 2. She later claims that 'a number of regulatory scholars predict that the 'new' regulatory state will turn from being predominantly concerned with compliance with technical rules to a concern with accomplishing the substantive regulatory goals by whatever means is appropriate and feasible': Parker (1999), 12.

[30] McBarnet and Whelan (1991).

[31] Parker (1999a), 4–5.

the collective goal or goals of a regulatory scheme, and regulatory *enforcement* to refer to any action taken with the aim of securing compliance with the regulatory standards embodied within a regulatory scheme. In order to understand the relationship between these two activities, it is helpful to conceive of the process of regulatory implementation (once the collective goals underpinning a regulatory programme have been identified) as typically encompassing three stages: institutional design,[32] standard setting[33] and the monitoring and enforcement of regulatory standards. Enforcement can thus be seen as one component, a crucially important component, of the overall process of regulatory implementation. Although the general public may tend to think of enforcement predominantly in terms of the formal process of prosecution and the imposition of punitive sanctions for violation, in practice the bulk of enforcement activity, in both regulatory and criminal contexts, is largely informal in nature, typically hidden from public view. In the context of regulatory enforcement, there may also be a tendency to emphasise the enforcement of legal prohibitions operating within a command and control framework,[34] but as several commentators have pointed out, no regulatory scheme is entirely self-enforcing. Thus, even techniques involving schemes of prior approval through licensing, mandatory disclosure and even those relying upon market-based instruments such as the levying of taxes or the offering of subsidies, require some form of enforcement. Some kind of monitoring is required to ensure that non-licensed activity does not occur, that all required information is disclosed and that relevant taxes are collected and so forth. Given that the predominant model for competition regulation entails a command and control system of rules and sanctions, most of my discussion occurs in that context, but our understanding of the enforcement process in general need not be so limited.

Now that we have clarified our terms, we can begin constructing the framework of principles against which the legitimacy of various dimensions of regulatory enforcement may be evaluated. It is clear from the preceding discussion, however, that although the legitimacy of regulatory enforcement is a necessary condition of legitimate regulatory implementation, it is not a sufficient condition, given that enforcement constitutes only one component of the overall implementation process. Although my analytical framework is employed in this book to evaluate enforcement practices, it might also be usefully adapted as a basis for evaluating the legitimacy of regulatory implementation in its entirety

[32] Institutional design includes designing both the institutions and techniques used as the means of regulatory implementation, and thus may entail considering whether to adopt, for example, market-based incentives, prior approval through a licensing regime, by introducing a mandatory disclosure regime or a classical 'command and control' regime: Below, ch 6, Part B.

[33] Within a command and control regime, the content of the rules must be specified, the kinds of rules thought suitable and the appropriate sanctions for breach must be determined. Even techniques that do not entail a classical 'command and control' approach, require the setting of standards. For example, if market-based incentive techniques are used, then the level of incentives must be specified, as well as eligibility to participate and so forth.

[34] Below, ch 4, Part B (2), and ch 6, Part B (1).

or—to use the language of public administration—for full programme evaluation. What it does *not* do, however, is provide a basis for evaluating the legitimacy of the collective goals themselves. Rather, it simply assumes the validity of the collective goals underpinning a regulatory programme, confining the scope of its inquiry to the implementation of those goals. Thus, before proceeding to the framework itself, we need to identify what the collective goals of competition regulation are, and to which we now turn.

2

Competition Law and Policy

A. THE PURSUIT OF ECONOMIC EFFICIENCY THROUGH COMPETITIVE MARKETS

THE PURPOSE OF modern competition law is generally claimed to be the promotion of economic efficiency by facilitating competitive markets. Given that society's resources are limited, it is in the community's interest to produce and allocate those resources efficiently. When this occurs, all economic resources are allocated between different goods and services in precisely the quantities which consumers wish (their desires being expressed by the price they are prepared to pay on the market) and produced at the lowest possible cost.[1] According to microeconomic theory, competition is required in order to ensure that markets operate efficiently.[2] In competitive markets, producers compete with each other in order to satisfy the demands of consumers: each producer striving for custom, thereby constantly seeking to produce better goods and services (as indicated by consumer's tastes and preferences) at the lowest possible cost. Under conditions of competition, if a producer is to survive, it must be responsive to the demands of its customers, suppliers and the policies of its rivals. The antithesis of a competitive market is a market with only one producer, a monopolist, which can dictate its terms of supply. It does not face the threat of being 'outperformed' by its rivals, and is thus free to reduce its volume of production to levels below that demanded by consumers in order to bump up the price of its produce, thereby maximising its profit.[3] The result is inefficiency: the quantity of production is lower than would be the case under conditions of perfect competition,[4] depriving

[1] Economic efficiency can be divided into allocative and productive efficiency. Allocative efficiency refers to the allocation of resources between different goods and services in precisely the quantities that consumers wish. Productive efficiency means that goods and services are produced at the lowest possible cost: see Scherer and Ross (1990), 19–29 and 661–67; Whish (2003), 2–4.

[2] Efficiency can be defined more precisely in terms of partial equilibrium welfare economics, that is the maximisation of the sum of the discounted present value of consumer and producer surpluses. This definition encompasses the trade-off between static and dynamic efficiency: current and welfare losses may be acceptable, if the market structure or conduct which gives rise to the losses will also generate efficiencies in the long run, so long as the prospective benefits are not too delayed in realisation and the social discount rate is not too high: see Hay and Morris (1991), chs 16–17.

[3] Scherer and Ross (1990), 15–17, 21–29.

[4] Perfect competition requires four conditions: a) a very large number of buyers and sellers on the market; b) all products are homogeneous; c) consumers have perfect information about market conditions; and d) there are no 'barriers to entry or exit' which might prevent the emergence of new competition or hinder firms from leaving the industry. Under the conditions of perfect competition, the price at which a good or service is sold never rises above the marginal cost of production: *ibid*, 29–49 ; Cooter and Ulen (1997), 29–30.

consumers of goods and services which they would be willing to pay for at the competitive price, generating what is known as the 'deadweight loss' of monopoly.[5] Because the monopolist is not constrained by the threat of competition, it faces few incentives to drive down its costs to the lowest level or to innovate in order to attract and retain custom. The result is a misallocation of resources, wasteful expenditure and hence a loss to society at large.

Competition is therefore essential to the pursuit of economic efficiency.[6] The antithesis of competition is market power. A firm possesses market power when it is free to act independently of its competitors, customers, and suppliers.[7] A firm with market power is thus able to 'give less and charge more',[8] exploiting the conditions of the market to maximise its own profit, thereby reducing society's general welfare. Because firms can generate higher profits if they possess significant market power, rational profit-maximising firms can be expected to pursue strategies that will enhance their market power. Economists have identified three kinds of market power enhancing strategies: collude with competitors, merge with competitors or deter competitors from entering the market (or induce existing competitors to leave the market). Modern competition law seeks to block these three routes to market power, in order to safeguard the competitive process and thereby promote economic efficiency.[9]

[5] Scherer and Ross (1990), 15–17 and 21–29; Cooter and Ulen (1997), 30–31.

[6] Although competition has traditionally been understood in terms of price competition, non-price competition can also occur in various guises. Firms may compete on the number of brands they put on the market, in product quality, after-sales service, marketing and so forth. Over time, firms may compete in physical investment or in research and development.

[7] *Hoffman La-Roche v EC Commission* [1979] ECR 461, para 38.

[8] *Re Queensland Co-operative Milling Association Ltd, Defiance Holdings Ltd* (1976) ¶ATPR 40–012 citing Attorney General for the USA, *Report of the National Committee to Study the Antitrust Laws* (1955), 320.

[9] Williams (1993), 94. Although competition is generally conducive to the pursuit of economic efficiency, there are some situations (known in economic parlance as 'market failure') in which this may not be the case: Bator (1958). First, there are some industries which require considerable capital investment in order produce the desired goods or services yet the strength of demand for those goods or services may be small in relation to the costs of production. It may even be that industry can only operate efficiently by a single supplier, which is known in economics as a natural monopoly, and is particularly common in relation to network industries: Sharkey (1982); Prosser (1997); Foster (1992). Even if an industry is not a natural monopoly, the reduction in costs of production achieved through economies of scale and scope arising from fewer firms supplying a large proportion of the product may outweigh the corresponding loss to consumers arising from pricing at levels above the competitive price: Scherer and Ross (1990), 80. Secondly, in competitive markets rational profit-motivated firms will strive to reduce their costs of production to the lowest possible level. However, this fails to account for external costs (or 'externalities') which may be generated from the production process but which are not reflected in the prices which the supplier charges for products: Ogus (1994), 35–36. For example, a factory may pollute the surrounding environment, thereby imposing costs on residents. In the absence of legal restrictions, a rational firm will not take these external costs into account in pursuing its production strategy, and hence the overall impact of its production on social welfare may not be efficient. Thirdly, firms in competitive markets may engage in excessive non-price competition, such as multiple branding, after-sales service and marketing (including advertising), the provision of which may exceed the level demanded by consumers. Because consumer preferences are not accurately reflected in the price mechanism, excessive services are produced, leading to inefficiency. Fourthly, some goods can be characterised as 'public goods'. A public good is a commodity, the benefit of which is shared by the public as a whole, or by some

It is important to acknowledge, however, that there is a lack of consensus between different schools of economic thought concerning how general welfare is best promoted through the operation of competitive markets. The theory of competition set out above reflects current mainstream industrial organisation, which regards economic efficiency as the exclusive goal of competition law and policy. There is a second, smaller but nonetheless vociferous school of thought known as the Austrian approach, claiming that the merits of the market mechanism stem not from the outcome of static allocative efficiency but from the market as a dynamic device leading to innovation and welfare gains from creative entrepreneurship.[10] The theory of contestable markets, on the other hand, emphasises the importance of ease of entry into an industry, rather than market structure. This theory posits that even if there are few firms in an industry each firm having a high market share, they cannot exploit their high market share if entry is easy.[11] The appropriate design and operation of a scheme of competition regulation will thus depend upon which strand of economic thought is preferred. Indeed, the emphasis of competition policy in various western industrialised economies has shifted over time, partly in response to developments in underlying economic theory.[12]

B. COMPETITION REGULATION AND NON-ECONOMIC GOALS

Despite differences in their approach to welfare maximisation, economists are nonetheless united in their belief that the primary purpose of competition

group of it. Thus, consumption by one person does not leave less for others to consume. The supplier may find it either too costly or simply impossible to exclude consumption by 'free riders', ie those who consume the good without paying for it. A national defence system is a frequently cited example of a public good. The market method of allocation cannot be relied upon to determine the desired quantity of supply of a public good, because willingness to pay does not provide a measure of demand and fails to provide incentives for suppliers to produce the public good: Ogus (1994), 30–32. Thus, given that there are some circumstances in which the promotion of competition may not lead to economically efficient outcomes, the design and application of competition law and policy should be capable of accommodating them if it is to be effective in promoting economic efficiency.

[10] Williams (1993), 95; Hay (1989), 3; Kirzner (1973); Littlechild (1990).

[11] Baumol (1982).

[12] Even if consensus concerning the underlying economic theory of competition regulation could be reached, there remain problems in applying the theory to real world markets. The conditions of perfect competition are unlikely to prevail in practice: consumers lack perfect information, significant barriers to entry and exit may exist and there may not be a large number of buyers and sellers. Between the two extremes of perfect competition and monopoly is a range of industry structures displaying differing levels of competitiveness. In recent years, there has been considerable debate concerning the appropriate response of competition policy to oligopolistic industries, that is, industries characterised by a small number of suppliers, each possessing a significant share of the market. Oligopolistic industries pose a particular challenge for competition policy. On the one hand, each firm possesses significant market power because its production policies are likely to have a significant impact on the industry. On the other hand, each firm cannot act completely independently, and is constrained by the actions of its rivals, albeit few in number.

regulation is to ensure the integrity of the competitive process as a means to securing economic efficiency. In contrast, it has sometimes been claimed (generally by non-economists) that competition policy should seek to pursue other goals, although these other goals may not necessarily be in conflict with the pursuit of economic efficiency. For example, some argue that competition policy should seek to protect small business, to protect consumers from exploitation by big business, to protect consumer choice, to protect domestic industries against foreign take-overs, to encourage domestic producers in order to enable them to compete more effectively in global markets, to implement regional policy and regulate regional unemployment and even to promote the pursuit of 'justice' by ensuring equality of opportunity for all business actors irrespective of size.[13] While economists frequently deride the use of competition policy to pursue non-efficiency based goals, there is no doubt that in practice, competition policy has been used in various jurisdictions to further such ends. For example, it is well known that the interpretation and application of EU competition law has been driven by a concern to achieve single market integration across EU member states.[14] In the UK, prior to the reform of merger regulation with the commencement of the Enterprise Act 2002, the regulation of mergers under the Fair Trading Act 1973 required an assessment of whether or not a merger was (or was likely to be) in the 'public interest', a term very broadly defined to include 'maintaining and promoting the balanced distribution of industry and employment in the UK.'[15] A review of the merger reference reports of the Monopolies and Merger Commission ('MMC')[16] indicates that it has taken various non-economic considerations into account in evaluating whether a merger was likely to be in the 'public interest', including managerial efficacy, regional unemployment, foreign ownership and the likely risks associated with leveraging and financing an acquisition.[17]

In identifying the appropriate role of non-economic goals in competition law and policy, it is helpful to situate competition regulation in its broader historical and political context. Modern competition law largely originated from United States antitrust law, beginning with the Sherman Act 1890, which emerged from the industrial revolution.[18] At that time, there was considerable popular dissatisfaction in the US with the expanding railroad companies that formed cartels, established in the form of trusts. Using these trusts, stocks held in competing companies were transferred to trustees who then managed and coordinated the affairs of the industry, enabling them to exploit their economic power to drive many small businesses out of the market while charging prices

[13] Whish (2003), 17–20; Amato (1997); Bork (1978); Fox (1981); Schwartz (1979).

[14] Goyder (1998), 15–16.

[15] Fair Trading Act 1973 (UK), s 84.

[16] The MMC's functions under the Fair Trading Act 1973 were taken over by the Competition Commission.

[17] Williams (1993), 103.

[18] Fox (1981), 440.

disproportionate to the value of their services. The Sherman Act was introduced in this context, making it illegal to enter into contracts in restraint of trade or to monopolise (or attempt to monopolise) a market, but it was not particularly effective in overcoming populist concerns, largely due to the US Supreme Court's relatively narrow interpretation of its provisions. The 1912 Presidential election was fought mainly on the antitrust issue, with Woodrow Wilson promising the 'New Freedom' through antitrust reform in order to give the 'little man' the chance to succeed and assuring greater certainty for business.[19] The Clayton Act 1914 was then enacted, making particular restrictive trade practices (such as price discrimination and some mergers) unlawful and an administrative agency, the Federal Trade Commission, was established to investigate competition problems, regulate business and provide guidance on competition policy. The protectionist era of the 1930s saw the enactment of the Robinson-Patman Act 1936, reinforcing the view that smaller business needed protection to prevent its bigger rivals from using their buying power to secure superior trading terms. Concerns about the perceived undue power of big business continued into the early 1940s following World War II, in light of the wave of vigorous merger activity, and the merger provisions of the Clayton Act were strengthened as a result.

A central theme pervading the early decades of US antitrust was freedom of economic opportunity, and a particular concern for the protection of small business from the superior economic power of large enterprise. It was not until the late 1940s that the influence of economic analysis began to emerge, and the conceptual basis of antitrust law shifted from political concerns relating to the power of large enterprise and the vulnerability of small business to the discipline of economic analysis and the pursuit of competition in order to secure economic efficiency. In particular, the influence of the so-called 'Chicago School' of economics began to take hold in the 1970s, reaching its zenith in the mid 1980s during the Reagan administration.[20] Those associated with the Chicago School emphasised that economic efficiency should be sole and exclusive concern of antitrust law, for by so doing consumer welfare would be maximised.[21] Thus, trade restrictions which were apparently restrictive could nonetheless have the overall effect of enhancing economic efficiency and thus to prohibit them would be harmful to consumer welfare. Increasingly sophisticated economic arguments began to predominate in antitrust disputes, and it is now the norm for economic argument to play a critical role in antitrust cases in the US.

The history of modern competition law demonstrates that the collective goals of competition law and policy have shifted over time. Although originally conceived as providing a legal framework for protecting the freedom of individual consumers and small business from the influence of large enterprise, competition

[19] *Ibid.*
[20] Amato (1997); Posner (1979a).
[21] Bork (1978).

law is now almost universally regarded as the primary legal mechanism for preserving and maintaining the competitive functioning of markets. The regulation of competition between private enterprise can be situated within a deeper political debate in liberal democratic theory concerning the appropriate boundaries between public and private power.[22] In a liberal democracy, citizens have the right to freedom from coercion: both from the state and from interference by other citizens to which they have not assented. But here lies a dilemma: to what extent can government legitimately intervene to safeguard individual liberty from the economic power of private actors, without itself unduly encroaching on the affairs of its citizens?[23] The attraction of economic theory is its analytical rigour and apparent neutrality in seeking to identify when it is legitimate for the state to intervene in the business activity of private actors. But the image of political neutrality is illusory, given the deeper political and philosophical roots of the fundamental issues lying at the foundation of competition policy.

This book is not concerned to identify the appropriate boundaries of substantive competition law, for its focus is on the enforcement and application of competition law rather than on its substantive content. Nevertheless, it is important to identify the collective goal (or goals) underpinning competition regulation in order to provide the basis for evaluating how those goals have been implemented and enforced. This book adopts the orthodox view that the collective goal of competition law and policy is the pursuit of economic efficiency by preserving and maintaining the competitive functioning of markets. This assumption is made for the sake of simplicity, primarily to illustrate my analytical approach to regulatory enforcement—I could equally have chosen a different collective goal. In so doing, however, I recognise that any society faces considerable difficulties in identifying the collective goals to which it aspires, a task that has long troubled political theorists in attempting to identify how societal ends should be defined and by whom, in order for those ends to lay claim to legitimacy.[24] In other words, my analysis takes the basic collective goal (or goals) of a regulatory programme as given, and thus confines its examination to the manner in which those goals are implemented.[25]

By assuming that the collective goal of competition law is the pursuit of economic efficiency, I am not thereby assuming that economic efficiency is valuable in its own right: it is only valuable to the extent that it promotes the welfare of the community. In other words, it is important to distinguish between the collective goals of any regulatory regime (including competition policy), and broader questions of social welfare. There will inevitably be a multiplicity of collective goals that a society may validly wish to pursue in promoting the welfare of the community, of which economic efficiency in production and resource allocation is but one. In situations where these other social goals conflict with

22 Amato (1997).
23 *Ibid.*
24 Black (2000); Vincent-Jones (2002); Baldwin (1996), ch 3.
25 Above, ch 1, Part B (4).

the goal of economic efficiency, then the community must decide which goal should prevail: if it decides that, in situations of conflict, the pursuit of other social goals should take priority over economic efficiency, then competition policy must give way. What is important is that the choice between competing collective goals is made explicitly and in accordance with principles of democratic governance, although devising procedures that satisfy the requirements of democratic legitimacy may well be a complex and contestable task. By confining the goal of competition law and policy to the pursuit of economic efficiency, any conflict with other social goals is made visible, so that trade-offs between them are more likely to be explicit rather than hidden or disguised.

C. AN OVERVIEW OF AUSTRALIAN COMPETITION REGULATION

1. Why Australian Competition Law?

The framework of analysis presented throughout this book is predominantly general and conceptual in nature, so that it may be readily adopted as a lens through which formal and informal enforcement practices in a wide range of contexts (including competition regulation) may be examined. In order to illustrate how my analysis may be applied to a specific regulatory context, I draw primarily (but not exclusively) from the Australian experience of public competition law enforcement for it provides a particularly valuable illustrative context for several reasons. Although each of the enforcement practices focused upon in this book occurs within the two most prominent competition regimes, the EU and USA, the Australian experience may be a more helpful site for illustrating conceptual tensions that are commonly encountered by regulators in general when seeking to secure compliance with regulatory standards. While EU competition regulation is highly developed, and provides the basic institutional framework upon which most EU states have modelled their domestic competition laws, it is heavily influenced by the complex dynamics of national and institutional politics that afflicts EU policy-making and practice.[26] Although the enforcement of US antitrust law is not as overtly subject to political influences, it is unique throughout competition regimes for the sharp incentives provided to those harmed by antitrust violations to commence private enforcement actions, arising from the availability of treble damages. The greater prominence of private enforcement within the overall structure and operation of US antitrust enforcement significantly affects the role of public antitrust enforcement.[27] Although the institutional dynamics of the EU, and the relationship between public and private enforcement, are important issues that have been the subject

[26] Eg Bulmer (1994); Cini and McGowan (1999).

[27] For an economic analysis of the relationship between public and private enforcement, see Landes and Posner (1975); Shavell (1993).

of considerable scholarly reflection, one of the primary purposes animating my inquiry is to identify the values that ought to inform the regulatory enforcement process. Because the Commission's experience of enforcing Australian competition law reflects practical and theoretical difficulties that commonly confront competition regulators in other jurisdictions (including the EU and USA[28]) but is not subject to either of these two rather atypical influences, its experience may highlight the significance of constitutional principles more sharply than its prominent transatlantic counterparts.

In addition, Australia's system of competition regulation, which is based primarily on the Trade Practices Act 1974 ('the Act'), largely reflects the primary institutional model adopted as the basis for competition regulation by many major industrialised economies, consisting of a body of substantive legal prohibitions that are both crafted and interpreted in accordance with economic reasoning, and—if violated—may result in the imposition of very significant financial penalties. Although private litigants may institute court proceedings to recover (single) damages if harmed by a violation, the primary responsibility for investigating and enforcing the legal prohibitions rests with the Commission, a specialist and independent public enforcement agency invested with considerable discretionary power to carry out this task. Australian competition law has also reached a stage of relative maturity. The interpretation and scope of its substantive provisions have been fleshed out in the courts and are now widely known by the Australian business community. The Commission has flourished in both size and stature, growing from fairly small and rather humble beginnings to become the most powerful regulatory agency in the nation, drawing from over three decades of practical experience in enforcing the legislative prohibitions. The Act has been universally hailed as a success by commentators in significantly reducing the use of anti-competitive agreements and practices that, at the time of the Act's introduction, had become widespread and endemic to the operation of Australian industry. Finally, in political and economic terms, Australia is a small, open economy that has followed in the footsteps of the Thatcher/Reagan era in seeking to emphasise a laissez-faire approach to economic policy, pushing for deregulatory reforms and emphasising market forces (and hence competition) as the primary driver of business activity. To that extent, Australian economic policy (including competition policy) reflects trends enthusiastically advocated by the OECD, WTO and largely adopted by western industrialised democracies.

[28] For example, in both the EU and USA, very significant financial penalties are payable by those found to have contravened competition laws, the competition authority in both jurisdictions allows scope for 'plea bargaining' enabling violators who co-operate with the regulatory authority to receive some form of leniency in the formal enforcement response adopted, and both authorities resolve the vast majority of suspected violations informally through some kind of administrative settlement, rather than pursuing all suspected violations through the formal enforcement process.

2. Australian Competition Regulation in Outline

By comparison to its US counterpart, Australian competition regulation is relatively young. The origins of modern Australian competition law can be traced to the 1960s when concern about the extensive range and form of restrictive agreements which had become characteristic of many Australian industries began to emerge.[29] In response to these concerns, the Liberal administration (which is traditionally pro-industry and more conservative than the Australian Labor Party, its principal political opponent) enacted the Trade Practices Act 1965, largely modelled on its British counterpart.[30] The 1965 Act, described by one leading commentator as 'tentative and experimental',[31] made little impact, and when the current competition laws were introduced into Parliament the then Attorney-General, Lionel Murphy, described the 1965 Act as 'one of the most ineffectual pieces of legislation ever passed by this Parliament.'[32] The Australian Labor Party was elected in 1972, having been in the political wilderness since 1949, and one of its principal policies was to reform restrictive practices legislation to give it (and the administering body) the 'teeth' which it had previously lacked. The result was the Trade Practices Act 1974, which continues to form the basis of contemporary Australian competition law.

The Act contains a series of competitive conduct rules and establishes the institutional framework for regulating anti-competitive conduct. Part IV of the Act sets out the competitive conduct rules, prohibiting certain specified conduct unless 'authorisation' is granted, including anti-competitive agreements (such as price-fixing agreements between competitors), the misuse of market power, resale price maintenance and anti-competitive mergers. The institutional framework established under the Act adopts a system of dual adjudication. On the one hand, it is for the ordinary courts to determine whether or not the Part IV prohibitions have been contravened in proceedings brought by either private litigants harmed by conduct alleged to be in breach of the Act, or by the Commission as public enforcement agency. If the Commission brings formal enforcement action resulting in a formal finding of contravention, the court is empowered to make a wide range of orders, including orders for the payment of civil penalties of up to $10 million (for corporations) and $500,000 (for individuals).[33] On the other hand, it is for the Commission (and on appeal, the Australian Competition Tribunal) to evaluate and determine whether conduct notified to it in advance by the parties should be authorised (and thus excluded

[29] Norman traces the history of Australian competition law and notes that in the 1950s it was reported that horizontal agreements had become a nation-wide phenomenon: Norman (1993), 529; Brunt (1994), 486–93.

[30] Restrictive Trade Practices Act 1956 (UK).

[31] Brunt (1994), 491.

[32] 27 September 1973, cited by Brunt (1994), 491.

[33] Trade Practices Act 1974, s 80 (injunctions); s 80A (corrective advertising); s 81 (divestiture in relation to anti-competitive mergers) and ss 76–77 (pecuniary penalties). Pecuniary penalties can only be ordered at the suit of the Commission. Below, ch 4, n 147 and associated text.

from the statutory prohibitions) on the basis that its public benefits would outweigh its anti-competitive detriment.

Central to the Act's purpose is the regulation of market power by maintaining and promoting the competitive process.[34] Despite its apparent youthfulness, Australian competition law is relatively mature in terms of its appreciation of economic analysis. Although non-economic considerations are relevant to the interpretation and application of the Act[35], it is difficult to overstate the importance of economic efficiency in the general thrust of modern Australian competition law and policy and the prevailing political climate, powerfully evidenced by the support given by the federal and all state governments for most of the sweeping and controversial recommendations set out in the 'Hilmer Report'[36]. The Hilmer Report (named after the chairman of the committee responsible for the report, Professor F G Hilmer) resulted from a broad-based inquiry by an ad hoc independent committee established at the request of the then Prime Minister and all State premiers to produce guidelines for the role of competition policy as a major element underlying Australia's push for deregulation and micro-economic reform. Although its recommendations need not be canvassed here, it is worth noting that one of its key principles was that there should be no regulatory restrictions on competition unless such restrictions can be justified in the public interest as assessed by an appropriate transparent assessment process[37]

[34] The economic justification of the Act was powerfully affirmed by the High Court of Australia in *Queensland Wire Industries v BHP* (1989) 167 CLR 177.

[35] Non-economic considerations are explicitly recognised by the Act. In determining whether conduct notified to it should be authorised, the Commission is required to evaluate whether or not proposed anti-competitive conduct is likely to result in any 'benefit to the public', after receiving representations from the public. Although it is clear from decisions of the Commission and the Tribunal that economic efficiency is the most common criteria in assessing public benefit, the test has been broadly interpreted as 'anything of value to the community generally, any contribution to the aims pursued by the society': *Re Queensland Co-operative Milling Association Ltd, Defiance Holdings Ltd* (1976) ATPR ¶40–012 at 17,242. Thus, authorisation has been granted not only where there is market failure in the technical sense of microeconomic analysis, but also where the market fails adequately to protect other social values, such as the need to maintain perceived standards of integrity within professional disciplines, the preservation of public safety and the protection of children from certain forms of advertising: Brunt (1994), 507. The Act's approach is consistent with the view that the central purpose of competition law is to facilitate economic efficiency by promoting competitive markets. In evaluating whether notified conduct is likely to be of benefit to the public, the Commission is required to invite public comment and must make its assessment in light of any representations received. In granting or denying authorisation, the Commission is required to give a full statement of reasons for its decision, and the Tribunal may review the merits of the Commission's decision if an appeal is made. Thus, where authorisation is granted on the basis of social goals other than the pursuit of competitive markets, the Commission (and, on appeal, the Tribunal) makes this explicit in its decision, following public consultation, and openly acknowledges that, in the limited circumstances of the application, the goals of competition policy are overridden by other social goals.

[36] Report by the Independent Committee of Inquiry (1993) ('the Hilmer Report').

[37] The Hilmer Report at xix. For an illuminating discussion of the impact of this recommendation, see Morgan (2003). The Hilmer Report also recommended that the test for authorisation should be amended to make explicit the primacy of economic efficiency considerations in determining questions of public benefit, although it noted the relevance of 'other valued social objectives': The Hilmer Report, 88 and 121.

and implementation of the Report's recommendations has shaped the contours of national microeconomic reform policies ever since.

In addition to its role of enforcing the competitive conduct rules under Part IV of the Act, the Commission has a range of other statutory functions (made even more extensive following the process of microeconomic reform implemented following the Hilmer recommendations), requiring it to: adjudicate applications for authorisation and access to essential facilities; arbitrate disputes concerning access to essential facilities; enforce product safety standards; enforce the Act's consumer protection provisions; monitor and inquire into prices of goods and services under the Prices Surveillance Act 1983; liaise with the Commonwealth, State and Territory governments and other regulatory authorities on economic reform issues; provide guidance to business and consumers about the legislation that it is responsible for administering and (most recently) to oversee the implementation of the new national goods and services tax.[38] Because this book focuses on competition law enforcement, it does not examine the Commission's other statutory functions. The breadth of the Commission's statutory responsibilities nonetheless serves to underline the critical role now played by the Commission in regulating Australian business activity and industry structure. It is widely accepted that it is one of the most powerful institutions in the country, and firms proposing to engage in conduct that may have a significant impact on the shape of an industry's structure or operation invariably approach the Commission for its views on the proposal before proceeding.[39] Notwithstanding its powerful position, the Commission is constitutionally independent of government, it carries out its statutory duties in an autonomous manner and it is not subject to day to day direction or political intervention from the government.[40] It is directly accountable to the Australian

[38] The Commission also has a range of other statutory responsibilities under related legislation. Under the Airports Act 1996, it is responsible for quality of service monitoring and reporting, facilitating access to airport services of national significance and to receive accounts and reports which facilitate its price oversight role. Under the Australian Postal Corporation Act 1989 the Commission conducts inquiries into disputes as to the amount of postal rate reduction given by Australia Post to bulk mailers interconnecting or attempting to interconnect to the Australian postal system. Under the Broadcasting Services Act 1922 the Commission reports on the allocation of subscription television broadcasting licences to applicants and monitors (in conjunction with the Australian Broadcasting Authority) the cross-media ownership of the holders of subscription television broadcasting licences. Under the Gas Pipelines Access (Commonwealth) Act 1998, the Commission is responsible for regulating third party access to national gas pipeline systems under the National Third Party Access Code for Natural Gas Pipeline systems. Under the Moomba-Sydney Pipeline System Sale Act 1994 it arbitrates disputes over the existence of spare capacity, the interconnection of a pipeline to the Moomba-Sydney Pipeline, increases in capacity and terms and conditions of provisions of haulage service. Under the Telecommunications Act 1997, the Commission is responsible for competition matters in the supply of telecommunications services. Under the Trade Marks Act 1995 the Commission is responsible for the approval of Certification Trade Marks.

[39] Below, ch 7, Part D (2) (a).

[40] The overall administration of the Act currently lies within the portfolio of the Assistant Treasurer of the Commonwealth of Australia. The use of independent agencies to oversee the administration and implementation of regulatory law has been common in Anglo-Australian public administration since the 1960s. Below ch 3, Part B (2) (c).

Parliament and is required to report to it on a regular basis in the form of its annual report that is laid before both Houses of Parliament.[41]

D. ENFORCEMENT DISCRETION

A cursory review of the legislation establishing Australia's regime of competition regulation may convey the impression that the courts play the central role within the regulatory framework. The Federal Court of Australia determines whether the Part IV prohibitions have been contravened and, if so, the appropriate remedy (including the amount, if any, of pecuniary penalties payable for contravention). But actions cannot come before the Court unless and until either the Commission or a private litigant institutes proceedings against those suspected to have contravened the Act. Unless a private party is particularly disadvantaged by an alleged contravention and sufficiently motivated to institute litigation, it is unlikely that conduct at risk of contravening the Act will be brought before the Court.[42] In addition, it is the Commission which is entrusted with the task of investigating suspected contraventions, a task underlined by its intrusive statutory powers of investigation which extend well beyond those available to litigants in private suits.[43] While the Court may appear to occupy the primary role in the enforcement of the Act, in reality, the Commission's role is of critical importance.

In carrying out its enforcement functions, the Commission wields enormous discretionary power, yet the Act itself provides very little guidance as to how this discretionary power should be exercised. These two features, the breadth of the Commission's enforcement powers, and the absence of specific legislative guidance concerning the exercise of that power, are fairly typical of the institutional framework within which regulatory agencies and law enforcement officials are expected to operate, both in Australia and elsewhere. Accordingly, regulators are confronted with a number of very significant decisions in enforcing regulatory standards, which may not only have a serious impact on those against whom enforcement action is targeted, but may also profoundly influence the overall implementation of regulatory policy objectives. Some of these choices involve questions of general enforcement policy, while others are more operational in nature, relating to specific complaints. In relation to the former, for example, the regulator may wish to formulate a structured policy that prioritises certain types of violation or suspected violators but, if so, it must then determine the criteria for shaping its priorities. How are these to be decided? On the other hand, the reg-

[41] The Commission's first three annual reports have been reviewed by Parliament: see House of Representatives Standing Committee on Financial Institutions and Public Administration (1997); House of Representatives Standing Committee on Financial Institutions and Public Administration (1998); House of Representatives Standing Committee on Economics, Finance and Public Administration (2001).

[42] Yeung (1998).

[43] The Commission has strong statutory power to require the production of documents and the examination of witnesses: Trade Practices Act 1974, s 155.

ulator might prefer to respond to instances of alleged contraventions on an ad hoc basis, opting for a reactive strategy rather than adopting a more focused approach to its enforcement priorities. If an enforcement policy is favoured, should that policy be driven by third-party complaints or is a pro-active self-investigation to be preferred? Should the regulator attempt to divide its enforcement efforts equally amongst the regulatory standards that it is required to enforce, or should a strategic approach be adopted by emphasising those provisions considered more harmful to the community than others? Should the regulator adopt a strategy of seeking to deter contraventions by pursuing formal enforcement action with a view to imposing punitive sanctions, or should it proceed by negotiation, seeking to persuade firms to comply with regulatory standards?[44]

At the level of specific complaints, the regulator's role displays considerable similarities to that of a prosecutor in 'traditional' criminal proceedings,[45] for the criminal prosecutor (at least within an Anglian adversarial system) possesses considerable discretionary power, the exercise of which will have a direct bearing on the outcome of the case. For example, the prosecutor must decide whether or not to lay charges, which evidence should be relied upon to prove the charges, what type of sanction should be sought, and so forth. Even after the regulator has made the threshold decision to investigate an alleged contravention it is then confronted with a series of further choices. It must decide whether the evidence gathered from a preliminary investigation warrants the making of a full-blown investigation. After extensive investigations have been carried out, it is then faced with the choice of pursuing formal enforcement action against those responsible for an alleged infringement or to proceed more informally. And, having decided on the particular strategy to be adopted in any given case, it is then faced with further decision-points throughout the enforcement process before the matter is brought to a close: what kind of sanctions (if any) should be sought? Against whom should the action be brought—the firm (or firms) alone or should individuals (where applicable) who have been involved in the alleged conduct also be subject to formal action? Should the action be settled or should the formal action be pursued to its conclusion, and if the former, then what terms of settlement should be regarded as acceptable?

The above examples are but a small sample of the wide spectrum of issues confronting regulators when enforcing regulatory standards. While the analytical framework constructed in the following chapter is applied to three specific enforcement activities,[46] it may be applied more broadly, providing a useful lens through which a range of enforcement decisions and activities may be examined. Now that the foundational assumptions upon which my exploration rests have been laid bare, we can now proceed to construct the analytical framework forming the basis of my evaluation.

[44] For a thorough literature review of the findings of socio-legal research concerning the various approaches that regulators have taken in response to such questions: see Kagan (1994).

[45] Below, ch 5, Part D (2).

[46] Above, ch 1, Part A.

3

Analysing Regulatory Implementation: A Principled Framework

A. INTRODUCTION

IN SETTING OUT to construct a framework of principles for evaluating regulatory implementation, I am not asserting that it is the best, let alone the only such framework. Grandiosity of this kind would be misplaced. Rather, I am simply setting out one valuable framework, drawn from liberal democratic premises, which may facilitate analysis of this kind, and which will hopefully provide a helpful springboard for provoking further inquiry and reflection.

B. A FRAMEWORK FOR ANALYSIS: REGULATORY GOALS AND CONSTITUTIONAL VALUES

In Chapter 1, I defined regulation as the sustained and focused attempt by the state to alter behaviour thought to be of value to the community.[1] Two important features arising from this conception of regulation provide the foundations for my analytical framework. First, because regulation is an instrument through which the community seeks to pursue the collective goals underlying a regulatory scheme, the primary criteria for evaluating a regulatory programme is the extent to which it effectively achieves those goals. Secondly, the means by which these collective goals are pursued is through the use of state resources, and may thus include the state's unique power of compulsion. In such circumstances, the regulated community is compelled by the state to behave in particular ways with the threat of sanctions if they do not comply. When regulation entails the imposition of sanctions upon those who violate regulatory standards, it may be conceived as a form of 'public law' in that regulatory rules are promulgated and enforced by the state and which cannot be overreached by private agreement.[2]

[1] Above, ch 1, Part B (1) (a).

[2] Regulation can thus be distinguished from private law in that the latter has a primarily facilitative function—it offers a set of formalised arrangements with which individuals can 'clothe' their activities and relationships. The arrangements carry with them mutual rights and obligations which a court will enforce if necessary. Although in this context the law controls conduct in one sense, it can be regarded as 'private' law in so far as the obligations are incurred voluntarily by the parties and can always be displaced by agreements between the affected parties if they so wish: Ogus (1994), 2.

These two characteristics of regulation, its instrumental nature and its public aspect, enable us to analyse and evaluate regulatory programmes at two different levels. At one level, it is possible to amplify the overarching purpose of regulation in effectively securing its collective goals by reference to more specific regulatory goals. At another level, it is possible to identify a series of factors that influence and constrain regulatory decision-making arising from the public aspect of regulation that rest on broader constitutional values which are themselves rooted in liberal democratic theory. In liberal constitutional democracies, state intervention in the private activities of its citizens must be exercised in a manner that is consistent with democratic governance and the rule of law.[3] Accordingly, because regulatory implementation involves the exercise of public power affecting the community and individuals, it must be consistent with public law principles or 'constitutional values', as I shall describe them. Regulatory goals and constitutional values together provide the foundation for normative standards through which regulatory programmes can be examined and evaluated, and to which we now turn.

1. Regulatory Goals

The essential purpose of regulation is to fulfil the collective goals justifying regulatory intervention. In general terms, effectiveness concerns the extent to which a regulatory scheme is successful in achieving its collective goal or goals.[4] Thus, for example, the success of any scheme of competition regulation will depend on whether, and to what extent, it secures economic efficiency through the promotion of competitive markets. The goal of effective regulation can, however, be pinned to the following more specific regulatory goals or clusters of goals, namely (a) efficiency; (b) clarity and predictability; and (c) flexibility, responsiveness and timeliness. This list is not intended to be exhaustive. Nor are these goals distinct and mutually exclusive, for there are many ways in which they overlap and cohere with each other. But, taken together, these goals encapsulate the essential elements that are likely to feature in assessing the effectiveness of regulatory implementation.

(a) Efficiency

Efficiency refers to the relationship between resources and outcomes. A decision is efficient if it generates the desired outcome at the lowest cost.[5] In the regulatory context, efficiency has two dimensions. First, regulation is a costly activity

[3] The term 'rule of law' is used here to refer to a set of political principles that reflect a collection of inter-related values and are discussed more fully in subsection 2 below.

[4] Galligan (1986), 285–6.

[5] *Ibid,* 129. I am using the term here to refer specifically to efficiency in public administration, rather than in its technical sense as per ch 2, n 1 and n 2.

and involves the expenditure of public funds. Given that public funds are limited, the implementation of regulatory programmes should endeavour to secure the desired outcomes at the least possible cost to the public purse. Secondly, regulation imposes compliance costs on the regulated community and others affected by regulation. Regulatory implementation should seek both to minimise these costs and to ensure that they are justified and outweighed by their benefits, thereby achieving effective outcomes at the lowest cost to the community in general.

In common parlance, the terms 'efficiency' and 'effectiveness' are often used interchangeably, yet they are theoretically distinct. Although both concepts are defined by reference to specified goals,[6] effectiveness concerns the realisation of given goals whilst efficiency is concerned with the deployment of resources in the realisation of goals. Accordingly, the collective goals of any regulatory programme must be identified in order to assess whether or not the scheme is efficient and/or effective. In private enterprise, the goal of the enterprise is clear and readily quantifiable: the aim is to maximise profit, which is directly measured by the excess of revenue over expenditure. The position is, however, considerably more complex when applied to regulation and other forms of public administration.[7] In the regulatory context, the goal is not to profit from some marketable commodity, but to achieve its stated collective goals.[8] However, the collective goals of a particular regulatory scheme may not be readily identifiable, or may be various and even conflicting—in which case the goals need to be ranked in relation to each other before any meaningful assessment of efficiency or effectiveness can be made.[9] Even if the goals are clear, assessing efficiency and effectiveness may be difficult because either or both the goal sought to be pursued and the costs and benefits of regulation may be inherently difficult to identify, let alone quantified in numerical terms with any degree of precision.

Difficulties in the practical application of these concepts to the public sector have not, however, prevented them rising to prominence in sweeping reforms to public administration that have become known as the 'New Public Management' (NPM) and the associated 'deregulation' movement. NPM refers to a series of related reforms in public administration occurring in various countries (including Australia and the UK and actively promoted by the OECD), underpinned by a desire to replace the perceived inefficiency of hierarchical bureaucracy with the presumed efficiency of markets, and a drive to make the state more entrepreneurial.[10] Deregulation is an elusive concept, but its general

[6] *Ibid*, 130.

[7] This is not to deny the conceptual and practical complexities which can arise in identifying and quantifying whether any given item should be classed as a revenue or expenditure item in order to calculate profit in any given financial reporting period.

[8] Conflict in regulatory goals has plagued utility regulation in the UK: Prosser (1997); Foster (1992); Department of Trade and Industry (1998).

[9] Galligan (1986), 131.

[10] The literature is considerable. Eg Hood (1996); Lewis (1993); Oliver and Drewry (1996); Freedland (1994); Taggart (1991); Bayne (1988); Pildes and Sunstein (1995).

essence refers to the process of reducing state control over an industry or activity so as to make it structurally more responsive to market forces.[11] Both trends can be seen within a broader movement beginning in the late 1970s concerned with 'rolling back the frontiers of the state'.[12] Hood has commented that underlying these reforms (and particularly the NPM) is a focus on the 'cold, calculating and relentlessly functional' values of 'economy, efficiency and effectiveness' (otherwise known as the 'three Es').[13] The design and conduct of regulation has experienced the full force of these reforms.[14] For example, the Australian Office of Regulation Review was established as the Commonwealth government's regulatory reform 'watchdog', with the responsibility of promoting the government's objective of 'effective and efficient legislation and regulations . . . from an economy wide perspective'.[15] All Commonwealth government departments, agencies, statutory authorities and boards are required to prepare a regulatory impact statement for all reviews of existing legislation, proposed new or amended regulation and proposed treaties involving regulation which will 'directly affect business, have a significant indirect effect on business, or restrict competition.'[16] The regulatory impact statement requires a cost-benefit analysis, an economic technique used to assess the net benefit of a project or proposal, and therefore requires a detailed analysis of the benefits and costs of the proposed action (and its alternatives), with each item being quantified in numerical terms.[17] The regulatory proposal is then evaluated primarily (although not exclusively) in terms of its efficiency.[18]

In order to implement these reforms, auditing institutions have assumed an increasingly important role.[19] In the conduct of 'value for money audits' of public sector programmes, Power observes that there is a fundamental tension

[11] Baldwin (1987), 24; Harlow (1999), 3–4.

[12] Prosser (1997).

[13] Hood (1990).

[14] The impact on regulation not only includes 'regulation' in the narrow sense adopted here, but extends to other forms of regulation.

[15] Office of Regulation Review (1998), B11. In the UK, similar bodies have been established: the Regulatory Impact Unit operates within the auspices of the UK Cabinet Office, in conjunction with the Better Regulation Task Force, which is independent of the UK government. See www.cabinet-office.gov.uk/regulation/.

[16] However, there are limited exceptions. A regulatory impact statement is not mandatory for regulation that is 'minor or mechanical in nature and does not substantially alter existing arrangements; involves consideration of specific Government purchases, is required in the interest of national security; is primary or delegated legislation which merely meets an obligation of the commonwealth under an international agreement by repeating or adopting the terms of all or part of an instrument for which the agreement provides, or is excluded from consultation in the Legislative Instruments Bill, or is a regulation of a state or self-governing territory that applies in a non-self governing territory.': Office of Regulation Review (1998), B3–B4.

[17] *Ibid*, B5 states that, 'where possible, the various costs should be quantified. Where quantitative data about costs are unavailable, there are various estimation techniques that can be used. Where it is not possible to prepare a quantitative estimate, a qualitative assessment of costs and benefits should be undertaken.'

[18] *Ibid*.

[19] Power (1997), 49.

between the logic and language of effectiveness and that of the concepts of economy and efficiency. Efficiency lends itself more readily to the audit process, in so far as it can be more readily translated (albeit roughly and imperfectly) into the measurement of inputs and observable outputs. By contrast, effectiveness requires a more complex evaluation of the quality of the overall outcomes achieved by reference to a programme's specific goals, and thus sits more uncomfortably with audit concepts and techniques. Thus, Power notes that there has been a tendency for the three Es to be related hierarchically such that economy and efficiency 'oversee' those of effectiveness.[20] The result has been that in many areas of public administration the conduct of value for money audits of public programmes has tended to focus on measurable outputs, despite the essentially arbitrary nature of these standards, rather than on their effectiveness.

It is therefore important to avoid conflating the concepts of efficiency and effectiveness and to bear in mind the shortcomings of their practical application in the regulatory context. While regulatory implementation should strive to be efficient, the overarching purpose of regulation is the effective achievement of its collectivist goals: the fulfilment of these goals may not be readily observable or measurable. Qualitative evaluation of a regulatory programme is critical to assess its effectiveness in a meaningful way. A crude comparison of the cost of inputs to observable outcomes will not suffice.

(b) Clarity and Predictability

Given that the primary purpose of regulation is to modify economic and social behaviour so as to promote its collective goal(s), a regulatory scheme must be capable of providing useful and reliable guidance to the regulated community concerning the scope of permissible conduct and the consequences of non-compliance. Clarity and predictability in both the content and application of regulatory standards contribute to the latter's ability to provide such guidance. This is true not only of legal rules, but also to all rules intended to provide guidance in any system of social organisation.[21] Guidance is provided most directly and completely by a system of precise rules that are stable, applied consistently, not changed too often, known publicly and not unduly complex.[22]

The importance of predictability in the framework of the law was emphasised by Max Weber in his analysis of the law and social action.[23] Weber sought to

[20] *Ibid*, 117. See also McEldowney (2000). Power's observation is paradigmatically demonstrated in the literature of the Office of Regulation Review which states that '[r]egulation should not only be effective, but should also be the most efficient means for achieving relevant policy objectives. In this context, there is a public perception that rule makers too often concern themselves with the issue of effectiveness, ignoring efficiency issues', Office of Regulation Review (1998), B1.

[21] Galligan (1986), 91; Twining and Miers (1991), 159–66; Schauer (1991), 155–58.

[22] Raz (1977); Diver (1999).

[23] Weber (1954).

explain the nature and forms of social action associated with western capitalism and the reasons for their development.[24] He was particularly concerned with the significance of law in facilitating the forms of rational planning and calculation that underpin capitalist enterprise. Weber argued that law is accepted in modern western societies, not primarily because it expresses society's deeply held values, but because it provides a commonsensical and comprehensive framework of predictable rules that enables individuals to pursue rational social action, and thereby fulfil self interest in a rational way. Whether or not one accepts Weber's view on the social basis of the law's acceptance, his instrumentalist view of the law is particularly apposite in the context of regulation. Because regulation seeks to implement collective goals by controlling behaviour, it is particularly important that a regulatory scheme provides the regulated community with clear and predictable rules within the confines of which they are free to pursue their own ends and purposes.[25] Clarity and predictability is particularly important in regulation because the regulated activity is valued by the community. The intention is to control how that activity is undertaken, rather than to eliminate it altogether. A lack of clarity and predictability in the interpretation and application of regulatory rules may deter some socially desirable activity, and this may undermine regulatory effectiveness.

(c) Flexibility, Responsiveness and Timeliness

Although clarity and predictability in regulatory standards facilitate effective regulation, flexibility and responsiveness are also required—both in the nature and content of regulatory rules and standards, and in their interpretation and application, if regulation is to be effective.[26] Flexibility is required in order to avoid formalism in implementing policy goals. Formalism involves a rigid and literal adherence to rules, emphasising form rather than substance and may undermine the effectiveness of rules in realising their desired objects.[27] In contrast, flexibility implies a willingness to adopt a more purposive approach to the interpretation and application of rules, in order to give effect to their underlying purpose or 'spirit'.[28] Regulatory implementation characterised by flexibility rather than formalism is more likely to be effective in securing its collective goals.[29] Flexibility demonstrates a commitment to the overall spirit of the regu-

[24] Weber (1954).

[25] Cotterrell (1992), 159.

[26] The relationship amongst regulatory goals is discussed at subsection (d) below.

[27] McBarnet and Whelan (1991), 850; Schaeur (1989).

[28] The need for flexibility in any system of social organisation, including legal regulation, provides one of the principal justifications for conferring some degree of discretion on those who are required to interpret and apply the relevant rules. See generally Galligan (1986) and below Part B (2)(a).

[29] Formalism in rule interpretation and application may also lead to 'creative compliance' whereby those subject to regulation rely on the formalistic application of rules to escape legal control without actually violating them: McBarnet and Whelan (1991).

latory scheme rather than a mechanistic adherence to rules, and encourages the regulated community to have confidence that regulatory rules and standards will be reasonably applied.[30]

Regulatory programmes should also strive to be responsive, by this I mean capable of adapting to the dynamic environment in which they operate.[31] When a regulatory scheme is designed and established, it is not possible to foresee or anticipate all potential contingencies which may affect the future regulatory environment. Developments may occur not only in the way in which the regulated activity is carried out, but also in the academic theory and social values that justify regulating that activity. A regulatory scheme therefore needs to be capable of adapting and responding to such developments as and when they arise, otherwise it risks becoming stultified and outdated, thereby failing to secure its collective goals.[32]

The legitimacy of regulatory implementation also depends on its timeliness. Undue delay in regulatory decision-making impedes the ability of those affected by the decision to plan their activities. Extended delay creates uncertainty and instability in the regulatory environment, and can thereby undermine its effectiveness. Prompt decision-making enables affected parties to act upon the decisions so made and avoids unnecessarily impeding socially desirable activity.[33]

(d) The Relationship Amongst Regulatory Goals

The series of regulatory goals set out above serve to amplify and inform the conditions of legitimate regulatory implementation. Pursuit of these regulatory goals together contributes to the effectiveness of a regulatory programme. In order to ascertain whether a regulatory programme is effective, it is useful to assess the extent to which these three clusters of specific goals, namely (a) efficiency; (b) clarity and predictability and (c) flexibility, responsiveness and timeliness, are achieved. These goals generally operate in harmony, so that the pursuit of one goal may also facilitate the fulfilment of another. For example, clarity and predictability in regulatory decision-making are likely to enhance the

[30] Black (1997).

[31] Galligan (1986), 137.

[32] In their well-known monograph, Nonet and Selznick claim that responsiveness should be distinguished from opportunistic adoption or capitulation to pressure. A responsive institution maintains its integrity while acknowledging the legitimacy of an appropriate range of claims and interests. A spirit of consultation must prevail and authority be subject to criticism and reconstruction, while the institution's basic commitments, and its capacity to function, are preserved and protected: Nonet and Selznick (1995), ch 4. Their notion of 'responsive law' is a much richer, thicker conception of responsiveness than that adopted here. Likewise, Ayres and Braithwaite have developed a specific set of programme recommendations which they collectively term 'responsive regulation' but this is not the sense in which the notion of responsiveness in regulation is used here: Braithwaite and Ayres (1992).

[33] It is often asserted that speed is particularly important in the commercial context, but as Black and Mulchinksi point out, it is difficult to see why speed is any more important in the determination of commercial matters than in the determination of applications for asylum by immigration officials: Black *et al* (1998).

efficiency of a regulatory scheme as well as reducing the uncertainty faced by the regulated community in planning their affairs, thereby reducing the risk, and hence costs, associated with engaging in the regulated activity. But on occasion regulatory goals may antagonise each other. In particular, the need for flexibility and responsiveness in regulatory decision-making invariably pulls in the opposite direction to the need for clarity and predictability. To emphasise one is to play down the other. Given the inherent tension between these two clusters of regulatory goals, how should this dissonance be resolved?

It is suggested that the guiding principle is to be found in the collective goals that constitute the overarching purpose of the regulatory scheme. It is not possible to determine in the abstract whether or not one goal should be emphasised in favour of another. Conflicts can only be meaningfully resolved in the particular circumstances in which they arise. Given that the fulfilment of specific regulatory goals is subsidiary to the achievement of the overarching collective goals of a regulatory scheme, any conflict between them should be resolved in favour of the goal more likely in the long term to lead to effective substantive compliance. So, for example, consider a situation in which the regulator is required to evaluate a proposed a transaction that may entail a technical breach of regulatory rules, but does not detract from or threaten their general underlying purpose or 'spirit'. In such circumstances, there is a legitimate basis for the regulator interpreting and applying the rules in a flexible and responsive manner, although this might detract from their clarity and predictability. This is because a broader, flexible and more context-sensitive approach may reasonably be expected to promote the regulatory scheme's collective goals in the long term, although this may generate some lack of clarity and predictability in the short term. There will inevitably be considerable scope for reasonable disagreement concerning whether the long term effectiveness of a regulatory scheme is more likely to be secured by favouring one regulatory goal over another in such situations of conflict. Provided that such policy trade-offs are openly articulated while constantly bearing in mind that the overarching collective goal(s) of any regulatory scheme, then those trade-offs cannot legitimately be faulted.

2. Constitutional Values

The above regulatory goals amplify and elucidate in more specific terms the demands of effective regulatory implementation and its primary goal. The pursuit of effectiveness is, however, shaped and constrained by the public aspect of regulation. This public aspect of regulation generates a series of values, or clusters of values, derived from what I shall refer to as constitutional principles. By this I refer not to the rules and precepts contained in the written text of a democratic constitution, but to those ideals and principles that are largely common to liberal democratic legal systems and are often referred to collectively and encapsulated by the idea of 'constitutionalism'. Constitutionalism springs from a belief in limited government.[34] It embraces the various ways in which it is possible to be committed to the notion that in any democratic political system, there are certain values that possess special 'constitutional' status, embodying a collection of values that democracy itself presupposes and therefore cut across the political programme of particular governments.[35] Although these values are more deeply rooted in liberal democratic conceptions of the nature and requirements of justice and democratic governance, they have become so embedded in the political structure and practice of western democratic legal systems that their existence and importance may often be taken for granted. While it would be naïve to think that these values might be stated exhaustively, it is nonetheless possible to identify five clusters of constitutional principles that together represent the essential constitutional values that are of importance in the regulatory context. Regulatory implementation should thus be (a) authorised by law (b) certain and stable (c) accountable and transparent (d) procedurally fair, and (e) proportional, consistent and rational. In many circumstances, these clusters of values may also be overlapping and mutually reinforcing, and they should not therefore be regarded as distinct and mutually exclusive. Each cluster is more fully described below.

(a) Authorised by Law

The rule of law requires that all government action should be authorised by law.[36] Because regulation involves state intervention in private affairs, regulatory decisions must be legally authorised, typically requiring a legislative mandate from the state's primary legislature and thereby investing the regulatory scheme with democratic legitimacy.[37] Although this requirement is simple to state, it may not always be simple to apply in practice, particularly in the context of regulatory decision-making. The conferral of broad discretionary powers on regulatory officials has become increasingly prevalent in the modern state[38] and where this occurs, the legal boundaries of that discretion must be identified in order to assess whether their action has been legally authorised. This may be a difficult task, particularly where the statute conferring power on the official is vaguely worded in the broadest of terms.

Broad administrative discretion appears to threaten values underlying the rule of law, particularly its concern for certainty and stability.[39] It should not be

34 Sajo (1999).

35 Loughlin (2000), Part IV.

36 Raz (1977). The concept of the rule of law captures a set of normative ideas about the nature and operation of law in society: see Craig (1997) and the literature cited therein.

37 Majone (1996), 291–93; Baldwin and McCrudden (1987); Baldwin (1996).

38 Raz (1977); Dicey (1961). Galligan explains the discretionary trend in the allocation and exercise of power on the basis of general historical factors, a belief that many regulatory tasks are to be approached as technical or scientific matters to be settled by specialists, and a tendency away from formal to substantive authority: Galligan (1986), 73.

39 The principal critique is by Davis (1969).

thought, however, that the conferring of broad discretion and broadly worded legislative standards are evils to be avoided.[40] There are sound reasons why a legislature may wish to confer broad discretionary powers on regulatory officials. It may not be possible for the legislature to set out precise objectives and appropriate standards for regulation and regulatory decisions as the tasks involved in regulation are frequently complex, requiring specialised knowledge and the exercise of judgement.[41] Thus it may be both legitimate and desirable for legislatures to delegate the task of fleshing out in more specific terms the content of regulatory rules and their application to the enforcement agency, provided that the latter is accountable for its decisions and actions.[42]

(b) Certainty and Stability

The rule of law not only requires that regulatory action must be authorised by law, but also that laws should be clear and certain, in order to allow those affected to know the laws in advance before being subjected to them *ex post facto*.[43] Certainty and stability may be considered one of the virtues of rules.[44] When officials act according to rules, the scope for arbitrariness and inconsistency in decision-making is reduced. Secondly, certainty and stability in regulatory law enables those affected by those laws to plan their affairs. Regulatory laws should not be changed too frequently, otherwise it will be difficult for those affected to find out what the laws are at any given moment and will inhibit them from planning for the future.[45] Stability in the law is particularly important in economic regulation because business decisions are often based on long-term time frames, the fruits of which are unlikely to materialise for several years.[46] Thirdly, the principle of legal certainty is particularly important where criminal sanctions apply for failure to comply with the law. It reflects our strong moral convictions that no one should be punished for conduct that was not unlawful

[40] The culture of British understandings of the rule of law may be attributed, ultimately, to Aristotle's idea of the rule of law: see Loughlin (2000), ch 5 and see generally Galligan (1986); Nonet and Selznick (1995), ch 4. As H L A Hart points out, all legal systems compromise between two social needs: the need for certain rules which can safely be applied by individuals to themselves without fresh official guidance or weighing up of social issues and the need to leave open, for later settlement by an informed official choice, issues which can only be properly appreciated and settled when they arise in a concrete case: Hart (1961), 130.

[41] Baldwin (1987), 35.

[42] Below section (c).

[43] Dicey (1961); Jowell (2000); Craig (1997). The principle of legal certainty is closely connected to the regulatory goals of clarity and predictability. Indeed, the two values may be regarded as two sides of the same coin. Viewed in constitutional terms, it is the moral dimension associated with certainty that is of particular importance in safeguarding the liberty of the individual. But when viewed as a regulatory goal, it is the instrumental value of legal certainty in enabling individuals to plan for the future that is emphasised.

[44] Rules have, however, been associated with a number of limitations which are discussed below at ch 6, Part C (1) (a).

[45] Raz (1977).

[46] *Ibid.*

at the time of its occurrence.[47] In the regulatory context, legal certainty is therefore particularly important where criminal sanctions may be imposed for violating regulatory rules. Even where sanctions are civil rather than criminal in nature and cannot therefore lead to restrictions upon, or deprivation of, the liberty of persons and tend not to carry the same degree of moral censure, legal certainty and stability is nonetheless important because civil sanctions nevertheless constitute a form of state-imposed hard treatment.[48]

(c) *Accountability and Transparency*

Accountability and transparency together constitute a cluster of values that is essential within any democratic system of governance. In a broad sense, to be accountable is to be liable to be called to account (or to answer for responsibilities and conduct) and to be capable of giving an account, to a person or institution. Within a democratic system, accountability requires that public officials to whom powers have been delegated must account for their actions to the community. The underlying assumption is that all government powers are held on behalf of the community and therefore account must be made to it.[49] Governmental accountability can be considered from a variety of perspectives. In the regulatory context, accountability can be usefully divided into five core (and overlapping) categories: political, administrative, financial, legal and professional—each category referring to the particular aspect of governmental accountability in issue. For example, legal accountability refers to the obligation of a public body to justify its actions in terms of compliance with the general law and the legal mandate conferred upon it.[50] But common to all these categories of accountability are the structural features of the mechanisms for accountability. 'Accountability is about requiring a person to explain and justify—against criteria of some kind—their decisions or acts, and then to make amends for any fault or error'.[51] Davies therefore argues that an accountability mechanism consists of four key components: setting standards against which to judge the account; obtaining the account; judging the account; and deciding what consequences (if any) should follow.[52] When assessing the quality of accountability

47 Dicey (1961).

48 Below ch 4, Part C (1).

49 Galligan (1986), 4.

50 Political accountability broadly refers to obligations to account for the exercise of political power, including the way in which powers are exercised so as to distribute benefits and burdens amongst individuals and groups in society. Financial accountability refers to obligations to account for the expenditure of resources and the financial controls that limit the use of public funds. Administrative accountability is closely related to financial accountability, encompassing the internal management of government agencies and institutions, but is concerned with administrative matters other than merely financial. Professional accountability refers to obligations to account for the exercise of decisions in accordance with professional expertise in relation to activities which require specialist knowledge and judgement. For a careful analysis of accountability, see Davies (2001), ch 1.

51 Oliver (1994), 245.

52 Davies (2001).

mechanisms in regulatory programmes, regard can usefully be had to these structural features to identify whether, and to what extent, they satisfy the requirements of accountable, and hence democratic, governance.

While it is important that mechanisms for ensuring that legal, financial, administrative and professional accountability are secured in relation to regulatory decision-making, it is political accountability that has tended to be the focus of discussion in the regulatory context.[53] This is largely due to the prevalence of the independent regulatory agency—an institution that rose to prominence in Australia, the UK and perhaps most notably within the EU, in the 1970s and 80s.[54] These agencies (including the Commission) are 'independent' in the sense that they are not directly elected by the electorate and are generally invested by the legislature with broad discretionary powers to carry out their regulatory tasks in a largely autonomous manner, with little (if any) specific or detailed guidance from the legislature or responsible Minister. In consequence, they often wield considerable power and their decisions often have very significant effects on the distribution of benefits and burdens between individuals and groups.[55] Within a democratic system, we would therefore expect that effective mechanisms for securing political accountability would apply to them. In practice, however, such mechanisms have been claimed to be either absent or ineffective. Here lies a tension between two concerns frequently expressed in relation to such agencies. On the one hand, the establishment of independent regulatory agencies is often motivated by a desire to insulate or at least distance them from the vagaries of politics, reducing the scope for politicians to intervene in the regulatory process to pursue self-serving political gain.[56] On the other hand, such agencies are frequently called on to make polycentric decisions that have a differential impact on individuals and groups so that their independent status sits rather uncomfortably with democratic principles.[57]

Even if this tension cannot be satisfactorily resolved, it is to some extent reduced if there is a high level of transparency in regulatory implementation and decision-making. Transparency refers to the visibility of regulatory decisions, referring to the extent to which the reasons or basis for particular regulatory decisions can be identified. Transparency is directly linked to accountability in that the latter requires the body being called to account to explain the reasons for its actions, and to justify them in accordance with a particular set of rules or standards for evaluation. Transparency is important at two levels: to enable those affected by the decision to know the reasons for the decision and for democratic governance. Those affected by regulatory decisions are entitled to an account of the reasons for the decision so as to demonstrate to them that the

[53] Graham (1998); Foster (1992), ch 8; Corry (1995).
[54] Majone (1996); Harlow (1999), 307–09.
[55] Graham (1998), 495.
[56] Foster (1992), ch 3; Harlow (1999), 307–09.
[57] Baldwin (1987); Graham (1998); Fuller (1978); Mashaw (1983), ch 3.

decision was made properly and that they were fairly treated.[58] Transparency in regulatory decisions is essential to their democratic legitimacy, by enabling the general public not only to be guided by regulatory decisions but also to assess their quality. By enabling the public to scrutinise regulatory decisions, transparency and accountability in decision-making enhances public confidence in the quality of those decisions.

(d) Procedural Fairness or Due Process

Procedural fairness can be interpreted in two senses. In one sense, it refers to a legal doctrine in Anglian administrative law more commonly referred to as natural justice. In this sense, the term procedural fairness refers to specific legal doctrines about procedures that express fundamental principles about the fair treatment of persons and the procedures needed to give effect to fair treatment.[59] The legal doctrine of procedural fairness has two limbs: decisions by public officials should be made in an unbiased manner and those affected by such decisions should be given an opportunity to participate in the decisions that affect them.[60] The particular procedural requirements demanded by these two limbs vary depending on the circumstances of the relevant decision. A range of factors are relevant to that end, such as the nature of the decision to be made, the range of affected interests, the extent of the interest of the person or persons affected and the seriousness of the implications of the decision.[61]

But the term 'procedural fairness' can be used in another sense, referring to the values justifying the legal rules of procedure, rather than the specific rules themselves. A range of different justifications for procedural fairness have been suggested, that vary in their perception of the role of fair procedures in leading to accurate outcomes and the role of non-outcome based values.[62] Strongly instrumentalist justifications claim that decision-making procedures must be fair for the purpose of, and to the extent that they promote, accurate outcomes.[63] At the other end of the spectrum, it has been argued that the instrumental role of fair procedures in facilitating accurate outcomes is merely incidental. Their primary purpose is to express in a direct and unmediated way society's respect for the dignity of persons: fair procedures are an essential expression of respect for the individual because it recognises the individual as a

[58] Galligan (1996), 431–34.

[59] Craig (1999), chs 13–14.

[60] *Ibid*, ch 14.

[61] *Ibid*, 425–38. For example, where criminal sanctions are contemplated, procedural fairness requires that a person alleged to have committed the contravention is accorded the full set of procedural rights associated with the criminal trial process. In contrast, if an applicant has but a mere hope that an administrative discretion will be exercised in one's favour, then the applicant's entitlement to a fair hearing will be less extensive. See below, ch 5, Part C.

[62] Richardson (1994).

[63] Bentham's writings on evidence and procedure are scattered, but some of the most important ideas are found in Dumont (1827); Dumont (1837) cited by Galligan (1996), 9.

moral agent who is entitled to be treated with dignity and respect.[64] In between this spectrum of views is a variety of intermediate positions. For example, Galligan argues that the primary purpose of procedural fairness is instrumental: to secure accurate outcomes, and thereby uphold normative expectations generated by society concerning the achievement of the standards established by law. But, by upholding the normative expectations generated by the law, procedures also serve the purpose of ensuring that other values (both outcome-based and non-outcome based) are respected in the legal process. Those values rest on the basic principle of respect for persons, drawing on moral and political ideas and are also shaped by the social and cultural context of each society.[65]

For the purposes of this book, we need not explore further the various justifications for procedural fairness. It is sufficient to acknowledge that procedural fairness is required in order to serve both outcome-based and non-outcome based values that are grounded on the basic principle of respect for the dignity of persons. The extent to which outcome-based and non-outcome based values feature in the justification for procedural fairness may, however, influence the resolution of conflicts between regulatory values and goals and amongst constitutional values in any given context, an issue discussed more fully below.[66]

(e) Proportionality, Consistency and Rationality

Regulatory implementation often entails matters of significant complexity, requiring consideration of diverse, disparate and often conflicting interests. Thus the decisions that regulators may be required to make when implementing regulatory programmes may not throw up obvious, simple solutions so that it is not meaningful to insist upon 'correct' decisions. Nonetheless, regulatory decision-makers should strive to ensure that their decisions are substantively fair in content and application. In other words, fairness is important not merely at the procedural level, but also at the substantive level. This is not to suggest that there is a clear analytical distinction between substance and procedure, but simply to point to the need for regulatory decisions to be responsive to moral principles and thus conform to some substantive notion of fairness (or justice) in rationally pursuing regulatory goals.[67]

The concept of fairness can be regarded as having both a substantive sense and a formal sense, exemplified or expressed in the maxim 'treat like cases alike'.[68]

[64] Galligan (1996), 74. In a well-known passage, Tribe expresses the principle thus, '. . . the right to be heard from, and the right to be told why, are analytically distinct from the right to secure a different outcome; these rights to interchange express the elementary idea that to be a *person* rather than a *thing*, is at least to be *consulted* about what is to be done with one.' Tribe (1978), 503.

[65] Galligan (1996).

[66] Below, subsection (f).

[67] Galligan (1996), 50; Dworkin (1985), 58.

[68] Hart refers to the idea of justice as consisting of two parts: a uniform or constant feature, summarised in the precept 'treat like cases alike' and a shifting or varying criteria used in determining when, for any given purpose, cases are alike or different: Hart (1986), 160.

One part of the maxim concerns the substantive principles as to what constitutes, for a particular purpose, justifiable categories of likeness and difference. Identifying those substantive principles, that is, identifying the basis upon which benefits and burdens should be distributed, must ultimately rest on some background political theory of justice.[69] The second part of the maxim concerns the even-handed application of those principles to specific situations. Compliance with this second part, which Galligan refers to as formal fairness, can thus be regarded as a direct sense of fairness, quite apart from whether the substantive principles are themselves justifiable.[70] It is therefore possible to identify more specific principles of formal fairness which are likely to feature in any plausible account of substantive fairness, and which should therefore guide and inform public administration, including regulatory decision-making, independently of the principles or content of the notion of substantive fairness. Such principles of formal fairness include proportionality, consistency (including equality of treatment) and rationality.

Proportionality requires that regulatory action seeks to pursue a legitimate aim, and that there is a reasonable relationship between that aim and the means used to achieve it.[71] It involves some idea of balance between competing interests and objectives, and the appropriate relationship between means and ends.[72] The principle of proportionality should be supplemented by the principle of consistency (although the latter is arguably implicit in the former). Consistency is often reflected in the maxim 'treat like cases alike' or the principle of equal treatment. Although consistency in decision-making does not necessarily guarantee that the decision will be substantively fair according to the chosen background theory of justice, nonetheless general adherence to the principle of consistency demonstrates a commitment to equality in the treatment of persons and groups, reducing the existence and appearance of arbitrariness. Consistency also promotes stability and certainty in regulatory decision-making, providing firmer guidance to those likely to be affected. Rationality is a complex notion, but at minimum, it requires that there be plausible and relevant reasons of sufficient weight to justify a decision. The notion of rationality is perhaps illuminated by considering its antithesis—irrationality, which denotes arbitrary or capricious action, or action lacking a reasoned and adequate foundation.

(f) The Relationship Amongst Constitutional Values: Rights in Regulatory Enforcement

Unlike regulatory goals, which are purposive in nature and thus amplify how the collective goals of regulation can best be achieved, constitutional values

[69] Craig (1999), 606.
[70] Galligan (1986), 152–53.
[71] de Burca (1993).
[72] Craig (1999), 590–91.

serve as *constraints* on society's pursuit of collective goals. Accordingly, resolving tension and conflict amongst constitutional values is somewhat more complex than resolving conflict amongst regulatory goals. Each constitutional value, or cluster of values, rests on deeper notions of constitutional and liberal democratic values derived from political theory and moral philosophy. It follows from their common foundation that they tend to operate in harmony with each other so that to pursue one value or cluster of values also enhances the fulfilment of other constitutional values. For example, transparency in decision-making is required so that those affected by the decision may know the underlying reasons for it and the broader community is enabled to scrutinise and evaluate regulatory decisions in general. To promote transparency in this way also promotes procedural fairness in decision-making, by confirming that due consideration has been given to any representations made by interested parties, enhancing public confidence in the decision-making process.

On the other hand, circumstances may arise in which some constitutional values may operate in tension, pulling in opposite directions. For example, in the course of evaluating the likely competitive impact of a proposed merger, the regulator may be provided with sensitive commercial information by the merging parties and from various persons and groups of persons (such as trade unions) likely to be affected. The public disclosure of confidential information may enhance the transparency of the regulator's ensuing decision, but it may be unlawful. In order to resolve such tensions, it is important to be clear about the nature of these constitutional values. Apart from the requirement that regulatory decisions must be authorised by law, the other constitutional values should not be seen in binary terms. In other words, identifying whether or not they are satisfied in any particular case is not a question of absolutes but a question of degree. It is more accurate to speak of the *degree* to which the values are fulfilled in the regulatory process, rather than whether or not they have or have not been fulfilled. It is this variable quality, the variable success of our efforts to realise values, that provides one basis for distinguishing constitutional values from legal doctrines that define legal rights and obligations. Although the content of legal doctrines may be variable in their application to different factual circumstances, they must be applied in binary terms when determining whether or not a legal right has been infringed or a legal duty complied with. So, for example, we can meaningfully enquire into whether or not the common law requirements of procedural fairness have been complied with in a particular situation. But this is not the same as enquiring into the extent to which the *values* of procedural fairness, or due process values, have been fulfilled in a particular situation. Mere compliance with legal rules may not necessarily ensure the adequate fulfilment of values upon which the rule is based, for it cannot be assumed that legal rules fully and completely give flesh to the deeper values which they are intended to reflect. For the purpose of constructing a normative framework, I am primarily concerned with the *values* that constrain and influence regulatory decision-making, rather than specific legal doctrines. My concern is to ensure that, within the regulatory process, constitutional values are respected at least to the extent necessary within a liberal democratic society.

The only constitutional value that does not take this continuous analytical form is the constitutional requirement that regulatory decisions must be authorised by law. This is because the requirement of legality is perhaps more accurately characterised as a legal doctrine, its underlying value resting on a respect for the rule of law[73] and democratic governance. Therefore, unlike the other constitutional values, this requirement can be seen in binary terms so that it is possible to assess whether any given regulatory decision is or is not authorised by law. But the binary nature of the requirement of legality should not be allowed to disguise the flexibility lying within it. I have already noted that where the legislature has conferred very broad discretionary powers on the regulator, determining whether a particular decision is legally authorised may be difficult to assess. In such cases, a plurality of considerations is likely to bear upon the requirement of legality, and these considerations may well vary from case to case.[74]

Although antagonism amongst constitutional values is likely to be infrequent, it may nonetheless occur. Just as conflict between regulatory goals cannot be resolved in the abstract, likewise whether or not one constitutional value should be emphasised so as to play down another can only be determined in light of the particular circumstances in which the tension arises. It is suggested that any such conflict should ultimately be resolved in favour of the constitutional value considered to be of greater importance, given the particular circumstances in which the conflict arises. Because I am not suggesting that there is any a priori hierarchy of constitutional values, a careful exploration of context is vital to determining which constitutional value should be given prominence in situations of conflict. In the following discussion, I will attempt to explain how conflict between constitutional values may be resolved by reference to the concept of individual rights, by facilitating an evaluation of the relative importance of constitutional values in a specific context. It is not necessary to embark on a detailed analysis of the nature and function of rights for the purposes of my examination. Nevertheless, because competition regulation and its enforcement may involve the exercise of the state's coercive power to control private activities in the pursuit of collective goals, there are circumstances in which individual rights may be implicated and it is therefore necessary to give brief consideration to their nature and function. But before elaborating on the idea of rights, we should pause to consider whether, and to what extent, it is meaningful to discuss the notion of rights in the context of regulatory enforcement, in which firms are typically the primary target of regulatory controls.

In considering the appropriate role (if any) of rights in the implementation of commercial regulation, it is useful to focus on the right to 'due process' (often

[73] Above, subsection (a).
[74] Above subsection (a).

referred to as the 'right to a fair trial'), which lies at the heart of the constitutional value of procedural fairness, for it is this right that is likely to be of greatest relevance in the enforcement context. Throughout regulatory compliance scholarship, relatively little attention has been paid to procedural fairness, and this may be partly attributed to the fact that those subject to enforcement proceedings are typically corporate entities rather than individuals. To the extent that due process rights are directly founded on essentially human needs and aspirations, on the nature of individual persons as moral agents, then they may seem inapplicable to corporate defendants.[75] But even if one accepts this premise, two responses are possible. First, even if due process rights are rooted in human dignity, they also derive force, at least in part, from other values—including the value of fairness and rationality implicit in the structure of the legal process, and also from instrumental concerns that the legal process should generate accurate outcomes. To the extent that due process rights derive their justification from instrumental concerns, there appears to be no reason why they should not then be accorded to all persons—whether individual or corporate in nature.[76] But, to the extent that such rights are justified on instrumental grounds, they are likely to be more readily *outweighed* by competing public interest considerations in lacking the peremptory force to which appeals to human dignity and individual autonomy typically give rise. Secondly, even if we ignore instrumental justifications for due process, it might plausibly be argued that a corporate entity is ultimately reducible to its owners as natural persons and *their* right to respect and recognition as moral agents is sufficient to ground a corporation's right to due process protections.[77]

For present purposes, we need not explore further the thorny and as yet unresolved question whether non-human entities can legitimately lay claim to due process and other so-called 'human rights' guarantees. In any event, regulatory proceedings are not always confined to corporate actors. For example, in Australian competition law the Commission frequently institutes proceedings seeking heavy sanctions against individuals suspected of direct involvement in alleged contraventions, so that the importance of ensuring that the fairness of procedures for determining liability remains intact.[78] In other jurisdictions, including the US and UK, some contraventions of competition law constitute criminal offences and may therefore result in the imprisonment of individuals. But although the typically corporate identity of those subject to enforcement action does not justify ignoring procedural fairness altogether, the fact some such actors may be well-resourced organisations with ready access to quality legal advice suggests that they do not belong to a vulnerable class for whom the protection offered by rights is of particular importance. One of the difficulties

[75] Feldman (1996), 366.
[76] *Ibid*, 367.
[77] O'Kelly (1979).
[78] But see Wils (2003) for a discussion of the liability of individuals for violations of EU competition law.

in prescribing the appropriate role for rights in the commercial setting arises from the enormous breadth and diversity in the character of those subject to regulatory requirements. Commercial actors come in all shapes and sizes, ranging from the giant multinational corporation controlling resources far exceeding the wealth of many developing nations, through to individuals practising a profession or trade upon which their livelihood depends.[79] Yet all of these actors may be affected by the same regulatory scheme and competition law is a prime example of this. Accordingly, it is difficult to argue in favour of a 'typical' case in identifying the significance of rights in commercial settings, and reliable generalisations are likely to be elusive. With this in mind, we can proceed to explore the idea of rights, and their role in resolving conflict within and between constitutional values.

The idea of rights, that individuals possess entitlements which it is incumbent upon others, and society at large, to acknowledge and respect, has become central to contemporary moral and political thinking, although the concept and content of rights remains surrounded by controversy.[80] For present purposes, rights can be defined as justified claims which relate to the interest of persons and which give rise to the duty of another person or persons in respect of that interest.[81] To have a right in moral and political reasoning is to indicate what people are entitled to do and how they are entitled to be treated.[82] The function of moral rights is primarily to justify action and restraints upon action, based on the critical morality of a society.[83] Fundamental (or human) rights are a species of moral right. They represent those minimum conditions under which human beings can flourish (that is as moral agents) and which ought to be secured for them, if necessary by force.[84] Rights thus have a special status, for to deny a person's right is to inflict upon them an injustice, a special kind of harm or 'moral harm'.[85] Because of their special status, rights operate to prevent the individual

[79] In particular, there is an increasing trend towards introducing court-ordered disqualification orders, prohibiting individuals from engaging in certain forms of employment or activity. von Hirsch and Wasik observe that there is a 'veritable forest of regulatory disqualifications, found throughout the law' noting that they often have a serious debilitating impact on the person disqualified: von Hirsch and Wasik (1997). For example, under the UK Enterprise Act 2002, individuals involved in certain violations of the Competition Act 1998 may be subject to 'Competition Disqualification Orders', prohibiting individual directors of companies which have breached UK or EU competition law from acting as a company director or taking on certain other management roles for up to 15 years.

[80] Different ways have been proposed of trying to pin down exactly what it means to have a right, which need not be canvassed for the limited purposes of this book. Some writings of importance are Dworkin (1978); McCormick (1973); Raz (1986), Part III.

[81] Raz (1986), ch 7.

[82] Jones (1994), 48.

[83] The critical morality of a society can be contrasted with its popular or 'positive' morality. To be concerned 'critically' with morality is to be concerned with what is right and wrong according to some substantive theory of justice. Positive morality is to be concerned with the empirical matter of what people believe to be right and wrong: Dworkin (1985), ch 7.

[84] Kleinig (1978), 45–6.

[85] Dworkin refers to bare harm as the harm a person suffers through punishment, whether it be just or unjust. Moral harm is the further injury suffered by a person when his or her punishment is unjust. Moral harm is thus a particular form of injustice: Dworkin (1985), 80.

from being used merely as a dispensable pawn in the collective decision-making of society.[86] When society is confronted with social and political decisions which impact upon individuals, rights stand in the way of a simple consequentialist calculus—their peremptory force prevents society from simply aggregating the costs and benefits of a particular course of action in deciding whether or not to pursue that course. Hence rights carry special weight in a case of conflict with other social goals or values and cannot lightly be overridden.

While fundamental rights are justified by reference to deep and abstract notions concerning the inherent dignity of persons, the particular rights recognised by a society will invariably be a product of local, historical and cultural factors. Thus it is not surprising that the catalogue and content of fundamental rights recognised and enshrined as constitutional by democratic societies differ from each other, and may differ over time.[87] It is also important to locate rights within the rough and tumble of politics and the messy practicalities of life and to resist the 'current tendency to accord rights an exaggerated role in moral life.'[88] Rights cannot be given complete protection in all circumstances because society recognises a multiplicity of different fundamental rights, which may sometimes come into conflict, and because fundamental rights may in some cases ground a justified claim on society's limited resources. It is therefore impossible to give fundamental rights complete protection, despite our noblest aspirations. Nonetheless, it may be possible to identify the minimum threshold level of protection that should be accorded to each right in order to preserve its fundamental core.[89] The degree of protection will vary, depending on the nature and content of the right, and the justification for its recognition. In some circumstances, to strengthen the protection of one right necessarily entails an encroachment on the scope of protection accorded to another right. In such situations, we must apply the principle of proportion, by assessing the relative importance of the moral harm arising from the infringement of rights,[90] guided by the critical morality of society.[91] Any unavoidable encroachment on rights should be the minimum necessary so as to provide adequate protection to the countervailing right. If it transpires that, in order to provide adequate protection to the right deemed more important, we cannot even secure the minimum level of protection to the countervailing right, then, although the infringement of the latter right is regrettable, it is nonetheless justified in order to protect the more important but conflicting right.

So conceived, fundamental rights may assist in the resolution of conflict between competing constitutional values arising in the context of regulatory

[86] Dworkin refers to bare harm as the harm a person suffers through punishment, whether it be just or unjust. Moral harm is the further injury suffered by a person when his or her punishment is unjust. Moral harm is thus a particular form of injustice: Dworkin (1985), 80.

[87] Bleckmann and Bothe (1986); Steiner (2000).

[88] Kleinig (1978), 46.

[89] Wellman (1978), 53.

[90] Dworkin (1985), 88.

[91] Galligan (1996), 120.

implementation, by enabling us to ascertain which value may be of greater importance in any given context. If only one of those constitutional values grounds a fundamental right while the other does not, then in general the former must prevail in order to avoid infringing the fundamental right. On the other hand, if we find that constitutional values ground competing fundamental rights, then we must balance these rights in relation to each other in the manner described above. For example, although restraining the publication of potentially prejudicial comment and opinion concerning the forthcoming trial of several firms and individuals charged with engaging in a price fixing cartel may infringe the right to freedom of expression, such an infringement may be justified in order to ensure that the right to a fair trial is adequately protected. Although the restriction on the right to freedom of expression is regrettable given its importance in a liberal democratic society, such restriction is unavoidable in order to protect those whose trial might otherwise be seriously prejudiced if no such restraint were imposed.

3. The Relationship Between Regulatory Goals and Constitutional Values

Having examined the nature of the internal relationship amongst regulatory goals and constitutional values *within* each level, an account must also be given of the relationship *between* the two levels. In many instances, regulatory goals and constitutional values converge and coexist in harmony with each other. This is because constitutional values are to some extent shaped by important moral and social values within the community. These same values may well nurture the particular collective goals of the community so that, in many situations, constitutional values can fulfil both regulation's instrumental purposes and the demands of democratic governance and the rule of law. The construction of these two levels of analysis is not therefore intended to set up a false and rigid dichotomy between them. The typology is adopted merely as a useful analytical tool for understanding and evaluating regulatory implementation decisions. In short, some of the specific regulatory goals that contribute to effective regulation not only operate in harmony with the dictates of democratic and lawful governance, but may actively serve the demands of the latter. Thus, for example, the regulatory goals of clarity and predictability overlap and inhere in the constitutional value of certainty and stability. When viewed as a regulatory goal, our concern is with their instrumental function in facilitating regulatory effectiveness by enhancing the likelihood that regulation will lead to a modification of behaviour in the desired manner. But when viewed as a cluster of constitutional values, the importance of certainty and stability lies in safeguarding individual liberty, by enabling individuals to plan their lives so as to protect them from the arbitrary exercise of state power. Regulatory goals and constitutional values should not therefore be portrayed as locked in conflict.

Nevertheless, there are likely to be circumstances when constitutional values may come into conflict with particular regulatory goals. Whether or not particular constitutional values harmonise with, or are antagonistic to, regulatory goals, will depend upon the particular context and circumstances in which those values arise. For example, the constitutional value in procedural fairness includes a concern to enable those affected by decisions to participate in the decision-making process.[92] Participation may entail giving a fair hearing to persons likely to be affected by a decision. The information acquired from the hearing process may, in turn, facilitate effective regulation by improving the quality of information upon which the decision is based. On the other hand, conducting a hearing is a time-consuming and resource-intensive task, and this can conflict with the demands of swift and responsive decision-making and may therefore tend to detract from efficiency in regulation.

In situations of conflict between constitutional values and regulatory goals, we must resist the temptation of thinking that, because the entire purpose of regulation is to pursue its overarching goal or goals effectively, constitutional values must be subordinated to the primary instrumental purposes of regulation and thus yield to regulatory goals. Such a claim is mistaken, for it overlooks the fundamental character of constitutional values as *constraints* on the extent to which society may legitimately pursue its instrumentalist goals. It is thus suggested that in situations of conflict between regulatory goals and constitutional values, regulatory goals may be promoted *provided* that constitutional values are respected to the extent necessary in a liberal democratic society. In this way, the collective goals of regulation may be maintained and promoted while ensuring that public power is legitimately exercised. In situations of conflict where the constitutional value in issue provides the foundation for rights, then regulatory goals may be promoted *provided* that the right implicated in the conflict is given the minimum protection necessary to ensure that its fundamental core is respected and preserved.[93] So for example, the successful conviction of a high profile businessperson for a serious regulatory violation may be expected to promote effective regulation, by deterring others from engaging in similar violations. If, in the course of securing such a conviction, the regulator discovers potential exculpatory evidence, the promotion of instrumental goals of the regulatory scheme may suggest that such evidence should not be disclosed. But, a failure to disclose this evidence and provide the suspect with an opportunity to establish her innocence would entail an infringement of her right to due process and encroach upon the right of an innocent person not to be wrongfully convicted. In the absence of any overwhelming reasons justifying the infringement of the suspect's rights, then the goal of effective regulation should give way to ensure that individual rights are adequately protected, and the evidence should therefore be disclosed.

[92] Galligan (1996), ch 4.

[93] On the relationship between rights and resources, see Dworkin (1985) ch 3 *cf* Galligan (1996) 101–18.

Before concluding this chapter, it is worth recapping the preceding discussion. I have sought to map out a structured framework of principles upon which my analysis of regulatory implementation will be based. In short, the instrumentalist nature of regulation and its public aspect provide the foundation for two sets of normative standards: regulatory goals and constitutional values. Because the first and essential purpose of regulation is to secure the attainment of its collective goals, the primary criterion for evaluation is that of effectiveness. The goal of effective regulation may be pinned to more specific goals, namely (a) efficiency (b) clarity and predictability and (c) flexibility, responsiveness and timeliness. The relentless pursuit of effectiveness in regulatory outcomes is, however, shaped and constrained by a series of constitutional values arising from the public aspect of regulation. These constitutional values require that regulatory decisions should be (a) authorised by law (b) certain and stable (c) accountable and transparent (d) procedurally fair and (e) proportional, consistent and rational. Although these regulatory goals and constitutional values will often act in harmony with each other, some conflict between norms is inevitable, both within each level, and between the two levels. Identifying how such conflict and tension should be resolved cannot be determined in the abstract, divorced from the practical and political context in which the conflict arises.

My proposed framework adopts a two-layered hierarchy of norms in which regulatory goals are given prominence, provided always that the constitutional values that constrain the pursuit of those goals are given adequate expression. While conflict between regulatory goals should be resolved in favour of the goal more likely in the long term to lead to effective regulation, resort to a simple consequentialist calculus cannot be used to resolve conflict amongst constitutional values. This is because constitutional values act as *constraints* on state power and may, in some circumstances, provide the foundation for individual rights. Where rights are implicated in regulatory decision-making, then we should strive to ensure that they are given sufficient protection to ensure that their fundamental core is maintained intact. Given the demands on society's resources and the existence of a broad range of rights that society may be duty-bound to protect, it may not be possible to give rights the fullest possible protection in all circumstances. If we find that constitutional values come into conflict with each other, then the constitutional value considered of greater importance in the individual circumstances of the case should be given priority, provided that the countervailing value is given adequate expression. In identifying which constitutional value is of greater importance in any given context, the concept of rights may again be of assistance.

C. GENERAL THEMES

Now that I have sketched out the normative framework that will be relied upon as the basis for our evaluation, I wish to conclude this chapter by foreshadowing some of the key themes that emerge as the book unfolds, and to point the direction of subsequent chapters. One of the animating motivations for constructing and drawing upon the above framework of regulatory goals and constitutional values as the lens through which the three enforcement activities focused upon in this book are examined is to stimulate reflection and debate concerning the values that ought to inform and shape regulatory processes. Although there are some stirrings within recent contemporary regulatory compliance literature that have implicitly begun questioning the role of values in regulatory processes,[94] most such scholarship still tends to assume (often without explicit acknowledgement), that regulatory implementation must be understood as a technocratic process, and is thus centrally concerned with identifying 'what works'. But although the effective achievement of policy outcomes is appropriately given prominence in light of the instrumentalist nature of the regulatory enterprise, there are other values, notably constitutional values, that have an important role in moulding and limiting the relentless pursuit of society's collective goals.

In this respect, both academic and policy prescriptions concerning the design and reform of regulatory processes appear to stand in stark contrast to equivalent literature concerned with the criminal justice process, where debate about its underpinning set of values tends to be both vigorous and contested. By examining a range of formal and informal regulatory enforcement practices, this book sheds light on why this rather sharp disjunction may have arisen. It will be suggested that, at the heart of this bifurcated approach lies the uncertain character of regulatory violations, with consequential implications for how the regulatory process is to be understood. Regulatory violations are generally distinguished from 'traditional crimes' because they are not typically thought to involve the same kind or degree of moral repugnance. Yet there is a corresponding reluctance to regard regulatory violations as simply a form of 'private' wrong, akin to the civil wrong occasioned by a breach of contract. The 'public' quality of regulatory violations, combined with the absence of strong moral antipathy, render the task of characterisation both slippery and elusive. Even within a command and control scheme involving the imposition of very significant sanctions for regulatory violations, there is apparent resistance to view regulation as part of a society's formal system of justice. Unlike traditional crimes, regulatory violations tend to be thought of as avoidable by-products of otherwise laudable economic and social activity, to be discouraged but not condemned. As a consequence, they tend to be viewed as constituting part of society's social-harm reduction system, rather than as a distinct component of a formal justice system. Yet in the course of analysing several formal and informal enforcement activities, it appears that regulatory programmes sit uncomfortably on the cusp of both systems. They are not central to the community's system of justice (unlike the criminal justice system), yet they cannot

[94] Eg Vincent-Jones (2002); Black (2000); Braithwaite (2002).

be accurately conceptualised exclusively as systems of social-harm reduction (unlike, for example, infant immunisation programmes aimed at community-wide disease prevention).

Difficulties in identifying which values ought to inform regulatory processes may be directly attributed to the ambiguous character of regulatory violations. To the extent that they resemble traditional crimes, the greater the emphasis that may appropriately be placed on constitutional values. But to the extent that they resemble private or 'civil' wrongs, the greater the emphasis that may appropriately be placed on regulatory goals in securing effective outcomes. Because there is considerable scope for reasoned disagreement about the characterisation of regulatory violations, dispute and dissent is only to be expected in specifying the values that ought to shape and constrain regulatory processes, quite apart from disagreement concerning the underlying political theory upon which a democratic society should build its foundations.

Before proceeding further, it is worth foreshadowing some potential objections to my approach. Some may regard my emphasis on constitutional values as inappropriate, claiming that other 'non-legal' values should be accorded priority. My approach acknowledges that there are a number of factors that appropriately inform and constrain the exercise of regulatory enforcement discretion, and these are not confined to legal and ethical considerations. They may include the need to secure effective and efficient policy outcomes, to respond sensitively to political influences and organisational factors, and, of course, the limitations arising from resource constraints,[95] some of which, as the preceding section demonstrates, are explicitly incorporated within my normative framework of principles. Others might object to the particular set of values that I focus attention upon, or to the principles I employ in seeking to resolve conflict within and between the values that I give allegiance to. Such disagreement is only to be expected, given that the values selected for priority will ultimately depend on some underlying political vision. In setting out a set of values and principles drawn largely from liberal democratic theory, I seek to encourage debates about the values, and the political vision underlying them, that ought to be given expression *within* the regulatory implementation processes, a debate which has hitherto tended to occur only at the level of identifying a community's collective goals. Still others may object to the scope of my inquiry by focusing on the state's role in regulatory implementation, pointing to the profound influence of private, non-state actors and civil society on regulatory processes, particularly in the face of globalisation, deregulation and the consequent hollowing out of the state. It is beyond doubt that non-state actors are important participants in the regulatory process. But this book is not the occasion for attempting to map out a framework for normative evaluation of regulatory processes in their entirety. That would be too ambitious a task to embark upon here. Furthermore, it is unlikely to expect the complete

[95] Galligan (1986), 128–37.

withdrawal of the state from regulatory activity. Even in the face of vigorous enthusiasm by legislators and policy-makers for rolling back its frontiers, the state has retained a critical role, albeit in the form of 'steering but not rowing', as Osborne and Gaebler's famous metaphor reminds us.[96] The state's grip over regulatory policy and implementation is likely to remain strong, and is therefore worthy of exploration in its own right.

Irrespective of the particular set of values that should inform and shape regulatory implementation, subjecting competition law enforcement to a normative evaluation of this kind is nonetheless valuable for several reasons. Not only does it challenge some of the typically unarticulated assumptions upon which a considerable body of existing regulatory compliance scholarship rests, but it also illuminates the intersection between two bodies of law—criminal law and administrative law—that are often thought of as largely independent and unrelated. As the subsequent chapters unfold, regulatory scholarship emerges as a bridge between administrative law and criminal law norms, revealing the shared constitutional foundation of these well-established bodies of law. This common bedrock of constitutional values, which may be more deeply anchored in liberal democratic political theory, is particularly striking in the context of an analysis of enforcement discretion. Although both these bodies of law fall within the general category of 'public law', they are not typically viewed side by side, so that the commonality between them has been largely overlooked.[97] Although the analysis of the discretionary power of public officials forms the staple diet of much administrative law scholarship, a vast swathe of existing literature takes an essentially abstract and doctrinal approach, attempting to locate the appropriate scope and content of the principles of judicial review. Attempts to undertake a more context-sensitive approach, setting out to evaluate the extent to which the demands of administrative law are met, particularly in the context of enforcement discretion, have been surprisingly few in number.[98] Criminal lawyers might also be thought guilty of neglect. Their neglect lies, however, not in a failure to appreciate the pervasiveness and importance of enforcement discretion in the criminal process, but rather in their tendency to view the criminal law and criminal procedure as autonomous, rather than anchored in, and infused by, the constitutional values upon which administrative law is also rooted. While numerous scholars from within the criminal law tradition have warned of the dangers associated with the informal resolution of criminal proceedings, noting that such practices risk overriding important procedural rights of the accused such as the right to a fair trial, they have interpreted these rights in a 'thin' fashion.[99] They have not generally tended to look beyond the conventional list of common law rights of the criminal defendant to the 'thicker' and deeper constitutional value of due process from which such catalogues of

[96] Gaebler and Osborne (1992).
[97] A notable exception is Richardson (1993).
[98] For an example of such an approach, Galligan (1994).
[99] Eg Belloni and Hodgeson (2001); Wadham (1994); Greenawalt (1978).

rights find their justification. As an analysis of the exercise of discretion by public enforcement officials, this book highlights the common wellspring of constitutional values from which the critiques of both the criminal and administrative law traditions are drawn.

Before embarking on our evaluation, it is useful to map out the direction of the ensuing chapters. Part II of this book contains a detailed analysis of the three enforcement activities focused upon throughout this inquiry. Chapter four begins by considering the appropriate quantum of regulatory penalties from a theoretical perspective, situating it within the normative framework outlined above. In chapter five, the focus shifts away from the controversy concerning the quantum of penalties to the *process* by which those penalties may be determined. In particular, it seeks to evaluate the use of 'plea bargains' or 'negotiated penalty settlements', in which the regulator and defendant in competition proceedings seek to negotiate liability for violation and/or the severity of the penalty payable for violation. These settlements can be seen as a specific manifestation of the use of bargaining and negotiation between the regulator and defendant in order to resolve disputes concerning alleged regulatory violations. In chapter six, the general technique of bargaining and negotiation in regulatory enforcement forms the central focus, with the aim of evaluating the use of 'administrative settlements' in responding to suspected violations. The analysis of administrative settlements set out in chapter six, which is largely abstract and theoretical in nature, is illustrated in a more concrete fashion in chapter seven, by examining the Commission's experience in using court-enforceable statutory undertakings in securing compliance with Part IV of the Act. Part III consists of chapter eight, the concluding chapter. It draws together the various strands of the detailed critique that form the body of this analysis in Part II, and briefly pauses to reflect upon its potential implications for the practice of regulatory implementation, enforcement, academic scholarship concerning regulatory enforcement in particular, and regulatory scholarship more generally.

Part II

4

*Quantifying Competition Law Penalties**

A. INTRODUCTION

WE BEGIN OUR examination of competition law enforcement by focusing on financial penalties as a sanction for competition law infringements. For the purposes of this discussion, sanctions may be broadly defined as the imposition of adverse consequences on those who contravene the law. In the realm of 'traditional' crimes, we tend to think of strongly punitive criminal sanctions, such as imprisonment, involving substantial deprivations of liberty of the person. But in the regulatory context, the sanctions relied upon to secure compliance may range from strongly punitive measures (including imprisonment for criminal wrongdoing) to administrative measures which are not (if at all) strongly punitive in their legal form, justification and effects. The competition laws of most OECD countries provide for the imposition of significant financial penalties for competition infringements[1] but their formal classification varies. In some jurisdictions (such as the USA and UK) they are formally classified as criminal in nature, while in others (such as Australia and the EU) they are formally classified as civil in nature.

Irrespective of differences in their formal classification, there is a noticeable trend across jurisdictions in favour of increasing the magnitude of these penalties, particularly in recent years.[2] For example, a recent spate of enforcement actions across several jurisdictions resulted in several pharmaceutical firms being subject to record fines for taking part in an international vitamin cartel involving price fixing, market rigging and market allocation, in which the US Antitrust Division extracted almost three-quarters of a billion US dollars in criminal fines from vitamin manufacturers,[3] the EC Commission imposed total fines of almost one billion US dollars on eight firms involved in the conspiracy,[4] and the Commission extracted almost US$17 million from three

* This chapter is based on an earlier article by the author: Yeung (1999)

[1] OECD (2002).

[2] Below ch 4, section C.

[3] See US Department of Justice, Antitrust Division, 'Sherman Act Violations Yielding a Fine of $10 Million or More' available via http://www.usdoj.gov/atr/public/criminal/12557.htm.

[4] See EC Commission Press Release, IP/01/1625 'Commission imposes fines on vitamin cartel', 21 November 2001, available via http://www.europa.eu.int/rapid/start/cgi/guesten.ksh?p_action.gettxt=gt&doc=IP/01/1625|0|AGED&lg=EN&display=.

Australian animal vitamin manufacturers.[5] But while a recent OECD report welcomes the 'noticeable trend towards stronger sanctions for cartel conduct', there is continuing debate concerning whether the severity of sanctions for competition law infringements is being set at the appropriate level. In both the EU and Australia, several commentators have called for increases in the severity of sanctions for competition law infringements, as well as calling for enhanced transparency in relation to the basis upon which penalty levels are determined.[6] In the USA, where criminal fines have long been available for certain antitrust violations, there has been a significant increase in the level of fines imposed, leading some commentators to question whether such penalties have now become excessively high.[7] The primary purpose of this chapter is to shed light on these debates by seeking to construct a principled basis for quantifying regulatory penalties.

By adopting a theoretical approach to penalty quantification, I draw heavily from the extensive jurisprudential literature concerning theories of punishment that have been expounded in relation to the traditional criminal law. This theoretical perspective is adopted for several reasons. First, although not all penalties imposed for competition law violations are formally characterised as criminal, they are clearly punitive in nature, constituting a form of hard treatment imposed by, and payable to, the state against those proved to have contravened the law, sought or imposed by the competition regulator either in its capacity as a law enforcement authority or as the state authority responsible for administering such sanctions. Accordingly, attempts by theorists to identify the philosophical foundation for criminal punishment and its severity have considerable potential to shed light upon the values and principles which should shape and constrain the quantification of competition law penalties. Secondly, the theoretical underpinnings of punishment bear directly upon the controversy concerning the magnitude of these penalties. Although various perspectives might be adopted to investigate the issue of penal quantification, recent controversy (both in Australia and elsewhere) has focused on whether penalties are excessively high or low. Thirdly, regulatory lawyers, and competition lawyers in particular, have paid scant attention to theories of criminal punishment when reflecting upon regulatory penalties. Although there is a considerable body of literature concerning regulatory enforcement and compliance, much of it is empirical in orientation, devoted to investigating the behavioural styles of regulators rather than seeking to evaluate regulatory sanctions from a principled perspective.[8] On the other hand, theoretical accounts of punishment have tended to focus on more 'traditional' crimes that are considered to lie at the core

[5] See ACCC Press Release 'Federal Court Imposes Record $26M Penalties Against Vitamin Suppliers', 1 March 2001, available via http://203.6.251.7/accc.internet/digest/view_media.cfm?RecordID=267.

[6] In the EU, see Van Bael (1995); Richardson (1999). In Australia, see ALRC (2002), ch 29.

[7] Kobayashi (2001).

[8] Below ch 5, Part B (3).

of the criminal law, rather than on regulatory contraventions.[9] Accordingly, the application of theories of criminal punishment to the regulatory context not only furthers our understanding of recent controversy concerning penalty severity, but also casts competition law penalties in a fresh light.

The following analysis is divided into three principal parts. In the first part, I draw upon theories of punishment expounded in the criminal sentencing context that have sought to explain not only why the law is justified in punishing those who commit crimes, but also to determine the appropriate severity of punishment. It focuses on two alternative theoretical approaches, each resting on strikingly different philosophical foundations: the 'deterrence' approach (as expounded by advocates of the economic analysis of law) and the contrasting 'desert' model. While the deterrence approach regards effectiveness and efficiency as its central values, the desert approach emphasises the need for proportionality. The second part explores the possibility of identifying which (if any) of these two models best explains the justification and severity of penal sanctions in the regulatory context, highlighting two characteristics of regulatory law which pose serious difficulties for penal theory: the absence of a strong degree of moral improbity attached to the commission of regulatory offences and the frequent use of 'strict liability' offences in the regulatory context. Having explored both penal theories in light of these two characteristics, I argue that neither theoretical model provides an entirely satisfactory and exhaustive account of regulatory penalties. Rather, there is a plurality of values, including effectiveness, efficiency and proportionality, that should be reflected in the punitive measures invoked to secure regulatory compliance. On this basis, part two situates the central values of both theories within the basic normative framework of this book to suggest how they might usefully be reflected in the severity of regulatory penalties. The third and final part of this chapter seeks to make more concrete the rather abstract theoretical discussion to demonstrate how my suggested model may assist in the practice of quantifying the level of penalty payable for competition law infringements by examining the Australian Federal Court's approach, although my suggested theoretical framework is general in nature and may be applied to any regulatory scheme where financial penalties are payable for violating regulatory standards.[10]

B. THEORIES OF PENAL SEVERITY

1. Theories of Criminal Punishment

Any attempt to answer the question '*how much* should we punish?' is determined, at least in part, by the separate but related question, '*why* do we

[9] Eg Ashworth (1998), Duff and Garland (1994).

[10] In relation to EU competition law fines, see Wils (2002). This framework suggested here was adopted by the ALRC as the basis for its recommendations in ALRC (2002), ch 25.

punish?'[11] Accordingly, in our quest for principles to inform and guide the quantum of penalties for contravening the law (whether regulatory law or otherwise), we must make some attempt to grapple with the difficult and as yet unresolved debates concerning the theoretical justification for punishing those who break the law ('the offender'). Even in jurisdictions (such as the EU and Australia) where competition law violations are not formally characterised as criminal,[12] civil penalties imposed for such violations are nevertheless 'punitive' in nature in that they involve state-imposed 'hard treatment' on those found to have disobeyed the demands of the law.[13] Hence, the various and often conflicting theories expounded to justify criminal punishment may bear directly upon the justification for competition law penalties, irrespective of their legislative designation.[14]

Before engaging in the philosophical conundrums surrounding the institution of criminal punishment, we must acknowledge that they raise deeply-rooted and fundamental questions concerning the nature of, and the relationship between, the state, individual and community that have troubled moral philosophers and legal theorists for centuries. Although the literature is rich and vast, little consensus has yet been reached, not only between theorists from different philosophical camps, but even between theorists from the same or broadly similar philosophical camp. The restricted nature and purpose of my excursion into the theoretical fray must therefore be emphasised: to explore the theoretical justification for criminal punishment with the aim of developing a principled approach to setting competition law penalties. Rather than embark on an extended and detailed critique of theories of punishment, it will suffice to limit this examination to two theories which seem to offer the most promise for shedding light on the issue of penal severity. Each theory is thus described and presented in a deliberately stylised and simplified fashion, for I could not possibly draw out all, or even most, of the nuances and complexities within each theory, given the scope of this book. More importantly, perhaps, by presenting the models in a simplified form we can emphasise their core values, which may assist in focusing more closely on their application to the regulatory context.

In the criminal law context, at least five possible theoretical justifications for punishment have been identified: deterrence (which seeks to deter people from committing crimes), incapacitation (which seeks to incapacitate offenders so as to render them incapable of re-offending for substantial periods), rehabilitation

[11] Hart (1968), 14; Hart (1962), 37.

[12] In Australia, see Trade Practices Act 1974, s 78; In the EU, see Regulation 17/62 First Regulation Implementing Arts 81 and 82 of the Treaty [1962] OJ Special Edition 204/62, Art 15(3).

[13] For present purposes, we may adopt Hart's definition of punishment, ie (i) it must involve pain or other consequences normally considered unpleasant; (ii) it must be for an offence against legal rules; (iii) it must be of an actual or supposed offender for his or her offence; (iv) it must be intentionally administered by human beings other than the offender; (v) it must be imposed and administered by an authority constituted by a legal system against which the offence is committed: Hart (1968), 4–5 *cf* Feinberg (1970), 95–118.

[14] Below, ch 5, Part C (1).

(which seeks to achieve rehabilitation of the offender), desert (which seeks to ensure that offenders receive their 'just deserts' for crime committed) and restoration or reparation (which is concerned to affect restoration for victims of crime).[15] Three of these theories are prima facie unsuited to setting penalties for regulatory contraventions. Incapacitation is usually confined to particular groups, such as 'dangerous' offenders and career criminals and thus appears to have little application to economic and social regulation. Rehabilitation provides little direct guidance on the issue of penal severity, although the idea of rehabilitation may have a useful role in promoting good 'corporate citizenship' where corporations may be the primary offenders.[16] Restoration may have a role in regulatory enforcement, in seeking to restore and heal those adversely affected by regulatory contraventions by, for example, enabling them to recover compensation for harm.[17] But it provides little if any guidance for determining the severity of financial penalties payable to the state at the suit of a public regulator.[18] This leaves deterrence and desert as possible theoretical bases for determining the quantum of penalties for regulatory offences and it is to these two theories which we now turn.

(a) The Deterrence Approach

Deterrence as a justification for punishing crime is based on the notion that punishment is warranted by reference to its crime-prevention consequences.[19] The deterrence approach to punishment has historically been associated with classical utilitarian philosophy, famously advocated by the English jurist and philosopher Jeremy Bentham in the eighteenth century, based on utilitarian goals of deterring future unlawful behaviour.[20] According to Bentham, punishment was justified primarily in order to prevent others from committing the same offence, the disutility visited on the offender being outweighed by the utility to society arising from the deterrent effect of punishment, thereby preventing future crime.

A modern variant of the utilitarian theory of deterrence is advocated by proponents of the economic analysis of law.[21] An economic approach to sentencing

[15] Ashworth (2000), ch 3. Although these theories are concerned with the justification of punishment generally, the appropriate severity of punishment is in part determined by the general justification for punishment: Hart (1968), 14.

[16] Bilmes and Woodbury (1991), 195 but *cf* Fisse and Braithwaite (1993) and Wells (1993), 21.

[17] Braithwaite (2002).

[18] Restorative theories of punishment are not solely or necessarily concerned that victims of crime should receive financial compensation. Restorative theories also encompass the perception that crime involves a conflict between the offender and victim which requires resolution in which the victim is given rights to participate in the process of dispute resolution. See Ashworth (1998), 300–11, Braithwaite (2002).

[19] Ashworth (1998), 395.

[20] Bentham (1838), 165–66.

[21] The pioneering work is by Becker (1968). In general, see Cooter and Ulen (1997); Posner (1977). Posner claims, however, that the economic analysis of law differs crucially from utilitarianism in that its normative goal is wealth maximisation rather than the maximisation of happiness: Posner (1979).

is primarily concerned to minimise the social costs caused by crime. Because crime imposes costs on society, both directly (in the damage wrought by criminal conduct) and indirectly (in the costs incurred by society in apprehending, convicting and punishing offenders), punishment should be set so as to deter crime to the level at which total social costs are minimised. Although not all advocates of deterrence theory necessarily support the economic theory of crime deterrence, it is focused upon here because it provides specific guidance for determining the severity of punishment and therefore provides a theoretical basis for the quantification of regulatory penalties.

(i) Penalties as Prices for Violations

The economic variant of the deterrence approach to punishment (the 'deterrence model') regards law-breaking conduct as a commodity that may be effectively 'purchased' by requiring the offender to pay a penalty for breaking the law. It depends crucially on the assumption that individuals and firms are rational actors who act in the pursuit of self-interest in order to maximise their welfare. In other words, it assumes that an actor will only undertake a particular act if the estimated benefits *to the actor* of so acting will exceed the estimated costs to the actor of engaging in it. Thus, if the estimated benefits of unlawful conduct outweigh its estimated costs, then the actor will rationally decide to break the law.[22] Because law-breaking conduct may harm others, thereby imposing costs on society, it is to be discouraged. By effectively increasing the estimated cost of violating the law, the imposition of penalties for unlawful conduct creates financial incentives that deter firms and individuals from breaking the law.[23] A penalty is simply the 'price' of violating the law.

The fundamental aim of the deterrence model is the pursuit of economic efficiency, that is, to allocate society's resources efficiently, based on the view that this maximises society's total welfare.[24] The essential decision-making criteria in economics are based on a cost-benefit analysis: if the benefits *to society* of a particular activity outweigh the costs to society, then the activity is efficient and should be encouraged because it enhances the overall welfare of society. If this analytical approach is applied to penalty setting, then the correct quantum of penalty is that which will deter unlawful conduct to an 'efficient' level.

Assuming that detecting and penalising violators is costless, then the efficient level of unlawful conduct occurs where the net costs to society arising from the unlawful conduct are minimised.[25] If the unlawful conduct in question has no beneficial effects on society while imposing costs on society, or if the costs of the unlawful conduct always outweigh its benefits, then the efficient level of unlawful conduct is zero.[26] Therefore, the aim of penalty setting should be 'absolute

[22] Cooter and Ulen (1997), 389–94.
[23] *Ibid;* Posner (1977).
[24] Efficiency is used here in the technical sense of allocative efficiency: Above, ch 2, n 1.
[25] Becker (1968); Posner (1977); Cooter and Ulen (1997).
[26] Becker (1968); Dau-Schmidt (1990), 11–13.

deterrence' of the unlawful conduct in question. On the other hand, if the unlawful conduct, although costly to society, also confers some benefits on society, then penalties should be set at a level which will deter unlawful conduct that imposes net social costs but not conduct generating a net social benefit. Therefore, the aim of penalty setting in such cases should be 'optimal' rather than 'absolute' deterrence. These two possible interpretations of the effects of unlawful conduct reflect the two different policy prescriptions or variants of the deterrence model: the 'unlawful gain' model and the 'injury to others' model.

(ii) The Injury to Others Model ('Optimal Deterrence')

The 'injury to others' variant of the deterrence model of penalty setting seeks to achieve 'optimal' deterrence by deterring only inefficient violations of the law. This variant of the deterrence model assumes that conduct that violates the law may have some beneficial effects which may potentially outweigh its costs.[27] If the net gain to society arising from the unlawful conduct in any given instance exceeds its social harm, then it is welfare-enhancing and should not be deterred. For example, a factory's production operations may pollute a nearby river in breach of environmental laws, harming others. However, the factory's production also benefits society, generating employment for factory workers, profits for the factory owner and providing consumers with goods that might not otherwise be available. If that benefit exceeds the harm so caused, then the factory ought not to be deterred from operating, albeit in a polluting fashion. It is important to note that the benefits accruing to the offender as a result of the unlawful conduct may be characterised as a social benefit: the mere fact that such gains are generated as a result of unlawful conduct is immaterial.[28]

In order to achieve its objective of optimal deterrence, the penalty for unlawful conduct should be set at a level equalling the total cost of the harm which it causes. When an actor's activity imposes costs on others that are not borne by the actor, these costs are known as 'externalities'.[29] Legal regulation seeks to ensure that these externalities are attributed to the actor. By imposing penalties set at a level which reflects the injury caused to others, this causes the actor to 'internalise' the cost of these harms by ensuring that the actor bears the full cost of its unlawful action.

Because unlawful activity may generate social benefits, the injury to others variant of the deterrence model seeks to avoid the problem of 'over-deterrence' arising from excessively high penalties. Over-deterrence should be avoided because it deters welfare-enhancing (albeit unlawful) behaviour. Accordingly, the offender's gain and the offender's ability to pay the penalty are not relevant to the calculation of penalties. Taking account of the former would result in

[27] Becker (1968).

[28] The generally accepted view among economists is that, even in the realm of traditional crimes, the criminal's unlawful benefit should be factored into a determination of the optimal quantum of punishment: Cooter and Ulen (1997), 396.

[29] Ogus (1994), 33–35.

over-deterrence, whilst taking account of the latter would over-deter larger more profitable firms, while under-deterring smaller, less profitable firms.[30]

(iii) The Unlawful Gain Model ('Absolute Deterrence')

Likewise, the 'unlawful gain' variant of the deterrence model also seeks to deter firms and individuals from unlawful action because of the harmful effects of such conduct. But it differs crucially from the injury to others model, in seeking to achieve 'absolute', and not merely 'optimal' deterrence of unlawful conduct. Its aim of absolute deterrence follows from the premise that the unlawful conduct is either utterly without any redeeming social benefits, or the social benefits of unlawful conduct are always outweighed by its costs, so that total social costs are minimised by its complete elimination.[31]

To achieve absolute deterrence, the penalty for unlawful conduct should be at least equal to the net gain to the offender arising from that conduct.[32] By effectively disgorging the offender's ill-gotten gain, this eliminates any incentive to violate the law. If the actor knows that there is no opportunity to gain from unlawful behaviour, then the rational actor will refrain from so acting.

Because the unlawful gain variant of the economic model is based on the premise that the unlawful conduct in question always imposes a net cost on society, this model does not contemplate the possibility of over-deterrence arising from excessively high penalty levels.[33] The crucial determinant for setting the appropriate penalty level is the gain arising from the offender's unlawful conduct. Accordingly, the harm to others caused by the unlawful conduct is irrelevant: even if the harm to others exceeds the gain to the offender, it is sufficient if the penalty equals the offender's gain, thereby eliminating any incentive to violate the law, and deterring all such violations. It also follows that the gain to the offender represents the *minimum* penalty level: a penalty exceeding the gain to the offender is consistent with the unlawful gain model because it eliminates the incentive of would-be offenders to act unlawfully.

(iv) Enforcement Costs, Detection Rates, Risk Neutrality and Legal Error

The two variants of the deterrence model described above assume that the probability of detecting a violation of the law and levying a penalty on the offender is 100 per cent. The above models also assume that there are no costs involved in enforcing the law. In other words, it is assumed that all violations of the law are detected without costs being incurred in the detection process. But, because neither assumption is realistic, the deterrence model requires adjustment to account for the cost of enforcing the law ('enforcement costs') and the probability of detection.[34]

[30] Bilmes and Woodbury (1991), 202–03; Becker (1968).
[31] Dau-Schmidt (1990), 11–13.
[32] Bentham's first rule: 'the value of the punishment must not be less in any case than what is sufficient to outweigh that of the profit of the offence': Bentham (1838), 166.
[33] Cooter (1984), 1532–33; Schwartz (1980), 1079–80.
[34] Cooter and Ulen (1997).

Enforcement costs may be taken into account in determining the appropriate enforcement strategy required by the deterrence model in the following ways. For the 'injury to others' variant of the model, then enforcement costs are added to the penalty calculated under the assumption of zero enforcement costs, thus ensuring that those contemplating violating the law 'internalise' the enforcement costs involved in detecting and penalising the violation.[35] For the 'unlawful gain' variant, the existence of enforcement costs may affect the enforcement strategy adopted by the enforcer, rather than quantum of penalty. Although the unlawful gain variant of the deterrence model should be applied to conduct that is always welfare-reducing to ensure absolute deterrence, if the cost of harm caused by the conduct is less than the enforcement costs incurred in eliminating the conduct, then no enforcement action should be taken.

In addition, it is impossible in practice to detect and pursue all unlawful conduct, particularly given the limited resources available to enforcement agencies. In deciding whether to comply with the law, rational actors calculate whether the expected benefits of violating the law exceed its expected costs. Because the assessment is made *ex ante*, based on *expected* rather than the actual costs and benefits, the relevant costs to the actor of violating the law are based on the *expected* penalty from violation. Where the probability of detection for violating the law is less than 100 per cent, then this lowers the actor's expected costs of violating the law. It is therefore necessary to adjust the penalty according to the probability of detection. For example, if the optimum penalty assuming a 100 per cent probability of detection is $1000, then if the probability of detection is 50 per cent, then the penalty must be increased to $2000 ($1000/0.5). It follows that the same level of deterrence can be achieved by raising the penalty level in response to a decline in the probability of detection.[36]

The preceding analysis has also assumed that offenders are risk neutral. However, if potential offenders are risk averse, they will be deterred by lower penalties, and thus the penalty required to achieve the requisite level of deterrence should be reduced accordingly. Correlatively, if potential offenders are risk-taking, then they will need to face higher penalties before they will be deterred from violating the law, and thus the penalty should be increased by the relevant risk aversion factor.[37]

Finally, the deterrence model of penalty setting assumes that legal error is avoided. In other words, the model assumes that legal rules are perfectly formulated and applied so that all relevant conduct that inflicts harm on others is detected and penalised but no benign conduct is penalised. However, some legal error is inevitable in practice, because legal decisions are inevitably based on incomplete information.[38] Thus, some conduct may be penalised although it

[35] *Ibid.*

[36] Posner (1976), 223–24; Becker (1968). For a more detailed discussion of the multiplier principle, see Craswell (1999).

[37] Cooter and Ulen (1997); Becker (1968).

[38] Cooter and Ulen (1997), 110.

may in fact be benign. Likewise, some conduct may escape penalty although it is in fact harmful. The possibility of legal error means that firms may substitute away from marginal conduct which is at risk of contravening the law if faced with the threat of penalties for contravention.[39] Legal error therefore results in the misallocation of resources, imposing costs on society. Moreover, the higher the penalty levels, the greater the costs arising from legal error as firms increasingly substitute away from marginal but benign activities.[40]

(v) Some Strengths and Limitations of Deterrence-Based Theories

Deterrence-based theories of punishment, including the economic theory described above, rest on its crime-prevention consequences, thus providing a forward-looking, consequentialist justification for punishment. One of the most significant strengths of the economic model of deterrence is its theoretical capacity to generate a specific quantum of penalty. Because it is based on a series of theoretically quantifiable variables, it appears to provide a non-arbitrary, principled and systematic approach to the real and practical problem of penalty-setting. On the other hand, deterrence-based theories of punishment have come under attack in a number of respects, but the principal criticisms appear to coalesce around two concerns. The first set of concerns raise important matters of principle, identifying serious moral difficulties inherent in deterrence-based accounts of punishment, while the second refer to their practical limitations and cast doubt upon their efficacy.

Of these objections, perhaps the most serious is their difficulty in explaining why punishment should be limited to those who wilfully break the law. Although legal systems recognise an increasing number of offences which do not require responsibility in the sense of proof of subjective intent to commit a criminal offence, the main body of criminal law insists that a person cannot be punished unless he or she is guilty in the sense of being responsible for the commission of the criminal act (the 'responsibility principle').[41] But the confinement of punishment to the guilty offender is a costly constraint on pursuit of the general aim of preventing future crimes.[42] Given that the underlying aim of deterrence-based theories is to protect society against the harms caused by crime,[43] they cannot explain why society may not, for example, take preventive measures by punishing those who have not yet committed a crime but are at risk of so doing in the future. Deterrence-based theories would seem to condone the punishment of an innocent person if the pain of punishment imposed on the innocent person were outweighed by its harm-prevention effects. As such, they

[39] Posner (1985).
[40] Cooter and Ulen (1997), 286–87; Block (1980).
[41] Below, Part B (2) (b).
[42] Galligan (1981), 147.
[43] The economic variant of deterrence theory adds a further gloss on this aim, by specifying the goal more precisely in terms of protecting society against the commission of crime that generates net social costs.

seem to fall foul of the Kantian injunction that persons should be treated as ends in themselves, and never only as a means to an end. Yet even staunch advocates of deterrence-based theories would be unlikely to support the punishment of the innocent for this is clearly immoral and unjust. Deterrence theorists have thus sought to explain why punishment is properly limited to the guilty-offender. Bentham, for example, claimed that punishment of those who were not responsible for crime would be ineffective.[44] But such attempted justifications nevertheless seem to fall short of fully meeting the objection that society would be justified in departing from the requirement of responsibility and punishing an innocent person, at least on occasion, if this would improve the general level of utility or efficiency.[45]

In a similar vein, deterrence-based accounts of punishment have also been criticised for permitting the excessively severe punishment of individual offenders so as to promote the perceived greater good of general crime prevention. This concern tends to arise in the context of debates relating to the legitimacy of exemplary sentences, that is, where an individual offender is punished with exceptional severity, often in response to a particular kind of criminal behaviour of public concern.[46] The objection is not that the offender was not responsible for the crime, but that the offender is dealt with by the state in an unduly harsh manner: the offender's punishment is determined entirely by the expected future behaviour of others, not by his or her own past behaviour. Nevertheless, the objection shares the same root as the objection to punishing the innocent, for the imposition of punishment of an individual in excess of that warranted by his or her offence involves the sacrifice of an individual for the benefit of the general community. Deterrence-based theories thus fall short of the liberal requirement of respect for individual autonomy and the separateness of persons. They fail to accord due recognition to the moral worth of individuals by treating citizens merely as numbers to be aggregated in an overall social calculation.

The second group of concerns are rather different. They relate not to the moral deficiencies of deterrence-based accounts but, instead, cast doubt on the plausibility of the theory's underlying assumptions and by so doing question the efficacy of deterrence as a crime prevention strategy. Deterrence-based theories of punishment assume that the rational offender, in response to the fear of punishment, responds to the threat of punishment by adjusting his or her behaviour to avoid the punishment which is likely to ensue for the commission

[44] Hart points out that Bentham only proves that the threat of punishment would be ineffective in relation to those with a defective will—others might still be deterred: Hart (1968), 24. Others have suggested that the responsibility principle can be accommodated within deterrence-based theories of punishment by suggesting that deterrence is achieved through respect for law. Unless the administration of justice, including criminal justice, is in accord with community values, then the law falls into disrespect. But even this instrumental account of the law cannot explain why occasional departures from the responsibility principle could not be justified if this would further the aim of crime prevention: Galligan (1981).

[45] Galligan (1981), 150.

[46] Ashworth (1998), 47–48.

of a criminal act ('general deterrence'). In particular, the economic model of deterrence assumes that an offender decides to violate the law on the basis of an explicit *ex ante* calculation that the expected benefits of violating the law outweigh the expected costs. But this assumption of rationality and rational calculation may not accurately reflect reality.[47] Moreover, it is assumed that the rational offender responds to variations in the severity of punishment so that a greater level of deterrence will be achieved by raising the severity of punishment ('marginal deterrence'). In the criminal context, empirical studies have failed to provide reliable findings about the relative deterrent effects of various types and levels of penalty for various offences.[48] A 1999 study of empirical research on the deterrent effects of punishment (which focused primarily on custodial sentences for individual offenders) concluded that while criminal punishment has been shown capable of having deterrent effects,[49] current research provides no definitive answers to whether and to what extent substantial increases in the severity of punishment enhance marginal deterrence.[50] The assumption of rationality may, however, be more readily accommodated within the area of economic and social regulation, given its primary focus on the commercial behaviour of profit-maximising firms rather than individuals.[51] But even in the corporate context, empirical studies suggest that corporations are not solely driven by self-seeking individuals concerned exclusively with the pursuit of profit, but who may be motivated, at least partially, by non-financial concerns, including a sense of social responsibility and respect for the rule of law.[52] If so, then attempting to deter commercial firms from committing offences on pain of punishment may be only weakly effective, and perhaps less effective, than the use of non-punitive strategies to encourage compliance.[53]

Doubt surrounding the effectiveness of deterrence-based theories have also been presented in a somewhat different cast. One difficulty with deterrence-based accounts of punishment, and the economic variant of deterrence theory in particular, is that it is prone to generating counter-intuitive outcomes which may appear at odds with the community's perception of fairness and morality. For example, the economic model of deterrence posits that there is a direct and interchangeable relationship between the probability of detection and the sever-

[47] Bilmes and Woodbury (1991), 205.

[48] Ashworth (2000), 60–61; Beyleveld (1979).

[49] Bottoms *et al* (1999), 47.

[50] It concluded that the absence of strong and consistent negative statistical correlation between severity and crime rates diminishes the plausibility of expecting large deterrent benefits through increases in penal severity: *ibid.*

[51] Ashworth (2000), 60; Goldstein (1992); Fisse and Braithwaite (1984).

[52] Braithwaite (1992), 19–23; Martin (1993). Note however that the focus on the firm as economic actor compounds the rationality problem, because the firm is controlled by directors, whose objectives and motivations may not be wholly aligned with that of the firm. The relationship between company shareholders and managers generates a classic principal-agent problem. But arguably, the rationale is consistent: shareholders can incur greater monitoring costs as the penalty level rises, per Bilmes and Woodbury (1991), 203; Fisse and Braithwaite (1993).

[53] Below ch 4, Part B (2).

ity of the penalty. Thus if an actor is risk-neutral, the same level of compliance can be achieved by varying the severity of the penalty in response to a variation in the probability of detection. But if this approach is applied to achieve a desired outcome it can result in the calculation of penalties which the general community would regard as excessively harsh and oppressive. Imagine, for example, that one aim of the law was to eliminate street litter, and that if all instances of street littering were detected, absolute deterrence would be achieved if a penalty of $10 applied to the offence of littering. However, if in fact because the risk of detection for littering is tiny (say, 0.001 per cent), then according to the deterrence model a $1 million penalty ($10/0.001 per cent) is required in order to ensure that littering is sufficiently deterred. Imposing penalties of such extreme magnitudes are likely to be perceived by the community as both unrealistic and oppressive.[54]

Likewise, the injury-based (optimal deterrence) penalty model prescribes that repeat violations by the same offender imply that penalties should be lower for that offender, because a finding of violation raises the probability of detection. In so doing, the injury-based penalty model ignores the social meaning of repeat offences and is directly contrary to the approach taken by some advocates of the desert model. The latter claim that, up to a point, repeat offences lead to a gradual loss of the sentence discount which is applied to the offender's first offence, so that the penalty level gradually increases for repeat offences.[55] The benefit-based (absolute deterrence) penalty model may also generate counter-intuitive results given that the loss caused to others arising from the offence is irrelevant to the calculation of penalty. Rather, the crucial variable is the offender's unlawful gain. Accordingly, even if the offence inflicts massive harm to others but confers only a small benefit on the offender, the penalty should be correspondingly small. It may therefore appear that the offender has 'got off lightly', particularly by the victims of the criminal conduct.

These concerns, that economic deterrence theories prescribe a level of penalty that may diverge significantly from community's perception of fairness, appear to raise moral concerns akin to the Kantian objections referred to above. They nonetheless differ from these deeply-rooted moral objections because they are based on popular conceptions of fairness rather than the liberal concern for individual autonomy and respect for persons. They adopt an instrumentalist view of the law, identifying the importance of sustaining the community's respect for law in order to ensure its effectiveness in crime prevention. It is feared that if the level of punishment which is dictated by the economic model of deterrence persistently

[54] This point is powerfully put by Mckay (1998). See also Hart (1968), 25. Even economists acknowledge that threatening competition law violators with draconian sanctions may not be optimal due to the inevitability of legal error: Block and Sidak (1980).

[55] This problem is avoided by the unlawful gain variant of the economic model, because it aims to achieve absolute deterrence. Thus, while under-deterrence is possible, over-deterrence is not. Note, however, that the relevance of prior convictions has been the subject of debate between desert theorists: see von Hirsch (1998).

involves substantial departures from popular conceptions of fairness, then over time the community may lose confidence in the criminal justice system and a respect for law. As a result, the level of obedience to the law may be weakened and the deterrent effect of punishment in crime prevention eroded.

Another objection to the economic variant of deterrence theory of a practical kind raises doubts about its application in reality. While the deterrence model provides a theoretically coherent and complete basis for penalty setting, applying the model to real world circumstances generates intractable practical difficulties. Quantifying variables such as loss, gain and probability of detection with any degree of precision may be impossible to achieve at reasonable cost. Indeed, precise objective calculation may be impossible. For example, calculating the extent of the harm arising from a violation may inevitably require some subjective assessment of harms that cannot be precisely quantified. As a result of such estimation problems, the penalties thereby calculated may in practice be no less arbitrary than penalties assessed under a less scientific model.[56] One may legitimately question the usefulness of a model that is theoretically precise, but fails to generate reliable and consistent results in the real world.

(b) The Desert Approach

Many of the characteristic features of deterrence-based accounts of punishment are sharply illuminated when viewed alongside their desert-based counterparts. Although there are several different variants of desert-based theories of punishment, their essential concern is to offer a backward-looking, retributive justification for punishment. They seek to explain punishment not by reference to its future crime-prevention consequences, but by reference to the core albeit somewhat nebulous notion that the offender's punishment is 'justly deserved'.

(i) Desert as a Justification for Punishment

In their strongest form, retributive theories claim that society has an *obligation* to punish the offender and is not merely authorised to do so, based upon little more than an intuitive moral belief that wrongdoers ought to be punished.[57] Such strongly intuitive retributive accounts have, however, largely fallen out of favour with more subtle and sophisticated yet nonetheless retributive accounts being offered by modern theorists. These theorists recognise the necessity to go

[56] Bilmes and Woodbury (1991), 208.

[57] One of the most influential statements of retribution theory was given by Immanuel Kant in the eighteenth century, who stated in his *Philosophy of Law*, 'Even if a Civil Society resolved to dissolve itself with the consent of all its members—as might be supposed in the case of a People inhabiting an island resolving to separate and scatter themselves through the whole world—the last Murderer lying in the prison ought to be executed before the resolution was carried out. This ought to be done in order that everyone may realise the desert of his deeds, and the bloodguiltiness may not remain on the people; for otherwise they might all be regarded as participators in the murder as a public violation of justice.' Translated by W Hastie (Edinburgh, 1887) cited by Honderich (1969) 22. For a more modern exposition of strongly retributive accounts, see Moore (1998).

beyond the mere assertion of a moral intuition and to provide social reasons that justify the retributive idea of punishment for wrongdoing. For example, Finnis attempts to justify punishment by reference to the notion of fairness and social balance, claiming that the offender acquires an unfair advantage which punishment 'neutralises', restoring the social balance.[58] By violating the law, the offender is thought to obtain an unfair gain, consisting of the wrongful appropriation of self-will or free choice of action that other law-abiding citizens deny themselves through self-restraint in remaining within the confines of the law. Punishment does not involve the actual disgorgement of the offender's ill-gotten gain, but rather seeks to restore the distributively just balance of advantages between the criminal and the law-abiding.[59]

Other recent desert-based accounts seek to follow a middle path, appealing to moral intuition more strongly than those who subscribe to the unfair advantage account of punishment, but who also accept the need to supplement moral intuition with social justification. These theorists claim that the social balance or fair play account of punishment is inadequate because it seems to distort the essential character of the wrongdoing by condemning the offender essentially for free-riding. When an offender is condemned for murder, what is communicated to the murderer is not that she has free-ridden, that she has not done 'her part' in sustaining the rule of law through which she and others benefit—but that she has committed murder and that *this*, not the free-riding, is wrong. So, for example, von Hirsch relies upon the alleged communicative feature of punishment to explain why society is justified in punishing those who commit crimes. He claims that punishment primarily expresses moral blame or censure, thus conveying disapprobation of the offender and concurrently acknowledging to victims and potential victims that they have been wronged by criminal conduct.[60] This censure-based account of punishment appears to be based on an assumption that, not merely is censure and reprobation an appropriate moral response to criminal wrongdoing, but that it is a proper and appropriate role for the state to perform, although the basis for this assumption remains somewhat obscure.[61] It seems to find historical antecedents with what was once known as the 'denunciatory theory' of criminal punishment, its essence being that the ultimate justification of punishment is the emphatic denunciation by the community of the offender's crime.[62]

[58] Finnis (1980), 262–64.

[59] *Ibid.*

[60] von Hirsh dismisses unfair advantage based accounts of retributionist theory, claiming that it is not clear how depriving the offender of rights *now* offsets the extra advantage the offender arrogates for herself *then* by offending. Nor does it make clear why preserving the balance of supposed advantages provides a reason for invoking the coercive powers of the state: see Duff and Garland (1994), 116–17.

[61] It is interesting to note that von Hirsh clearly rejects that the state has a legitimate penitential function in his rejection of Duff's attempt to justify the hard treatment aspect of punishment as a form of 'secular penance'. Yet von Hirsch does not himself make clear why the state has a legitimate reprobative function: von Hirsch (1999).

[62] Hart associates the denunciatory theory of punishment to the Victorian judge James Fitzjames Stephen: Hart (1968),169–70.

But this communicative or expressive function raises deeply rooted and difficult questions concerning the status of judgements of right and wrong, particularly given that people differ in their views on what kinds of things are right and wrong, and in what they believe to be the status of moral judgements. The mere existence of different moral understandings raises a prima facie problem for communicative accounts of punishment. The legitimacy of communicative accounts depends on the judge and the law being properly regarded as speaking for a community (that is, they give voice to shared values) and that their language is at best that of offenders, at worst comprehensible to them, so that they can 'hear' what is being said.[63]

(ii) The Proportionality Principle

For retributivists, the principle of 'just deserts' provides not merely the justification for punishment, but also lays the theoretical foundation for determining penal severity by requiring adherence to the principle of proportionality. The proportionality principle requires that the severity of the punishment be commensurate with the seriousness of the offence, seriousness being defined in terms of the twin elements of harm and culpability. Harm refers to the extent of the injury caused by the offence while culpability refers to factors of intent, motive and the circumstances that bear on the degree of the offender's blameworthiness.

But just as there are variations in the invocation of desert as the justification for punishment, so too there are variations in the particular content and function of the principle of proportionality.[64] For example, von Hirsch claims that it plays a central and determining role in prescribing the appropriate severity of punishment. In his view, because punishment embodies blame, then how much one punishes conveys how much one is condemned.[65] Others deny the centrality of the principle, perceiving its role as setting the outer limits or constraints on the severity of punishment. Morris argues, for example, that when we claim that punishment is deserved we rarely mean that it is precisely appropriate. Rather, we mean that it not undeserved; that it is neither too lenient nor too severe, that it neither sentimentally understates the wickedness or harmfulness of the crime nor inflicts excessive pain or deprivation on the criminal in relation to the wickedness or harmfulness of the crime. For him, proportionality operates as a limiting, rather than a defining, principle.[66] Finnis also rejects that there is an absolute or 'natural' measure of due punishment.[67] In his view, talionic notions of life for a life, an eye for an eye and so forth are misguided in their focus on the material content or consequences of criminal acts, rather than their formal wrongfulness which consists in a will to prefer unrestrained self-interest

[63] Matravers (1999), 109.
[64] Below, ch 6, Part B (2) (b).
[65] von Hirsch (1993), 17.
[66] Morris (1998).
[67] Finnis (1980), 263.

to the common good.[68] Nonetheless, Finnis recognises that a rough and ready scale of *relatively* appropriate punitive responses can be devised, because some unlawful acts are premeditated while some are impulsive, some involve trivia while others are big choices for high stakes. In other words, the principle of proportionality informs the relative severity for punishment in relation to criminal offences of different levels of seriousness, but does not provide any precise guide to the absolute measure of penal severity warranted in any given instance.

(iii) Strengths and Limitations of Desert-Based Theories

Desert-based accounts of punishment, being firmly grounded in moral notions of retribution, avoid many of the principled difficulties associated with deterrence-based justifications. Their starting premise is that the offender is a moral agent, and therefore do not lay themselves open to allegations of failing to acknowledge the moral worth of individuals and the importance of the responsibility principle that is regarded as central to the criminal law. It is the strong moral appeal of retributive accounts of punishment that arguably represent their greatest strength. But, like their deterrence-based counterparts, retributive theories of punishment are not free from difficulty, only some of which can be touched upon here.

One of the most pressing difficulties faced by retributive theories lies in explaining why the assertion of a moral principle justifies the social practice of punishment. By adopting a backward looking model rather than consequence-based view of punishment, it is not obvious why condemnation of the offender should take the form of penal hard treatment. Whilst retributive accounts provide convincing reasons why society may be justified in singling out the offender and condemning her for her wrongdoing, they may not provide a wholly adequate explanation for why such condemnation should take the form of penal deprivation.[69] In other words, the harm of punishment requires further justification.

Desert theorists have offered a range of different responses in order to meet this objection. But a common feature of these responses is an acknowledgement (albeit often implicit) of the necessity to have recourse to forward-looking concerns in seeking to explain the hard treatment element of punishment. For example, Duff claims that penal hard treatment can itself be explained in desert terms, the deprivation of punishment providing a 'kind of secular penance'.[70] He claims that punishment seeks to focus, through force, the offender's attention on his or her wrongdoing, so as to induce repentance, reform and reconciliation. Whilst it is seriously questionable whether one can fairly regard penal deprivation as a 'communicative process', Duff himself acknowledges that this penitential function of punishment is forward-looking and not confined to

[68] Finnis (1980), 264.
[69] Galligan (1981), 155.
[70] Duff (1999).

looking backwards to the past offence. Finnis's fair play account of retributive theory appears to hold more promise, for it is possible to interpret the restoration of social balance as a justification for penal hard treatment.[71] But when seen in this way, his argument from fairness has a forward-looking dimension, through its concern to preserve and maintain social institutions and standards on a continuing basis.

The difficulties in finding an adequate justification for penal hard treatment have led some desert theorists to concede defeat, and to look explicitly to deterrence-based justifications to supplement their retributive claims. Thus von Hirsch, well-known for the strength of his commitment to a desert-based account of punishment, rejects Duff's attempt to explain penal deprivation solely in retributive terms regarding Duff's notion of secular penance as implausible. For von Hirsch, to regard penal hard treatment as serving a penitential purpose involves entrusting the state with functions that are simply inappropriate to it.[72] Rather, his response is openly to concede that moral censure is not in itself sufficient to justify penal hard treatment.[73] Hence he relies upon the forward-looking function of deterrence, providing a 'prudential supplement' to the censuring function of punishment, designed to reduce offending by offering to those who do not find the law's moral appeal compelling an additional, prudential reason to obey through penal hard treatment.[74]

In addition to these difficulties, the concept of proportionality is itself beset with theoretical uncertainty and practical limitations. Unlike the economic deterrence theory, desert-based accounts are simply not theoretically capable of assigning a particular penalty to a particular offence. I have already briefly alluded to the lack of consensus concerning whether proportionality provides a central or merely limiting principle. von Hirsch's belief that proportionality is a central and determining principle relies critically on the alleged communication of censure through punishment. It is argued that if punishment embodies blame, then how much one punishes will convey how much one is condemned. But von Hirsch's claim that punishment communicates blame may require further examination. Why is it that punishment communicates blame, rather than, say, a communication of the need for such offences to be avoided in future?

Even if the principle of proportionality should play a central (rather than merely limiting) role, applying it to determine the actual level of penal severity is fraught with difficulty. Desert theorists have identified two forms of proportionality, both of which must be met in order to fulfil the demands of the proportionality principle.[75] Ordinal proportionality relates to comparative punishment, requiring that those convicted of crimes of like gravity should receive punishments of like severity and that those convicted of crimes of

[71] Above n58 and associated text.
[72] von Hirsch (1999).
[73] *Ibid;* von Hirsch (1993).
[74] von Hirsch (1993), 13.
[75] *Ibid,* ch 2 for an extended discussion.

differing gravity should receive punishments correspondingly graded in their degree of severity. Cardinal proportionality, on the other hand, refers to the severity of punishment relative to the offence committed. Although the two concepts are themselves reasonably straightforward, in translating these requirements of proportionality into practical terms, complexity and subjectivity abound. For example, in seeking to devise a scale of ordinal proportionality we are faced with intractable difficulties in comparing crimes of an entirely different nature. Nonetheless it might be possible to devise a rough scale of offences according to their relative seriousness although structuring such a scale of ordinal proportionality will inevitably be a controversial and complex task.[76] More fundamentally, there is no particular level of punishment which suggests itself as uniquely appropriate to a particular offence (ie cardinal proportionality) because, as von Hirsch himself acknowledges, the amount of disapproval conveyed by a penal sanction is a social convention.[77] In other words, 'anchoring' the penalty scale cannot be achieved on any principled basis, even if it were possible to devise an acceptable scale of relative offence seriousness.[78] Despite this, von Hirsh rightly claims that there are nonetheless limits to cardinal proportionality, so that to impose drastic intrusions on the liberty of the individual for the most trivial of crimes would fall short of the demands of cardinal proportionality. For this reason, cardinal proportionality operates as a constraint on penal severity, determining its outer limits rather than providing a central and determining role in prescribing the severity of punishment for any particular offence.

2. Regulatory Penalties and Penal Theory

The above discussion merely scratches the surface of some of the deep and long-standing debates concerning the institution of punishment, particularly in relation to fundamental issues of justification and severity. I have deliberately avoided making definitive evaluations of either model (or their variants), for this would require a considerably more detailed and exacting critique, which is beyond the limited purposes of this book. Nonetheless, the core features of each model, and some of their principal weaknesses, may be identified, drawing out the complexity and tension lying within and between them. The central concerns of the economic deterrence model are effective and efficient deference: the aim is to minimise the social costs of crime by deterring would-be offenders through the threat of punishment. The appropriate severity of punishment is determined primarily by the costs of crime, enforcement costs and the probability of detection: the aim is to 'price' offences at the level which deter offences to

[76] Hart (1968), 162–63.
[77] von Hirsch (1993), 19.
[78] For an attempt to construct a principled scale, see von Hirsch (1991).

the level which will minimise the social costs of crime. By contrast, desert-based theories claim that the punishment of an offender is a 'justly deserved' social response to the offender's wrongdoing, expressing disapprobation of the offender and maintaining standards of fairness within the community. In determining the severity of punishment, the guiding principle is that of proportion, possibly as a central and guiding principle, but at the very least as a constraint on the outer limits of the severity of punishment which may be imposed on any given offender for past wrongdoing.

Armed with an understanding of these core concepts, we are now in a position to reflect upon the severity of penalties for the commission of regulatory offences for they offer a fruitful starting point from which to draw in developing a framework of principles. But, in so doing, we must bear firmly in mind that the theories of punishment discussed above were espoused in relation to 'traditional crimes', that is, the types of crime typically thought to be central to the criminal law, such as intentional violations of the physical integrity of persons or their property. At this juncture, it is useful to recall the definition of 'regulation' adopted in this book and outlined in the previous chapter. It refers to the sustained and focused attempt by the state to alter behaviour generally thought to be of value to the community, with the aim of achieving certain collective goals.[79] For present purposes, two features of this definition call for closer scrutiny. First, the regulated activity is thought to be of value to the community—the aim of regulation being primarily to modify that behaviour, rather than to punish or censure those engaging in it.[80] It may therefore be possible to exclude conduct sanctioned by the traditional criminal law if we accept that one of the principal purposes of the criminal law is to censure conduct considered to be anti-social or otherwise morally reprehensible[81] although, as we shall see, the line between traditional crime and regulatory offences is rather unstable and fuzzy-edged. Secondly, regulation thus conceived is undertaken by the state as purposeful actor, drawing upon its available resources, including the state's unique power of compulsion. The use of sanctions underwritten by state compulsion in response to a breach of regulatory standards is typically referred to as 'command and control' regulation.[82] These two features may tend to pull in opposite directions in reflecting upon the application of penal theory to regulatory offences. On the one hand, the focus of regulatory law on conduct considered to be of 'value to the community', which primarily seeks to modify behaviour, rather than censure, may suggest that searching for guidance within penal theory is simply wrongheaded. Yet if regulation encompasses the use of sanctions for failure to comply with legal rules, backed by the coercive power of the state, this suggests that penal theory may be a fertile and fruitful source of guidance in our quest for principles.

[79] Above, ch 1, Part B (1) (a).
[80] Baldwin *et al* (1998).
[81] Ashworth (2000); von Hirsch (1993).
[82] Below ch 6, Part B (1).

In order to grapple with this tension,[83] we need to explore the assertion that regulatory offences may be distinguished from traditional crimes. I have defined regulation by reference to its underlying enterprise, that is, to modify rather than condemn conduct thought to be of value to the community. On this basis, the strong degree of moral improbity typically associated with traditional crimes appears largely absent in relation to regulatory offences. This alleged distinction may be reinforced by the fact that regulatory offences are often 'strict liability' offences, so that liability may be established without proving fault or culpability.[84] The following discussion examines these two issues of moral probity and strict liability more deeply, in light of the core ideas encapsulated within the two theoretical models described above. It then seeks to identify how we can best explain the punishment of regulatory offences in our endeavour to identify principles for determining the severity of regulatory penalties. Given the deeply entrenched disagreement that continues to plague attempts by legal theorists and moral philosophers, despite centuries of reflection, to explain the basis and severity of punishment for traditional crimes, we should not be surprised that what emerges from this examination is nothing so concrete as a formula for determining the severity of regulatory penalties. Rather, arguments are presented in favour of a structured and principled approach to quantifying regulatory penalties, recognising the plurality of values implicated in the regulatory process and the practical difficulties arising at the level of application.

(a) Moral Probity and Regulatory Offences

Much of the academic literature concerned with identifying the moral and theoretical basis for punishment has typically focused upon traditional crimes. There is, however, a perceived distinction, made by some judges and rooted in early nineteenth century case law emerging from the industrial revolution, between conduct that is *mala in se* and that which is *mala prohibita*.[85] The former refers to conduct considered 'wrongful in itself' and thus treated as 'criminal' in societies with very different social and economic values, whilst the latter refers to conduct that is not so characterised but which is the subject of specific proscription.[86] While we cannot expect to find sharp-edged principles for clearly delineating the proper scope of the criminal law,[87] we can nonetheless accept that the paradigm of criminal responsibility involves the notion of individual wrongdoing, generally with a degree of awareness of the act or its consequences.[88] A

[83] The appropriate characterisation of regulatory law as forming part of a broader 'social harm reduction system', or as part of a distinct 'criminal justice system' is explored more fully below.

[84] Cane (2002), 82.

[85] Green claims that the first common law judicial recognition of the distinction appeared in 1496 but was originally drawn by Aristotle, Augustine and the early ecclesiastical courts, see Green (1997), notes 114–17.

[86] Ogus (1994), 79; Hart (1968), 236; *Sherras v De Rutzen* [1895] 1 QB 918, 922 per Wright J.

[87] Ashworth (2000).

[88] Richardson *et al* (1984), 56.

breach of regulatory law, as I have defined it, does not, however, commonly attract the same degree of moral condemnation typically accompanying the commission of traditional crimes.[89] On this definition, regulatory law is primarily concerned to facilitate the achievement of collectivist goals. Regulated activities are thought to be of general value to the community, but require direction and modification (in this case, through the instrument of the law) so as to promote regulation's collective goals. The punishment of regulatory offences is simply a practical means of exerting control over an activity, without necessarily implying the element of social condemnation that is characteristic of traditional crimes.[90] Seen in this light, regulation may appear to be part of a broader system of 'social harm reduction' or 'social hygiene', to promote certain social 'goods' and/or to guard against identified social 'bads'. However, if a regulatory scheme embodies a system of punishment for violating the law, it may also be seen as part of a distinct criminal justice system for reasons which shall shortly be explained.

Before proceeding further, it is worth sounding a note of caution. The relatively narrow definition of regulation adopted here should not be taken to suggest that failure to comply with all laws and standards relating to the regulation of economic and social activity are trivial, at least not in terms of the extent to which non-compliance may wreak harm on individuals and/or the community. Perhaps more fundamentally, implicit in the alleged distinction between the moral content of traditional crimes and regulatory offences is an assumption that an assessment of moral virtue and propriety is, if not unitary, than at least the subject of widely held and shared moral values within the community. The mere existence of different moral understandings raises a prima facie problem in distinguishing traditional crimes from regulatory offences on the basis of an alleged difference in their moral reprehensibility. Some commentators argue, for example, that moral opprobrium should attach to regulatory offences, claiming that traditional crimes arouse moral disgust partly because they have been labelled criminal for so long.[91] Such commentators emphasise historical, cultural and social conditioning and convention in shaping our moral convictions.[92] Others, such as Kadish, distinguish regulatory laws that seek to protect economic interests, from those concerned to promote other social interests (such as public health, industrial safety and a sustainable environment).[93] In his view, moral reprehensibility is not naturally associated with regulatory laws

[89] Richardson *et al* (1984), 117; Ashworth, (1995), 1; Hart (1968), 236 *cf* Wells (1993), 7–8. Of course, social/community understandings of what is morally bad is not frozen, but constantly evolving: Coffee (1991), 200.

[90] Ashworth (1995), 1. Feinberg argues that penal sanctions for such regulatory offences do not constitute 'punishment' although the imposition of such sanctions visits 'hard treatment' on the offender because they do not convey reprobative symbolism, which he regards as the essence of punishment: Feinberg (1970).

[91] Aubert (1952); Wells (1993), 26.

[92] Wells (1993), Ch 2.

[93] Kadish (1963).

protecting economic interests (such as competition law, securities regulation, export controls and the like) but this cannot be said of regulatory laws protecting non-economic interests.[94]

Despite the existence of a broad spectrum of moral beliefs which may coexist within any community, and their dynamic and constantly changing nature, it is nonetheless possible to appeal to the critical morality of society[95] to distinguish between the level of wrongdoing associated with traditional crimes in comparison with regulatory offences. While it is mistaken and misleading to suppose that a bright-line distinction clearly separates one from the other, we should avoid throwing out the proverbial baby with the muddied bath-water. Both types of offences may be situated on a continuum of legal offences along which particular crimes and regulatory offences may be located. Crimes involving deliberate and brutalising violations of physical integrity such as murder, rape and other sexual offences might lie at one end, while minor and often unintentional offences, such as parking infringements, minor traffic misdemeanours and other similarly trivial offences might lie at the other end. The fact that there is considerable scope for argument in the middle-ground is not a fatal flaw. We may therefore accept that there is considerably less moral stigma attached to the commission of regulatory offences when contrasted with traditional crimes, at least in relation to regulatory offences which are aimed primarily at safeguarding collective economic interests or where the consequences of a regulatory offence are minor or trivial in their effects.

It follows that, as one moves along the scale, away from the most serious, brutalising crimes in the direction of the most trivial offences, the degree of social censure and condemnation associated with punishing the offence declines. What, then, are the implications of this sliding scale of moral opprobrium in seeking to apply the theories of punishment outlined above to regulatory offences? One notable difficulty arises in seeking to locate regulatory offences along this sliding scale. While some regulatory offences, such as parking infringements and minor traffic violations, are clearly trivial, others (such as a manufacturer's negligent release of toxic emissions into the atmosphere) may be less so, and therefore lie further towards the centre of the scale.[96] In other words, the objectionable nature of the activities proscribed by regulatory law will vary from the pragmatically inconvenient at one end of the spectrum, to the

[94] *Ibid.* Richardson, Ogus and Burrows attempt to find a middle-ground by arguing that an element of blame can be attached to many regulatory offences in so far as the commission of an offence amounts to a failure by the offender to take reasonable care in carrying out the regulated activity: Richardson *et al* (1984).

[95] The critical morality of a society can be contrasted from its popular or 'positive' morality. To be concerned 'critically' with morality is to be concerned with what is right and wrong according to some substantive theory of justice. Positive morality is to be concerned with the empirical matter of what people believe to be right and wrong. Dworkin (1985), ch 7.

[96] As Friedman states, 'there are vast differences among regulatory crimes in their moral status within society. There is a huge gulf between what people feel about a corporation that pours poison into a river and how they feel about someone who pulls the tag off a mattress', Friedman (1993), 285.

more morally dubious on the other rather than being firmly anchored at the 'morally neutral' end of the scale.[97]

Desert theorists are confronted with a further difficulty. While desert-based accounts of punishment may readily explain the justification for punishing offences at the violent and brutish end of the scale, for which the purpose and degree of moral censure is very powerful, they appear to run into a significant dilemma as they move further along the scale towards the most trivial offences. For those who adhere to its stronger variants, the difficulties loom very large indeed. If punishment is warranted solely by virtue of an intuitive moral belief that offenders ought to be punished for wrongful and blameworthy conduct, then it follows that punishment is not justified if moral impropriety is only weakly associated (if at all) with the commission of a regulatory offence.[98] The dilemma appears less acute, however, for those who subscribe to the unfair advantage or social balance account of penal retribution. On this account, it might be argued that those who commit regulatory offences gain an unjust advantage by virtue of the violation which other law-abiding citizens are deprived of through exercising self-restraint in obedience to regulatory law thereby upholding the common good. Thus, punishment of regulatory offenders might be justified in order to maintain the social balance between the offender and the law-abiding members of the community.

Deterrence theorists, on the other hand, do not face what we may term the 'condemnation dilemma'. Because the purpose of punishment is the prevention of harm (and its associated social costs), the punishment of regulatory offences is justified in order to deter others from committing such offences.[99] The fact that there is little (if any) moral impropriety attached to the commission of some regulatory offences is largely irrelevant. If the commission of regulatory offences impose net costs on society, then punishment is justified in order to deter their occurrence. But while deterrence theorists remain untroubled by the 'condemnation dilemma' confronting those advocating retributivist accounts of punishment, they face a different, perhaps equally troubling problem. If the justification for punishment is to deter socially harmful conduct, irrespective of its moral repugnance, then what deterrence theorists cannot readily explain is why punishment should be confined to those who have committed an offence. Why not punish those who pose the gravest *risk* of harm, rather than those who

[97] Harding (1993), 130.

[98] Ashworth (1995), 50; Richardson *et al* (1984),17; Kadish (1963), 445. Feinberg argues that the imposition of sanction without moral culpability does not generate any dilemma because sanctions for regulatory offences do not constitute 'punishment' because the essence of punishment is its reprobative symbolism, which is not attached to regulatory sanctions. However, he concedes that where the penalties are 'severe' then the argument loses cogency, and cannot justify regarding the safeguards of culpability requirements and due process requirements as irrelevant: Feinberg (1970).

[99] For this reason, Hart has observed that many modern retributivists concede that 'in the vast area of criminal law where what is forbidden by the law is so remote from familiar requirements of morality', punishment is to be justified and measured mainly by utilitarian consequences: Hart (1968), 236. See also Richardson *et al* (1984), 17.

have committed an offence, thereby promoting the most efficient level of deterrence? Those who are most at risk of committing offences (whether regulatory or otherwise), and who thus pose the gravest risk of the particular kind of social harm which regulatory law seeks to prevent, need not be those who have already committed an offence. Yet attempts to find a way out of this 'distribution dilemma' appear to yield little success.

(b) Strict Liability and Regulatory Offences

Difficulties in seeking to justify the punishment of regulatory offences are compounded by the fact that many are strict liability offences.[100] While criminal offences typically depend on proof of some form of mens rea, be it intent, knowledge or recklessness, strict liability offences disregard mens rea so that there is no need to prove the offender's mental state in establishing the offence. Criminal liability is visited on the offender without proof of his or her culpability or subjective wickedness. Even those who take all due care to avoid committing the offence, but nevertheless accidentally engage in the proscribed conduct, act unlawfully and may therefore be punished.[101]

Given that the purpose of this chapter is not to engage in a detailed critique of strict liability, it will suffice to outline the nature of the claims made in its defence and in opposition to it. Academics have been stinging in their critique of strict liability for criminal wrongdoing, with Lacey claiming that it is 'generally mentioned in hushed tones as an embarrassing and uncivilised exception to the general principles of the criminal law.'[102] To criminalise conduct on the basis of strict liability is thought, at least within the rhetoric of English criminal law, to be in fundamental opposition to the 'responsibility principle' already alluded to, requiring that one should not be condemned without proof of fault.[103] The principle is grounded in the liberal requirement of respect for individual autonomy and is regarded, at least by legal scholars if not by legislatures, as a well-established and core principle of criminal law.

It must be acknowledged, however, that the harshness of strict liability may be mitigated in practice through the judicious exercise of discretion by enforcement authorities.[104] Several empirical studies, particularly in the regulatory

[100] Richardson *et al* (1984), 16 and 57. On the growth of strict liability offences, see Leigh (1982), 14–16. Although many regulatory offences that are classed as criminal are strict liability offences, they should not be equated: some regulatory offences require proof of intent, and some strict liability offences are not 'regulatory' in the sense defined here. For example, EU competition law only provides fines for 'intentional or negligent violations of Articles 81–82 of the EU Treaty: Regulation 17/62 First Regulation Implementing Articles 81 and 82 of the Treaty [1962] OJ Special Edition 204/62, Art 15(2).

[101] Ashworth (1995), 160.

[102] Lacey (2001), 354; Cane (2002), 109–10.

[103] It has been claimed that the 'one golden thread' running through English criminal law is that the prosecution bears the burden of proving guilt: per Viscount Sankey, L C in *Woolmington v DPP* [1935] AC 462.

[104] Cane (2002) 239–41.

context, have observed a noticeable reluctance by regulatory authorities to prosecute offences which they regard as politically and morally ambivalent.[105] Formal prosecutions tend to be regarded as a strategy of last resort, reserved for offences of the gravest kind, especially where a one-off violation is thought to be a genuine accident. But while the practice of regulators may help alleviate the unfairness associated with strict liability, the deeply principled objections remain, quite apart from the legitimacy of such a stark disjunction between law 'on the books', promulgated by democratically elected legislatures, and law 'on the ground' as it is applied by unelected and politically unaccountable enforcement officials in a less than transparent manner.

Unlike its objections, the justifications for strict liability appear to rest exclusively on pragmatic grounds of economy and expediency. Whilst the rhetoric of criminal law vehemently objects to strict liability, legislators do not appear to have been much moved by such concerns, as the number of strict liability offences has multiplied, and continues to grow, particularly in recent years.[106] Freiberg and O'Malley point to the industrial revolution as the genesis of a proliferation of sources of harm and injury in modern society, of such a degree that safety and related abuses can only be effectively remedied if mens rea requirements are suspended.[107] It is often claimed that the difficulty of proof of mens rea, and the fact that strict liability is typically confined to 'minor' offences, provide sufficient justification for strict liability as a basis for criminalisation. For example, Ogus argues that 'whatever the strength of the moral arguments against strict liability, economic considerations would seem to favour it, at least in the corporate sphere'. In his view, proof of the mental states of intention, recklessness or negligence can impose prohibitively high administrative costs, so that dispensing with the requirement of proof of fault is justified.[108] But such reasoning is lamentable. It cannot be right that pragmatic considerations of economy and expediency simply outweigh moral objections without pause to consider the strength of those moral objections. Nevertheless, there may be something more to his claim that such moral objections pose less of a stumbling block when imposing criminal liability for trivial offences and upon large corporate offenders.[109] The latter might be appropriately regarded as extremely serious from society's point of view because the aggregate harm-causing potential of a large corporation may be very great.[110]

For desert theorists, or at least those of a strongly retributivist bent, the absence of any requirement to establish the offender's culpability necessarily

[105] Hawkins (1984); Richardson (1984); Hawkins (2002).

[106] For example, Ashworth (2000), 228 provides statistics of the number of criminal offences introduced by the UK Parliament in 1997.

[107] Freiberg and O'Malley (1984).

[108] Ogus (1994), 82. Ashworth has pointed out the fallacy of this argument, however, on the basis that an assessment of fault is required (at least in relation to serious offences) in order for a court to pass sentence on a proper basis: Ashworth (1995), 51 and 163.

[109] Horder (2002).

[110] Cane (2002), 205–06.

implies that punishment of the offender cannot be justified. If it has not been shown that the offender is morally responsible or blameworthy, then no appeal can be made to the intuitive moral claim that wrongdoing deserves punishment.[111] When cast in terms of unfair advantage, however, desert theory appears, at least at first sight, to be capable of accommodating strict liability offences. One might argue that those who commit strict liability regulatory offences gain an unfair advantage in the form of freedom to engage in conduct which is not shared by self-restrained law-abiding citizens and which therefore justifies punishment of the offender in order to restore the social balance. But this argument is ultimately unsustainable, for the advantage illegitimately acquired by the offender is regarded by proponents of the theory as lying in the offender's wilful and deliberate flouting of the law, so that the punishment of accidental or inadvertent non-compliance cannot be explained.[112]

These apparently insoluble difficulties cannot, however, be simply avoided by recourse to deterrence-based accounts of punishment. Just because deterrence theory is not troubled by the fact that moral improbity is only weakly present (if at all) in relation to regulatory offences, it does not follow that deterrence theory is similarly unmoved by the use of strict liability for regulatory offences. It has largely been assumed that strict liability strengthens the deterrent effect of the law by encouraging extreme care to be taken in the carrying out of the regulated activity.[113] But the deterrence impact of strict liability is unclear, not merely in empirical terms, but also in terms of logical reasoning. Given that strict liability offences may occur through mere accident or misfortune, why should strict liability strengthen the incentive to take care, since liability will arise if the proscribed conduct occurs, however careful the actor may have been?[114]

(c) Hybrid Models and Regulatory Offences: Suggested Principles

The preceding discussion reveals the inability of either the theory of deterrence or desert to provide a complete, coherent and principled justification for the punishment of regulatory offences. This is unsurprising, given that complexity and uncertainty arises at two levels: within the penal theories themselves, and in relation to the arguably distinctive nature of regulatory offences in contrast to more traditional crimes. The prevalence of strict liability as a basis for imposing penal liability in the regulatory context poses insurmountable hurdles for both theories, albeit for different reasons. The primary concern of desert theory in singling out and censuring the offender for the moral wrongdoing associated

[111] It might, however, be argued that there is a moral obligation to obey the law, encompassing an obligation to take precautionary measures to avoid breaking the law. On this basis, it might be argued that even an inadvertent failure to obey the law is morally blameworthy in so far as the failure may have been avoided by adopting precautionary measures.

[112] Kadish (1963), 445 *cf* Smith (1996), 109.

[113] Smith (1996), 112–18.

[114] Richardson *et al* (1984), 16–17.

with his or her crime leaves no room for punishing conduct without proof of fault. Although the logic of deterrence does not demand proof of fault, in the sense of moral culpability, it cannot account for the punishment of purely accidental conduct. In other words, deterrence theories fail to explain why the punishment of accidents should serve to strengthen the deterrent effect of punishment rather than to weaken it. But the inability of both models to provide complete or even partial explanations of strict liability is not so much a reflection of their conceptual weaknesses, but of the deeply problematic nature of strict liability, and we should avoid dismissing them on this basis.

On the other hand, it follows from the instrumentalist nature of regulation that deterrence-based theories of punishment can more readily explain the use of regulatory penalties in two respects. First, the consequentialist, forward-looking logic of deterrence theory reflects the instrumentalist purpose of regulation. Both are concerned with seeking to modify future behaviour. Secondly, I have suggested that offences may be located on a sliding scale representing their relative moral repugnancy, with violent, brutalising offences against the person lying at one end and trivial offences such as car parking infringements and so forth at the other. Therefore, as one moves away from the most serious crimes and towards less serious offences, the degree to which retributive concerns justify the imposition of punishment declines, reflecting the declining degree of social and moral censure associated with the commission of the offence. Thus, desert theories have intractable difficulties in seeking to explain why offences at the trivial end of the scale ought to be punished. By contrast, the lack of any strong degree of moral improbity associated with regulatory offences does not preclude the applicability of deterrence-based explanations because, unlike their desert-based counterparts, their primary concern is to prevent future wrongdoing rather than primarily to condemn past wrongfulness.

On its face, then, deterrence theories appear to provide the best explanation for the punishment of regulatory offences. Seen in this light, penalties payable for regulatory violations may be regarded as simply the price of doing business. Yet, as we have seen, while deterrence theories are untroubled by the 'condemnation dilemma' confronting retributivists, they are faced with a different, but equally difficult conundrum, in explaining why punishment is limited to the guilty offender, rather than those who pose the greatest risk of harm to the community. While deterrence may provide the primary *justification* for punishing regulatory offences, retributivist concerns limit the *distribution* of punishment to the guilty offender. In other words, deterrence may provide the primary explanation of *why* we punish regulatory offences, but retributivist concerns must be relied on to explain *whom* we punish. It is the retributive constraints on punishment, limiting its imposition to the guilty offender, which distinguishes the criminal justice system from other social harm reduction systems. If, for example, deterrence provided the sole and exclusive justification for punishing regulatory offences, then we could legitimately punish those who had not yet committed any offence, but who posed a serious risk of committing such offences in future. Yet such a regime would amount to a system of taxation, imposing some form of burden for undertaking *lawful* behaviour, rather than a system of punishment for *unlawful* behaviour. One of the distinctive characteristics of punishment is its retributive nature: punishment is imposed as a response to law-breaking, although this need not be its primary feature.[115] While a regulatory scheme which does not involve penal sanctions for unlawful conduct[116] might be characterised as part of the general system of social harm prevention, akin to quarantine laws and so forth which may impose hard treatment on those who pose a serious health risk to others, a regulatory scheme that seeks to punish those who violate regulatory laws should not be seen solely and exclusively as forming one component of a broader system of social harm prevention. Its retributive nature means that it may also be characterised as part of a distinctive criminal justice system. While the criminal justice system might intersect with the broader system of social harm prevention, the former is not a complete subset of the latter.[117]

Accordingly, it seems that *both* deterrence and desert theories must be relied upon to explain the punishment of regulatory offences. While deterrence theory provides the primary justification, in seeking to deter others from offending, desert theory constrains the pursuit of the consequence-based goals of deterrence by restricting punishment to the guilty offender. Many of those who attempt to provide an account of criminal punishment seem to be searching for a single, complete, conclusive and incontestable justification. But this quest seems doomed to failure. We cannot expect to find more than tentative reasons for punishing which will inevitably pull in different directions, at least on occasion. For just as there are a multitude of values, goals and ideals to which any community may aspire, so also are there likely to be a plurality of different, often deeply rooted and sometimes contestable values and aims which the criminal justice system may seek to pursue and reflect through the institution of punishment. What we have, then, is a hybrid or mixed theory of regulatory penalties, demonstrating the validity of HLA Hart's claim that, 'any morally tolerable account' of punishment 'must exhibit a compromise between distinct and partly conflicting principles.'[118] We might therefore expect that some values

[115] Wood (2002), n 16.

[116] For example, a regulatory scheme which imposed a tax on specific kinds of prescribed activities.

[117] It might be argued that one of the distinctive features of the 'hard treatment' associated with criminal punishment is the so-called moral stigma associated with its imposition. For example, quarantining a person with a contagious disease for three months does not carry the same moral stigma as imprisoning a person for three months for criminal wrongdoing. The distinctive quality of punishment underlines the importance of the proportionality principle in circumscribing its severity. But, when regulatory offences are punished, there is typically very little moral stigma associated with the offence, making regulatory offences appear, superficially, more analogous with social harm prevention measures (such as quarantine) rather than with sanctions for traditional crime. But because only those guilty of regulatory wrongs are subject to regulatory sanctions, retributive notions are clearly at play.

[118] Hart (1968), 1. For a communitarian approach which recognises that the social practice of punishment seeks to further a plurality of values, see Lacey (1998).

will be more strongly or weakly implicated depending upon which distinct aspects of the penal process are under consideration.[119]

What then, are the implications for determining the severity of punishment for regulatory offences? As a matter of logical consistency, the answer to this question ought primarily to be determined by reference to the reasons *why* we punish regulatory offenders. On this basis, we would expect that the severity of punishment, should be guided by deterrence as its primary aim. The pursuit of deterrence is constrained, however, by retributivist concerns. In providing his well-known account of punishment, Hart identified two questions associated with the distribution of punishment: questions of liability (*whom* do we punish?) and questions of quantum (*how severely* do we punish?). In relation to the former, we limit liability to the guilty offender for restributive reasons—the innocent do not 'deserve' to be punished, however grave the risk that they might do so in the future. It is this retributive constraint on the distribution of punishment that distinguishes punishment from other 'social harm reduction' institutions, such as the quarantine of those with life-threatening contagious illnesses.

In relation to questions of penal severity, retributive concerns are also at play, but for slightly different reasons. The punishment of regulatory offenders involves imposing a form of hard or burdensome treatment on citizens, backed by the coercive power of the state. In liberal democratic societies, the imposition on citizens of state-imposed hard treatment (whether in the form of penal deprivation for the commission of an offence, or in the form of restrictions on liberty, such as quarantine, in order to protect others from serious, foreseeable risks to health) not only requires particularly strong justification, but its scope must itself be clearly and narrowly circumscribed.[120] In other words, the moral worth and autonomy of citizens in a liberal democratic society demands adherence to the principle of proportionality, so that encroachment on individual liberty and freedom cannot simply be traded off in the ordinary social calculus in order to further the general welfare.[121]

[119] Hart's 'hybrid' or 'dualist' theory of criminal punishment, which attempts to accommodate both retributivist and utilitarian considerations has been criticised on at least two grounds: (1) that it does not take retributivist concerns seriously enough by confining them to the distribution of punishment rather than as forming part of the general justification for punishment; and (2) that the link between the general aim and the principle of distribution is not established : Wood (2002) n 16; Galligan (1981), 350. My hybrid account of regulatory penalties overcomes the claim in (1) because retributivist concerns do not feature strongly in the justification for punishing regulatory offences. But it is, however, vulnerable to the criticism in (2). On this basis, it is more aptly described as what Wood calls 'mere conjunction' dualism, entailing a genuine compromise between irresoluble tension between deterrence and desert: see Wood (2002).

[120] Brigham and Brown (1980).

[121] Hart (1968), 25; Ashworth (1998), 17. In the context of a system of social harm prevention, for example, the proportionality principle demands that hard treatment is justified only if it satisfies the requirement of necessity. So, for example, a liberal democratic society may quarantine a person with smallpox, to prevent the spread of this highly contagious fatal disease, but it is not justified in quarantining a person with a common cold, to prevent others from catching a cold.

Thus, while the quantum of regulatory penalties should, in the first instance, be guided by the goal of deterrence, the proportionality principle is an important delimitation on the intrusive powers of the state.[122] Because the imposition of penalties for a regulatory offence does not serve primarily to convey moral censure or reprobation associated with the regulatory offence, the severity of penalty does not communicate the degree of blame attached to the offence. Hence the principle of proportionality does not have a central or determining role, but instead operates as a limiting principle. It acts as a constitutional constraint, setting an upper limit on the extent to which the goal of effective deterrence can be pursued by the imposition of increasingly severe penalties on an individual offender.

My suggested framework of principles for determining the severity of regulatory penalties can be summarised thus.[123] Assuming that the state is justified in regulating the proscribed activity by the imposition of penal sanctions, those sanctions should be sufficiently severe to deter would-be offenders from engaging in the proscribed conduct, otherwise the regulatory scheme is unlikely to be effective. Hence the quantum of regulatory penalties should, in the first instance, be set high enough to deter the offender and others from contravening the law in order to promote the first and primary purpose of regulation in securing its collective goals. Any 'morally tolerable' system of punishment is constrained, however, by the requirements of fairness.[124] That there is little or no moral condemnation attached to the commission of a regulatory offence, nor a need to prove culpability by the offender to establish liability, does not necessarily imply that moral considerations and issues of culpability are irrelevant to the penalties levied thereunder.[125] Although conceptions of fairness and morality do not play a central justification for regulatory law, liberal democratic societies require that the moral autonomy and agency of its citizens are respected when penal sanctions are to be imposed. This is the foundation for the responsibility principle lying at the heart of the criminal law, which, in turn prohibits the punishment of the innocent so that the distribution of punishment is restricted to the guilty offender. Because punishment involves the visitation by the state of penal deprivation on its citizens, the scope of such deprivation must be clearly and narrowly circumscribed[126] thereby according due respect to the individual's right to fair treatment.

[122] This invocation of the proportionality principle differs slightly from the proportionality principle arising from the 'just deserts' model of punishment, because its primary concern is to avoid the use of oppressive or unfair state power against the citizen, rather than to ensure that the degree of censure or blame attributed to those who violate the law is commensurate with the seriousness of the violation: Hart (1968), 181–82.

[123] See ALRC (2002), chs 25 and 30 for a discussion of this approach.

[124] Zedner (1994), 243.

[125] The ALRC identified four different functions which a remedial court order for contravention of the Act is designed to serve, which included 'deterrence and, as a secondary outcome, retribution': ALRC (1994), 29.

[126] Brigham and Brown (1980).

Thus, in any given case, if the severity of a deterrence-based penalty would be disproportionate to the seriousness of the offence, then the goal of deterrence (be it 'absolute' or 'optimal, depending on whether or not the unlawful conduct is potentially welfare-enhancing) must give way to the principle of proportionality. In other words, the proportionality principle circumscribes the outer limits of the range of acceptable penalties. Within that range, the deterrence model can be used to determine a particular quantum of penalty.[127] An effective penalty regime for regulatory offences should be based on a hybrid of the two models, so that the severity of punishment reflects the goal of deterrence provided that it is not unfairly disproportionate to the seriousness of the offence. Although the proportionality ceiling, which is grounded in the constitutional value of substantive fairness, may limit the deterrent effect of penalties, it might in the longer term promote the deterrent-effects of penalties. As the preceding section demonstrates, the application of the deterrence model of penalty setting may generate unfair results. If a penalty scheme departs too greatly from moral consensus, this can (particularly over time) undermine the perceived legitimacy of the regulatory regime within which penalties operate.[128] Not only does this bring the law into disrepute, but may eventually undermine the legitimacy of the regulatory system.[129] Without the confidence and support of the regulated parties, and the society in which they operate, the regulatory system will inevitably fail to achieve its objectives.[130] A penalty scheme must not be too out of step with intuitive conceptions of fairness and justice lest it lose the support of the regulated parties and the general community that it is intended to serve.

C. COMPETITION LAW PENALTIES

Armed with a general framework of principles for determining the severity of regulatory penalties, we are now in a position to assess whether, and to what extent, the level of penalties imposed for competition law infringements may be regarded as fair and effective. Thus the final section of this chapter seeks to illustrate in more concrete terms how the theoretical models examined above may assist in seeking to quantify competition law penalties. Laws aimed at regulating competition provide a prime example of regulatory law: the purpose of compe-

[127] The use of the desert principle to locate the outer limits of penal sanctions has been advocated by several criminal law theorists: Allen (1981), 139; von Hirsch (1981) *cf* von Hirsch (1993), ch 6. The proposed solution is a compromise one, and may be criticised by purists on that basis. See for example Galligan's criticisms of Hart's hybrid account of punishment: Galligan (1981), 161. However, I share the view of Judge Frank Easterbook who stated that, 'there is no first best solution to the enforcement of anti-trust laws. If one existed in theory, it probably could not be achieved in the face of very expensive litigation. Fancy rules are costly to administer and they breed error. Only second-best solutions are available. This is my excuse for offering marginal adjustments in existing rules rather than some thoroughgoing revamp,' Easterbrook (1987), 353.

[128] Hart (1968), 25.

[129] McKay (1998).

[130] Grabosky (1993), 5; Brigham and Brown (1980), 6.

tition law is to eliminate certain restrictive market outcomes, not primarily because such outcomes are worthy of moral condemnation, but because they are inefficient, diminishing the overall welfare of society. Although debates concerning the magnitude of penalties for competition law infringements have also arisen in the EU and US,[131] disquiet arising in Australian competition law sharply illuminates the scope for tension between the deterrence and desert models, reflected in judicial uncertainty concerning the role of 'punishment'. This examination proceeds in two parts, firstly, by describing the Australian framework for regulating competition and penalising contraventions with a view to identifying how the models of deterrence and desert models might be expected to apply and secondly, by examining the Federal Court's approach in determining the quantum of penalties in light of both theoretical models in order to assess whether judicial reasoning conforms to my suggested approach.

1. The Australian Regulatory Framework

In the previous chapter, I described the Australian framework for regulating competition law as a system of a 'dual adjudication': it is for courts to determine whether the Part IV prohibitions have been contravened and to impose pecuniary civil penalties on offenders, but it is for the Commission to determine whether conduct which would otherwise contravene the Act confers a net public benefit on the community and should therefore be granted legal immunity from the prohibitions.[132] The Commission cannot grant such legal immunity unless the conduct has first been notified to the Commission or the parties have applied to the Commission for authorisation of the proposed conduct.[133] Thus the prohibitions contained in Part IV are not absolute. Immunity from the prohibitions is available in relation to net welfare-enhancing conduct (with the exception of conduct in breach of section 46) via the authorisation and notification process.

(a) The Deterrence Model

If the deterrence model is applied to competition law violations, should the aim of penalty setting be 'optimal' or 'absolute' deterrence? As we saw in the preceding section, the economic model of deterrence prescribes that if the practices sought to be prohibited may in some circumstances be welfare-enhancing, then the 'injury to others' variant of the model should be applied so as not to deter welfare-enhancing violations. Apart from price-fixing and bid-rigging agreements between competitors, which are universally condemned as economically

[131] Above, Part A.
[132] Brunt (1994).
[133] Trade Practices Act 1974, s 93.

inefficient, not all horizontal restraints (ie where competition is restricted by co-ordination between firms operating at the same level in the supply chain) are unequivocally anti-competitive and inefficient.[134] The same is true of vertical restraints (ie where a restraint is imposed by one firm on another operating at a different level in the supply chain). A vertical restraint implemented by a firm with market power may be inefficient and thus welfare reducing, but the same type of restriction by a firm lacking market power may be benign, and might even have net pro-competitive effects.[135] Thus an evaluation of the market power of the firms engaged in the restrictive practice in the particular case may be required before the restraint can be condemned as inefficient.[136]

There is a considerable body of literature (largely written in the USA) which is concerned with identifying the optimal basis for determining the penalty level for 'antitrust' violations (ie competition violations) so as to provide the appropriate level of damages payable in a private antitrust suit against an offender. A recurring theme in this literature is a concern to avoid 'over-deterrence' due to a belief that welfare-enhancing violations of the law should not be deterred.[137] Posner cites, by way of example, a market-power enhancing merger imposing costs of $1 million on society but confers benefits, as a result of the lower costs of the merged entity arising from economies of scale and scope, of $2 million. Posner argues that if the purpose of antitrust law is to promote efficiency, such a merger should be permitted but if the penalty is set substantially above the social cost of the violation then the merger will be deterred.[138] Thus, it is widely assumed by such theorists that some unlawful anti-competitive practices may have net welfare-enhancing effects.[139]

If this strand of economic reasoning is adopted,[140] it follows that competition law penalties should aim to achieve optimal deterrence, rather than absolute

[134] Warner and Trebilcock (1993); Easterbrook (1985).

[135] For an analysis of vertical restraints, see Scherer and Ross (1990), ch 15.

[136] This distinction may be reflected in the way in which substantive rules are constructed. For example, horizontal price-fixing is illegal per se (ie on proof that the price-fixing conduct occurred) while exclusive dealing is only unlawful if it has the purpose or likely effect of substantially lessening competition in a market: Trade Practices Act 1974, s 45, s 45A and s 47. See Posner (1977).

[137] Easterbrook (1985), 450.

[138] Posner (1976), 222.

[139] Landes (1983), 22; Posner (1976); Easterbrook (1985); Elzinga and Breit (1985). The underlying reason why some economists claim that anti-competitive conduct may, in certain circumstances, be efficient and thus welfare-enhancing occurs because efficiency is not a unitary concept. Efficiency has three possible dimensions: allocative efficiency, productive efficiency and dynamic efficiency: see *Re 7 Eleven Stores* (1994) ATPR ¶31–357, 42,677. Allocative efficiency arises when economic resources are allocated between different goods and services in precisely the quantity which consumers wish (their desires being expressed by the price they are prepared to pay on the market). Productive efficiency occurs when goods and services are produced at the lowest cost possible using current technology. Dynamic efficiency refers to the capacity of the market to adapt to change and incorporate new processes and products. There may be circumstances in which a reduction in allocative efficiency resulting from anti-competitive action may be outweighed by the gain in productive or dynamic efficiency accompanying such action.

[140] Some economists take the view that monopoly pricing can never be welfare-enhancing. For example, Schwartz is unconvinced that the exercise of monopoly power could result in cost savings to the monopolist and thus generate social benefits, basing his view on the standard deadweight loss

deterrence. The 'injury to others' variant of the deterrence model therefore appears to provide the preferred basis for penalty setting.[141] An exception to this approach could be made in relation to horizontal price fixing and bid rigging for which penalties should be set so as to achieve 'absolute deterrence', thus utilising the 'unlawful gain' model, based on universal acceptance that such conduct is inefficient and confers no redeeming benefits on society.[142]

The goal of 'optimal' rather than 'absolute' deterrence appears to underpin the Australian institutional framework for regulating competition because restrictive practices which would otherwise breach the statutory prohibitions may be immune from penalty if the practice is notified to, or authorised by, the Commission. It does not, however, follow that the courts should adopt the injury-to-others model (which aims to achieve optimal deterrence) as the basis for quantifying penalties for contraventions of the Act. The task of evaluating whether the public benefits alleged to arise from proposed anti-competitive conduct does not rest with the courts, but with the Commission as independent competition regulator entrusted with the responsibility for evaluating whether specific anti-competitive practices notified to it should be permitted on the basis that they constitute a benefit to the public.[143] The courts' task, when applying the legislative prohibitions, is merely to consider the effect or likely effect of the

argument against monopoly. Schwartz (1980), 1081–82; On this view, it follows that competition law penalties should aim to ensure absolute deterrence, and thus the unlawful gain model for penalty setting is to be preferred. Yet Schwartz then goes on to argue that a loss-based penalty measure is to be preferred because a gain-based remedy will not fully reflect the harm to society caused by the monopolist's conduct, and thus fails to achieve the objective of efficiently allocating enforcement resources to minimise the harm associated with monopoly. However, he concedes that if a loss-based remedy is adopted, there is a possibility that the gain to the violator may exceed the loss to others and therefore fail to deter monopoly conduct, but he claims that this will rarely occur in practice, at 1083. In other words, although Schwartz favours absolute deterrence of monopoly conduct, he nonetheless supports the injury to others model for calculating penalties rather than the unlawful gain model. Schwartz seems to conflate two distinct ideas: i) the quantum of penalty; and ii) the allocation of enforcement resources. He implicitly assumes that the allocation of enforcement resources will logically be determined by penalty size. But this is not an inevitable or necessary link.

[141] Posner favours the injury to others variant of the deterrence model, recognising that monopoly pricing may yield cost savings for the monopolist, so that if such cost savings exceed the deadweight loss to society which is caused by monopoly pricing, it is inappropriate to deter the conduct because it is net welfare-enhancing. The New Zealand Ministry of Commerce, however, rejects Posner's reasoning without providing any adequate justification for so doing, simply stating that '[g]iven that this is a contentious argument and that the size of the deadweight loss is usually small compared with the monopoly profit, for the purposes of this document we have adopted the illegal gain rather than the 'total harm' approach': New Zealand Ministry of Commerce (1998), 9.

[142] The adoption of two different penalty standards could generate some counter-intuitive results. If the gain to the violator in a price-fixing case is very small, but the loss inflicted is very large: according to the absolute deterrence standard, the penalty should be that of the small gain. By contrast, if in a rule of reason case, the same dimensions of gain and loss arise, then according to the optimal deterrence model the penalty should be the large loss. From an outsider's perspective, the result seems inequitable. But, this could be adjusted to allow for the greater loss-based penalty to be awarded in the price-fixing case because the absolute deterrence model knows no concept of over-deterrence. It would therefore be possible to set penalties for price-fixing at the greater of the loss to others or gain to the violators.

[143] Officer and Williams (1995).

relevant conduct on competition; it does not extend to examining any other effects (whether welfare-enhancing or otherwise).[144]

Penalties should therefore be structured so that firms proposing to engage in allegedly welfare-enhancing anti-competitive conduct face appropriate incentives to notify or to seek authorisation from the Commission, thereby enabling the alleged social benefits to be evaluated and weighed against any potentially harmful anti-competitive effects. In other words, penalties should be set with the aim of absolute deterrence, thereby encouraging firms to seek authorisation for anti-competitive practices that may provide net social benefits.[145] If this view is adopted, then penalties for contravening Australian competition law should be set according to the unlawful gain variant of the economic model, rather than the injury to others variant.

(b) The Desert Model

If the desert model is applied to competition law penalties then it is necessary to establish both 1) the seriousness of competition law violations relative to other violations of the law that are punishable by monetary penalty and the relative seriousness of specific competition law violations relative to each other (thereby establishing a scale of ordinal proportionality) and 2) the magnitude of the penalty scale itself, which involves specifying the monetary amount that fairly reflects society's disapproval of the unlawful conduct (thereby establishing a scale of cardinal proportionality). Once ordinal and cardinal proportionality scales have been established, the quantum of penalty for any given violation of the prohibitions can be determined by reference to the seriousness of the violation.

[144] For a discussion of the Australian institutional approach, see Brunt (1994), 510–12.

[145] However, conduct which is authorised or notified in relation to conduct pursuant to Trade Practices Act 1974, s 45, s 45B, s 47 and s 50 is immune from contravening the Act. The only conduct that cannot be authorised is the misuse of market power, which is prohibited by s 46 of the Act. In order to establish a breach of s 46, the applicant must establish that the respondent: a) had a substantial degree of power in a market; b) has taken advantage of that power; c) for a proscribed purpose. If the conduct in question can be explained on grounds of productive efficiency then the respondent has not 'taken advantage' of its market power: *Queensland Wire Industries Pty Ltd v BHP* (1989) 167 CLR 177; Hanks (1990). Thus the substantive prohibition contained in s 46 has been structured and interpreted such that conduct which is productively efficient and thus net welfare-enhancing is not caught by the prohibition. Assuming that legal error is avoided in applying s 46 so that only welfare-reducing conduct is prohibited, then conduct which contravenes s 46 should be prohibited absolutely and penalties for breach should be assessed in accordance with the 'unlawful gain' model so as to secure absolute deterrence. Economists might criticise the Australian institutional scheme on the basis that requiring the public competition regulator to scrutinise *ex ante* all conduct alleged to be welfare-enhancing (assuming that an authorisation application is made) is more costly than a regime in which courts evaluate whether particular anti-competitive conduct is welfare-enhancing if challenged in litigation. The latter regime underlies the approach taken to misuse of monopoly power in s 46 of the Act—it places the onus on individual firms to assess for themselves whether their conduct is likely to be efficiency-enhancing: Warner (1993). But such a criticism is empirical in nature, and it is by no means certain that an alternative institutional regime would be less costly in total than the existing regime.

It is immediately apparent, however, that the establishment of a penalty scale which ranks the severity of competition law violations relative to other violations of the law is a complex task which is practically impossible to achieve with any scientific precision. Nonetheless, in theory it may be possible to rank the seriousness of competition law violations relative to other types of regulated commercial conduct punishable by monetary sanction, such as laws relating to insider trading, disclosure of corporate information and so forth, by reference to the potential harm caused by such practices valued in monetary terms. The relative culpability of offenders as indicated by the offender's actual mental state, such as the deliberateness of the offence and knowledge of the illegality, may also provide some assistance in ranking the 'seriousness' of specific violations of the law.

However, establishing the magnitude of the penalty scale in financial terms so as to reflect the extent of society's disapproval cannot be achieved in any principled, non-arbitrary way. There is no quantum of penalty that suggests itself as uniquely appropriate for competition law violations.[146] Australian competition law currently sets the statutory maxima for penalties at $ 10 million for corporations and $ 500 000 for individuals,[147] but these penalty ceilings largely reflect the legislature's intuitive perception of the suitable magnitude of penalties, perhaps influenced in this task by a comparison of the penalty levels applicable to other types of regulatory offences.[148]

Assuming that reasonable solutions can be found to overcome the difficulties inherent in establishing a scale of proportionality, then a penalty scheme which is based on the just desert model could rest on the proportionality principle in order to determine the quantum of penalties, with the 'seriousness' of violations determined by the extent of the harm caused by the violation and the culpability

[146] von Hirsch (1993), 19.

[147] The Dawson Review recommended that the Act should be amended so that the maximum pecuniary penalty for corporations be raised to the greater of $10 million or three times the gain from the contravention or, where the gain cannot be readily ascertained, 10% of the turnover of the body corporate and all its interconnected bodies corporate (if any); and that the Court be given the option to exclude an individual implicated in a contravention from being a director of a corporation or being involved in its management, and that corporations be prohibited from indemnifying, directly or indirectly, officers, employees or agents against the imposition of a pecuniary penalty upon an officer, employee or agent: Trade Practices Review Committee (2003), recommendation 10–2. The Australian government has indicated that it supports this recommendation: Commonwealth Government Response to the Review of the Competition Provisions of the Trade Practices Act 1974 (2003).

[148] Under EU competition law, the negligent or intentional infringement of the prohibitions contained in Art 81(1) and Art 82 of the EC Treaty range from ECU 1000–ECU 1 mil or up to 10% of the turnover in the preceding business year of each of the undertakings participating in the infringement: Council Regulation (EEC) No 17/62, First Regulation implementing Arts 85 and 86 of the Treaty OJ L13, 21.2.62; Under USA antitrust law, breach of the Sherman Antitrust Act,15 USC §1–7 by fines of up to $US 10 million (for corporations) and $US 350 000 (for individuals). In the USA, the setting of fines for antitrust offences is subject to the guidelines laid down in the USA Federal Sentencing Guidelines 1998, Part R as amended by the Criminal Fine Enforcement Act 1984, which allows an alternative maximum fine equal two times the gain made or harm caused: 18 USC §3571(d).

of the offender. Hence the greater the loss caused by the violation, the greater the quantum of penalty. Similarly, an 'innocent' breach of the law would be penalised less severely than a breach arising from deliberate action taken by the offender in knowing violation of the law.

2. The Federal Court's Approach

Having briefly identified how we might expect the two models of deterrence and desert to be applied to Australian competition law penalties, we can now examine whether the Federal Court's approach resembles either of the two models. While the responsibility for initiating and conducting civil enforcement proceedings to obtain penalties from suspected offenders lies with the Commission,[149] it is the Federal Court of Australia which decides whether a breach of the Act has occurred and, if so, the quantum of penalty to be imposed.[150] Statutory guidance is provided to the Court in determining the level of penalty for a breach of Part IV in section 76(1) of the Act which confers on the Court a very wide discretion to determine the quantum of penalty but sets out a list of relevant matters which the Court must take into account when exercising its discretion. For this purpose, relevant matters include, but are not limited to: the nature and extent of the act or omission; any loss or damage suffered as a result of the act or omission; the circumstances in which the act or omission took place; and whether the person has previously been found by the Court in previous proceedings under the Act to have engaged in any similar conduct.

The statutory criteria do not, in and of themselves, appear strongly to reflect either of the theoretical models of punishment described above. However, it could be argued that they fit more comfortably with the desert model of penalty setting, for all the stated criteria concern matters which pertain to the 'seriousness' of the unlawful conduct. On the other hand, the listed criteria might broadly be interpreted as the basis for taking into account specific quantifiable variables utilised by the deterrence model.[151] The statutory criteria are not exhaustive, however, and the Court's ultimate task is to determine a penalty 'as it determines to be appropriate having regard to all relevant matters'.

[149] Trade Practices Act 1974, s 78 provides that criminal proceedings do not lie for breach of Part IV of the Act. Hence the rules of civil rather than criminal procedure apply in the conduct of penalty proceedings.

[150] In recent years, however, the quantum of penalty has largely been determined by negotiation between the Commission and the respondent, subject to the court's approval: see Thorpe (1996). Below ch 5.

[151] The ALRC recently recommended the introduction of legislative guidance setting out 'broad but comprehensive factors' governing all civil penalties in Australia with the aim of assisting courts 'to assess the penalty from the dual perspectives of the seriousness of the contravention and the culpability of the offender': ALRC (2002), para 29.24. The relevant factors are set out in Recommendation 29–1.

Accordingly, we must look more closely at the case law to identify how the Federal Court has approached the task of penalty setting in order to identify the theoretical basis upon which it has proceeded.[152]

The controversy concerning Part IV penalties has centred upon the actual level of penalty imposed, rather than on the various factors which the Court takes into account in determining the appropriate penalty. There have been a significant number of decisions in which the Court has applied section 76 so that its general reasoning in setting Part IV penalties is now well established, stemming from the judgment of French J in *TPC v CSR Ltd*[153] where he elaborated on the criteria relevant to a determination of the appropriate level of penalty.[154] These criteria, which have become known as the 'French factors', now provide the general reference point used by the Court in determining the appropriate penalty, based upon the key passage of French J's judgment:

> The assessment of a penalty of appropriate deterrent value will have regard to a number of factors which have been canvassed in the cases. These include the following:
>
> 1. The nature and extent of the contravening conduct.
> 2. The amount of loss or damage caused.[155]
> 3. The circumstances in which the conduct took place.
> 4. The size of the contravening company.[156]
> 5. The degree of power it has, as evidenced by its market share and ease of entry into the market.
> 6. The deliberateness of the contravention and the period over which it extended.[157]
> 7. Whether the contravention arose out of the conduct of senior management or at a lower level.[158]
> 8. Whether the company has a corporate culture conducive to compliance with the Act, as evidenced by educational programs and disciplinary or other corrective measures in response to an acknowledged contravention.
> 9. Whether the company has shown a disposition to cooperate with the authorities responsible for the enforcement of the Act in relation to the contravention.[159]

[152] See generally Frieberg and O'Malley (1983).

[153] *TPC v CSR Ltd* (1991) ATPR ¶41–076.

[154] The factors considered by courts to be relevant to a determination of penalties for price-fixing agreements have been analysed in detail by economists Round *et al* (1996), 300–01.

[155] In particular, courts may consider the economic impact of the contravening conduct on the market—a greater effect warranting a heavier penalty. Compare *TPC v Allied Mills Pty Ltd* (1981) ATPR ¶40–241 with *TPC v Malleys Ltd* (1979) ATPR ¶40–118.

[156] Courts have taken the view that the larger the corporation, the larger the appropriate penalty, on the basis that what would deter a small company might have little effect on a very large one: *TPC v Carlton & United Breweries Ltd* (1990) ATPR ¶41–037; *TPC v TNT Australia Pty Ltd & Ors* (1995) ATPR ¶41–375 at 40,168.

[157] Systematic, deliberate defiance of the law is considered to warrant heavier penalties: *TPC v TNT* (1995) ATPR ¶41–375.

[158] The higher the level of management responsible for participation in the contravention, the more serious the infringement and the higher the level of penalty: *TPC v TNT* (1995) ATPR ¶41–375.

[159] Cooperation with enforcement authorities has been regarded as a mitigating factor which justifies a reduction in penalty: *TPC v TNT* (1995) ATPR ¶41–375.

> The first three factors are all expressly mentioned in s.76. They can be regarded as measures of the scope and impact of the conduct and it is conducive to deterrence that the greater the significance of these elements, the heavier the penalty should be.[160]

In addition to setting out the various factors which should inform the penalty setting process, French J also made a number of strong statements of principle concerning the determination of Part IV penalties which, at first blush, suggest that the deterrence model informs the Court's approach. In his view, the sole purpose of such penalties is to deter future contraventions of the Act. Moral considerations have no role to play,

> Punishment for breaches of the criminal law traditionally involves three elements: deterrence, both general and individual, retribution and rehabilitation. Neither retribution nor rehabilitation, within the sense of the Old and New Testament moralities that imbue much of our criminal law, have any part to play in economic regulation of the kind contemplated by Pt IV. Nor, if it be necessary to say so, is there any compensatory element in the penalty fixing process . . . The principal, and I think probably the only, object of the penalties imposed by s. 76 is to attempt to put a price on contravention that is sufficiently high to deter repetition by the contravenor and by others who might be tempted to contravene the Act.[161]

The view that 'punishment has no role' in the determination of penalties under section 76 was endorsed by the majority of the Full Federal Court in *NW Frozen Foods Pty Ltd v ACCC*.[162] The majority rejected the approach taken by Heerey J at first instance in comparing the culpability of the appellant with that of another corporation in an earlier price-fixing case in which sizeable penalties were imposed. By so doing, Heerey J had, in the Full Federal Court's opinion, engaged in an exercise of punishment, which was not the purpose of penalties imposed under section 76.[163]

By claiming that the only object of penalties imposed by section 76 is to 'price' contraventions so as to deter future contraventions by the offender (ie specific deterrence) and other would-be offenders (ie general deterrence), French J appears powerfully to endorse the deterrence model as the theoretical basis for penalty setting for Part IV contraventions, although he does not make clear which variant of the deterrence model is to be applied. The express rejection of morality and punishment as having any relevance to the determination of penalties also appears to reject outright the desert model as the basis for penalty setting. Despite these statements, an examination of the general body of case law, the specific criteria enumerated by French J as relevant to penalty setting, and the reasoning adopted by French J in the *CSR* case itself, indicate that this may not be the case.

[160] *TPC v CSR Ltd* (1991) ATPR ¶41–076 at 52, 152–3.
[161] *TPC v CSR Ltd* (1991) ATPR ¶41–076 at 52, 152.
[162] (1996) FCR 285.
[163] (1996) FCR 285, 297.

Although the majority of the Full Federal Court in *NW Frozen Foods* stated that notions of morality and punishment have no role to play in the setting of penalties under section 76, the issue is by no means settled, with conflicting judicial statements concerning the matter. So, for example in *ACCC v ABB Transmissions & Distribution Ltd*[164] Finkelstein J stated that 'in antitrust cases retribution has no real role to play' while Goldberg has stated that 'in an appropriate case where there has been a flagrant and wilful contravention [a court] might take the view that a severe penalty was warranted having regard to the deliberateness and wilfulness of the contravention'[165] and thereby pointing to the offender's culpability as relevant to the determination of penalty. More recently, in *J McPhee & Son (Aust) Pty Ltd v ACCC*[166] the Full Federal Court deliberately left open whether punishment is a relevant factor in quantifying penalties under section 76 on the basis that it was not necessary for them to decide the issue for the purposes of the appeal. Nonetheless, the Court accepted that matters relating to the deliberateness of the conduct and the manner in which the contravention occurred were relevant to penalty setting, although the Court made the somewhat puzzling claim that such considerations do not involve 'moral issues'.[167]

A closer examination of the comments made by French J in *CSR* reveals that he conflated the substantive rules for determining whether a contravention of the Act has occurred with the principles to be applied in determining the level of penalty for contravention. Put differently, he confused the question of breach with the question of penalty.[168] These are separate and independent questions. There are two strands of reasoning which led French J to his conclusion that morality has no role to play in penalty setting. First, because the purpose of the Act is directed to regulating competition, the statutory provisions are regulatory rather than penal in nature. Secondly, the High Court in *Queensland Wire Industries v BHP*[169] expressly rejected the view that morality was relevant when determining whether section 46 of the Act has been contravened. According to French J, it therefore followed that morality was irrelevant to setting penalties for contraventions of the Act. But both strands of reasoning are concerned with the issue of breach: the first goes to the subject matter of the Act, and the second to the substantive rules which define unlawful behaviour. While French J correctly stated that morality has no place in determining whether a *breach* of the

[164] (2002) 190 ALR 169.

[165] (1997) ATPR ¶41–562 at 43,811. Goldberg J reiterated his earlier comments in *ACCC v George Weston Foods* [2000] FCA 690, but nevertheless considered himself bound by the authority of the Full Federal Court in *NW Frozen Foods* (1996) FCR 285 not to take account of punishment in determining the appropriate level of penalty.

[166] [2000] FCA 365.

[167] [2000] FCA 365, para 170.

[168] This error is referred to by Goldberg J in *ACCC v Australian Safeway Stores Pty Ltd* (1997) ATPR ¶41–562 at 43,811.

[169] (1989) 167 CLR 177. See also *TPC v Commodore Business Machines Pty Ltd* (1989) ATPR ¶40–976 at 50,672 and *TPC v TNT* (1995) ATPR ¶41–375.

Act has occurred, it does not necessarily follow that morality has no place in determining the appropriate *penalty* which should apply in respect of a breach.[170] Furthermore, of the nine factors cited by French J as relevant to a determination of penalty setting, six are concerned with matters of culpability and cannot easily be reconciled with the deterrence theory of penalty setting nor regarded as wholly devoid of moral content. For example, the deliberateness of the contravention is irrelevant to the deterrence model. Indeed, the injury to others variant of the deterrence model is grounded on the notion that deliberate contraventions of the law are desirable and should occur if their net effect is welfare-enhancing. Because the deterrence model assumes that each actor is rational, all contraventions are assumed to be deliberate. By contrast, the deliberateness of a contravention lies at the core of the concept of culpability, which is fundamental to a determination of the penalties levied in accordance with the desert model.[171] Similarly, the adoption of a compliance programme and culture by the offender has no bearing on the calculation of penalties under the deterrence model. If the law is violated, then the offender must pay. All other things being equal, an offender who provides evidence of a culture of compliance should be penalised to the same extent as the offender who sets out deliberately to contravene the law.[172]

In addition, the comments of Smithers J in *TPC v Stihl Chain Saws* were quoted by French J with approval, thus implicitly acknowledging that morality and fairness have a legitimate role in determining penalties under section 76:

> The penalty should constitute a real punishment proportionate to the deliberation with which the defendant contravened the provisions of the Act. It should be sufficiently high to have a deterrent quality, and it should be kept in mind that the Act operates in a commercial environment where deterrence of those minded to contravene its provisions is not likely to be achieved by penalties which are not realistic. It should reflect the will of Parliament that the commercial standards laid down in the Act must be observed, but not be so high as to be oppressive.[173]

Accordingly, the Federal Court's overall approach to determining the quantum of penalties under section 76 appears to be guided by a combination of the principles upon which the deterrence model and the desert model are founded. Some of the criteria which the Court has taken into account in penalty setting can be accommodated within the deterrence model, while other criteria appear to fit more comfortably within the desert model. In the first instance, the Court claims

170 See n105 (above).

171 Cf *J McPhee & Son (Aust) Pty Ltd v ACCC* [2000] FCA 365, para 170.

172 The other criteria which appear to have no apparent relevance to the economic model are: the nature and extent of the contravening conduct, the circumstances in which the conduct took place, whether the contravention arose out of the conduct of senior management or at a lower level, and whether the company has shown a disposition to co-operate with the authorities responsible for the enforcement of the Act in relation to a contravention. But, as in Round's study, economists could simply assign economic value to judicial criteria as proxies for economically relevant variables: Round *et al* (1996).

173 (1991) ATPR ¶41-076, at 52,152.

to be guided by the principle of deterrence, which it defines as requiring penalties to be set sufficiently high so as to deter both the particular respondent and those contemplating contraventions of the law in future. On the other hand, the Court has also referred to the importance of penalties being proportionate to the seriousness of the offence, thus indicating that the notion of 'just desert' which underlies the desert model should also guide the Court in determining the quantum of penalty.

Ultimately, the Court has correctly acknowledged that:

> the fixing of the quantum of penalty is not an exact science. It is not done by the application of a formula, and, within a certain range, courts have always recognised that one precise figure cannot be incontestably said to be preferable to another.[174]

In general, the framework of principles which the Court has developed to determine the appropriate quantum of penalty strike a reasonable balance between the need to ensure that penalties serve to deter future contraventions, while avoiding penalties which would be disproportionate or oppressive.

D. CONCLUSION

While considerable attention has been given to the appropriate role of punitive strategies and mechanisms within regulatory compliance scholarship, relatively little discussion addresses 'how severe' those sanctions should be. Although the issue of penal severity has been the subject of considerable debate by legal philosophers, they have tended to concentrate on the punishment of 'traditional' crimes, rather than regulatory offences. By setting out to identify how regulatory penalties should be quantified, this chapter has sought to identify whether there are any unique and distinctive features of regulatory offences that point to the application of specific principles for determining the penal severity and which may then be applied to determine the appropriate level of penalty for competition law violations.

Two theoretical models have been examined: the 'deterrence' model and the 'desert' model. The deterrence model is based on economic efficiency, seeking to 'price' unlawful conduct at a level that will deter firms from engaging in such conduct so as to minimise the social cost of unlawful conduct. Two variants of the deterrence model can be identified. The 'injury to others' model aims to deter unlawful conduct to its optimal level, by deterring only unlawful conduct which is net welfare-reducing to society. Thus, the relevant quantum of penalty is measured by the cost of harm to others caused by the offender's wrongful conduct. On the other hand, the 'unlawful gain' model is concerned to achieve 'absolute' deterrence, in order completely to eliminate unlawful conduct, based

[174] *TPC v TNT* (1995) ATPR ¶41–375 per Burchett J. See also *ACCC v George Weston Foods* [2000] FCA 690, para 37.

on the assumption that such conduct is always net welfare-reducing. Thus the relevant quantum of penalty is measured by the size of the offender's unlawful gain, for by disgorging the offender's ill-gotten gain, the incentive to violate the law is eliminated. By contrast, the 'desert' model regards punishment as a means for censuring offenders for wrongdoing and thus seeks to punish offenders in proportion to the seriousness of their unlawful conduct, as indicated by the offender's culpability and the extent of the harm thereby caused.

Neither theoretical model provides a complete and consistent account of the social practice of punishment. Both have certain strengths and shortcomings. Although the deterrence model is theoretically capable of generating a specific quantum of penalty and recognises the need to take account of the probability of detection in the calculation of penalty, it assumes that firms and individuals are solely motivated by rational welfare-maximisation: an assumption which may not accurately reflect reality, even in the commercial context. It also generates intractable problems in practice when attempting to quantify variables that are inherently incapable of precise quantification. Its main limitation, however, is its failure to respect the moral worth and autonomy of persons and its disregard for concepts of fairness and justice. In contrast, this is the greatest strength of the desert model given its deliberate concern that penalty levels should be fair. But while the logic of desert justifies singling out the offender for differential treatment, it fails to explain why that treatment should take the form of penal deprivation. Moreover, the desert model is unable to generate a precise quantum of penalty in any given situation so that attempts to apply the desert model to real factual situations are fraught with imprecision which might lead to inconsistency and arbitrariness in penalty setting.

Although it may be tempting to suggest that the deterrence model is preferable to the desert model as the basis for quantifying regulatory penalties because regulatory law is primarily concerned with achieving economic and social goals, rather than to express moral outrage at the proscribed conduct, this overlooks the important distinction between liability and penalty. While issues of fairness and morality may have little or no role to play in determining whether the relevant conduct is unlawful, such notions are inevitably implicated in the process of state penalisation of unlawful conduct. The powers of a liberal democratic state in meting out penal hard treatment must be constrained by the requirements of fairness so as to respect the individual's right to fair treatment. In addition, a penalty scheme must not be too out of step with societal notions of fairness and justice, lest it fail to inculcate in those who violate the law a sense of the wrongfulness of their conduct, and lead to an erosion of public confidence in the regulatory system. Accordingly, it is suggested that a fair and effective regulatory penalty regime should combine the essential features of both models: penalties should be set at a level which is sufficiently high to deter future contraventions of the law, provided that any given penalty award is not unfairly disproportionate to the seriousness of the offence. The approach thus reflects the principle framework set out in chapter three: regulatory goals may be promoted provided that constitutional values implicated in the regulatory implementation process are given adequate expression.

By exploring the approach of the Australian Federal Court in setting penalties for violations of Part IV of the Act, we have seen how the framework of principles developed in this chapter may provide a valuable contribution in seeking to assess whether the penalties imposed are fair and effective. While Australian case law is replete with incantations of the aim of deterrence and the irrelevance of morality, suggesting that the Federal Court adheres to the deterrence model in quantifying penalties, a closer examination indicates that both the desert and deterrence models inform the Court's approach to penalty setting, striking a reasonable balance between the need to deter future contraventions of the Act while avoiding oppressive or unfairly disproportionate penalties.

5

Negotiated Penalty Settlements

A. INTRODUCTION

WE HAVE SEEN how the justification for penalising regulatory offenders sheds light on the principles that inform and constrain the severity of punishment. In this chapter, we shall see how the reasons why we single out and penalise law-breakers also contributes to another facet of our quest for principles in the enforcement of regulatory law. But our focus now shifts away from examining the severity of punishment to the *process* by which liability for, and quantum of, such penalties ought to be determined.

One common feature of the framework for regulating competition established throughout OECD countries, including the USA, UK, EU and Australia, is that the prescribed procedure for imposing penalties on those violating competition law involves formal determinations first, that a violation has occurred and secondly, of the penalty to be imposed.[1] In some jurisdictions, such as the USA and Australia, the public authority empowered to make these determinations is a judicial body invested with jurisdiction to hear competition matters, whilst in others, such as the EU and UK, the legislative framework provides for such determinations to be made by the competition regulator.[2] But the formal structure of these regulatory schemes should not be allowed to obscure the fact that, in practice, proceedings to penalise those in violation of competition law are often resolved, not in formal adjudicative proceedings, but by some form of 'plea bargain' or negotiated settlement. These 'negotiated penalty settlements' may take a variety of forms, ranging from the defendant agreeing to admit liability in return for leniency[3] through to agreement between the regulator

[1] See OECD (2002) for an outline of the sanctions for competition law violations across OECD countries.

[2] In the USA, jurisdiction is divided between the Department of Justice (Antitrust Division) ('DoJ') which is empowered both to prosecute criminal antitrust violations and enforce civil violations, and the Federal Trade Commission, which has civil enforcement powers. Where the DoJ brings enforcement action, it is the Federal Courts which determine whether a violation has occurred.

[3] Formal 'leniency' policies have been established by the DoJ (Department of Justice Individual Leniency Policy, issued 10 August 1994; Department of Justice Corporate Leniency Policy, issued 10 August 1993), the EC Commission (Commission Notice on Immunity from Fines and Reduction of Fines in Cartel Cases, 19 February 2002; OJ C45/3) and the ACCC ('ACCC leniency policy for cartel conduct', June 2003). The primary aim of these policies is to encourage those involved in suspected violations to come forward and admit involvement in the violations in exchange for more lenient treatment by the enforcement authority. Where such leniency takes the form of a complete exemption from the application of the legal provisions and ensuring sanctions that would otherwise

and defendant on the specific quantum of penalty payable.[4] This might seem surprising, given that it is rare for the legislation establishing the framework for competition regulation to make provision for such settlements. So, for example, in the Australian context, section 76 of the Act clearly entrusts the Federal Court with the task of determining both penal liability and quantum.[5] The Commission's role in relation to penalties, at least on the face of the Act, is simply to apply to the court for an order for the recovery of a pecuniary penalty. The Act makes no mention of negotiated penalty settlements.[6]

Yet the use of negotiated penalty settlements is well-established in the practice of public competition law enforcement, in Australia and elsewhere. Variability arises, however, in the nature and form of such settlements, and the procedures by which such settlements are reached and given legal force. For example, in EU competition enforcement, such settlements typically take the form of a 'sentence discount', reducing the level of fine that would otherwise be payable by the offender in respect of the violation.[7] By contrast, the resolution of criminal antitrust cases in the US has often been concluded by a full-blown 'plea bargain' between the US Department of Justice and the accused person, which is provided in written form and submitted to a court for formal approval before it takes effect.[8]

The primary purpose of this chapter is to examine critically the use of such plea bargains or, as I prefer to call them, 'negotiated penalty settlements' in the public enforcement of competition law. This issue is of considerable salience in the Australian context in light of the considerable disquiet[9] surrounding them,

apply, this amounts to the conferral of legal immunity on the person seeking leniency, discussed below at n.14. Due to limitations of length, a fuller examination of official leniency policies in regulatory enforcement is beyond the scope of this inquiry. For a discussion of the EC Commission and DoJ leniency policies, see Arp and Swaak (2003).

[4] In the USA, all DoJ prosecutions since 1990 seeking criminal fines under the Sherman Act have been resolved by negotiated settlements: Klaiwiter (2001).

[5] Section 76(1) provides that 'If the Court is satisfied that a person—

(a) has contravened a provision of Part IV;
(b) has attempted to contravene such a provision;
(c) has aided, abetted, counselled or procured a person to contravene such a provision;
(d) has induced, or attempted to induce, a person, whether by threats or promises or otherwise, to contravene such a provision;
(e) has conspired with others to contravene such a provision,

the Court may order the person to pay to the Commonwealth such pecuniary penalty, in respect of each act or omission by the person to which this section applies, as the Court determines to be appropriate having regard to all relevant matters including the nature and extent of the act or omission and of any loss or damage suffered as a result of the act or omission, the circumstances in which the act or omission took place and whether the person has previously been found by the Court in proceedings under this Part or Part XIB to have engaged in similar conduct.'

[6] S 77(1) of the Act provides that 'The Commission may institute a proceeding in the Court for the recovery on behalf of the Commonwealth of a pecuniary penalty referred to in section 76.'

[7] See EC Commission Notice on Immunity from Fines and Reduction of Fines in Cartel Cases, 19 February 2002; OJ C45/3; Van Bael (1995); Richardson (1999); Arp and Swaak (2003)

[8] Klaiwiter (2001); The DoJ's role in plea-bargain discussions are governed by the Federal Rules of Criminal Procedure, r 11 and r 43(a) which provide for a series of detailed rules formalising the plea bargaining process, including court approval of any plea bargaining agreement.

[9] Featherston (1995); Featherston (1997); Kench (1998).

with critics claiming that they are secretive, unfair, and involve an abuse of the Commission's discretionary powers of enforcement. In the course of this examination, we shall seek to understand the apparent polarisation between academics critiques of bargaining and negotiation as a means for resolving law enforcement proceedings. Although criminal law scholars typically express stinging condemnation of such practices, regulatory scholars tend to sing their praises. The explanation for this sharp disjunction appears to rest, at least partly, in the civil/criminal divide lying deep within the historical core of western legal thought and tradition. As we shall see, important procedural consequences follow from categorising liability for violating the law, and the ensuing sanction, as either civil or criminal, with considerably more rigorous and demanding procedural requirements applying in criminal proceedings than those applicable to enforcement proceedings of a civil nature. Yet the contours of this divide prove much more elusive than its longevity may suggest, particularly when used to distinguish between civil and criminal sanctions for unlawful conduct. It is nonetheless possible to distil several criteria underlying the civil/criminal labels from which we can draw in developing a principled approach to the process and procedures by and through which liability and punishment for regulatory violations ought to be determined. In so doing the challenge is to find a principled way of mediating between the regulatory goals of efficiency, responsiveness and effectiveness, which the use of negotiated penalty settlements tends to promote, and the constitutional values of accountability, transparency and, most importantly, procedural fairness, which such settlements tend to antagonise.

While the first part of this chapter illuminates how these constitutional values may be strained by the negotiated settlement process, it is necessary to understand in more concrete terms how they might best be protected in negotiating practice, thereby enhancing its legitimacy. Much will depend on the practice and conduct of the institutions involved in the negotiated settlement process and thus the discussion then shifts to a different, somewhat less abstract plane, by outlining various safeguards that may assist in ensuring the fairness and integrity of the settlement process. Three such safeguards are briefly discussed, drawing on the Australian regulatory enforcement framework to provide a more concrete focus for the discussion: the separation of prosecutorial and judicial functions, the ethical obligations of enforcement officials and judicial oversight of settlement agreements.

B. BARGAINING IN THE CRIMINAL AND REGULATORY ENFORCEMENT PROCESS

The prevalence of bargaining and negotiation by enforcement officials in response to 'traditional' crimes and regulatory offences is well documented.[10]

[10] Eg Ashworth (1998), Ch 9.

Although enforcement bargaining and negotiation in both social contexts have attracted extensive scholarly attention, a comparative examination of the literature demonstrates a stark cleavage in opinion concerning their desirability. In order to make sense of this disjunction, the assumptions and reasoning underpinning these critiques require exploration, and it is to this task that we now turn.

1. Plea Bargaining in Criminal Proceedings

Plea bargaining refers to a variety of practices that are sometimes used in criminal proceedings.[11] The central feature of plea bargaining is that the person alleged to have violated the law (the 'accused') is offered some form of inducement or benefit by the enforcement authority (the 'prosecution') in exchange for a plea of guilty in a criminal case. A distinction may be drawn between:

(a) *charge bargaining*, which involves negotiations between the prosecution and the accused's legal representative, frequently resulting in the prosecution agreeing not to pursue a more serious charge if the accused pleads guilty to a lesser charge. There is no judicial involvement in the negotiations;
(b) *sentence discounting*, which involves imposing on an accused who pleads guilty a lesser sentence than would otherwise have been imposed had the accused denied the charge but is found guilty at trial;
(c) *agreement on sentence*, which involves agreement between the prosecution and the accused on the appropriate sentence. Court approval of the agreed sentence is typically required prior to its implementation;[12]
(d) *sentence indication*, which involves some form of active participation by the judge in plea negotiations usually to give the accused an idea of the likely penalty if the accused pleads guilty as opposed to the likely sentence if convicted after trial.[13]

Each practice may occur independently, or may be used in conjunction with the others. For example, the prosecution and counsel for the accused may reach an agreement on sentence incorporating a sentence discount following a charge bargaining agreement. Although each practice raises slightly different issues, criminal law scholars have demonstrated that each practice raises common and often deeply-rooted concerns, which shall shortly be explored. The term 'plea bargaining' is used in the following discussion to encompass the broad range of practices that involve the accused forgoing strict entitlements

[11] This discussion considers plea bargaining in the context of an adversarial system of justice, in which the trial by a neutral and independent court plays the central and pivotal role in determining the accused's guilt or innocence and, if found guilty, the appropriate type and severity of punishment.

[12] Strictly speaking, an agreement on sentence need not involve plea bargaining in the sense of involving an offer of inducement to the accused in return for agreement on sentence, but in practice such an inducement is likely to be involved.

[13] Sallmann (1984), 150.

within the enforcement process in return for greater leniency in expected sentence.[14]

Negotiated penalty settlements in regulatory enforcement proceedings constitute a form of plea bargaining, in that the defendant agrees to co-operate with the regulator by admitting a contravention in return for leniency, be it in the form of a reduction in number or severity of 'charges'. In Australia and the USA, where such settlements require court approval, then the regulator typically agrees not to press for a penalty beyond the agreed sum, rather than seeking a higher penalty in contested proceedings.[15] In such circumstances, the defendant substantially eliminates the risk that a higher penalty may be imposed as well as saving the costs of contesting the proceedings. By so doing, however, the defendant forgoes the possibility of being found innocent of the allegations[16] and, even if found to have committed a contravention, forgoes the possibility that the relevant decision-making body may have ordered a lower penalty in the absence of such agreement. In some Australian cases, the defendant may agree with the Commission on the facts and admit liability, but then leave the quantum of penalty to be determined by the court in contested proceedings. If the agreement on facts is the result of a charge bargain, this eliminates the defendant's risk of being found liable for a greater number of charges in fully contested proceedings. Even in the absence of a charge bargain, the defendant who admits liability is likely to benefit from a sentence discount as a result of its co-operation with the Commission in making admissions.

2. The Benefits of Plea Bargaining and Negotiated Settlements

The prevalence of bargaining and negotiation in both criminal and regulatory enforcement practice can be readily explained. The precise nature of the benefits

[14] This definition excludes agreements that involve the grant of immunity from prosecution to the accused. Immunity agreements are different in nature from plea agreements. In the case of plea agreements, the consideration flowing from the accused is always a guilty plea and the consideration flowing from the prosecutor may vary. By contrast, the consideration given by the accused pursuant to an immunity agreement may vary but the consideration flowing from the Crown is constant—it is always the promise of immunity: Law Reform Commission of Canada (1992). The use of immunity agreements raise deep ethical, philosophical and legal questions, the consideration of which is beyond the scope of this book. See for example Law Reform Commission of Canada (1992); Temby (1985); Kell (1997). Grants of immunity from prosecution are generally regarded as a necessary tool in the administration of justice, particularly in relation to the detection of organised crime. Commentators have, however, emphasised that such agreements should be used sparingly and only in exceptional circumstances and should be properly regulated in order to guard against abuse. The Commission has, on occasions, granted immunity to those who have cooperated with its investigations (see *TPC v CC (NSW) Pty Ltd* (1994) ATPR ¶41–352) and its recently adopted leniency policy allows for the granting of immunity: Above, n 3.

[15] Cf *TPC v Allied Mills Pty Ltd* (1981) ATPR ¶40–241 at 43,182: Below, Part D. See Klaiwitter (2001) for a discussion of DoJ settlement practice in antitrust proceedings.

[16] Where the formal determination of liability is made by the regulator, then the defendant forgoes the possibility that the evidence may prove insufficient to justify a finding of liability.

associated with their use depends, however, upon whose perspective is under consideration. From the state's perspective, there are two principal advantages, of a practical rather than principled kind, when law enforcement proceedings are resolved by plea negotiations. The primary advantage lies in the cost savings arising from the avoidance of a trial to determine the accused's guilt or innocence. Given that investigations and the trial process are time-consuming and resource-intensive for the prosecuting authority and the court adjudicating the matter, the avoidance of trial by plea bargaining enables these costs to be substantially reduced. The magnitude of such savings is likely to be greater the earlier the plea bargaining occurs, by avoiding prolonged and extensive investigations and the preparation of the case for trial.[17] Similar cost savings arise when negotiated penalty settlements are used to resolve competition proceedings, directly benefiting the defendant and regulator (in the form of saved litigation expenses), and indirectly benefiting the general public (through cost savings associated with contested proceedings). Secondly, in jurisdictions where liability and penalty are determined in court proceedings, plea bargaining not only avoids the costs associated with trial, but it may enable the state to secure a conviction without enduring the hazards of a trial whose outcome is uncertain. To the extent that securing convictions of the guilty may be regarded as a public good, then plea bargaining may promote the public interest. Plea bargains and negotiated penalty settlements may also be thought to promote the public interest in the early settlement of disputes and the prompt resolution of conflict.

From the perspective of the accused in criminal proceedings, the perceived advantages are somewhat different. Whilst both the innocent and the guilty-accused benefit from the cost savings associated with the avoidance of trial, and the consequent disruption and adverse publicity that may otherwise arise, from the accused's perspective the primary benefits of plea bargaining depend on his or her guilt or innocence. For the guilty-accused, the benefits of plea bargaining generally, and sentence discounting in particular, are clear: the accused receives a lower sentence than would otherwise have been imposed had a plea of not guilty been entered. Likewise, in the regulatory context, it is the guilty defendant who is most likely to regard negotiated settlements as particularly beneficial. Not only do they enable the guilty defendant to avoid the considerable expense associated with contested litigation, but the availability of a sentence discount means that, by admitting liability, the defendant may benefit from a lower penalty than would otherwise have been imposed. For the innocent-accused, however, the benefits of plea bargaining are rather more amorphous. The innocent-accused may accept a plea bargain rather than seek to establish her innocence at trial in order to avoid the prospect that she may fail in this endeavour,

[17] It should be noted, however, that empirical research has cast some doubt on the extent of such efficiency gains in the criminal context, due to the fact that in practice, most guilty pleas are made just prior to trial, thus investigation and preparation costs are not avoided ('cracked trials'). Nevertheless, even in the case of late guilty pleas, significant savings in court time are realised by the avoidance of trial: see JUSTICE (1993).

with the consequent imposition of a more severe sentence than would otherwise have been imposed had she pleaded guilty to fewer (or less serious) charges. In other words, for the innocent-accused the advantage of plea bargaining lies in the ability to exchange the risk of being found guilty and subject to a heavier sentence for the certainty of a more lenient sentence by accepting a plea bargain.

3. Bargaining in Regulatory Enforcement: To Punish or Persuade?

The benefits associated with the bargaining process referred to above highlight the advantages to each participant as a rational actor in the enforcement process. But the benefits from bargaining in the enforcement context can be seen in more general terms, and it is these benefits that tend to be emphasised by regulatory scholars. There is rich and well-developed literature documenting the findings of a large and varied range of ethnographic studies that have sought to investigate, understand and explain how regulatory enforcement officers seek to secure compliance.[18] Many studies have identified a notable reluctance on the part of enforcement officials to rely upon formal prosecution in responding to observed non-compliance, favouring a more accommodative, conciliatory approach involving counselling, negotiating and bargaining with those under investigation.[19] Resort to the formal legal process is perceived by many enforcement officials, at least in the UK context, as a strategy of last resort, to be called upon only when attempts to cajole and counsel the suspect into compliance have failed.[20]

The Australian experience of regulatory enforcement, at least during the mid-1980s, appears to conform to that of its UK counterpart[21] in so far as regulatory agencies in both jurisdictions have been identified as reluctant to prosecute and punish those in violation of regulatory norms. Grabosky and Braithwaite's Australia-wide study, based on a series of interviews with senior enforcement officials from 96 Commonwealth agencies involved in the regulation of commercial activity,[22] found that most Australian regulators did not see themselves as primarily concerned with enforcement of their legislation. Over 80 percent of

[18] These studies include: Hawkins (1984); Hawkins (2002); Hutter (1988); Hutter (1997); Richardson *et al* (1984); Rowan-Robinson *et al* (1990); Baldwin (1990); Genn (1993); Bardach and Kagan (1982); Vogel (1980). For a useful survey of the literature, see Kagan (1994).

[19] Kagan observes that studies of enforcement have most often focused on the penal style, but in fact there are two activities embedded in such descriptions of legal style (i) the way officials assess compliance or non-compliance with regulatory standards: do they interpret rules stringently and apply them in a literal fashion, or more flexibly? and (ii) what do they do once they have decided that the activities constitute a violation?: *ibid*. My present concern is with the latter activity. The use of administrative settlements that may involve a departure from regulatory standards is discussed more fully in chs 6 and 7.

[20] Vogel (1980); Hawkins (2002).

[21] Above n 18.

[22] Grabosky and Braithwaite (1985). I am not aware of a more recent systematic study of Australian regulatory enforcement.

the officials interviewed claimed that aid, education and persuasion were more important functions for them than law enforcement. The manners of a vast majority of such agencies were observed to be 'gentle indeed': they overwhelmingly rejected a law enforcement ideology, they trusted business as socially responsible and anxious to be law abiding, and they rejected adversariness in favour of a co-operative ideology. Compliance was fundamentally seen by field officers as a matter of persuasion, negotiation or simply reminding regulatees to do what they know they should do. Not only the use of formal enforcement measures, but even its threatened use, was generally viewed as an adversarial breakdown indicative of failure by the regulator.[23]

This conciliatory approach, referred to by Hawkins and others as a 'compliance strategy' is often contrasted with a more formal, adversarial approach that relies more heavily on invoking the legal process by seeking to punish and deter contraventions through the imposition of penalties for non-compliance.[24] This 'sanctioning'[25] or 'deterrence' strategy,[26] as it has been variously described, is often claimed to be less effective in securing compliance because it is thought to generate greater resistance from regulated firms, undermining the importance of generating a culture of shared commitment to regulatory goals between regulator and regulated which is claimed to provide the necessary foundation for compliance.[27] Hawkins is even more emphatic. In his view, not only is a compliance strategy likely to be more effective in achieving compliance, but it is 'morally compelled'[28] because the authority of regulatory officials is not secured on a perceived moral and political consensus about the ills they seek to control. A strategy of bargaining and negotiation is therefore essential in order to sustain the support of the regulated.[29]

[23] It is interesting to note, however, that the one prominent exception was the strategy of the Commission's predecessor, the Trade Practices Commission ('TPC'). No other regulator took injunction proceedings against offenders with the frequency of the TPC, and apart from the Australian Taxation Office, no other agency is as frequently litigated against by companies that wish to challenge their regulatory actions. No Australian regulatory agency spent as large a proportion of its budget on litigation as the TPC, nor demonstrated the same or similar level commitment to taking on large and difficult cases. Yet, despite this, even the TPC, like every other Australian regulatory agency studied, placed more emphasis on administrative action than on litigation: *Ibid*, 91–94.

[24] Hawkins (1984); Hawkins (2002); Hutter (1997).

[25] Hawkins (1984).

[26] Reiss (1984).

[27] In a very similar manner, Bardach and Kagan also perceive two basic models of regulation. At one extreme is the style of enforcement typified by the title of their study 'Going by the Book'. They see this as essentially unreasonable and excessively legalistic, involving the strict imposition of standards regarded as unrealistic. In direct contrast is a strategy of 'reasonable regulation', a more tolerant, flexible regime in which enforcement authorities are discriminating and pragmatic in their application of law. The basic goal is to achieve compliance without invoking the formal legal process: Bardach and Kagan (1982). In contrast to Hawkins, Bardach and Kagan regard the unreasonable, legalistic model as the predominant style of enforcement in the USA: also Vogel (1980). Haines observes that regulatory theory has shifted, seeking to maximise 'corporate virtue' in which moral persuasion plays an integral party in regulatory enforcement strategies: Haines (1997), 10–11.

[28] Hawkins (1984), 128. The influence of moral judgement on the decision to prosecute is explored more fully in Hawkins (2002).

[29] Above, ch 4, Part B (2).

But academic support for the compliance approach is by no means universal. For example, Pearce and Tombs, arguably its most vocal opponents, claim that a punitive strategy is a necessary, practical and desirable response to corporate wrongdoing.[30] They challenge the assumptions underlying the compliance approach, alleging that it reflects an implicit conservative political ideology that illegitimately perceives corporate illegality as morally and qualitatively different from more traditional crimes. Nor is it clear, as Kagan points out, that discretion and dialogue, as opposed to strict application of law, invariably improve regulatory effectiveness, noting the potential for a compliance approach to degenerate into intolerable laxity.[31]

To some extent, the debate concerning the necessity or desirability of either a compliance or deterrence strategy in the enforcement of regulatory law has been overtaken as academic reflection in this area has matured, recognising that a combination of different enforcement approaches may be desirable, rather than dogmatic adherence to any particular style.[32] Although there have been various refinements to the deterrence versus compliance heuristic, with academics constructing more nuanced typologies to encapsulate the range of observed regulatory styles,[33] reliable generalisations and predictive models remain elusive.[34] Yet this has not prevented regulatory scholars from attempting to construct normative models prescribing strategies claiming to secure compliance most effectively.[35] One notable attempt is that proposed by Ayres and Braithwaite, who draw from a combination of game theory and the results of sociological investigation to argue that the relevant question is not *whether* to punish or persuade, but *when* to punish and when to persuade.[36] While their prescriptive model is the subject of more detailed scrutiny in the following chapter, its salient feature for our immediate purposes is the centrality accorded to the use of bargaining and co-operation. In their view, co-operative solutions between regulator and regulated firm provide the most effective means for securing compliance, being the most timely and least costly means by which the regulator may secure compliance.[37] It is only when such co-operation is not forthcoming, that the regulator should adopt a more punitive stance, with the threat of more

[30] Pearce and Tombs (1990); Pearce and Tombs (1991).

[31] Kagan (1994), 386; Gunningham (1987).

[32] A number of different factors are claimed to influence whether a compliance or deterrence style is adopted by regulators, including the nature of the breach (one-off or persistent), judgements as to seriousness, assessments of the nature of the regulatees (whether ill or well-informed and well-intentioned), whether the breach was careless, negligent or malicious, the social and moral legitimacy of the regulations being enforced and the existence of a continuing relationship (or the 'relational distance') between the regulator and regulated firms: Hutter (1997); Baldwin (1990); Black (1993).

[33] See Black (2001), 4.

[34] Kagan (1994), 386

[35] Braithwaite and Ayres (1992); Braithwaite (2002); Gunningham and Grabosky (1998); Gunningham and Johnstone (1999); Sparrow (2000).

[36] Braithwaite and Ayres (1992).

[37] *Ibid*, 35.

punitive approaches serving to encourage co-operation between regulated firms and the regulator.[38]

Taken together, the potential benefits from negotiated penalty settlements loom large. Where such settlements are employed in competition proceedings, the cost savings can be very substantial, given that formal legal proceedings are often expensive and protracted, particularly where the effects of the defendant's conduct on competition in the relevant market must be proved.[39] Negotiated penalty settlements may thus be seen as promoting the public interest, by freeing up law enforcement resources, facilitating the early resolution of disputes, and, to the extent that the emphasis on co-operative relationships between the prosecuting authority and those under investigation avoids fuelling resistance and hostility between them, may help promote lasting compliance.

4. Critiques of Plea Bargaining

Unlike regulatory scholars, who have tended to emphasise these benefits in the regulatory enforcement process, academics working within the criminal law tradition have typically expressed strenuous objections to plea bargaining in criminal proceedings, at best expressing grudging tolerance of such practices in the interests of pragmatism and expediency. As we shall see, their objections tend to focus around the following claims, that plea bargaining may undermine the procedural rights of the accused, impose undue pressure on the accused, lead to inaccurate or inappropriate outcomes and diminish the transparency of the criminal process due to their lack of visibility.[40]

(a) The Procedural Rights of the Accused May be Undermined

In most western legal systems, it is a fundamental right of an accused to have the prosecution prove the case against the accused at trial, a right associated with the basic presumption of innocence applicable in criminal proceedings. Acceptance of a guilty plea arguably encroaches on the basic presumption of innocence and right to trial. This is not a direct objection to plea bargaining, but with the ability of the court to accept a guilty plea instead of insisting on proof of guilt by the prosecution in all cases. Nonetheless, the objection is directly applicable to the use of sentence discounts, which may be seen as improperly penalising those who avail themselves of the right to trial rather than pleading guilty. Sentence discounting not only imposes institutional pressure on the innocent-accused to plead guilty, but it also enables the variation of sentence for

[38] Braithwaite and Ayres (1992), 40–41.

[39] For example, see *TPC v TNT Management Pty Ltd* (1985) ATPR ¶40–512, a massive case which was commenced in 1976 and took nine years to reach its conclusion.

[40] Ashworth (1998), 286–97; Clark (1986); Curran (1991); JUSTICE (1993); Langbein (1978); Mack and Anleu (1995); McDonald (1985); Schulhofer (1992); Scott and Stunz (1992) *cf* Easterbrook (1992).

reasons unrelated to the accused's wrongful conduct, thus conflicting with the right to fair treatment, which lies at the heart of fundamental sentencing principles that sentence should be based on the accused's conduct and personal characteristics, reflecting the gravity and seriousness of the criminal conduct in the particular case.[41]

(b) Improper Pressure

Perhaps the most serious objection to plea bargaining lies in its potentially coercive effect on the accused. Because it may involve a reduction in the number or seriousness of charges against the accused, plea bargaining provides the accused with incentives to accept a plea bargain rather than put the prosecution to proof at trial, foregoing the prospect of acquittal. While one might question whether the imposition of some pressure on guilty persons to plead guilty is improper, there are indisputably grave risks associated with pressuring innocent persons to plead guilty. The innocent-accused may accept a plea bargain, notwithstanding her innocence, fearful that she may be found guilty at trial and thus more severely punished than had she pleaded guilty to a lesser charge and so limited the severity of the ensuing sentence. This pressure to plead guilty, even for the innocent-accused, may well be considerable. By strengthening the incentives to plead guilty, sentence discounting exacerbates the pressure. Thus, the greater the sentence differential, the greater the risk of undue pressure being exerted, so heightening the risk of undermining the voluntariness of the accused's plea and rendering suspect its genuineness or factual accuracy.

(c) Inaccurate or Inappropriate Outcomes

Plea bargaining may result in a determination of guilt and the imposition of a sentence which do not accurately or appropriately reflect the true circumstances of the case or the quality of available and admissible evidence. The injustice associated with such inaccurate or inappropriate outcomes is at its gravest if plea bargaining induces an innocent person to plead guilty, resulting in conviction and punishment. If procedural fairness means anything, then at the very least it means that the procedures for determining guilt must ensure that the innocent accused is not exposed to an undue risk of wrongful conviction.[42] Similarly, plea bargains may also result in unjustified disparities and inconsistencies among accused persons in relation to the charges laid, convictions entered and/or the size of the sentence or penalty imposed for similar conduct. These disparities or inappropriate outcomes may result from the use of inducements, reflect lack of skill or professionalism on the part of legal representatives

[41] Van Bael (1995). The theoretical and moral justification for criminal punishment is, however, a heavily disputed issue. See Ashworth (1998); Duff (1994). Above, ch 4, Part B (1) (b) (ii).

[42] Below Part C.

and/or wider social power imbalances such as racial or ethnic bias. Where plea bargains are struck, the evaluation of the case by legal representatives is based almost exclusively on written records, including admissions, raising the spectre of inaccurate or inappropriate outcomes. This may be particularly acute in the criminal context where the written records are prepared by the police, who may operate with an informal presumption of guilt and pay insufficient attention to exculpatory information. Police investigation and interrogation replaces trial as the fact finding process, and the prosecution and defence counsels' shared sense of fairness can replace the legislative and sentencing policy of the criminal justice system.[43]

From a constitutional perspective, these concerns can be recast in terms of the right to fair treatment, embodied in the values of proportionality, consistency and rationality. In particular, where proceedings are resolved by agreement, rather than by impartial court adjudication, this generates a risk of inconsistency between settlements concluded with accused persons in different proceedings. This is not to deny that inconsistency may arise in judicial decision-making. But where disputes are resolved by negotiation, the resulting settlement will inevitably be, at least to some extent, a product of the relative bargaining strengths and capacities of the negotiating parties. As a consequence, the likelihood of inconsistent treatment of persons is enhanced when penalty proceedings are resolved by plea bargaining rather than by the court in contested proceedings. This may tend to undermine the apparent rationality of plea bargaining practice, suggesting that the relevant enforcement authority is unfairly discriminatory in conducting its negotiations.

(d) *Invisibility*

Plea bargaining discussions usually occur in secret. Only the end result is open to public scrutiny. The Canadian Law Reform Commission has observed that perhaps the most serious objection to plea bargaining has arisen from the 'secretive aura' that has enveloped it.[44] The bargaining process is invisible, occurring outside the court between the parties' legal representatives, unlike contested court proceedings which are public and the admissible evidence laid bare.[45] There is little or no judicial supervision except in the actual imposition on sentence or penalty.[46] Too much power can be concentrated in the enforcement authorities and too much of an obligation imposed on the defendant's legal representatives. If legal counsel are unprofessional, the invisibility of plea bargaining discussions can lead to sloppy practices, resulting in abuses such as charge reduction unwarranted by likely trial or sentence, or facts concealed from court

[43] Mack and Anleu (1995), 11.

[44] Law Reform Commission of Canada (1989), 9.

[45] Mack and Anleu (1995).

[46] With the exception of sentence indication, which entails judicial involvement in providing an informal indication of likely sentence on a guilty plea and after conviction.

to ensure an agreed outcome. Resolution by private discussion can mean that criminal laws defining right and wrong conduct are not seen to be clearly stated and enforced, potentially leading to greater public misunderstanding of the legal system and eroding public confidence in the administration of justice. The development of the law by application, testing through argument and judicial exposition may be stifled.[47]

The objection to invisibility in the criminal justice system arises from the essential requirement that justice must not only be done, but it must also be seen to be done.[48] Given the enormous breadth of the discretionary powers vested in law enforcement officials, it is important within a democratic system that they can be called to account to the community for the way in which those powers are exercised. If the law enforcement process is not sufficiently transparent, this diminishes the accountability of the enforcement authority and may tend to lower the level of public confidence in the legal process.[49] Couched in the language of procedural fairness, the lack of visibility in the bargaining process may undermine, or at least diminish, public confidence in the fairness of the enforcement process.

C. NEGOTIATED PENALTY SETTLEMENTS AND PROCEDURAL FAIRNESS

The above objections to plea bargaining are rooted in concerns that such practices may antagonise several constitutional values, particularly those of accountability, transparency, due process, legality, proportionality, consistency and rationality. Of these, the constitutional value under the gravest strain is that of due process, for each objection may be traced, at least in part, to concerns that the negotiation process may fail to respect its demands. The following discussion therefore seeks to understand the tension between the practice of negotiating penalty settlements and the requirements of due process, in the hope of integrating the sobering critiques of plea bargaining in the enforcement of 'traditional' crime with their considerably more optimistic counterparts writing from a regulatory compliance perspective. But before integration can be attempted, it is first necessary to examine why the literature from these two fields of inquiry reach such strikingly discordant policy prescriptions and, to this end, we must examine the relationship between the nature of sanctions and the demands of due process, to which we now turn.

[47] Mack and Anleu (1995), 10.
[48] Jaconelli (2002).
[49] Braithwaite (1993), 92.

1. Sanctions and Procedural Fairness

In chapter three, I referred to the range of different theoretical justifications for procedural fairness, which vary in their perception of the role of fair procedures in leading to accurate outcomes and the role of non-outcome based values. Strongly instrumentalist justifications claim that decision-making procedures must be fair for the purpose of, and to the extent that they promote, accurate outcomes.[50] Others argue that the instrumental role of fair procedures in facilitating accurate outcomes is merely incidental. Their primary purpose is to express in a direct and unmediated way society's respect for the dignity of persons: fair procedures are an essential expression of respect for the individual by recognising her as a moral agent who is entitled to be treated with dignity and respect.[51] For our purposes, we need not form a conclusive view on the extent to which procedural fairness is justified in either or both instrumental or deontological terms. It will suffice to acknowledge that procedural fairness is required in order to serve both outcome-based and non-outcome based values, the latter being grounded on the basic principle of respect for the dignity of persons.

Thus the extent to which procedures may be regarded as fair depends, at least in part, on the extent to which they ensure accuracy in outcome, and partly on the extent to which they give effect to non-outcome based values. Given that mistakes are unavoidable in the process of legal decision-making, due to human frailty in decision-making and the inevitable incomplete and imperfect nature of the information upon which legal decisions are based, we can never be certain that the correct outcome has been reached in all cases. Once we acknowledge that some risk of mistaken outcomes is unavoidable and may therefore cause injustice, two further consequences follow. First, we must assess the seriousness of a mistaken outcome: for in establishing the requirements of procedural fairness we must take care to ensure that no person is exposed to an unacceptable risk of the harm that follows from a mistaken outcome. Secondly, that risk must be fairly distributed among possible victims. In this regard, the guiding principle is to treat people with equal concern and respect—and what constitutes equal concern and respect in this context should be the relative importance of the substantive rights at issue. A mistaken conviction for a serious crime generates a more serious injustice than the wrongful denial of a welfare benefit, even though the latter might be very important, and this difference ought to be reflected in the distribution of risk.[52] Because conviction for a serious crime is not only

[50] Bentham's writings on evidence and procedure are scattered, but some of the most important ideas are found in *A Treatise on Judicial Evidence,* Dumont, M (ed), London, 825; *Principles of Judicial Procedure* (Works 1837, ii), and *Rationale of Judicial Evidence* (Works, 1827, vi) cited by Galligan (1996) 9.

[51] Galligan (1996), 74. Above, ch 3, Part B (2) (d).

[52] *Ibid.*

associated with considerable moral stigma, but with restrictions upon, or deprivation of, the liberty of the individual, it is the practice of western legal systems to demand the most exacting and rigorous standards of fairness when a person is charged with a serious crime, reflected in the requirements of a jury trial and the extensive rules of criminal evidence and procedure.

If we accept that the specific demands of procedural fairness vary in proportion to the seriousness of the consequences flowing from a mistaken outcome, then we must clarify what, in this context, constitutes an accurate outcome. This depends not only on the severity of sanction, but also upon its nature or character. Armed with a fuller understanding of the nature of sanctions, we can then evaluate the seriousness of the harm associated with mistakes in the sanctioning process. While the previous chapter explored the issue of penal severity, the task of exploring the nature and character of regulatory sanctions remains, forming the focal point of the following discussion.

(a) Hybrid Sanctions and the Civil/Criminal Divide

A fruitful starting point for exploring the nature of sanctions is the basic distinction drawn in western legal systems between criminal and civil liability. One reason why this distinction has been considered so fundamental lies in the procedural consequences of characterisation, with the criminal process insisting upon more exacting procedural standards than those typically required in civil proceedings. In his endeavour to identify the 'principled core' of the English criminal law, Ashworth acknowledges that the contours of the criminal law are in many respects a product of historical contingency rather than principled characterisation and development.[53] Yet he nevertheless suggests that two leading and defining features of criminal liability lie in its censuring and punitive functions. Similarly, in the North American context, Mann claims that the primary purpose of the criminal law is to punish wrongdoers, unlike the civil law, which is primarily aimed at compensating harm.[54] Mann illustrates the distinction between civil and criminal liability by representing them in paradigmatic forms. According to the paradigm criminal law sanction, the state is responsible for instituting proceedings, the conduct is wrongful because it violates a collective rather than a private interest, the enforcement authority possesses stronger information gathering and investigative powers, more rigorous procedural requirements apply in determining liability than in civil proceedings, the purpose of the sanction is to punish the defendant and some form of moral or social stigma attaches to the remedy so imposed.[55] In contrast, the paradigm civil sanction is instituted by the private citizen, the conduct is wrongful because it violates a private interest, information gathering powers are

[53] Ashworth (2000a).

[54] Mann (1992). For an illuminating discussion of the civil and criminal law paradigms of responsibility, see Cane (2002).

[55] Mann (1992); Coffee (1992); Zimring (1992).

relatively weak, and the purpose of the sanction is to restore and compensate the wronged party rather than to punish the wrongdoer.[56]

Although these two paradigms provide useful heuristic tools, applying them to particular legal forms is far from straightforward. In particular, the growing use of the law as an instrument of social control in the modern state has led to the proliferation of hybrid legal forms and remedies, defying rigid classification. Both Ashworth and Mann observe the increased blurring of the distinction between civil and criminal liability in the social practice of modern western legal systems, in which punishment no longer appears to be a distinctive attribute of the criminal law. This blurring of legal forms is particularly prevalent in the regulatory sphere, in that regulatory schemes often provide for the imposition of punitive sanctions for legal violations, primarily for protective purposes, with the aim of deterring economic and social activity thought to be harmful to the collective welfare, rather than primarily to censure morally wrongful conduct.[57] This expanding use of hybrid sanctions reflects a largely functionalist view of the law, in which the coercive force of law is seen as merely one of several instruments available to the state in exerting social control over individuals and the broader community. Where sanctions display this hybrid quality, their formal classification as either civil or criminal in nature may fail to reflect their true character, requiring us to probe more deeply, behind their formal label. The challenge then is to identify whether there are certain characteristics or features, underlying the civil/criminal tag, that may illuminate the quality of sanctions in a manner which may be of greater assistance in seeking to identify the appropriate procedures that ought to apply when such sanctions are imposed.[58]

While it would be unrealistic to expect some kind of mechanical formula for identifying the character of a sanction, it is nevertheless possible to identify at least three independent but related questions that recur throughout academic and judicial discussion that are of considerable assistance in responding to this challenge. First, why is the sanctioned conduct considered 'wrongful'? Secondly, what is the social purpose of the law in sanctioning the proscribed conduct? Thirdly, what consequences follow from the decision to impose the sanction and for whom? In answering each of these questions, we can draw upon previous chapter's examination of the justifications for penalising regulatory violations in order to delve beneath the surface of Mann's paradigmatic depictions of civil and criminal sanctions.

(i) Why is the Sanctioned Conduct Considered 'Wrongful'?

In describing the paradigm criminal sanction, Mann draws attention to the kind of conduct paradigmatically regarded as criminal, identifying two characteris-

[56] Mann (1992); Coffee (1992).

[57] Above ch 4, Section B (2).

[58] Mann states the 'fundamental jurisprudential question' as 'what is the degree of 'punitiveness' required for state-invoked punitive civil sanctions to trigger heightened due process, and what are the indicators of such punitiveness?': Mann (1992), 1842–43.

tic features: the effects of the sanctioned act and the need for proof of fault. The criminal paradigm sanctions wrongful acts because they are public wrongs, violating a collective rather than an individual interest[59] and typically require proof of mens rea (subjective wickedness) to establish the commission of a wrong. By contrast, the wrongful conduct to which the civil sanction paradigmatically attaches requires actual damage before liability arises, and depends principally on the notion of objective liability rather than requiring subjective fault.[60] These two characteristics resonate strongly with the previous chapter's discussion of moral probity and strict liability in seeking to understand the justification for penalising regulatory offences. By portraying the wrong to which the paradigm criminal sanction attaches as harmful to the general community, Mann emphasises the shared or collective nature of the moral values reflected in traditional criminal law norms. In other words, conduct that is paradigmatically sanctioned by the criminal law fits the description of the kind of wrongdoing referred to in the previous chapter as 'traditional crimes', wrongs which are typically seen as morally reprehensible and in violation of shared community norms.[61]

While the two characteristics associated with the criminal paradigm were discussed in the previous chapter in distinguishing traditional crimes from regulatory offences, they are now being used to carve out a different but related set of distinctions: between criminal and civil wrongdoing. Both pairs of distinctions share similar structural qualities: although they readily lend themselves to heuristic depictions of the core ideas encapsulated within them, there remains a substantial patch of middle ground in which attempts to apply the distinctions in a clear and concrete fashion prove elusive. It is into this middle ground that regulatory sanctions often fall. Although the 'wrongfulness' associated with regulatory offending does not rest primarily in its moral reprehensibility, such acts are considered wrongful largely because they harm collective interests, rather than because they directly harm individuals.[62] Indeed, there is often no

[59] In relation to the first criteria, Coffee observes that the standard 'black letter' law distinction between public and private wrongs is deeply problematic, in that private and public injuries are correlative (for example, an individual's private interest in the enforcement of a contract can also be described as the collective public interest in the security of transactions), but accepts that there is nonetheless a kernel of an idea within it: Coffee (1991), 221

[60] Mann (1992), 1805; Cane (2002).

[61] Coffee claims that the factor that most distinguishes the criminal law from tort law is its operation as a system of moral education and socialisation, a system for the public communication of values: Coffee (1991).

[62] This is not to suggest that moral culpability is irrelevant in the enforcement of regulatory law. Many ethnographic studies of regulatory enforcement officials indicate that the perceived moral culpability of breach strongly influences whether a 'compliance' or 'deterrence' approach is adopted in pursuing the violation, particularly where the violation is a 'one-off' occurrence and does not generate an immediate risk to health, safety or the environment, or a direct harm has already resulted. If the violation is deemed accidental, then it is unlikely that a sanctioning approach will be used unless the breach was severe in nature or consequences. Prosecutions for persistent failures will be brought even in the context of a heavily compliance-based approach, but they are seen as failures, and tend to be sought in order to punish not the breach itself so much as the symbolic assault on the legitimacy of the regulatory authority that the persistent non-compliance represents: Hadden (1970).

identifiable and specific 'victim' associated with regulatory wrongdoing in situations where the harm is widespread and diffuse. This is particularly true of conduct proscribed by competition law: the harm generated is the impairment of the efficient functioning of markets, rather than harm to an identifiable individual. In other words, although the collective or 'public' nature of the wrong may suggest that regulatory sanctions tend towards the criminal end of the spectrum, the absence of any strong degree of moral reprehensibility (particularly where the offence does not require proof of fault) associated with regulatory wrongdoing tends to pull in the opposite direction, suggesting a greater resemblance to civil wrongdoing.[63]

(ii) What is the Social Purpose of the Law in Sanctioning the Proscribed Conduct?

Another related feature of sanctioning systems that Mann draws upon to distinguish civil and criminal sanctions lies in their underlying social purpose.[64] Although he acknowledges that primary justification for the criminal sanction has long been characterised by substantive normative disagreement, Mann asserts that there is broad agreement that punishment (which he defines as the public condemnation of the offender who experiences shame because of the notoriety of his punishment) is a distinctive feature of the criminal law, although not exclusive to it,[65] in contrast to the paradigmatic remedies of the civil law, which serve primarily restorative goals, seeking to restore and compensate the injured party for the harm caused by the defendant's wrong. Again, the issue of social purpose singled out by Mann echoes the previous chapter's endeavour to identify the justification for penalising regulatory offences. In particular, we have seen that retributive concerns feature much more prominently in the justification for punishing traditional crimes, for social censure and public condemnation is seen as an appropriate response to morally reprehensible acts, while the aim of preventing future wrongdoing by deterrence plays the leading role in penalising regulatory offences.

But if we accept that deterrence is the primary social purpose for sanctioning regulatory offences, this again pulls in two directions when locating regulatory sanctions along the civil/criminal divide.[66] On the one hand, the goal of deterring future violations may be seen as inherent in the more general aim of protecting the community by seeking to prevent future harm. Viewed in this

[63] Regulatory schemes may provide for the recovery of compensation by those directly harmed by regulatory wrongs, eg Yeung (1998). These statutory causes of action fit much more comfortably within the civil paradigm.

[64] Below, ch 6, Part 2 (a).

[65] Mann (1992), 1808.

[66] Mann comments that '[p]unishment is an overdetermined concept, for while the idea of punishment *qua* punishment and punishment for deterrence are conceptually distinct, it is difficult to unravel the two when imposing a sanction. Although policymakers and courts may seek primarily to achieve one of the alternative ends of the criminal sanction, the core retributive aspect of the criminal sanction remains (ie punishment): *Ibid.,* 1808.

way, deterrent-based sanctions closely resemble other techniques used in general social harm reduction systems, akin, for example, to the use of quarantine to protect society against highly contagious and potentially life threatening disease or requiring the registration and licensing of medical practitioners before they may lawfully practice their profession.[67] Although the goal of social protection is conceptually distinct from compensation, nonetheless it appears to stand in stark contrast to the notions of moral censure and condemnation underpinning retributive-based sanctions, thereby indicating that criminal classification is inappropriate. Yet, as we saw in the previous chapter, many claim that the deterrence of future wrongdoers is the primary justification for punishing both traditional crimes and regulatory offences, so that deterrence-based sanctions applied to regulatory offences may also be classed as criminal. Even for those who distinguish the primarily retributive justifications for traditional crimes from primarily deterrence-based justifications for regulatory offences, retributive purposes are nevertheless at play (albeit in a subsidiary manner) in sanctioning regulatory offenders, because only the guilty regulatory offender is sanctioned, thereby limiting the extent to which the goal of deterrence may be pursued.[68] Viewed in this way, the punitive and deterrent purposes underpinning regulatory sanctions appear to elide together, suggesting that they might be appropriately classified as criminal in nature.[69]

(iii) What are the Consequences of the Sanction?

A third dimension of Mann's paradigmatic forms focuses on the remedy provided, with Mann observing that the stigma of a criminal sanction has become a special kind of remedy due to its 'burdensome and sometimes destructive consequences for the individual'.[70] While he claims that this stigma is paradigmatically attached to imprisonment, a sanction that Mann acknowledges is less frequently imposed than other criminal remedies such as fines and probation,

[67] In determining whether certain measures constitute civil or criminal charges for the purposes of Art 6 ECHR, the European Court of Human Rights has distinguished punitive measures from preventative measures. For example in *Escoubet v Belgium* (2001) 31 EHRR 46, the Court examined a procedure which allowed a driving licence to be withdrawn for up to 15 days where a driver was suspected of being drunk. It held that this did not involve a criminal charge. The measure was preventative, there was no investigation, no finding of guilt, the impact of the penalty was limited in time and scope and not sufficiently substantial to amount to a criminal charge. It distinguished procedures involving the addition of penalty points to a driver's licence in the context of a criminal prosecution: *Malige v France* (1999) 28 EHRR 578.

[68] Above, ch 4, Part B (2) (a) for a discussion of the 'distribution dilemma' facing deterrence theorists.

[69] This has been the approach in ECHR jurisprudence, in which 'deterrence' is used interchangably with 'punishment' in seeking to characterise offences as civil or criminal in nature. For example in *Ozturk v Germany* (1984) 6 EHRR 409 the Court took the view that the purpose of an administrative penalty was 'punitive and deterrent' in effect. Likewise, *Maligne v France* (1999) 28 EHRR 578, an administrative imposition of penalty points on a driver's licence for exceeding the speed limit the court concluded was criminal because it had a punitive and deterrent purpose.

[70] Mann (1992), 1908. The so-called stigma associated with criminal punishment might be regarded as part of the 'hard treatment' aspect of punishment or as part of its 'communicative' dimension, but its precise role in the criminal justice process is unclear. See Walker (1980).

nonetheless he regards imprisonment and the special stigma associated with convictions as the core remedies used to achieve the purposes of the criminal sanction. The civil paradigm, in contrast, utilises two remedies, also closely linked to their social purpose: either a court order mandating a return to the status quo, or an order to pay money damages as compensation for the harm caused.

By emphasising imprisonment and stigma as paradigmatic features of the criminal sanction, Mann focuses attention on the distinctive 'moral harm' associated with their imposition, which is not typically associated with civil sanctions. This might best be illustrated by comparing the consequences arising from the mistaken imposition of sanctions involving the deprivation of liberty. Consider the use of civil quarantine orders to prevent the spread of contagious diseases with imprisonment for a criminal offence. While both orders involve the same 'bare harm', consisting of the deprivation of the individual's liberty, the mistaken imprisonment of an innocent person involves a more serious injustice, causing graver moral harm than that associated with mistakenly quarantining a healthy person. In a similar, albeit less striking vein, requiring a defendant in civil proceedings to pay damages for a specified sum by way of compensation for a breach of contract which the defendant did not in fact commit, and requiring an innocent person to pay a criminal fine of the same sum, may involve the same degree of bare harm, but the moral harm associated with a mistaken criminal conviction is significantly more serious than that associated with the mistaken imposition of a civil sanction. In other words, compared with its civil counterpart, criminal sanctions typically involve significantly more serious and burdensome consequences for the individual upon whom they are imposed, including the distinctive moral stigma commonly associated with criminal convictions.

Yet in reflecting upon the consequences of sanctions imposed for regulatory violations, we again encounter difficulties in locating them along the civil/criminal divide. In this respect, one commonly used regulatory sanction is the 'punitive civil sanction',[71] a financial penalty imposed upon those who act unlawfully that is intended to be punitive, but is formally classified as civil in nature.[72] Financial penalties imposed for violations of Australian and EU competition law appear to fall squarely within this category of sanctions. Although formally designated as 'civil', they clearly involve punitive consequences for the offender, imposing a form of hard treatment on those who unlawfully violate competition laws[73] yet, unlike a criminal fine, default in payment cannot lead to imprisonment, nor does the imposition of a financial penalty tend to generate the kind of stigma typically

[71] See Walker (1980), Freiberg and Gillooly use the term 'civil penalty' to refer to the same type of sanction: Freiberg and O'Malley (1984); Gillooly and Wallace-Bruce (1994).

[72] Mann (1992).

[73] The compensatory function is achieved by private Federal Court actions instituted by those who have been harmed by unlawful conduct by another in breach of Part IV of the Act to recover damages as compensation for harm. See Brunt (1990).

associated with criminal offending. Yet their formal 'civil' classification does not, in and of itself, render these sanctions analogous to private law civil damages. The latter are sought by private litigants seeking compensation for interference with their private rights while punitive civil sanctions, such as the civil penalty, are instituted by a public official on behalf of the state and are primarily intended to deter the offender, and others, from committing future violations.

(b) Hybrid Sanctions and Procedural Fairness

Although the above questions assist in illuminating the nature and character of legal sanctions, they hardly constitute a mechanistic formula capable of readily locating sanctions within either the civil or criminal paradigm. When applied to regulatory sanctions, it becomes clear that they often defy rigid classification, falling within the shadowy twilight zone bridging the civil and criminal divide and thus constituting a kind of hybrid, reflecting the increasingly unstable boundaries between civil and criminal liability. The existence of this middle-ground does not necessarily render otiose the existence of a qualitative distinction between these two forms of liability and sanction, at least in relation to their principled core.[74] But what is does suggest, is that, just as traditional crimes and regulatory offences may be situated along a continuum, depending on the extent to which an offence is morally reprehensible and thus subject to social censure and condemnation, so also can sanctions be situated along a sliding scale. Rather than construct a rigid and inflexible dichotomy between civil and criminal sanctions, we can construct a rough continuum between a range of sanctions, the ordering of which may depend upon why the nature of the sanction is relevant to the question posed.

Because our present concern is to identify the procedural requirements applying to the sanctioning process, then it is the consequences of the sanction for the individual upon whom they are imposed that is of particular importance, given that the protection of individual liberty underpins the need for due process protections. Mann refers to the procedural characteristics which apply to sanctioning systems as the fourth dimension of his paradigm legal forms, observing that:

> a fundamental principle of due process requires a positive correlation between investigative intrusiveness and severity of sanction on the one hand and stringency of procedural protections on the other.'[75]

This positive correlation arises from epistemological uncertainty associated with mistakes in the sanctioning process: the greater the seriousness of mistaken outcomes, the more rigorous the procedures needed to ensure accuracy in the sanctioning process.[76] Such an approach is reflected in the binary structure of Anglo-American procedural forms, with the formal classification of a sanction

[74] Ashworth (2000a).
[75] Mann (1992), 1811–12.
[76] Above, ch 3, Part B (2) (d).

largely dictating the content of the bundle of procedural rights available to the defendant in the determination of liability. So, for example, in Anglo-Australian criminal proceedings, it is for the prosecutor to establish the guilt of the accused beyond reasonable doubt, and the accused is accorded a range of procedural rights such as the presumption of innocence, the right to silence, the right to privilege against self-incrimination and so forth.[77] By contrast, in civil proceedings, liability need only be established on the balance of probabilities, and the defendant has fewer procedural grounds for resisting demands to disclose relevant but potentially incriminating evidence.

Yet this binary procedural structure fails to accommodate the diversity and range of legal sanctions utilised in the modern state, which, for the purposes of identifying the appropriate procedural standards, may be ordered along a rough continuum in which the consequences of the sanction for the individual are emphasised. At one end of our continuum lie strongly punitive criminal measures involving the deprivation of the liberty of the individual that are typically associated with a high degree of moral stigma and reserved for serious wrongdoing such as brutalising interferences with the person. At the opposite end lie civil sanctions typically involving a monetary penalty for minor infractions such as parking infringements and other similarly trivial contraventions of the law for which there is little or no moral stigma. Half-way along this continuum lie hybrid legal forms, variously labelled as civil or criminal, yet which display features which are typically associated with both paradigmatic legal forms.

Given the prevalence of hybrid sanctions, rigid adherence to their formal 'civil' designation may result in the use of procedures that fall short of the demands of procedural fairness, unfairly exposing the defendant to the risk of harm arising from mistakes in the sanctioning process. But the increasing use of hybrid sanctions has also been accompanied by a shift away from conceptualising legal processes in binary terms, with a limited but growing recognition from judicial and academic quarters that the level of procedural protections applicable in any given case ought not be determined solely by reference to the formal legislative designation of a sanction.[78] Rather than view the range and rigour of procedural protections in binary terms, as either importing the entire range of extensive procedural guarantees typically accompanying the criminal process or the correspondingly weaker protections of the civil process, the hybrid quality of such sanctions may require greater procedural protections than those applicable to the latter, yet less extensive than those adopted in the former.[79] While the notion of a hybrid procedural form may be largely alien to those working within the common law tradition, the so-called 'administrative proceeding' is familiar

[77] Ashworth (1995).

[78] *Benham v UK* (1996) 22 EHRR 293; *Ozturk v Germany* (1984) 6 EHRR 409; Goldstein (1992); Mann (1992); Gillooly (1994); Klein (1999), 679.

[79] Mann (1992) *cf* Coffee (1992); *Official Receiver v Stern* [2000] 1 WLR 2230; *Brown v Stott* [2003] 1 AC 681; *R v Benjafield* [2002] 2 WLR 235 *cf R (on the application of McCann) v Manchester Crown Court* [2003] 1 AC 787.

to many Western European legal systems rooted in the civil law tradition, constituting a separate enforcement regime falling outside the ordinary criminal justice system and used in relation to a discrete category of 'administrative' offences in which both penalty and procedural safeguards are appropriately lower than those applicable in criminal proceedings.[80]

Acceptance of a 'third way' form of procedure in the imposition of hybrid sanctions would not only be normatively consistent with our understanding of the demands of procedural fairness as varying in proportion to the consequences flowing from a mistaken outcome, but it would also avoid the artificiality of attempting to shoe-horn hybrid sanctions into the binary constraints of the civil/criminal paradigms.[81] The consequences of insistent adherence to a rigid and binary civil/criminal divide are well-illustrated in the jurisprudence generated from the extensive litigation surrounding Article 6 of the European Convention on Human Rights, which guarantees the right to a fair trial. Although the legal systems of several states which are party to the Convention recognise a discrete class of 'administrative offences', Article 6 expressly confines a set of specified minimum procedural rights (such as the presumption of innocence, the right to legal assistance and so forth) to criminal defendants, so that the European Court of Human Rights has often been called upon to classify such offences as either civil or criminal for the purposes of determining the range of procedural rights applicable in particular cases. In the leading case, *Ozturk v Germany*,[82] the applicant was fined for a minor road traffic offence. The offence in question had been decriminalised following legislative reform in order to benefit individuals (who would no longer be criminally liable for the relevant act and could avoid all court proceedings) and to facilitate the effective functioning of the courts (by relieving them from dealing with the high volume of such offences previously subject to court processes) in which responsibility for administering these fines rested with an administrative authority rather than a criminal prosecutor. Although the majority of the Court claimed the Convention was 'not opposed to moves towards decriminalisation', it concluded the punitive character of the sanction indicated that it was criminal in nature, thus entitling the applicant to the full set of procedural rights of the criminal accused guaranteed in Article 6(2) and 6(3).[83] In contrast, the minority

[80] Harding (1996).

[81] Although criminal fines may be less severe in financial terms than civil pecuniary penalties, they can nevertheless be regarded as more severe in that failure to pay a criminal fine may lead to imprisonment whereas failure to pay a civil penalty cannot. The difficulties in classifying competition law penalties as 'civil' or 'criminal' is illustrated in the contrasting decisions of the European Court of Human Rights. In *Stenuit v France* (1992) 14 EHRR 509 a finding by the French Competition Commission was held to constitute a criminal charge, yet in *Krone-Verlag GmbH and Mediaprint Anzeigen GmbH & Co KG v Austria* (1997) 23 EHRR 152 the imposition of a fine for failing to obey an injunction ordered in the course of civil proceedings for unfair competition was held not to impose a criminal charge, so the procedural requirements of Art 6(2) and 6(3) of the ECHR did not apply.

[82] (1984) 6 EHRR 409.

[83] *Ibid*, para 49.

of judges refused to recategorise the offence as criminal, concerned to preserve what they regarded as a worthy strategy of legislative decriminalisation, reflecting a 'humanising trend in the criminal law'.[84]

While the *Ozturk* ruling may be criticised for effectively thwarting legitimate legislative attempts at decriminalisation, the Court is rightly vigilant to insist on probing behind the formal legislative classification attached to a sanction. Although the rise of hybrid sanctions may sometimes be attributable to entirely appropriate concerns that sanctions should constitute a proportionate response to the 'quasi-criminal' quality of the wrongs for which they are imposed, their increasing prevalence may also be motivated by less noble aims. Undue deference to the label attached to a sanction by legislators would provide scope for illegitimate manipulation of the civil/criminal divide, in which a sanction may be formally designated as civil in nature with the deliberate aim of circumventing the onerous procedural requirements accompanying criminal proceedings, whilst imposing on guilty offenders many of the harsh and repressive consequences that ought fairly be regarded as criminal.[85] Without meaningful judicial oversight over the sanctioning process, particularly as the creation of hybrid forms of sanction continues to proliferate, then due process requirements may be systematically and surreptitiously flouted.[86]

2. Are Negotiated Penalty Settlements Procedurally Fair?

Now that we have explored the relationship between the nature of sanctions and the requirements of procedural fairness, we are better placed to evaluate whether negotiated penalty settlements in competition proceedings are consistent with the latter's demands. By exploring the civil/criminal divide, and the inherent fuzziness of its contours, we can make more sense of the apparent disjunction between the powerful opposition to plea bargaining practices

[84] (1984) 6 EHRR 409, dissenting opinion of Judge Liesch.

[85] One example of this cynical use by policy-makers of the instability in the civil/criminal divide is the recently developed 'anti-social behaviour order' adopted in the UK, which enables a court to make an order prohibiting a defendant from certain forms of behaviour for a minimum of two years, but if breached (without reasonable excuse) provides for a penalty of up to five years' imprisonment: Crime and Disorder Act 1998 (UK), s 1. Such orders were designated as civil by the British parliament, with the deliberate aim of avoiding the standard procedural protections applicable to criminal proceedings. The intention to avoid the normal procedural protections is apparent from the Labour Party's documents, *A Quiet Life* (1995) and *Protecting our Communities* (1996) which forms the background for s 1 of the 1998 Act: Emmerson and Ashworth (2001) n 34.

[86] It is arguable whether the level of judicial scrutiny provided under the Human Rights Act 1998 provides adequate protection. For example, in *Clingham v Kensington & Chelsea BC* [2003] 1 AC 787 the House of Lords upheld the civil classification of anti-social behaviour orders under the 1998 Act for the purposes of determining whether those subject to such orders were entitled to the procedural protections of Art 6(2) and 6(3). Nonetheless, their Lordships were willing, despite the civil nature of such orders, to accept that as the seriousness of such orders required that a heightened civil standard of proof applied which was 'all but indistinguishable from the criminal standard' so that the criminal standard of proof was to be applied.

expressed by criminal law scholars, and the heartening encouragement of regulatory scholars when reflecting upon regulatory compliance techniques that emphasise the centrality of bargaining. This cleavage in opinion may be attributable to the liability models underlying their respective critiques. While criminal scholars typically focus attention on plea bargaining where the charges in issue relate to offences that are central to the criminal paradigm, regulatory scholarship concerning enforcement practices may tend to view liability for regulatory violations as more closely aligned with the civil paradigm. As a consequence, while the former typically emphasised the dangers associated with negotiated enforcement in undermining the procedural rights of the accused, the latter may view the use of negotiation and bargaining practices as largely akin to the processes of consensual settlement that are actively encouraged in the resolution of disputes concerning civil liability between private litigants.

But, as we have seen, financial penalties for competition violations, such as those imposed for violations of Australian, British[87] and EU competition laws, constitute a form of hybrid sanction fitting neither the civil nor criminal paradigm comfortably. Thus, while their punitive character justifies the use of greater procedural protections than would otherwise apply in ordinary civil proceedings, procedural fairness may not demand the full range of procedural safeguards guaranteed to the criminal defendant.[88] In other words, the analogy between plea bargaining practices in criminal proceedings and the use of negotiated penalty settlements in competition proceedings is partial and incomplete. Although many of the objections to plea bargaining expressed by criminal law scholars may also arise in the regulatory enforcement context, they do not apply with the same powerful force.

But regulatory scholars may have been rather too willing to accept the validity of a conceptual distinction between true crimes/regulatory crimes and criminal/civil sanctions, thereby justifying a wholly differentiated approach to enforcement and procedural fairness. Underlying much of the literature concerned with identifying the most appropriate strategy for securing regulatory compliance is an assumption that the purpose of sanctioning regulatory violations is ultimately to protect society from the particular ills which the regulatory regime seeks to address. But even if we accept that the foundational motivation for sanctioning regulatory violations is to protect the general community from collective harm, there has been a tendency to overlook the coercive force underlying the mechanisms used to pursue those goals and the significant, albeit subsidiary, retributive goals that are concurrently pursued by limiting the imposition of sanctions to those found to have violated the law and the consequences for violators. In other words, regulatory scholars may have tended to assume that the civil law paradigm provides the background liability model against

[87] Competition law penalties under the UK Competition Act 1998 are formally classified as civil, with the exception of cartel conduct by individuals, which is expressly designated as criminal in nature under the Enterprise Act (2002), discussed by Harding (2002).

[88] Mann (1992); Gillooly (1994); Goldstein (1992).

which their evaluations of bargaining and negotiation in regulatory enforcement have been based, thereby failing to overlook some of the more criminal-like characteristics that regulatory sanctions also exhibit.

The apparent lack of attention paid to procedural fairness in regulatory compliance scholarship may also be partly attributed to the fact that the defendants in such proceedings are typically corporate entities rather than individuals. But, as we observed in chapter three, although the typically corporate identity of defendants in competition proceedings does not justify ignoring procedural fairness altogether, the fact such defendants are typically (although not always) well-resourced organisations with ready access to quality legal advice suggests that they are not vulnerable actors who are prone to being 'bullied' into settlement. Accordingly, concerns that negotiated penalty settlements (and other similar kinds of bargain) may impose unfair or undue pressure on innocent defendants are likely to have less force in the regulatory enforcement context, providing a basis for having more confidence in the voluntariness or genuineness of the defendant's consent than might be associated with plea bargaining with individuals accused of traditional crimes.

This argument for middle ground procedural protections also finds support in the influential work of American jurist Lon Fuller and later developed by Denis Galligan in his work on procedural fairness, explored more fully in the following chapter. Fuller argued that decision-making processes could be grouped according to their social form, and that each form generates a set of procedural requirements that protect the integrity of the form. Galligan, building upon this idea, argues that for each decision-making process, specific legal purposes can be identified. The set of procedures which secure those purposes protect the integrity of the decision-making form, thereby giving expression to the values of procedural fairness. Applying this approach to the preceding analysis suggests that, because competition law penalties possess criminal-like qualities, an important aim (although arguably not the predominant aim) of the sanctioning process is the application of legal standards. Just as it is contrary to the rule of law to convict an innocent person of a crime, so also it is contrary to the rule of law to extract a civil penalty from those who have not acted unlawfully. Thus we cannot claim that a negotiated penalty settlement is fair simply because it represents a genuine and consensual agreement between the parties. We must also have confidence in the accuracy of the outcome agreed to, and that the terms of the bargain itself accurately reflect the true facts giving rise to the allegations of contravention. In short, fair treatment in this context requires that the standards of the law are accurately applied so as to ensure that the individual is not exposed to an undue risk of being wrongfully or excessively penalised. Although regulatory violations may attract significantly less (if any) moral stigma when compared with the commission of more 'traditional' crimes, the use of the coercive power of the state to sanction regulatory offenders inevitably imports, at least in liberal democratic societies, limitations on the extent to which such power may be used, particularly when asserted against the individual. Accordingly, the process for determining the quantum of penalty imposed for regulatory offences should seek to ensure not only that innocent persons are not penalised, but also that the penalties imposed on an offender are not unfairly disproportionate or oppressive.[89]

3. Negotiated Penalty Settlements: An Assessment

As we have seen, the use of negotiated penalty settlements may impose significant strain on the constitutional values of procedural fairness, accountability, transparency, consistency and proportionality. Whilst these are serious concerns, there may be scope for instituting various safeguards that can reduce the risk of unduly pressuring innocent defendants to settle and promote transparency and accountability in the negotiation process, yet nevertheless allow the benefits of settlement to be reaped. These benefits are considerable: reducing the costs associated with enforcement, enabling the enforcement authority to respond to suspected contraventions with a greater degree of flexibility and responsiveness than is typically associated with contested adjudicative enforcement proceedings, allowing those under investigation to reduce the business disruption and adverse publicity associated with such proceedings and encouraging a co-operative relationship between the regulator and the regulated and so help to promote lasting compliance. Thus, if adequate safeguards are in place, concerns about such settlements do not appear to be so weighty as to justify their prohibition, particularly in light of the significant public benefits arising from the timely and early settlement of court proceedings. The remaining task, then, is to identify the requisite safeguards, to which we now turn.

D. SAFEGUARDING SETTLEMENTS

In the opening comments of this chapter, I noted that the resolution of competition enforcement proceedings by negotiated penalty settlements was widespread and pervasive throughout the practice of competition regulation in a variety of jurisdictions, yet the legislation establishing the regulatory regime typically makes no mention of them. To the casual observer, this disjunction between law 'on the books' and law in practice may be rather disquieting, suggesting that negotiated penalty settlements may be unlawful. But the legal authority underpinning such settlements typically arises, not from express legislative delegation, but from the broad discretionary powers conferred on the regulator in carrying out its enforcement functions. The conferral of broad discretionary power on governmental actors has become increasingly prevalent in the modern state, providing the flexibility necessary for bureaucratic

[89] Above, Ch 4, Part B (2) (c).

decision-making in an information-rich age characterised by complexity and rapid technological innovation.[90] Yet leading public law scholars have long been deeply suspicious of such broad discretionary power, fearing that its abuse may seriously threaten the liberty of the individual.[91] The resolution of enforcement proceedings by negotiated settlement exemplifies this well-known tension between the virtues of discretion in providing flexibility and expediency in decision-making, and the dangers of discretion in allowing scope for arbitrariness and inconsistency of treatment. But while the virtues and vices of discretionary power are well-known, devising and implementing mechanisms that enable the former to be reaped without generating undue risks of the latter remains a difficult and sometimes delicate task, requiring sensitivity to context. The following discussion explores three safeguards that may assist in promoting the fair yet effective use of negotiated penalty settlements in competition proceedings: the separation of prosecutorial and judicial functions, ethical constraints on prosecutorial discretion and judicial oversight.

1. The Enforcement Process and the Separation of Powers

The formal process through which competition laws are publicly enforced is broadly similar to the criminal process, and may be divided into three stages:

a) *investigation*: to identify suspected violations, which may initially consist of brief preliminary inquiries but later develop into full-blown investigations;
b) *prosecution*: the commencement of formal legal proceedings by the initiation of charges; and
c) *judgment*: the formal evaluation of evidence, followed by official decision and public pronouncement concerning whether or not a violation has occurred and the issuing of sentence following violation.

The 'regulatory space' within which settlement negotiations may occur, and the attendant risks associated with the settlement process, depend largely upon the role and powers of the regulator at each stage of the enforcement process and, in this respect, the allocation of the prosecutorial and judicial functions is of particular significance.

If broad discretionary power in the hands of governmental actors is viewed as the enemy of liberty, then the idea of constitutionalism may be viewed as liberty's companion. I referred in chapter three to the idea of constitutionalism, embodying the notion of limited government—a scheme of governance in which the exercise of state power is subject to stable and enduring institutional constraints thereby enabling democratic society to flourish. The separation of powers doctrine, famously expounded by Montesquieu, is considered foundational to this constitutional ideal, with one leading scholar describing the doctrine as

[90] Galligan (1986), Jowell (2000).
[91] Dicey (1961); Davis (1969).

a 'fence which can protect the citizen's liberties from the potentially oppressive power exercised by rulers.'[92] Although constitutional theorists have long debated the precise contours of the doctrine, it is generally accepted that, at its core, the doctrine prescribes the division of power between the legislative, executive and judicial organs of government and the mutual checking of power by each institution over the other.[93]

When applied to the enforcement of competition law, the separation of powers doctrine suggests that the judicial function—the formal determination that a violation of the law has occurred and the consequent imposition of a penalty—should be institutionally separate from the investigative and prosecutorial stages of the enforcement process. Were they to be combined in a single institution, the defendant would be left in a particularly vulnerable position, owing to the sharp conflict of interest that appears to confront the enforcement authority. Although the latter should act impartially and even-handedly in judging whether a violation has occurred, the temptation to favour a finding of violation would appear to loom large, given that its prosecutorial functions are directed towards securing the defendant's conviction.[94]

While an awareness of this danger underpins the well-established separation of the prosecutorial and judicial functions in the enforcement of traditional crimes, considerable variation is evident in the institutional framework within which competition enforcement takes place. Although this variation may be attributed to diversity in the local constitutional architecture, it may ultimately be traced to the jurisprudential character of competition law sanctions. In jurisdictions, such as the USA, where some competition sanctions are formally and substantively criminal in nature and thus punishable by imprisonment, a failure to separate the prosecutorial and judicial functions represents a serious violation of due process rights.[95] But where competition sanctions constitute a form of hybrid sanction, displaying a mix of both civil and criminal qualities, then a

[92] Loughlin (2000), 184.

[93] *Ibid.*

[94] For example, in recommending against giving the Office of Fair Trading ('OFT') responsibility for prosecuting criminal offences under the UK Competition Act 1998, the independent experts commissioned to consider how criminal sanctions for cartel perpetrators could best operate in practice stated that 'Perhaps the most potent risk is that there may be a temptation for such [OFT in-house] lawyers to become too close to the policy demands of the organisation which they serve and to develop a solicitor-client relationship rather than a relationship of prosecuting lawyer exercising an independent judgment': Hammond (2001), para 3.8.

[95] Under the Enterprise Act 2002, the UK has criminalised certain 'hard core' competition violations by individuals. In the White Paper setting out the proposals leading to the Act, the government proposed that the OFT would be the main prosecuting authority, given its primary responsibility for uncovering cartels. But, to ensure that the defendants received a fair trial, the government proposed that different divisions in the OFT would handle the investigation and prosecution phases of the case. The formal decision to prosecute would be made by a functionally separate part of the OFT with advice from the OFT's legal branch, which may also need to operate as a separate body: Cm 5233, paras 7.37–7.42. Although the independent expert report commissioned by the OFT recommended against these proposals, in favour of the Serious Fraud Office as the prosecuting authority (Hammond 2001), the government chose not to adopt this recommendation.

lack of functional separation may not necessarily amount to unacceptable encroachment on due process values. Within such a sanctioning regime, the determination of liability and consequent imposition of a sanction might plausibly be regarded as merely 'quasi-judicial' in nature, and therefore strict functional separation may not be thought necessary. So, for example, although Australian and US competition regulation confines the role of the regulator to the investigation and prosecution of suspected violations of the Act, with the courts determining liability and penalty,[96] this functional separation is not reflected in the structure of EU competition enforcement, with the European Commission's competition directorate bearing responsibility for all three enforcement functions.[97]

That said, the EU experience is particularly instructive, in light of the litany of complaints that the European Commission treats those subject to competition infringement proceedings unfairly, with several scholars arguing that the existing framework of enforcement violates the due process guarantees set out in Article 6 of the ECHR.[98] Complaints of unfairness in the European Commission's enforcement practice are exemplified by Montag, who states that:[99]

> Under antitrust infringement procedures, undertakings are frequently given the impression that their defenses have not been heard because the wording of the Commission's final decisions is often almost identical to the wording of the Commission's statement of objections. This practice raises serious doubts as to the practical value of the parties' rights of defence in proceedings before the Commission. Although the undertakings have a right to an oral hearing before an independent hearing officer, practice has shown that it is extremely difficult for the hearing officer to influence the position of the case handlers within DGIV. It appears similarly difficult to influence the Commission's decision by submitting written answers to the statement of objections. Again, practice shows that the Commission rarely changes its position during the course of the administrative procedure . . .
>
> It appears that the fundamental reason for this problem may be the fact that the Commission officials handling infringement cases function both as investigators and as those responsible for drafting the final decision. Being responsible for the case from the beginning of the investigation until the drafting of the final decision imposing fines would appear to make any Commission official less open to the defenses put forth by the undertakings. As a result, the burden of proof in the administrative proceeding is practically reversed.

[96] Because the Australian Constitution requires rigid adherence to the separation of powers doctrine, judicial powers cannot be invested in an executive body: *The Queen v Kirby; Ex parte Boilermakers' Society of Australia* (1956) 94 CLR 254. Above n. 2.

[97] The EC Treaty does not provide scope for private law subjects (be they natural or legal persons) to be the subject of infringement proceedings before the European Court of Justice or the Court of First Instance. Cases may only be brought before the EC courts against acts or omissions of Community institutions as defined in Art 4(1) of the EC Treaty, or institutions deemed equivalent in the Treaty (such as the European Central Bank) and Member States: See EC Treaty, Arts 169 and 173: Montag (1996), 15.

[98] Brent (1995); Montag (1996); Waelbroeck (1994); Van Bael (1995); Wilks (1995), 267; Wesselling (2001), 21.

[99] Montag (1996), 160.

Montag, like many other critics, attributes the root cause of these complaints to the perceived conflict between the European Commission's role as both prosecutor and judge, leaving it with almost untrammelled discretion.[100]

But while the EU experience highlights the risks associated with failing to separate the prosecutorial and judicial functions, separation in and of itself may not be sufficient. Despite the clear separation of functions within Australian competition enforcement, the Commission nonetheless retains extremely broad discretionary powers of enforcement. While this broad prosecutorial discretion ultimately enables the Commission to resolve enforcement proceedings expeditiously by negotiated settlements, thereby avoiding the time, expense and uncertainty associated with a fully contested trial, the breadth of this discretion carries with it the potential for unfair practice. Indeed, it is the danger of prosecutorial overreaching, even if not, strictly speaking, unlawful, that lies at the heart of the objections to plea bargaining expressed by criminal law scholars discussed above, calling into question the need for further safeguards.[101]

2. Prosecutorial Ethics and Regulatory Enforcement

Public law scholars are not alone in focusing attention on the virtues and vices of discretionary power. Scholars working within the tradition of professional ethics have also identified the value and inevitability of discretionary power, although the source of power forming the focus of their inquiry arises not from its governmental source, but from the specialist knowledge or expertise to which 'professionals' have access but which is not typically held by their clients. While there is considerable debate over which groups or occupations may fairly be classified as 'professionals' for this purpose, there is a well-established strand of literature specifically concerned with the ethics of lawyers, exploring the lawyers' powerful position within the adversarial system of justice upon which Anglo-American legal systems are based. In attempting to flesh out a series of ethical norms to guide and inform the exercise of lawyer's discretionary power, this rich body of scholarly reflection provides a fertile source from which to draw in exploring the appropriate boundaries of settlement negotiations by regulators in exercising their prosecutorial discretion. While the deeper moral, social and philosophical underpinnings of these ethical principles form the subject of extensive reflection in the sphere of applied ethics, a branch of moral philosophy, it will suffice for the purposes of this book to accept that these ethical norms or principles represent moral obligations which are dependent on conscience rather than legal sanctions which are, at least partly, a product of the responsibilities attached to professional office that seek to provide a focus for

[100] See n 98; Also, Lenaerts and Vanhamme (1997); Levitt (1997).
[101] Vorenberg (1981).

reconciling often powerfully conflicting moral values in a principled, rational and consistent manner.[102]

Within this literature, the criminal defence lawyer operating in an adversarial system of justice is typically thought to occupy a role of 'neutral partisanship', requiring single-minded zeal in the lawyer's pursuit of her client's cause, while simultaneously disavowing moral responsibility for the merits of that cause.[103] This ethic of 'zealous advocacy' which is claimed to arise from the professional role of the legal advocate, may require the advocate to act in ways that may contradict, rather than supplement, allegedly universal moral values (such as harassing and trying to undermine witnesses whom the advocate knows to be telling the truth). The prosecutor, on the other hand, is generally regarded as occupying a different role: the prosecutor's duty is to pursue justice, not merely to convict. While the adversarial ethic requires the zealous pursuit of the client's case, prosecutors do not really appear for any individual client. In a wider sense, their client is the community, and thus they occupy dual roles.[104] On the one hand, the prosecutor is required to be independent and objective in the pursuit of justice, but in an adversarial system, the prosecutor must also be an advocate for conviction at trial. The prosecutor's role in advocating conviction is, however, always subordinate to the primary duty to act fairly in the pursuit of justice.[105] They are therefore regarded as 'ministers of justice who ought not to struggle for a conviction . . . it is their duty to assist the court . . . to make certain that justice is done between the subject and the State.'[106] Two propositions thus reflect agreement between common law jurisdictions on the general role of the prosecutor within an adversarial system of justice:

(a) It is the duty of the prosecutor to forsake the partisanship implicit in the role of defence counsel and make justice his or her primary aim; and
(b) such a priority does not absolve the prosecutor from the duty to present the Crown case firmly, even vigorously.[107]

But while these propositions may be simply stated, applying them to particular circumstances confronting the prosecutor in individual cases may be a difficult and delicate matter. Although prosecutors are liberated from the need to embrace the ethic of neutral partisanship of the criminal defence lawyer, they also face ethical dilemmas, albeit of a different kind. Such dilemmas arise from the prosecutors' dual role within an adversarial system of justice, which may therefore pull in opposite directions in exercising their broad prosecutorial

[102] The following discussion of prosecutorial ethics applies to adversarial systems of justice that apply to Anglo-American legal proceedings. These ethical precepts may not be wholly opposite to systems of justices that are not based on an adversarial model.
[103] Luban (1994).
[104] Crispin (1995).
[105] Prosecution Policy of the Commonwealth 1992, paras 1.4 and 6.1; Hetherington (1989) Ch 8.
[106] *R v Lucas* [1973] VR 693, 705.
[107] Crispin (1995), 185.

discretion.[108] The dictates of the law, and some broader sense of 'justice', let alone compassion, do not always coincide, and in seeking to resolve such tensions, ethical principles and codes of conduct may have a valuable role to play by assisting prosecutors in the resolution of conflicting values in a consistent and rational manner.[109] Recognising this, most common law jurisdictions have established a prosecution policy encompassing a code of ethical conduct for informing prosecutorial decision-making.

To the extent that proceedings to enforce regulatory offences resemble the prosecution of 'traditional' crimes, ethical norms applicable to the exercise of prosecutorial discretion may also serve as a safeguard against unfairness and inconsistency in the enforcement process. Indeed, these ethical norms may be of greater significance in the regulatory enforcement context, given that regulators are often entrusted with the task of both investigating and prosecuting suspected violations, unlike the enforcement of traditional crimes in which the investigative role falls primarily on the police. In contrast, the regulator's investigative duties may, in practice, tend to accentuate its impulse to strive for conviction, and, to the extent that this renders even-handedness and objectivity in decision-making more difficult, may heighten the risk of unfairness in settlement negotiations.

But although the ethical norms applicable to prosecutorial discretion may assist in locating the boundaries of legitimate settlement practice in the course of competition enforcement proceedings, we cannot expect to devise hard and fast rules. At best, we can only hope to provide broadly-framed guidance, serving as an ethical focus in seeking to reconcile often powerfully competing demands in promoting the public interest in fair and effective enforcement. The following discussion thus considers in more detail various points in the enforcement process in which the regulator's prosecutorial functions may generate ethical dilemmas in drawing upon its discretionary power to negotiate settlements, seeking where possible to provide general guiding principles concerning how those dilemmas might fairly be resolved. It draws expressly on the experience of the Commission in negotiating settlements in the resolution of Australian enforcement proceedings under the Act, in order to give the discussion a more concrete focus, although one might readily extrapolate from the Australian experience in devising a set of ethical principles applicable to other regulatory contexts. Because the Commonwealth Prosecution Policy establishes the ethical code of conduct to guide Commonwealth prosecutors, it forms the primary Australian reference point in seeking to elucidate the boundaries of ethical

[108] Crispin (1995), 180; Ashworth (1998), 257.

[109] Craig notes that philosophers have criticised the notion of a self-derived professional ethic on the basis that, if an action is morally right, it should be susceptible of justification by the same moral arguments that apply to the behaviour of any other member of society. He acknowledges that, even if this claim is accepted, there are still arguments in favour of an ethical code specific to a given professional group in order to promote consistency among practitioners rather than leaving moral judgement to the fallible individual alone: Craig (1998), 735.

negotiated penalty settlement practice.[110] Rather than provide a comprehensive review of Commission practice, the following selection of issues are focused upon to highlight the risks associated with settlement negotiations: the initiation of proceedings, charge bargaining, 'false' confessions, penalty agreements, Commission recommendations on penalty, the sentence discount and failed negotiations.

(a) Initiating Proceedings

In the criminal context, the power to lay charges, to develop and disclose information to the accused, to reduce or withdraw charges and the possibility of playing a role in sentencing, are all areas in which the prosecutor can strongly influence, if not directly control, the outcome of the prosecution.[111] This is also true of the Commission's position in Part IV proceedings, given that the decision to initiate proceedings and the determination of the nature and number of charges to be made lies wholly within its discretion.[112]

An individual against whom charges have been brought faces considerable burdens in the form of cost, inconvenience and potentially adverse publicity.[113] As one leading commentator has stated:

> It is wrong for a person to be prosecuted if the evidence is insufficient. The essence of the wrongness lies in the protection of the innocent. If this principle is taken seriously, it should mean not merely that innocent people are not convicted, but also that innocent people should not be prosecuted. The reasons for this may be found in the dictum that 'the process is punishment': being prosecuted is an inconvenience at least, often a source of profound worry, and sometimes a considerable expense, and it may also lead to an element of stigma and loss of social esteem.[114]

It is therefore important that the discretionary power to lay charges, whether criminal or regulatory in nature, be fairly and properly exercised, and in particular, that charges should be made only where there is sufficient evidence to support them. In initiating formal enforcement proceedings, the Commission's task is thus to balance the demands of vigorous and effective enforcement with the need to ensure that persons are not unfairly subjected to the burden of such proceedings. On this basis, it is suggested that the Commission's responsibility is to ensure that it only initiates proceedings on the basis of allegations which can be

[110] Because of the importance of the initial charging decision and the width of the prosecutor's power in deciding whether or not to lay charges and the nature and number of charges, the Commonwealth Director of Public Prosecutions ('DPP') has developed formal prosecution policy guidelines, which must be adhered to in the criminal charging process (including charge bargaining) which are uniform throughout Australia (with a few exceptions).

[111] Mack and Anleu (1995), 74; Tombs (1984), 13; Potas (1984); ALRC (1980) 61; *Price v Ferris* (1994) 74 A Crim R 127, 130.

[112] This discretion is, however, subject to legal proceedings and can be challenged in judicial review proceedings: *R v Director of Public Prosecutions ex parte C* (1995) 1 Cr App R 136.

[113] Frieberg (1983), 25.

[114] Ashworth (1998), 180.

supported by evidence and there is a reasonable prospect of securing a finding of contravention at trial.[115] Although liability for pecuniary penalties is formally characterised as civil rather than criminal in nature, this cannot justify the institution or continuation of proceedings on the basis of insufficient evidence.

(b) Charge Bargaining

Charge bargaining, which involves the enforcement authority agreeing not to proceed with some of the charges, or not to proceed with more serious charges, in return for the defendant's agreement to admit liability to a lesser charge, also lies within the Commission's enforcement discretion. As we saw in the preceding section, although it is the guilty defendant who stands to gain the most from a charge bargain, an innocent defendant may nonetheless be willing to plead guilty to lesser charges, fearing conviction (and consequent punishment) of more serious charges. From the enforcement authority's perspective, charge bargaining may be attractive because it enables a contravention to be secured without risking failure to prove contravention at trial and also saves enforcement resources. Thus, the benefits of charge bargains are greatest for the guilty defendant and the enforcement authority with a weak case and it is in those circumstances that the incentive to engage in charge bargaining is strongest.[116] One of the invidious features of charge bargaining is that the enforcement authority's incentives to engage in it are greatest where the evidence is weak, that is, where there is a higher probability that the defendant is innocent.

One of the risks inherent in charge bargaining arises from prosecutor's temptation to 'overcharge' so as to provide leverage in subsequent plea negotiations. Charges can then be dropped or reduced in exchange for pleas without dropping the entire case.[117] In the criminal context, the Commonwealth Prosecution Policy sets out three requirements that are designed to guard against the improper use of charge bargaining and, in particular, to avoid the temptation for prosecutors to overcharge so as to provide leverage in plea negotiations. Under the Policy, charge bargaining is an acceptable practice provided that the charge-bargaining proposal is not initiated by the prosecution, that the charges to be proceeded with bear a reasonable relationship to the criminal conduct of the accused, and there is evidence to support the charge.[118] There is considerable value in applying similar restraints to the Commission in exercising its discretion to lay 'charges', thereby minimising the risks of unfairness yet leaving

[115] As public enforcer, the Commission is well placed to bring proceedings with the purpose of giving the Court an opportunity to clarify the scope of the law when giving reasoned judgment and deciding the case ('test cases'). Although there will inevitably be an element of risk which the Commission faces when bringing test cases, the legal argument put forward by the Commission in such cases should also satisfy the test of 'reasonable prospect of success' before such proceedings are instituted.

[116] Ashworth (1998), 274–75.

[117] McDonald (1985), 12.

[118] Commonwealth Prosecution Policy (1992), 19.

the Commission with moderate flexibility and scope for professional judgement in seeking to promote efficient and effective enforcement.

(c) 'False' Confessions

One particular practice that appears to have arisen in several Australian negotiated penalty settlements is the defendant's formal admission of contravention in order to bring proceedings to a swift conclusion, while publicly protesting innocence.[119] In criminal proceedings, it is clearly improper for a prosecutor and the court to accept a plea of guilty where the accused maintains his or her innocence, due to the danger of wrongfully convicting the innocent. For this reason, the Commonwealth Prosecution Policy prohibits the acceptance by the prosecution of a charge-bargaining proposal if the accused maintains his or her innocence with respect to the charges for which the accused has offered to plead guilty.[120] The proper course is to proceed with the charges and allow the evidence to be tested at trial so that the court can independently and impartially determine the accused's guilt or innocence.

Should similar constraints apply to the Commission? Clearly the Court lacks jurisdiction to impose penalties under section 76 unless it is satisfied that a contravention (or attempted contravention) of the Act has occurred.[121] However, the issue is not formal denial of liability, but the informal denial of liability while formally admitting a contravention and agreeing to a penalty. In criminal cases, the particular danger of accepting such 'false confessions' is the risk of punishing an innocent-accused because the evidence is not tested at trial to determine liability. But because Part IV penalties are 'quasi-criminal' in nature, the injustice arising from wrongfully penalising an innocent defendant in Part IV proceedings is less severe than that arising from wrongfully punishing an innocent person accused of a 'traditional' crime. We must also bear in mind that commercial pragmatism may be a strong motivation for making false confessions in Part IV proceedings[122]: an innocent defendant may face greater total costs even if it successfully establishes its innocence at trial than if it had accepted liability at an early stage and reached a negotiated penalty settlement.[123]

[119] *ACCC v J McPhee* (1998) ATPR ¶41–628; *ACCC v NW Frozen Foods Pty Ltd* (1996) ATPR ¶41–515 at 42,441.

[120] Commonwealth Prosecution Policy (1992) para 5.16.

[121] Trade Practices Act 1974, s 76(1).

[122] See the respondent's submissions in *TPC v TNT Australia Pty Ltd* (1995) ATPR ¶41–375 cited by Featherston (1995).

[123] Although a defendant which establishes its innocence in contested proceedings is generally entitled to an award of costs, these are generally awarded on a party-party basis so that the defendant is still required to bear a significant proportion of its own legal costs. Significant costs in management time are also involved in contesting proceedings which are also factored into the decision whether or not to submit to a negotiated settlement.

Arguably, the most effective safeguard against unduly pressuring the innocent defendant to plead guilty is to ensure that the discretion to institute penalty proceedings is exercised only when there is evidence to support the charge and a reasonable prospect of a finding of contravention and that this is kept under continual review. If, after initiating proceedings, the Commission forms the view that there is insufficient reliable and admissible evidence to support the charges, there is no longer any justification for continuing proceedings and they should therefore be discontinued. Nor should negotiated settlements be contemplated in the absence of formal admissions. If these principles are adhered to, then the risk of penalising innocent respondents by agreeing a penalty settlement should be quite small. In other words, the Commission may legitimately accept formal admissions *if* it has reliable supporting evidence of a contravention, notwithstanding that the respondents may thereafter publicly deny having contravened the Act.[124]

(d) Penalty Agreements and Recommendations

One particularly notable feature of Australian penalty settlements is the popularity of penalty agreements: the parties agree on the level of penalty, making joint submissions to the Court setting out the agreed facts and jointly recommending the appropriate level of penalty.[125] Although some negotiated settlements are only 'partial', in that the defendant may accept liability but dispute the quantum of penalty sought by the Commission, there are several reasons why 'full' penalty settlements have become so widespread. For defendants, they substantially diminish the risk of the Court imposing a higher penalty as well as avoiding the costs associated with contested penalty proceedings. For the Commission, penalty agreements reduce its enforcement costs, provide scope to secure a penalty higher than the amount imposed by a Court in a contested hearing,[126] and may bolster the Commission's bargaining power in settlement discussions by enabling it to reserve the right to seek higher penalties in contested proceedings if no agreement on the quantum of penalties is forthcoming.[127]

Yet in some US jurisdictions where sentence agreements have been used in criminal proceedings, critics point to the risk that judges may routinely accept agreed penalty recommendations, thus effectively usurping the court's role in sentencing and replacing it with 'trial by prosecutor'.[128] Likewise, if the Court in Part IV proceedings routinely accepts the Commission's recommendation on penalty without meaningful and independent assessment of whether the agreed penalty is legally appropriate, this risks conferring too much power on the

[124] The Court also has an important role in ensuring that admissions of liability are genuine and supported by reliable and admissible evidence. Below, section (3).

[125] The cases are discussed in section (3) below.

[126] Kench (1998).

[127] Featherston (1995); Featherston (1997).

[128] This is perhaps the principal criticism of American style plea bargaining: Mack and Anleu (1995), 98.

Commission. Even if the settlement agreement extends to liability only, there is still a risk that the agreed facts put to the Court may not be an accurate reflection of the true facts, resulting in a penalty amount that is not justified by the true circumstances giving rise to the contravention. So stated, the objections to sentence agreements or the making of sentence recommendations by the enforcement authority lie not in the fact of agreement or recommendation per se, but the lack of meaningful independent scrutiny by the Court to ensure that the agreed facts are supported by reliable and admissible evidence and that the quantum of penalty so recommended or agreed is legally appropriate.

While the most effective safeguard against these risks may lie in the keeping of the courts,[129] self-restraint by the Commission may go a considerable distance in reducing them. To this end, useful guidance may be found in the legal and ethical principles applicable to a prosecutor in the criminal sentencing process. In Australian sentencing proceedings, the prosecutor's role was historically very limited,[130] but the establishment of the office of the Director of Public Prosecutions and the availability of prosecution appeal against sentence has resulted in a more active role, summed up by the Australian High Court thus:

> the Crown is required to make its submissions as to sentence fairly and in an even-handed manner, and the Crown does not, as an adversary, press the sentencing court for a heavy sentence. The Crown has a duty to the court to assist in the task of passing sentence by an adequate presentation of the facts, by an appropriate reference to any special principles of sentencing which might reasonably be thought to be relevant to the case at hand, and by a fair testing of the defendant's case so far as it appears to require it.[131]

Yet expansion in the prosecutor's role at the sentencing stage has not generally extended to making specific recommendations on the actual level of the sentence, let alone reaching agreement on sentence with the accused.[132] If this conception of the prosecutorial role is applied to the Commission, its role in contested penalty proceedings is to make submissions on sentence which fully reflect the underlying facts, firmly based upon the legal principles of penalty setting. The Commission's role is not, therefore, to extract the maximum possible penalty but to seek an 'appropriate' penalty, one properly reflecting the relevant

[129] Below, Section 3.

[130] The traditional view has been that the prosecutor's task is complete once a conviction has been obtained and, in relation to sentence, is limited to outlining the facts, presenting an antecedents report and ensuring that the court makes no errors of fact or law: ALRC (1988), 105.

[131] *R v Tait and Bartley* (1979) 24 ALR 473, 477.

[132] Although it is generally accepted that the prosecutor should not present its views on the desired quantum of punishment in criminal proceedings, courts have been willing to hear the prosecutor's views on the appropriateness on various types of sentence: Fox and Freiberg (1999), 124–25. Cato claims that a prosecutor is entitled to refer to a range of sentences where there is one for a certain offence. The range is, however, only a guide to sentences that have been handed down in relation to a particular offence and is not binding on a sentencing court. Normally, a prosecutor will not urge a precise period of imprisonment in criminal sentencing proceedings because that is a matter within the discretion of the judge, taking into account the circumstances of the case: Cato (1998), 317.

facts and grounded in legal authority, drawing the Court's attention to any relevant aggravating and mitigating factors. Thus, in penalty negotiations, the level of acceptable penalty suggested by the Commission should be based on the same legal principles that inform a court's assessment of penalty in contested proceedings, subject to a modest reduction by way of sentence discount in recognition of the defendant's willingness to co-operate and forgo contested penalty proceedings.[133] Thus, any amount offered by the Commission by way of settlement in penalty negotiations should not exceed the level of penalty that could be justified on the basis of legal authority. To offer inflated penalty sums that are not properly grounded in fact and law would risk constituting an unfair use of the Commission's discretionary power.[134] Scope for compromise would arise from the inherently imprecise nature of the penalty-setting process, so that the Commission could legitimately offer to settle penalties at the upper end of the lawfully justified scale whilst permitting scope for downward revision in negotiations.

(e) *The Sentence Discount and Failed Negotiations*

For defendants, one powerful attraction of negotiated settlements lies in the availability of the so-called 'sentence discount' for co-operating with the Commission and admitting liability. Although many competition regimes utilise formal 'leniency policies' incorporating sentence discounting in offering full or partial immunity from penalty for those who voluntarily 'confess' to violations and assist with investigations, our present concern is with the use of informal sentence discounts falling short of full immunity, granted in return for the defendant's willingness to plead guilty rather than contest the proceedings.[135] Sentence discounting has long been used in criminal cases[136] but, as I have already noted, has been heavily criticised on the basis that it effectively penalises those who avail themselves of the fundamental right to trial.[137] Nonetheless, it has generally been accepted by most commentators in the criminal context,[138] provided that the sentence discount is modest in size to avoid imposing excessive institutional pressure on the accused to plead guilty,[139] owing to its pragmatic contribution to the speedy and cost-effective resolution of cases. Although

[133] The sentence discount is discussed below.

[134] Featherston (1995); Featherston (1997).

[135] See n 3 and n 14 above.

[136] However, it is also claimed that some judges play mere lip-service to the sentence discount: Ashworth (1998), 278 *cf* 282.

[137] ALRC (1988), 92.

[138] Although some commentators favour strict adherence to principle and thereby reject the use of the sentence discount altogether: Ashworth (1998), 292.

[139] ALRC (1988), 92–94; Mack and Anleu (1995), 173; JUSTICE (1993); Sallmann (1984), 130. Proponents of the latter view point to empirical studies of plea bargaining in criminal cases which indicate that the most significant factor influencing an accused to plead guilty is the strength of the prosecution's case, thus suggesting that fears of coercion due to sentence discounting are overstated: Mack and Anleu (1995), 110 and 170. However, the empirical research is inconclusive.

the possible injustice arising from sentence discounting in Part IV proceedings is considerably less severe than in criminal proceedings because the defendant's personal liberty and freedom are not at stake, sentence discounting is nonetheless a source of pressure on innocent defendants to admit liability therefore straining the constitutional value of procedural fairness. For this reason, the size of the sentence discount should be modest (as a proportion of the total penalty) in order to ensure that this pressure is not excessive.[140]

The availability of the sentence discount strengthens the Commission's negotiating position in attempting to reach an agreed penalty settlement with the respondent. If sentence discounting is available, then the absence of a penalty agreement enables the Court to impose a modestly higher penalty on the defendant who cannot plead full co-operation with the Commission as a factor in mitigation of penalty. It follows that if the Commission is unable to reach a penalty agreement with the defendant, it may be at liberty to recommend that the defendant should be penalised moderately more severely than the defendant with whom a penalty agreement has been concluded. On the other hand, the Commission is not justified in recommending a penalty out of proportion to the wrongfulness of the defendant's conduct, in light of the Commission's duty to the assist the court by reference to the facts and applicable legal principles, rather than pressing the sentencing court for a heavy penalty.[141]

3. Judicial Oversight

Although ethical norms may assist in reducing the risk of prosecutorial overreaching, professional self-restraint may fail to ensure that the constitutional values of transparency, due process, consistency and accountability are adequately preserved in settlement negotiations. To this end, external oversight by an independent tribunal may be necessary and desirable. But, as we have seen, there is considerable variation in the range of institutional structures and processes within which the settlement of competition enforcement proceedings occurs across different jurisdictions, reflecting the differential degree of 'criminality' reflected in the nature of sanctions imposed for violation. In jurisdictions where competition sanctions are formally classified as civil or 'administrative' in nature, than the degree of judicial involvement is patchy and uneven, despite the quasi-criminal quality which such sanctions typically display. In light of the hybrid character of such sanctions, procedural fairness would seem to require

[140] In *ACCC v NW Frozen Foods Pty Ltd* (1996) ATPR ¶41–515, Heerey J at first instance took the view that a sentence discount of $300 000 was warranted in relation to a legally appropriate total penalty which would otherwise have been awarded in the absence of cooperation of $1.5 million, representing a discount of 20%. However, his decision was overturned on appeal: *NW Frozen Foods Pty Ltd v ACCC* (1996) 71 FCR 285. In *Rural Press v ACCC* [2002] FCA 213 the Full Federal Court held that the respondent's co-operation in the conduct of the trial was irrelevant to the fixing of penalty, although it might be relevant in relation to cost orders.

[141] See *R v Tait and Bartley* (1979) 24 ALR 473, 477.

some degree of judicial oversight of the settlement process, although there is considerable room for debate about the form and intensity of that oversight.[142] Although there may well be a need for confidentiality between the parties in the course of negotiations, we must bear in mind that regulatory offences involve a violation of community standards and the settlement of enforcement proceedings involves the exercise of governmental power, underlining why they ought not to remain hidden from public view.

But, once a deal has been struck, it is in the parties' mutual interest to ensure that its terms are observed and they are therefore unlikely to welcome measures, such as judicial oversight, that might inhibit their freedom to bargain. Even if external judicial scrutiny of negotiated penalty settlements is required, both parties acting rationally in their own self-interest are likely to advocate approval of their agreement when bringing it before the court. The absence of adversarial incentives to challenge the validity of such agreements underlines the need for judicial vigilance in ensuring that court scrutiny is meaningful.[143] The following discussion of the Australian courts' approach to scrutinising negotiated settlements highlights this tension, illustrating their understandable disinclination to interfere with the parties' bargain, given its ostensibly consensual underpinnings, but which may therefore fail to provide an effective hedge against the general lack of transparency and consequent lack of accountability in regulatory settlement practice which arguably constitutes their most troubling feature. If judicial oversight is to safeguard the integrity of the enforcement process, then the intensity of judicial scrutiny adopted must be genuine and robust, rather than simply routine validation.

Although the resolution of Part IV proceedings by negotiated settlements is now the norm in Australian enforcement practice, such settlements are a relatively recent innovation, not gaining widespread judicial acceptability until the early 1990s.[144] Under the current legislative scheme, the Federal Court is entrusted with the power to determine liability and quantum of penalty but, as the regulatory scheme has matured, the Court has permitted the Commission to reach negotiated penalty settlements with the defendant, but which do not take legal effect until approved by the Court. In order to evaluate the extent to which the Court has discharged its responsibility to safeguard and supervise the integrity of negotiated settlements, three particular issues are focused upon: penalty agreements, admissions and the giving of reasons.

142 In relation to EU competition proceedings, see Brent (1995); Waelbroeck and Fossellard (1994).

143 In the USA, the Antitrust Procedures and Penalties Act 1974 (the 'Tunney Act') imposes various procedural requirements on the proposed settlement of antitrust enforcement action by the DoJ, including court approval of the agreement on the basis that the settlement is 'in the public interest'. Academic comment is divided on whether the courts have engaged in the appropriate level of scrutiny of consent decrees: Anderson (1996a); Savin (1997); Boyder (1983). For a discussion of the Tunney Act procedure, see ch 7, Part D (5) (a).

144 Such settlements were first approved in *TPC v Allied Mills Pty Ltd* (1981) ATPR ¶40–241, 43,182.

(a) Penalty Agreements

Although penalty agreements between the Commission and the defendant were largely unheard of during the first two decades of the Act,[145] since 1994 the Court has actively encouraged their use.[146] Its concern to avoid jeopardising penalty settlements is reflected in its extremely liberal standard of scrutiny, articulated by the Full Federal Court's when overturning a lower court decision to depart from the penalty agreed to by the parties in *NW Frozen Foods.*[147] The Court underlined the importance of encouraging penalty settlements owing to the significant savings in legal costs and court time they may generate, prompting it to adopt a more liberal test when approving agreements,[148] stating:

> The cases we have discussed earlier in these reasons unite in affirming the public interest in the promotion of settlements, especially in this area where litigation is likely to be very lengthy. We agree with the statement made in several of the cases cited that it is not actually useful to investigate whether, unaided by the agreement of the parties, we would have arrived at the very figure they propose. The question is not that; it is simply whether, in the performance of the Court's duty under s.76, this particular penalty, proposed with the consent of the corporation involved and of the Commission is one the Court should determine to be appropriate.[149]

(b) Admissions

In keeping with its deferential approach to penalty agreements, the Court has also taken a fairly relaxed view of the defendant's admissions in negotiated penalty cases. Because the Court's jurisdiction to order pecuniary penalties pursuant to section 76 is contingent on it being satisfied that a contravention (or

[145] For example *TPC v British Building Society* (1988) ATPR ¶40–880; *TPC v General Corporation of Japan (Australia) Pty Ltd* (1989) ATPR ¶40–722; *TPC v Australian Autoglass Pty Ltd* (1988) ATPR ¶40–881.The one exception is *TPC v Allied Mills Pty Ltd* (1981) ATPR ¶40–241 when penalties were negotiated.

[146] While the use of negotiation and bargaining to resolve competition proceedings has a long pedigree in US antitrust enforcement and EC competition regulation, the frequent use of negotiated penalty settlements is a relatively recent phenomenon in the Australian context. The practice first received judicial approval in *TPC v Allied Mills Pty Ltd* (1981) ATPR ¶40–241 and since then the practice has become so commonplace that, in recent years, they have outnumbered contested penalty cases. A review of the Commission's Annual Reports between 1992–1998, and the cases reported in the CCH *Australian Trade Practices Reporter* over the same period reveals that, since 1 January 1993 when the statutory penalty ceilings for contraventions of Part IV of the Act were raised from $250,000 to $10 million for corporations and from $50,000 to $500,000 for individuals, there were 29 incidents involving Part IV contraventions which were the subject of penalty proceedings by the Commission. Of those, only eight were concluded by a contested penalty trial—the remainder were resolved by negotiated penalty settlement. For a more detailed analysis, see Yeung (2001) ch 2 and Appendix A.

[147] (1996) 71 FCR 285, 296–7.

[148] The previous test required that, in order to approve a negotiated settlement agreement, the agreed penalty submitted by the parties must fall within the 'relevant range' of penalties that a court would have ordered: *TPC v TNT Australia Pty Ltd* (1995) ATPR 41–375, per Burchett J.

[149] (1996) 71 FCR 285, 298.

attempted contravention) of a Part IV provision has occurred, an agreed penalty cannot be approved without formal admissions of liability. Several judgments appear to suggest, however, that courts have doubted the authenticity of the formal admissions given in negotiated penalty cases, but have nonetheless endorsed the parties' agreement to enable the proceedings to be settled expeditiously.[150] For example in *TPC v CC (NSW) Ltd*[151] the defendant's senior counsel submitted that the defendant (Richmond) did not admit the allegations pleaded, but consented to orders against him under section 76 as sought by the Commission on the basis of those allegations without admitting their truth.[152] In approving the penalty orders, Lindgren J stated:

> The facts of the alleged contraventions by the corporations and of Richmond's involvement were not proved before me by evidence. Rather, the hearing proceeded on the basis that Richmond no longer traversed, for the purpose only of the fixing of penalty, the allegations made by the Commission in its amended statement of claim: see Order 11 r 13 of the Federal Court Rules. Accordingly, although it is necessary for me in fixing the amount of the pecuniary penalty payable by Richmond to refer to the relevant 'facts' of the case, it must be understood that the basis for these 'facts' is the Commission's *allegations* in its pleadings and Richmond's *non-traversal* of them for the limited purpose of the quantification of pecuniary penalty. (emphasis in original)[153]

The Court's willingness to approve penalty agreements despite a hint of unease about the formal admissions given in the absence of proof of contravention by the tendering and testing of evidence, may reflect its concern to respect the defendant's commercial autonomy. But, as I have already emphasised, it is contrary to the rule of law to penalise innocent firms and individuals, even if they 'voluntarily' accept punishment for reasons of commercial pragmatism. The risk of this occurring should be minimal if the Commission ensures that proceedings will only be continued if it has sufficient reliable and admissible supporting evidence of contravention. If the Court has significant doubts concerning the validity of the respondent's admissions, it should exercise its discretion to call upon the Commission to provide supporting evidence of the contraventions admitted to. This would enable the benefits of early and expeditious settlement to be realised while providing additional safeguards against the unfair punishment of innocent defendants. The Court could then acknowledge, without difficulty, that, whilst the existence of a contravention had not been proved in contested proceedings in light of the defendant's admissions, it was nonetheless satisfied that there was sufficient evidence to substantiate the allegations so admitted.

[150] *ACCC v NW Frozen Foods Pty Ltd* (1996) ATPR ¶41–515.
[151] (1994) ATPR ¶41–363.
[152] (1994) ATPR ¶41–363, 42,724.
[153] (1994) ATPR ¶41–363.

(c) The Giving of Reasons

Without full knowledge of the facts underlying a contravention, the Court cannot properly carry out its judicial role of determining whether the sanction imposed on the defendant accurately applies the standards of the law and fairly reflects the true circumstances of the contravention. It is therefore essential that the Court is fully apprised of the factual background to the contravention before imposing penalties, whether the proceedings are contested or negotiated. Yet in securing court approval for negotiated penalty settlements, the practice has developed of the Commission and defendant making joint submissions on both the factual background to the contravention, and their submissions on penalty (in cases where both facts and quantum of penalty are agreed).[154] Documentary evidence may also be tendered in support of the parties' joint submissions of fact, although the evidence is not tested in court by way of examination and cross-examination. In approving negotiated settlements, the Court therefore relies entirely on the facts as jointly submitted by the parties. While there is nothing objectionable to the submission to the Court of an agreed statement of facts that accurately reflects the circumstances giving rise to the contravention, it has, however, led to a tendency for the Court to provide only the briefest outline of facts in giving judgment, making it difficult to assess and evaluate the basis and reasons for the penalties so imposed in any given case.[155] Although the joint submissions are generally placed on the court file and are therefore available for public inspection, they do not always appear in the reported judgment. Furthermore, Kench has observed that the volume and quality of evidence put before the Court in negotiated penalty cases seems quite inconsistent and it is thus hard to see how a judge could determine the range of penalties that he or she would have ordered.[156]

Not only does the absence of a full factual account of the case reduce the transparency of the courts' penalty decisions, it may also reinforce the perception that penalties negotiated out of court between the Commission and the defendant lack adequate grounding in fact and legal principle. The deterrent impact of court judgments may also be weakened as a result. In approving settlements, the Court has sometimes tended to overlook the importance of publicly articulating the reasons for its decisions and the need for a full statement of the relevant facts, relying too heavily on placing the parties' joint submissions of fact and law on the court file.[157] As the Australian High Court has warned:

[154] In criminal proceedings, the court is not bound by parties' agreement on facts.

[155] For example, *TPC v Allied Mills Pty Ltd* (1981) ATPR ¶40–241; *ACCC v Hugo Boss Pty Ltd* (1996) ATPR ¶41–536, *ACCC v Foamlite (Australia) Pty Ltd* (1998) ATPR ¶41–615; *TPC v Amatek Ltd* (Federal Court of Australia, 24 November 1994).

[156] Kench (1998), 22.

[157] The ALRC has recommended more extensive requirements for the giving and recording of reasons in criminal sentencing: ALRC (1988).

> If a private communication is permitted to affect the sentence so that it appears to be discordant with the facts publicly related to the court, the sentence will not be seen to be appropriate, the deterrent effect of punishment will be impaired and public confidence in the process of sentencing will be diminished. As Sir Frank Kitto wrote in his essay 'Why Write Judgments?' (*Judicial Essays*, Law Foundation of New South Wales and Victorian Law Foundation 1975 p 9): 'It is not enough that the hearing of the case has been in public. The process of reasoning which has decided the hearing of the case must itself be exposed in the light of day, so that all concerned may understand what principles and practice of law and logic are guiding the courts, and so that full publicity may be achieved.[158]

4. An Evaluation

There is no doubt that the Court's willingness to approve negotiated settlements has encouraged the expeditious and efficient resolution of Part IV penalty proceedings. That the Court has only departed from a penalty agreement between the Commission and the defendant on one occasion may be wholly explicable on the basis that it has genuinely regarded the agreed quantum as legally and factually appropriate.[159] But its strikingly light-handed review of penalty agreements and willingness to approve penalty agreements in the face of occasional unease about the genuineness of the defendant's admissions, suggests that the Court may have been somewhat over-enthusiastic in encouraging penalty agreements. While cost minimisation is an important goal that the Court should seek to pursue by actively encouraging settlements, its current approach appears to constitute little more than a rubber-stamping exercise, thereby overlooking its constitutional duties.[160]

The Court's failure to engage in rigorous and open review of penalty agreements may have the somewhat paradoxical result of weakening the perceived legitimacy of the factual basis and legal appropriateness of the agreed penalty amount. If the agreed sum is legally and factually appropriate, then the agreement should withstand more rigorous Court scrutiny and pose no threat to the Commission's bargaining position in negotiating settlements.[161] By generally failing to engage in rigorous scrutiny of penalty agreements, there is a real risk that the Court has overlooked the quasi-criminal nature of Part IV penalty proceedings, inappropriately regarding Part IV penalties as largely analogous to ordinary civil damages. But, as we have seen, the analogy with civil damages is misleading. Because they constitute a form of hybrid penalty, a legally coerced sanction for unlawful behaviour, it is important that the Court does not

[158] *R v Tait and Bartley* (1979) 24 ALR 473, 492.

[159] The only instance of the Court departing from the agreed penalties referred to in the reported cases is *ACCC v Tyco Australia Pty Ltd* [2000] FCA 401, where the Court awarded penalties of $50,000 on two individual respondents, rather than the $75,000 jointly proposed by the parties.

[160] Eg *ACCC v Tubemakers of Australia* [2000] FCA 977; *ACCC v Simsmetal Ltd* [2000] ATPR 40–993 *cf* Dunning and Dean (1995).

[161] Featherston (1995); Featherston (1997); Kench (1998).

abdicate to the Commission its judicial and constitutional responsibility for punishing unlawful conduct. Its general approach not only fails to adhere to the constitutional requirement of the separation of judicial and executive functions but also fails to accord sufficient protection to the integrity, transparency and accountability of the regulatory enforcement process.

More recent judicial pronouncements, however, may suggest that the Court is beginning to recognise the risks associated with undue deference to negotiated penalty settlements. Individual Federal Court judges seem to be expressing a heightened awareness of the tension between the public interest in the efficient settlement of disputes, and the public interest in ensuring that public law is openly, accurately and fairly applied. For example, in the context of deciding whether to make orders by consent as jointly requested by the Commission and defendant (although not involving penalties) Weinberg J appeared to favour a more intensive degree of scrutiny, stating[162]:

> I cannot leave this matter without commenting briefly upon what I consider to be the somewhat undesirable practice on the part of the ACCC in presenting this Court with a specific figure as an 'agreed pecuniary penalty'. I acknowledge that both the ACCC and Colgate have accepted that the figure proposed is in no way binding upon the Court. However, when pressed to point to a single instance when the Court has not, in the past, endorsed such a figure, counsel found it difficult to do so.
>
> It is difficult to imagine that the parties would propose a pecuniary penalty that is so clearly beyond the permissible range that the Court would depart from it. As the authorities presently stand, the Court is bound to impose an agreed pecuniary penalty, save in such circumstances. I acknowledge that a contravention of s 48 is not a criminal offence. The liability is civil only. I also acknowledge the importance of the principles enunciated in *NW Frozen Foods v Australian Competition and Consumer Commission* (supra), and in particular the need for corporations to have certainty of outcome if they are to be encouraged to engage in negotiated settlements. I am bound by these principles, and a well established line of authority, to accept that the Court will not depart from an agreed figure merely because it might otherwise have been disposed to select some other figure.
>
> However, there are dangers associated with this approach. The Court may be seen, perhaps not altogether incorrectly, to act as a 'rubber stamp' in simply approving a decision taken at an executive level by a body charged with investigating and prosecuting contraventions of the Act, but having no role in actually imposing particular sanctions for those contraventions. Negotiated settlements are an important vehicle for resolving complex matters such as those involved in the present case. It must be borne in mind, however, that there is a public interest in ensuring that corporations that engage in behaviour of the kind that occurred in this case are dealt with appropriately, and that proper recognition is given to the need for specific and general deterrence. There are important parallels between the fixing of a pecuniary penalty under s 76, and the ordinary sentencing process which is quintessentially a matter for the courts: *Australian Competition and Consumer Commission v ABB Transmission and Distribution Limited* [2001] FCA 383 at pars 4—6 per Finkelstein J.

[162] *ACCC v Colgate-Palmolive Pty Ltd* [2002] FCA 619.

I should emphasise that nothing that I have said should be regarded as a criticism of a joint submission being received regarding what might be the appropriate range of pecuniary penalties to be imposed. A submission couched in those terms can assist in achieving a measure of certainty, and consistency of treatment with other like cases. At the same time, unlike what seems to have emerged as the more usual practice, namely putting forward an 'agreed penalty', the suggestions of an appropriate range of pecuniary penalties allows for the proper exercise of judicial discretion in what is fundamentally a matter for the courts to determine.

E. CONCLUSION

In reflecting upon the use of bargaining and negotiation in regulatory enforcement practice, we noted that a significant strand of contemporary regulatory compliance scholarship seeks to identify when regulators ought to punish and when they ought to persuade. Yet the use of negotiated penalty settlements within competition law enforcement may suggest that it may not be possible to characterise all enforcement strategies in terms of a dichotomy between formal punitive strategies, on the one hand, and informal techniques of negotiation and persuasion on the other. Negotiated penalty settlements appear to constitute a peculiar mix of both: negotiation and bargaining takes place between the regulator and suspect, but for the purpose of seeking to *impose* formal punitive sanctions, rather than as a means for *avoiding* punitive strategies.

The use of such settlements in public competition law enforcement appears to generate significant and far-reaching benefits: substantially reducing the costs associated with public enforcement, providing scope for a greater degree of flexibility and responsiveness by the enforcement authority in responding to suspected contravention, providing a means by which those under investigation may alleviate the business disruption and adverse publicity associated with contested enforcement proceedings and encouraging a co-operative relationship between the regulator and the regulated that may help to foster a culture of compliance within the regulated community. Couched in terms of the analytical framework constructed in chapter three, negotiated penalty settlements promote the regulatory goals of efficiency, responsiveness and predictability.[163] But while these benefits are readily identifiable, the risks associated with such settlements may not be so readily apparent, antagonising several constitutional values, including the values of transparency, accountability and proportionality. However, it is the constitutional value of due process that is placed under the most significant strain. In attempting to flesh out precisely what procedural fairness entails in the sanctioning process, intractable difficulties arise in characterising the nature of competition law penalties as civil or criminal, for they display a mixture of paradigmatic civil and criminal qualities, constituting a

[163] From the defendant's perspective, the availability of negotiated penalty settlements allows the defendant to reduce the uncertainty associated with contested enforcement proceedings.

form of hybrid quasi-criminal/quasi-civil sanction. Because the rigour of procedural protection varies in proportion to the gravity of the harm associated with mistakes in the decision-making process, the procedures for imposing 'middleground sanctions' demand middle-level protections: procedural safeguards that are more rigorous and demanding that those typically applied to civil proceedings, but need not import the entire range of procedural rights guaranteed to the accused in prosecuting 'traditional' crimes.

But although procedural fairness is required to ensure the accurate application of legal standards, it alone is insufficient to ensure the integrity of the negotiated settlement process. Because the value of procedural fairness is not wholly instrumental, but also rests on the need to ensure that certain non-outcome based values are respected in the decision-making process, these values must also be taken seriously in sanctioning offenders. As critiques of plea bargaining demonstrate, the values of transparency, accountability, consistency and proportionality may also be strained when penalty proceedings are resolved by negotiated settlements between the law enforcement authority and those charged with violating the law. The invisibility of settlements makes it difficult for the public to scrutinise the conduct of the enforcement authority in negotiating such settlements, with a consequent diminution not only in public confidence in the accuracy or fairness of the resulting settlement, but also in the extent of the authority's legal and professional accountability. Because the resulting settlement is a product of bilateral negotiations between the official and the firms and individuals under investigation, there is also considerable scope for inconsistent outcomes between similarly situated firms, given that the settlement agreement will be strongly influenced by the bargaining skills and strength of the parties involved, undermining the requirement of equality before the law.

Although these are serious concerns, we have explored several mechanisms which may assist in lowering the risk of unduly pressuring innocent defendants to settle while promoting transparency and accountability in the negotiation process, yet allowing the benefits of settlement to be reaped. In terms of regulatory enforcement architecture, the separation of prosecutorial and judicial functions in the penalty enforcement process may reduce the risk of unfairness, by avoiding the inherent conflict between these two functions that may otherwise arise when both functions are vested in a single authority. But even the institutional separation of powers still leaves the prosecuting authority with extremely broad prosecutorial discretion. In order to guard against the temptation for prosecutorial overreaching, two further safeguards have been outlined: ethical constraints on the exercise of prosecutorial power, and judicial scrutiny of settlement agreements.

Whether or not all three mechanisms are considered vital to securing the integrity and legitimacy of the negotiated penalty settlement process depends, to a large extent, in the degree of 'criminality' reflected in the sanctions used in any given scheme of competition regulation. In those jurisdictions where the relevant sanctions are both formally and substantively criminal in nature, providing for the imprisonment of offenders, then all three mechanisms would be of critical importance. But, where sanctions are formally designated as civil by the relevant legislature, then whilst all three safeguards would provide a valuable and welcome means for securing the fairness and integrity of the negotiated settlement process, there may be considerable scope for their implementation in a more diluted and less rigorous procedural form. In other words, in those jurisdictions where competition violations are treated as a form of administrative rather than criminal delinquency, the arguments for installing such extensive safeguards are significantly less compelling, and this is borne out in the use of purely 'administrative settlements' to resolve enforcement proceedings, which forms the focus of the following chapter.

6

Regulatory Bargaining and Administrative Settlements

A. INTRODUCTION

WE SAW IN the previous chapter that both liability for, and quantum of, penalty payable for competition law violations are often determined by agreement between the regulator and defendant, rather than by formal adjudication. Enforcement negotiations are not, however, confined to resolving matters concerning the defendant's formal liability and punishment. The vast bulk of the complaints received by competition regulators concerning alleged violations are 'settled', with only a small minority of complaints subject to detailed investigations, let alone formal enforcement proceedings.[1] There are many reasons why complaints concerning suspected violations may not be pursued through to formal adjudication: there may be no (or little) evidence of a contravention, the offending conduct may have been terminated or may have been so trivial or slight that formal enforcement action cannot be justified in light of the regulator's limited resources and enforcement priorities or the regulator may agree with the suspected offender ('suspect') not to pursue further enforcement action.[2] While each of these scenarios might be described as 'administrative settlements', for present purposes the term will be confined to

[1] For example, in Australia, the Commission received 10,942 complaints during 1997–98, but pursued only 2247 of them. A 'pursued complaint' includes all matters where additional information was sought to establish whether a possible contravention was involved and whether Commission action was appropriate. Of these, some were concluded after initial inquiries and others investigated in depth: ACCC Annual Report 1997–1998, Appendix 4. In the USA, Kauper observes that when enforcement actions are taken by the US Department of Justice, defendants have strong incentives to agree to a settlement by consent decree in order to avoid the effect of s 5(a) of the Clayton Act which essentially provides that court judgment in any civil or criminal action under US antitrust laws constitutes prima facie evidence of a violation, which may then be used in a private treble damages action: Kauper (1993), 104–5. In the EU, a review of the EC Commission's enforcement statistics published in its Annual Reports on Competition Policy demonstrate that between 1991–2001, the EC Commission handled a total of 6523 matters that involved the opening of a file. Of these, only 364 (5.6%) were resolved by a formal decision. The EC Commission states that the remaining complaints were resolved either by the issuing of a comfort letter, discomfort letter, rejection of the complaint and administrative closure of the file (the latter referring to cases closed because the agreements were no longer in force, the impact was too slight to warrant further investigation, the complaints had become moot or had been withdrawn or had not revealed any anti-competitive practice).

[2] Van Bael (1986); Bourgeoius (1993).

situations in which the regulator has reasonable grounds for suspecting that a contravention has occurred (or may occur in future), but agrees not to proceed with more severe enforcement action in return for the suspect's agreement to act, or to forbear from acting, in a specified manner. For example, the firm under investigation may agree to cease and desist from engaging in the suspect activity in return for the regulator's agreement not to pursue further and/or more formal enforcement action. In other words, the term 'administrative settlement' is restricted to situations where enforcement action is actually being 'settled' in consideration of concessions or commitments provided by the suspect. While the negotiated penalty settlements discussed in the previous chapter would appear to fall within this definition, they are nevertheless excluded because they result in an official determination of liability and the imposition of a punitive sanction on the offender. Administrative settlements, by contrast, entail neither of these consequences, although there may well be room for debate concerning whether the commitments offered by the suspect are tantamount to punitive measures.[3]

The primary purpose of this chapter is to subject the use of administrative settlements in regulatory enforcement to critical scrutiny, in an attempt to flesh out what principles, if any, ought to inform their use. This issue is of considerable importance with one leading commentator observing that

> negotiation and exchange pervade the regulatory process. Yet the full impact of negotiation and exchange has been overlooked to the extent that it pervades implementation and enforcement . . . Even in a command-and-control system, the regulatory process is deeply, if informally, contractual.[4]

The examination in this and the following chapter seeks to deepen our understanding of administrative settlements as a regulatory compliance tool and technique and, in so doing, enrich our understanding of the more general and widely used phenomenon of 'regulatory bargaining'. While the analysis presented in this chapter is largely abstract and theoretical, the following chapter seeks to illustrate how the various theoretical issues identified here are reflected in the practical reality of enforcement practice, drawing from the Commission's experience of accepting court enforceable undertakings in response to suspected violations of the Act.

I begin by locating administrative settlements within one well-known strand of the burgeoning compliance literature, in which regulatory theorists have sought to understand and prescribe 'optimal' strategies for securing regulatory compliance. As we shall see, while much of this scholarship is normative in orientation, the notion of optimality upon which they are constructed has been almost exclusively conceived in terms of achieving 'effective and efficient' outcomes. Constitutional values have been either marginalised or completely

[3] Below, ch 7, Part C (2) (b).
[4] Freeman (2000a), 191.

overlooked, typically given little more than passing reference to vague and often undefined notions of 'political acceptability' without further pause for thought. The following discussion endeavours to plug this gap, seeking to identify and illustrate how enforcement strategies driven by the quest for effectiveness and efficient outcomes may pull against several constitutional values, thereby detracting from their legitimacy. In so doing, it urges both academics and policy-makers to resist the inclination to bifurcate their approach to regulatory tools and techniques on the one hand, and their concern for regulatory legitimacy on the other. While scholarship concerning the former has typically been seen predominantly in functional, technocratic terms, the latter have demonstrated a greater awareness of the need to make explicit the values upon which the legitimacy of a regulatory programme rests. Although there are important values associated with the use of administrative settlements and the bargaining and negotiation process upon which such settlements rest—such as the values of deliberation, participation and consensus, these values may sit somewhat uncomfortably with the traditional rule of law ideal, an ideal more closely associated with adjudication. These tensions, between the virtues of negotiation and settlement, and the constitutional values of openness, transparency, due process, participation and fairness (including equality of treatment) which their use may tend to antagonise, are explored more fully throughout the ensuing discussion, thereby illustrating that questions of regulatory technique and sanction cannot be wholly divorced from normative values.

B. REGULATORY ENFORCEMENT TOOLS, TECHNIQUES AND PURPOSES

There has been considerable academic interest in the various tools and techniques employed by regulators in seeking to secure compliance with regulatory rules, spawning a growing body of literature that may be of assistance in our endeavour to understand and evaluate the use of administrative settlements in the regulatory enforcement process. One strand of this literature adopts a largely functional orientation, focusing on the broad and diverse array of legal and economic instruments available to policy-makers in designing the appropriate institutional framework for shaping regulatory processes with the aim of designing compliance tools and strategies that will secure effective compliance.[5] Another strand, discussed in the previous chapter, draws from the sociological tradition by exploring the behavioural style or attitude of regulatory officials through ethnographic studies seeking to identify and understand how regulatory officials approach their enforcement duties.[6] The following section begins by broadly outlining the first strand of this literature, before relating it to the second strand of literature by examining the well-known 'pyramid of enforcement' model

[5] Ogus (1994); Sinclair (1997); Baldwin *et al* (1998), 23–6; Breyer (1982), ch 2.
[6] Above, ch 5, Part B (3) and the literature cited there.

developed by Ayres and Braithwaite. While their model of regulatory enforcement was briefly alluded to in the previous chapter, it will be explored more fully in the following discussion, given its considerable influence in shaping both contemporary public administration practice and academic reflection on regulatory policy, enforcement strategy and institutional design.

1. Regulatory Design and Enforcement Tools

Throughout this book, I have largely focused on classical 'command and control' regulation, given that this is the basic structure of most schemes of competition regulation established throughout OECD countries. In this sense, the approach underlying these regulatory regimes relies primarily upon what might be described as first generation regulatory design. By this I refer to early social and economic regulation introduced by the state to control some of the harms and excesses accompanying the development of large scale industrialisation and laissez-faire capitalism in the late eighteenth and early nineteenth century and continued into the years immediately following the second world war.[7] The essence of command and control regulation is the legal proscription of defined social and economic behaviour, backed by the coercive force of either criminal or civil sanctions.[8] As a technique of social control, the command and control approach possesses strengths of both a practical and principled kind. From the practical perspective of the state, resort to legal rules backed by the criminal law may be thought of as a relatively simple and inexpensive technique of controlling economic and social activity.[9] In terms of principle, command and control regulation might be regarded as consistent with many of the virtues associated with the rule of law insofar as it relies centrally upon the use of precisely formulated legal standards of general application, publicised in advance.[10] The proscription of regulated conduct by legal rules backed by the criminal law may also have symbolic significance, by declaring that certain conduct should be regarded by the community as unacceptable and thus liable to be dealt with severely.[11]

Over time, however, experience of command and control regulation has thrown several of its shortcomings into high relief. These include difficulties in formulating legal rules with sufficient clarity and certainty so as to encompass the conduct considered harmful without suppressing benign or socially beneficial activity.[12] Similarly, reliance on specifically formulated legal rules

[7] Freiberg and O'Malley (1984); Baldwin *et al* (1998), 5–6. Although it is usual to trace the origins of modern regulatory law in Britain to the nineteenth century, the roots lie much deeper, particularly in the highly interventionist regimes of the Tudor and Stuart periods: Ogus (1992).

[8] Baldwin (1997).

[9] Ashworth (1995), 51.

[10] Richardson *et al* (1984), 22.

[11] Baldwin and Cave (1999), 117.

[12] Below, Part C (2).

may be prone to inflexibility and legalism in application which may stifle enterprise and generate resistance within the regulated industry or might be avoided by enterprise altogether by engaging in 'creative compliance'.[13] In particular, resort to the criminal law to sanction non-compliance is often thought to be an excessively blunt instrument to regulate conduct that is typically regarded with ambivalence in terms of its moral repugnance.[14] Doubts have also been expressed about the effectiveness of regulation to bring about desired outcomes in circumstances where the law was not rigorously enforced by officials entrusted with this task, partly due to their own perception of the apparent harshness of using criminal punishment to sanction the regulated conduct.[15]

A second generation of regulatory design was borne partly out of these perceived deficiencies. These techniques sought to rely less on coercion through the law (including the development of forms of sanction for non-compliance which do not involve the imposition of criminal punishment), in favour of 'constitutive', less restrictive and incentive based styles of control.[16] This interest in techniques that shy away from legal coercion in favour of reliance upon more flexible, individualised approaches which utilise suasion, 'voluntary' participation by industry through self-regulation and the economic incentive-based techniques of the market mechanism, cannot be attributed solely to disenchantment with traditional command and control techniques.[17] They should also be viewed in the context of the rise of a political ideology associated with liberal capitalism in which many governments of western industrialised democracies in the late 1970s and early 1980s sought to 'roll back the frontiers of the state' and remove or at least reduce the burdens of regulation from the shoulders of enterprise.[18] In terms of political and ideological rhetoric, these alternatives to command and control regulation may be seen as representing a move away from a paternalistic interventionist state, claiming to promote greater scope for free enterprise, participation and individual autonomy.[19]

More recent contemporary perspectives on regulatory design appear to reflect a maturing in academic thought. They caution against the adoption of a rigid dichotomy between command and control approaches and those reliant upon the voluntary and consensual participation of enterprise upon which systems of self-regulation are based. This literature adopts a more subtle and sophisticated approach advocating a combination of regulatory techniques and instruments, stressing the importance of sensitivity to the context in which regulation is intended to operate. For example, in the context of environmental regulation

[13] McBarnet and Whelan (1991).

[14] Above, ch 4, Part B (2).

[15] Hawkins (1984); Hawkins (2002); Baldwin (1990).

[16] Baldwin (1997).

[17] Daintith (1994); Shearing (1993).

[18] Above ch 3, Part B (1) (a).

[19] Many commentators have pointed out, however, that the so-called deregulation movement has paradoxically led to the introduction of a number of new schemes of statutory regulation responsible for overseeing the operation of the privatised industries: Majone (1992); Baldwin *et al* (1998), 7.

Gunningham and Grabosky advocate what they refer to as 'regulatory pluralism', which involves the use of a mix of complementary institutions and instruments, claiming that rarely will a single instrument be optimal in generating efficient, effective and 'politically acceptable' outcomes.[20] Likewise, Sinclair argues that the alleged dichotomy between command and control strategies and voluntarist strategies of regulation is false. Instead, he identifies a number of different variables that may be used to characterise regulatory policy instruments, including the nature and extent of regulatory compulsion, the extent to which regulatory flexibility allows firms to accommodate individual circumstances of regulatees and the opportunity for regulatees to participate in rule design.[21]

One of the valuable insights of this recent literature is its emphasis on the complex, intricate and often subtle ways in which different aspects of a regulatory system interact with each other and with the broader social context in which it operates. Thus we should be mindful of unduly rigid or simplistic classifications in distinguishing different regulatory tools and techniques, recognising that there are multiple and equally valid ways to conceptualise and characterise them, and which may intersect and overlap, contingent upon specific purposes and contexts. In seeking to describe and classify enforcement tools, we can identify a range of different functional, legal and practical ways of distinguishing between them. Thus, although the general structure of most schemes of competition regulation throughout western industrialised states rely primarily on the use of legal rules to proscribes certain conduct, contravention of which may result in the imposition of punitive sanctions, it does not follow that the enforcement of competition law relies solely on punitive means. Instead, the tools and techniques available to regulatory authorities in enforcing rules proscribing anti-competitive conduct display a variety of legal and functional characteristics, which may, in turn, affect their ability to promote effective regulation and their conformity with constitutional values.

2. Compliance Tools, Techniques and the Pyramid of Enforcement

The literature referred to above may be related directly to the body of regulatory scholarship discussed in the previous chapter that draws upon a broad and diverse range of ethnographic studies investigating the behaviour of enforcement officials in responding to regulatory contraventions. In my earlier discussion, I noted that these studies had given rise to academic debate concerning whether regulators ought 'to punish or persuade' in seeking to secure compliance, observing that, as academic reflection has matured, the debate is now generally cast in a less polarised fashion with Ayres and Braithwaite observing that the primary question is not whether to punish or persuade, but *when* to punish or persuade. Their approach to regulatory enforcement draws upon both these

[20] Gunningham and Grabosky (1998), 26–27.
[21] Sinclair (1997).

strands of literature, involving a combination of game theory and the results of sociological investigation.[22] They construct a two-dimensional 'enforcement pyramid': the first dimension being a static model, depicting various regulatory sanctions, while the second dimension is a dynamic model, depicting the appropriate strategy that regulators should adopt in seeking to secure compliance.

Ayres and Braithwaite's static pyramid sets out to characterise and order the tools and sanctions within a regulator's enforcement armoury by reference to their coercive backing, associated formality and expense. Informal, co-operative solutions between the regulator and regulated lie at the base of the pyramid, constituting the most numerous, most timely and least costly means by which the regulator may secure compliance.[23] As the pyramid ascends, the sanctions become increasingly severe in terms of their legal, coercive and deterrent effect on the regulated and the cost involved to both the regulator and the regulated in using those sanctions to secure compliance. In this way, the static pyramid of enforcement represents sanctions in a hierarchical fashion, reflecting the cost/benefit trade-off involved in regulatory compliance. The second dimension of the pyramid is dynamic in outlook, depicting a 'hierarchy of interventionalism in regulatory style'.[24] In their dynamic model, Ayres and Braithwaite advocate a 'Tit for Tat' strategy, combining suasion and punishment to secure compliance, contingent on the response of the regulated as co-operative or combative.[25] In their view, a dynamic pyramid of enforcement strategy is likely to be more effective the greater the number of tiers of sanctions of escalating deterrent impact which are available to the regulator (illustrated in the layers of the static pyramid)[26] because the escalating effect of the pyramid framework is claimed to encourage co-operation between the regulated and the regulator at the base of the pyramid, which is the least costly and most time-efficient method of securing compliance.[27] Drawing from the two dimensions of this pyramid, Ayres and Braithwaite suggest that regulators can and should be able to 'speak softly when they carry a big stick'[28]: provided there is a credible and severe body of sanctions, enforcement officers should be able to educate and persuade firms to comply, so that a mixed enforcement pattern is advocated, involving both punishment and persuasion, albeit in different measures.

This notion of an enforcement pyramid, with its simple yet evocative imagery, has proved a popular ordering structure for many government policy documents on regulation across a range of jurisdictions.[29] It provides a valuable

[22] Braithwaite and Ayres (1992).

[23] *Ibid*, 35.

[24] *Ibid*, 40.

[25] *Ibid*, ch 2.

[26] *Ibid*, 40–41.

[27] *Ibid*.

[28] *Ibid*, 19.

[29] Eg Industry Commission (1995) 694–5; Australian Taxation Office Compliance Model, referred to in ALRC (2002) para 10.18; United Nations: Economic and Social Commission for Asia and the Pacific, 'The Economic Regulation of Transport Infrastructure Facilities and Sciences' (2001).

framework for conceptualising the range of enforcement tools available to regulators in securing compliance and linking it to the level of 'punitiveness' reflected in various enforcement styles or strategies. Taken together, the two dimensions of the pyramid clearly depict several key characteristics of enforcement tools and techniques, including their varying levels of flexibility and rigidity, formality, expense, timeliness of response and reliance upon suasion, consent or legal coercion between the regulator and the regulated. By envisaging enforcement tools as situated within a graded pyramid structure, it also avoids drawing a rigid dichotomy between different enforcement tools and techniques, locating them along a continuum when viewed from different functional and legal perspectives rather than being discrete and discontinuous in form and structure. It suffers, however, from several significant shortcomings, both as a descriptive (or static) and a prescriptive-dynamic model, to which we now turn.

(a) Regulatory Compliance Tools and Social Purpose

Despite the enforcement pyramid's powerful descriptive force, it fails to provide an entirely comprehensive representation of regulatory enforcement tools, due to its tendency to overlook the distinct, related and sometimes overlapping social purposes for which they are best suited. At the highest level of generality, it may be claimed that the purpose of regulation in general, and thus all enforcement tools and techniques, is to 'secure compliance' with regulatory goals by securing the modification of behaviour in the desired manner.[30] But, as we saw in chapter one, the notion of 'securing compliance' may lend itself to a looseness in definition so that couching the aim of regulatory enforcement in this open-textured manner risks neglecting the breadth and complexity inherent in that broad enterprise. In particular, there may be various social goals that a regulatory scheme may wish to pursue in seeking to modify social and economic behaviour and which might (although not necessarily) be reflected in a spectrum of regulatory tools and instruments. Particular tools or instruments may be associated with the pursuit of distinct and sometimes multiple social purposes, which need not be exclusive to the tool in question. Thus, for example, a regulatory scheme may be variously concerned with preventing specific types of harm, compensating those harmed by the impugned conduct, restoring the status quo by placing the parties affected by the impugned conduct in the position they would have been in had the conduct not occurred, punishing wrongdoing or deterring future contraventions and so forth. These specific, albeit subsidiary, social goals are not adequately reflected in the pyramid of enforcement, largely because it remains caught up in the two-pronged discourse of 'punishment versus persuasion', conceptualising enforcement tools largely in terms of their coercive or harsh consequences for the suspect (and hence formality and associated expense). While Ayres and Braithwaite criticise economic rationalist

[30] Above, ch 1, Part B (4).

formulations by conceiving of sanctions only as monetary deterrence, they appear to be similarly guilty of restricting their portrayal of sanctions to one dominated by the notion of deterrence, albeit recognising that deterrence may take various forms, such as reputational deterrence or, in its most severe form, through incapacitation.[31]

In short, although we can usefully draw upon a pyramid of enforcement in classifying and characterising regulatory enforcement tools, we may supplement our analysis by considering their purposive dimension. But identifying the social purposes which any given enforcement tool or sanction may be thought to serve is not always a straightforward task, particularly given that some instruments may serve several purposes whilst the same purpose may in some cases be served by several different instruments.[32] In this respect, it may be more accurate to characterise enforcement tools in terms of the purpose or purposes for which they are most suited and least suited (or even unsuitable), rather than attempting to specify their social purpose(s) in a rigid and sharply defined manner. While socio-legal scholars have identified links between the behavioural response of regulatory enforcement officials to the social purposes motivating their conduct, social purposes may also be linked to legal sanctions based on the nature of the sanction itself. But as we saw in the previous chapter, characterising the nature of a sanction can be a complex matter, with several factors providing guidance, including their legal character (including degree of coerciveness), procedural requirements, visibility and the consequences of the sanction for the defendant and others. Because the primary aim of this chapter is to examine and critique the use of administrative settlements as a regulatory compliance tool, the following discussion draws upon these factors with the aim of identifying the social purpose(s) which administrative settlements might be best and least suited to securing. To this end, it is useful to compare administrative settlements with court-ordered sanctions in order to highlight the similarities and differences between them, and thus it is court remedies to which I turn first.

(i) Court Imposed Remedies and Social Purpose

When viewed as a regulatory compliance tool, court-imposed remedies may serve a variety of social purposes, depending primarily on the particular type of court order in question.[33] So, for example, court injunctions and declarations

[31] Braithwaite and Ayres (1992), 35.

[32] Above, ch 5, Part C (1) (ii).

[33] While it might be possible to rank court orders, as Ayres and Braithwaite's model implies, based on their degree of punitiveness vis a vis the defendant, this may be counterproductive to the extent that first, it overlooks the varied range of social purposes that different court orders may be suited to securing, and secondly, the pyramid's hierarchical structure suggests that some social purposes should be systematically prioritised over others in determining the appropriate court orders which should be sought or pursued, rather than selecting the appropriate social purpose(s) to pursue in any given case based on a careful and sensitive appreciation of the context in which the suspected contravention has arisen.

may secure the termination of specific conduct and thereby serve to eradicate (or at least reduce) the incidence of violation,[34] mandatory injunctions requiring the defendant to act in a specified way may promote restorative goals by 'correcting' and undoing the effects of past violations (eg by endeavouring to return the defendant and those harmed by the contravention to the position they would have been in had the contravention not occurred). Likewise, orders for the payment of damages may also promote restorative goals, enabling those harmed by unlawful conduct to recover monetary compensation for the loss or damage thereby suffered. In contrast, civil or criminal penalty orders serve to punish the offender for past violations, thereby deterring both the offender and other potential offenders from engaging in similar kinds of unlawful conduct and they might also been seen as promoting educational goals by raising public awareness of regulatory requirements. This broader educative purpose might also be reflected in a regulator's desire to pursue enforcement action through to formal court adjudication for the purposes of enabling a court to clarify uncertainties in the scope and content of regulatory rules.[35] The elucidation of the law by courts in judicial proceedings on a case-by-case basis serves not only to provide guidance to regulated firms, but may also promote responsiveness in the law, enabling the law to develop in response to the changing social environment in which it operates.

While the social purposes for which court orders are best suited may be readily identifiable, partly because they have the longest history as a means of responding to suspected contraventions, this may also be partly attributable to the narrow and precise way in which court orders must be formulated, given that the breach of a court order is a serious matter, constituting a contempt of court.[36] For this reason, court orders are unsuited to securing social purposes that are broad and aspirational in nature. For example, it may be socially desirable to encourage the regulated community to develop new and innovative methods of managing the particular risks associated with the regulated activity. But court-orders are ill-suited mechanisms for fostering innovation and encouraging creative entrepreneurship. This may be partly attributable to a court's reluctance to make orders which require on-going monitoring and/or third party participation. For example, in *ACCC v REIWA*[37] French J refused to grant consent orders requiring two colleges of further education who had violated the Act to publish a notice in a West Australian Department of Training publication stating (amongst other things) that colleges must increase their awareness of the application of trade practices law to their business activities. In the court's view, such orders were inappropriate because the State of West

[34] The Court's jurisdiction to grant injunctions requires that it must be satisfied that a persons has 'engaged, or is proposing to engage' in conduct in breach of Part IV of the Act: Trade Practices Act 1974, s 80(1).

[35] Below, Part C (1) (a).

[36] *ACCC v Z-Tek Computer Pty Ltd* (1997) 78 FCR 197, 201.

[37] (1999) 161 ALR 79.

Australia was not party to the proceedings and, because court orders cannot bind third parties, it could not therefore be compelled to publish the proposed notice. Furthermore, the proposed notice was directed to other colleges (not only those which were party to the proceedings), and assumed a systemic deficiency within the industry in understanding competition law, a burden which French J did not think should be shouldered only by the two colleges party to the proceedings, stating that

> [i]f there is a systemic deficiency that is a matter to be addressed by the Government of Western Australia which, through the relevant minister, can give directions to the colleges. I would add that in my opinion the proposed order also involves an unacceptable intrusion into the proper functions of the West Australian government.[38]

The pursuit of more aspirational goals may therefore lend themselves more readily to so-called 'voluntary' or market-based techniques that seek to harness the entrepreneurial impulse of firms by providing incentives for them to act proactively in furtherance of regulatory goals. Unlike court-ordered remedies, which are directly rooted in the coercive power of the state, enforcement tools and sanctions that rely on voluntary participation, including economic incentives, may be more suited to facilitating social goals that enrol actors other than the defendant or which require on-going monitoring.[39] So, for example, the aim of seeking to promote and inculcate a positive 'culture of compliance' within the regulated industry may be better implemented through consensual participation in which members of the regulated community agree to implement on-going compliance training programmes, rather than through the use of coercive-backed court orders. For similar reasons, if the relevant social goal is to guide and assist firms lacking the knowledge or expertise to ensure compliance, then administrative instruments and techniques may be more appropriate than coercive strategies and sanctions.

(ii) Administrative Settlements and Social Purpose

The preceding discussion of court-ordered remedies may assist our endeavour to understand the use of administrative settlements in regulatory enforcement, providing a valuable point of contrast when drawing upon both Ayres and Braithwaite's static enforcement pyramid and the notion of social purpose. If regulatory enforcement tools are conceptualised in terms of an enforcement pyramid, then court orders would sit at the top of the pyramid, constituting the most coercive, formal and resource-intensive means for responding to suspected violations. Given that administrative settlements do not rely heavily on the formal coercive power of the state, unlike court orders, they would appear to lie half way up the pyramid, constituting a form of 'middle-ground' instrument being a less coercive, less formal and less expensive means for responding to

[38] (1999) 161 ALR 79, 90.
[39] Black (2003).

suspected violations when compared to court orders, yet more formal, intrusive and severe than the kinds of highly informal mechanisms that regulators may resort to in the early dismissal of complaints, such as informal cautions or warnings.

Unlike court orders, however, the scope and content of administrative settlements are determined by agreement between the regulator and defendant, rather than being unilaterally imposed by an independent tribunal and defined in narrow and precise terms. Identifying the social purpose of administrative settlements is therefore considerably more difficult. Unlike the social purposes of court remedies, which are limited and largely dependent upon the range of court orders available to the regulator,[40] administrative settlements appear to be a product of consensus between the parties and may therefore seem capable of pursuing an infinite range of possible purposes, restricted only by the parties' creativity and imagination. But we must bear in mind that administrative settlements involve the exercise of state power and are therefore subject to administrative law constraints that seek to ensure that administrative power is lawfully exercised and thus circumscribe the outer limits of permissible settlement.[41] In other words, there may be some purposes for which administrative settlements are unsuited on the basis that they may amount to an abuse of administrative power. So, for example, administrative settlements could not lawfully provide for the payment of bribes or other forms of kickback to the regulator in return for its forbearance from more severe enforcement action.

As we saw in the previous chapter, the demands of procedural fairness suggest that prosecutorial powers should not be commingled with judicial functions in order to guard against the risk of punishing those who have not in fact violated the law. Whilst the line between 'administrative' and 'judicial' functions may be notoriously difficult to draw, at least at the margins, it is well-established that the imposition of punishment is a quintessentially judicial function. On this basis, it is suggested that administrative settlements are unsuited to securing penal purposes, at least in the absence of judicial oversight to oversee the fair and accurate application of legal standards so as to ensure that the innocent are not punished, a conclusion reinforced by the previous chapter's discussion of the grave risks associated with criminal plea bargaining.

But while due process concerns may exclude punishment from the range of social purposes for which administrative settlements may be suited, they would not seem to exclude the broad range of non-punitive purposes that may profitably be pursued by regulators in securing compliance. Accordingly, administrative settlements may also be seen as substitutes for court ordered

[40] For example, the ALRC has recently proposed that the range of court orders available for responding to regulatory contraventions should be expanded to enable courts to make orders (a) disqualifying the person from government contracts; (b) probation orders; (c) community service orders; (d) information disclosure orders; (e) orders to publish an advertisement; (f) adverse publicity orders: ALRC (2002) Recommendation 27–1.

[41] Below, ch 7, Part B.

remedies to the extent that they may be utilised to secure the termination of suspect conduct, to pursue restorative goals by enabling those harmed by the defendant's suspected unlawful conduct to obtain compensation or to otherwise undo the effects of the suspected violation. But, because administrative settlements are based upon the parties' agreement, rather than on the formal coercive state power, they might also be suited to promoting social goals that cannot readily be achieved by court order, such as the implementation of broad-based compliance programmes, stimulating regulatory innovation in the relevant industry, or implementing arrangements that involve third party participation or on-going monitoring.

(b) The Dynamic Enforcement Pyramid and Constitutional Values

By overlooking the distinct and sometimes overlapping social purposes which different regulatory instruments may seek to pursue, this weakens the potency of Ayres and Braithwaite's static enforcement pyramid as a descriptive device, generating a further weakness in the model's prescriptive (or dynamic) force. As we have seen, because a regulator's enforcement tools may be used to pursue a range of social purposes, selecting the appropriate instrument should be determined in the first instance by the purpose sought to be achieved.[42] Some enforcement instruments are specifically intended to achieve a particular purpose so that, if the enforcement authority seeks to promote that purpose in a particular case, the preferred choice of instrument will be clear. For example, if the regulator is properly concerned to punish the defendant, then the appropriate enforcement tool is to commence formal proceedings seeking punitive orders rather than by seeking to punish the suspect by the terms set out in an administrative settlement. But in any given situation it may be appropriate for the regulator to pursue a multiplicity of purposes, and this may justify the use of several different enforcement tools. Yet by relying upon the response of the regulatee as either combative or co-operative as the critical factor in determining the appropriate enforcement strategy and instrument to be used in any given case, Ayres and Braithwaite overlook the fact that, whilst the primary goal of regulation is to secure the collective goals which justify regulation, there may be several subsidiary social goals underlying the regulatory scheme. By downplaying the variety of social purposes that different enforcement tools may seek to secure, the pyramid of enforcement strategy may be less effective in securing the fulfilment of these subsidiary social goals.

But Ayres and Braithwaite's dynamic model suffers from a further and, in my view, potentially more dangerous weakness. Their dynamic prescriptive model

[42] Regulators typically possess considerable discretion in carrying out their enforcement functions and in determining the purpose they seek to pursue in any given case. This discussion proceeds on the assumption that the purpose sought to be pursued by the regulator is a proper one in the circumstances of the case. Factors which bear upon the seriousness of the contravention are likely to be relevant in determining the appropriate purpose of enforcement action.

is demonstrated by a subtle and formal game theoretic model, illustrating that the rational firm will comply rather than face sanctioning, leading to the conclusion that regulators should play a Tit-for-Tat strategy under which they co-operate with firms until the firm defects, at which point they should hit the firm with a heavy sanction. But in the next round the regulator should resume the pattern of co-operation. Rational firms will co-operate and the regulatory objectives will be met,[43] leading Ayres and Braithwaite to advocate a combination of suasion and punishment to secure compliance, contingent on the response of the regulated firm as co-operative or combative.[44] Underlying this approach is an assumption that the only concern of enforcement officials is to secure the collective goals underpinning the regulatory scheme, failing to take account of the constitutional framework and values within which regulation operates. If we recall that the enforcement of regulatory law involves bringing to bear the coercive power of the state against citizen, then it is vital that constitutional limits on the exercise of this power are recognised and respected.[45]

The essence of the Ayres and Braithwaite strategy is that co-operation with the regulator should be rewarded, whilst failure to co-operate should be punished. Where, in such a strategy, is consideration given to the notion of freedom under the law in which all citizens may act as they wish provided that they do not contravene the law? In the absence of specific legislative proscription, it is not unlawful to decline to co-operate with state authorities, be it the police or commercial regulators.[46] On this basis, Ayres and Braithwaite seem to ignore the implications of their model for a liberal constitutional democracy, failing to accord due respect to individual rights.[47] Even more worrying is the pivotal importance placed on the firm's co-operation as the primary guide to regulatory enforcement action. There is something seriously suspicious about a strategy in which very serious regulatory infractions causing widespread harm are not treated with the appropriate level of severity because the suspect chose at all times to co-operate fully with the regulator, whilst minor infractions are dealt with in a punitive and severe manner because the suspect refused to co-operate with the regulator in its investigations. These examples illustrate the risks of unthinking adherence to the Ayres and Braithwaite model without an awareness of its constitutional shortcomings. In particular, their model overlooks the constitutional values of proportionality and consistency, which are themselves rooted in the right to fair and equal treatment.

[43] Braithwaite and Ayres (1992), ch 2.

[44] *Ibid.*

[45] Although Ayres and Braithwaite acknowledge the risk of regulatory enforcement discretion being abused they conceive of abuse in terms of excessively co-operative relationships that generate the risk of capture and corruption: *ibid*, ch 3.

[46] Zuckerman (1989). Failure to co-operate with authorities may, however, lead to a more severe sentence in so far as the defendant is not able to claim the 'sentence discount' which might otherwise be available. Above, ch 5, Part D (2) (e).

[47] *Cf* Braithwaite claims that the restorative justice process should be 'constrained by all the rights that are foundational to liberal legalism', Braithwaite (2002), 12.

As we saw in chapter three, the proportionality principle requires that state action must be commensurate to the seriousness of the issue at hand. The concept of proportionality involves the evaluation of three factors: the suitability of the measure for the attainment of the desired objective, the necessity of the measure (in the sense that the state has no other option at its disposal which is less restrictive of the citizen's freedom) and the proportionality of the measure to the restrictions which are thereby involved, including the burdens imposed on affected persons.[48] In other words, proportionality entails some idea of balance, and of proper relationship between ends and means. The proportionality principle may, however, be inherently difficulty to apply because it is not an independent principle of review. Rather, it refers to the relationship between other specific and possibly competing substantive interests, requiring an articulation of the relevant benchmark for evaluating proportionality.[49] Given that the focus of the present inquiry is to identify the level of punitiveness that ought to inform the regulator's response to a suspected contravention, the relevant benchmark is the nature and seriousness of the suspected wrongdoing which, as discussed in chapter four, may be defined in terms of harm and culpability. Thus the seriousness of a contravention will be determined by a multiplicity of factors, including the degree of harm caused by the contravention, the deliberateness of the breach, the duration of the contravention, and the existence of prior contravening conduct by the firm concerned.[50]

While Ayres and Braithwaite invoke a form of proportionality in applying what they refer to as the 'minimal sufficiency' principle,[51] they adopt as their reference point the goal of effective future compliance, rather than the nature and seriousness of the defendant's violation. In other words, their proportionality assessment is largely functional and prospective in its orientation, rather than grounded in a concern for restraints on state power that are rooted in respecting individual rights. Their approach seems to suggest that a suspect who fails to co-operate with the regulator in response to a trivial contravention ought to be severely punished, whilst those who commit grave violations of the law but co-operate fully with the regulator should be left unpunished. The relentless quest for effective compliance pervades their policy prescriptions, reflected in their claim that:

> The trick of successful regulation is to establish a synergy between punishment and persuasion. Strategic punishment underwrites regulatory persuasion as something that ought to be attended to. Persuasion legitimates punishment as reasonable, fair, and even something that might elicit remorse or repentance.[52]

[48] Craig (1999), 586–598; de Burca (1993).

[49] de Burca (1993).

[50] See also the factors relevant to penalty setting set out by French J in *TPC v CSR Ltd* (1991) ATPR ¶41–076, cited in ch 3 above.

[51] Braithwaite and Ayres (1992), 40.

[52] *Ibid*, 25–26.

In liberal democratic societies, punishment is legitimated not by persuasion, as Ayres and Braithwaite suggest, but by a finding of guilt determined in accordance with the requirements of procedural fairness, and by proportionality between the severity of punishment imposed upon the offender and the seriousness of the offence. By failing to acknowledge the importance of offence seriousness as a matter properly informing the regulator's enforcement strategy, relying instead on the co-operation of the regulated as the determining factor, Ayres and Braithwaite neglect several essential constitutional values implicated in the enforcement process.

In short, Ayres and Braithwaite's pyramid of enforcement fails to live up to the normative requirements set out in this book that inform and constrain the enforcement authority's powers. Although I do not deny that it may be effective in promoting the overriding goals of regulation in securing its collective goals, it overlooks the variety of subsidiary social purposes that regulation may seek to secure and which may be reflected in a range of different enforcement tools. More importantly, it largely overlooks the constitutional values of proportionality and consistency which should restrict the extent to which regulation's instrumentalist enterprise may legitimately be pursued. These latter values suggest that, while regulatory officials should employ the enforcement tool most likely to be effective in securing compliance, that choice should also be informed by the desired social purpose(s) sought to be promoted, subject to the requirement that the choice of instrument constitutes a fair and proportionate response to the seriousness of the alleged offence.

3. Administrative Settlements, Responsive Regulation and Collaborative Compliance

The constitutional limitations of Ayres and Braithwaite's pyramid of enforcement strategy identified in the foregoing discussion points to a more deeply-rooted antagonism between techniques of 'consensual' regulation (of which administrative settlements may form part) and several constitutional values. Ayres and Braithwaite's pyramid of enforcement strategy forms only one plank, albeit a central plank, of a broader strategy which they refer to as 'responsive regulation', which they explain is

> not a clearly defined program or set of prescriptions concerning the best way to regulate. On the contrary, the best strategy is shown to depend on context, regulatory culture and history. Responsiveness is rather an attitude that enables the blossoming of a wide variety of approaches . . . bearing the marks of . . . flexibility, a purposive focus on competence, participatory citizenship, negotiation . . .

Although Ayres and Braithwaite originally claimed that responsive regulation is 'devoid of any grand theoretical aspirations',[53] 10 years later Braithwaite seeks

[53] Braithwaite and Ayres (1992), 5.

to clothe responsive regulation in more theoretical garb by setting out to integrate his 'restorative justice' approach to traditional crimes with his responsive regulation ideas formulated with Ian Ayres in the sphere of business regulation.[54] He now claims that 'the responsive regulatory approach is the framework for locating restorative justice in institutional spaces where it can best complement institutions of crime prevention, human and economic development, deterrence, incapacitation and care and love for the land'.[55] This refined notion of responsive regulation thus relies critically on what Braithwaite refers to as a restorative justice approach, which he defines as a:

> method of bringing together all stakeholders in an undominated dialogue about the consequences of an injustice and what is to be done to put them right . . . an alternative that has very different values framing than punitive justice.[56]

While this book does not allow for a fuller exploration and critique of responsive regulation or restorative justice, what is worth noting for our immediate purposes is that both ideas rely upon the centrality of dialogue and deliberation between stakeholders in the law enforcement process, primarily between the regulator and regulated, but in which other participants affected by the regulatory enterprise may (in certain circumstances) contribute. In this respect, Ayres and Braithwaite's responsive regulation may be viewed in the context of increasing calls to develop regulatory processes and institutional structures that will enhance deliberation and enable participation, which Black identifies as proceeding under the banners of reflexive law, responsive regulation, or most broadly, 'proceduralisation',[57] all of which ascribe a critical role to deliberative, participatory procedures as a means for securing regulatory objectives.

This emphasis on consensual, dialogic modes of resolving regulatory problems has not been the sole preserve of regulatory theorists, with policy-makers expressing similar enthusiasm for deliberative approaches, reflected in the emergence of North American regulatory 're-invention' initiatives introduced throughout the 1990s. These programmes were largely rooted in finding consensual solutions between the regulator and regulated firms (sometimes with input from affected third parties) characterised by a series of regulatory policy programmes piloted in a range of regulatory contexts fed by the Clinton administration's National Performance Review (NPR).[58] One commentator describes the underlying aims of the NPR as seeking to:

> replace confrontation with cooperation in both regulatory rule-making and enforcement by removing the [regulatory] agency from its traditional role as authoritative decision-maker and placing it on an equal footing with the regulated entity and then expect[ing] them to negotiate a settlement based on terms that all interested parties

[54] Braithwaite (2002).
[55] *Ibid*, viii.
[56] *Ibid*, 12.
[57] Black (2000), 297–98.
[58] Vice President Al Gore, Report of the National Performance Review, From Red Tape to Results: Creating a Government That Works Better and Costs Less (1993).

> will accept, rather than on the [regulatory] agency's own view of how best to implement statutory policy.[59]

Thus, initiatives such as the Environment Protection Agency's Project XL,[60] Habitat Conservation Projects,[61] innovation waivers,[62] and the Occupational Health and Safety Authority's Cooperative Compliance Program,[63] all share basic design features which may broadly be described as forms of 'collaborative compliance'.[64] Dana describes the central technique underpinning these initiatives as a form of contractarian regulation, in which legislators do not amend substantive regulatory statutes to address flaws (or even to grant regulators explicit authority to fashion new solutions on their own initiative) but instead the regulator and regulated firm strike a deal, in which regulators contractually commit not to enforce some requirements that are formally applicable to the regulated entities, in return for the latter's contractual commitments to take measures not required under existing formal law.[65] While these collaborative compliance techniques have been described as 'innovations' in regulatory policy, they rely upon a long-established technique of regulatory bargaining which, as Hazard points out, occurs in the everyday practice of regulatory enforcement when licences and permits are issued, and in the resolution of suspected non-compliance through settlement and negotiation.[66] What is new about these regulatory implementation initiatives is not their reliance on the technique of bargaining and negotiation between the regulator and regulated firm, but the desire to adopt contextualised consent-based regulatory enforcement techniques on a systematic, institutionalised basis.

[59] Werhan (1996).

[60] The Project XL programme invites firms to submit proposals to the Environmental Protection Agency which are aimed at achieving 'superior environmental results', in exchange for a relaxation or waiver in some regulatory laws and standards: see Hirsch (2001).

[61] The Endangered Species Act, s 10 authorises the Secretary of the Interior to permit what would otherwise be a formal violation of the Act (eg the destruction of the critical habitat of an endangered species) as part of a Habitat Conservation Plan, if the Secretary determines that the proposed action 'will not appreciably reduce the likelihood of the survival and recovery of the affected species in the wild'. These plans typically provide for the private landowner to provide some developmental protection for species and land which fall outside the reach of the Act, and in return the Secretary of the Interior agrees to allow what would otherwise be a major violation of the Act on some portion of land in question: see Dana (2000).

[62] Various environmental legislation authorises innovation waivers, which allow qualifying firms extensions of time beyond the deadline for meeting emission or effluent standards in order to develop innovative approaches to compliance: see Caldart and Ashford (1999).

[63] Under this programme, OHSA identified firms with the highest volume of workers making claims and placed them on a primary inspection list. These firms were notified that they would be subject to a comprehensive inspection, unless they agreed to participate in the voluntary co-operative compliance programme. To participate, each firm was required to agree to implement a 'comprehensive health and safety programme', incorporating voluntary industry standards which were more demanding that those required by law. In return, OSHA would remove the firms from the primary inspection list, thus reducing the probability of inspection by 70–90%.

[64] Others have variously described such techniques of 'negotiate and control': Dana (2000); 'command and covenant': Elliot (1997) and 'collaborative regulation': Seidenfeld (2000).

[65] Dana (2000).

[66] Hazard (2001).

In practical terms, resort to context-sensitive, case-by-case negotiation as a means of resolving regulatory problems provides a means for escaping the cumbersome and blunt-edged formalism that is often thought to accompany insistent adherence to prescriptive rules. It allows for the implementation and enforcement of regulatory rules in a tailored manner, negotiated to fit the particular needs and issues arising for the firm or industry sector in question. In this sense, collaborative compliance techniques represent a movement away from command and control approach in favour of voluntarist styles of control, akin to the market-based approaches fashionable throughout the 1970s–1980s. Collaborative compliance techniques are nevertheless distinguishable from market-based techniques on the basis that, while the latter rely on the invisible hand of the market to overcome the limitations of command and control technique, the former rely upon case-by-case negotiations between the regulator and regulated. But not only can collaborative compliance techniques be seen as a practical anti-formalist strategy, they may also be seen as promoting several ideological claims, embodying visions of deliberation between stakeholders as a form of democratic participation in which the public and private sector are depicted as operating together in collaborative 'public/private partnerships', rather than being portrayed as locked in conflict, visions resonating strongly in both Ayres and Braithwaite's responsive regulation and the notion of 'collaborative governance' advocated by Jody Freeman as the most promising form of designing, implementing and enforcing regulatory policy.[67]

Despite their practical and ideological appeal, academic critiques of these North American collaborative compliance initiatives have been rather ambivalent in their assessment, with two broad strands of criticism emerging. The first set of concerns draw attention to the practical limitations associated with collaborative compliance approaches, expressing scepticism about the feasibility of translating consensual/deliberative ideals into the practical operation of regulatory policy design, implementation and enforcement. So, for example, Dana suggests that it is more difficult for affected third parties and public interest groups to participate in regulatory dialogue, with the result that collaborative processes tend to favour regulated firms.[68] Likewise, Seidenfeld claims that the minimum conditions for 'truly collaborative regulatory processes' are unlikely to occur in practice, so that they should not be regarded as a panacea for all regulatory ills, lest such dialogue become a mechanism for regulatory capture.[69]

By contrast, the second set of concerns express unease about the submergence of what I have termed constitutional values. While these critics recognise the need to escape from formalism in regulatory policy implementation, reflecting the general 'delegalisation' trend in public administration throughout the 1990s, they warn of the dangers of collaborative compliance approaches in undermining the

[67] Freeman (1997).
[68] Dana (2000).
[69] Seidenfeld (2000).

values of transparency, accountability, consistency and the rule of law, exemplified in the Werhan's claims that[70]:

> It is the rule of law that legitimates administrative service.... Virtually all the reform efforts pursued by the National Performance Review threaten rule of law values. For example, the recent emphasis on consensual settlements of regulatory issues carries the potential of subtly undermining rule of law values. The[ir] attraction . . . is not only their informality, but also the removal of the agency as the authoritative decisionmaker. The reformist premise is that the parties know best how to solve their problems and will arrive at the best solutions if the [regulatory] agency largely leaves them free to do so. But this is troubling from a rule of law understanding of public law processes because [they] discount the public values that should be served by agency decision-making. They have been selected and provided authority in accordance with public law, not private agreement.

In a similar, albeit less emphatic vein, Farber observes that much important regulatory policy is made through regulatory inaction, settlement of litigation and other techniques that operate outside of full public view, techniques which do not contain the usual opportunities for public input or the normal mandates for deliberative decision-making. Such problems, he claims, have plagued the various 'reinvention' efforts referred to above, being repeatedly criticised for their procedural irregularity, opacity and lack of adequate public accountability. Although he claims that these criticisms are not insurmountable, efforts to bolster accountability are likely to hamper the very collaborative processes lying at the heart of reinvention, calling for sustained analysis of how to manage the trade offs between unhampered regulatory collaboration and values such as transparency and accountability.[71] Farber's observations point to a deeper clash of normative values which emerges once we begin to excavate beneath the surface of what appear to be largely functional debates concerning which regulatory techniques and strategies are likely to secure compliance most effectively. Because administrative settlements may be regarded as a collaborative compliance technique, the following discussion sets out to unpack the tension between the normative values which advocates of collaborative compliance approaches tend to prioritise, and the rule of law values championed by those who warn of its constitutional dangers.

C. BARGAINING, ADJUDICATION AND THE RULE OF LAW

In seeking to understand the disagreement concerning the desirability of collaborative compliance approaches, we may draw from the voluminous literature

[70] Werhan (1996).

[71] Farber (1999), 324 *cf* Freeman (2000) who argues that while the rising prominence of contract as a regulatory instrument may undermine accountability, it also provides opportunities for enhanced accountability through the involvement of private parties. Seidenfeld (2000) fears that the emphasis on contract as a means of providing accountability will seriously undermine the flexibility of the administrative process.

that has developed in response to the 'alternative dispute resolution' ('ADR') movement. Two distinct but related strands of this literature may help to enrich our understanding of administrative settlements as a compliance tool. One strand is concerned with institutional design, in which the central questions relate to the appropriateness of different methods of dispute resolution to various types of 'dispute' and which is represented in the pioneering work by Fuller, briefly mentioned in the previous chapter.[72] Another strand encompasses largely political debates concerning the desirability and necessity of encouraging and developing ADR on a large scale. By drawing from this literature, we may explore the nature of administrative settlements by reference to the underlying form of social ordering through which they are secured—that of bargaining and negotiation.

1. Forms of Social Ordering: Bargaining and Adjudication

Thus far, we have identified at least two bases for distinguishing between enforcement instruments: their degree of punitiveness (as reflected in the gradations of Ayres and Braithwaite's pyramid of enforcement) and their purposive dimension. Another possible basis for distinguishing between the various regulatory enforcement strategies and instruments is the *social process* upon which they are based. Administrative settlements are arrived at following a process of negotiation and bargaining between the regulator and party under investigation. In contrast, court-ordered remedies typically result from the process of adjudication, in which an impartial and independent judicial adjudicator is entrusted with the task of applying the law to the facts established by the evidence brought before it at trial. These two processes, bargaining and adjudication, represent two quite distinctive and in some ways strikingly different forms of reaching decisions, of settling disputes and defining individual's relations with each other.[73]

[72] Fuller (1978).

[73] Social and decision-making processes have been classified by commentators in a number of different ways. Fuller, for example, identified nine different processes or forms of social ordering (which he referred to as 'principles of social ordering'): customary law, contract, property, officially declared law, adjudication, managerial direction, voting, mediation and deliberate resort to chance: Fuller (1981). Galligan adopts a slightly different typology by distinguishing decision-making processes according to their legal purposes, ie according to the mode of resolution dictated within the legal system itself. He thus classifies processes according to whether their purpose is to apply authoritative legal standards; to decide as the official thinks best; to reach agreement between the parties; to decide by voting; and to decide by fiat or decree. He identifies two further 'step families' of decision-making processes: investigation and inquiry and proceduralism and participation: Galligan (1996), 24–32. For the purposes of this book, it is not necessary to adopt any particular typology, given that my aim is simply to explore and evaluate the nature, function and difficulties associated with the use of administrative settlements in regulatory implementation.

(a) Adjudication

In order to compare the two decision processes, it is perhaps useful to begin by considering the process with which legal scholars are perhaps most familiar—adjudication.[74] In his well-known work on adjudication, Fuller highlighted three forms of social ordering which could be used to settle disputes: contract, elections and adjudication.[75] In his view, the characteristic feature of each of these forms of social ordering lay in the manner in which the affected party participates in the decision reached. Thus, elections entail participation by voting, contract entails negotiation, and adjudication entails the presentation of proofs and reasoned arguments.[76] Of these forms of ordering, Fuller identified adjudication as the most rational, for it is the device that gives formal and institutional expression to the influence of reasoned argument in human affairs. By this he meant that adjudication is institutionally committed to a decision based on 'principle'.[77] It depends critically on governance through rules that are authoritatively applied by a neutral and independent arbitrator.[78]

With its reliance upon rules, adjudication is most closely associated with the so-called 'legal paradigm'[79] that draws heavily on Dicey's largely formalist conception of the rule of law.[80] Fixed, certain and precisely formulated legal rules constitute a critical (but not sufficient) component of the rule of law ideal, fulfilling one of the important aims of the law in guiding behaviour through the governance of rules. It provides that the citizen should be able to ascertain the rules governing his or her activities in relation to the state. In normative terms,

[74] In his overview of ADR literature, Twining observes that it is largely divorced from what is widely perceived to be 'mainstream' Anglo-American jurisprudence (as exemplified by positivists in the tradition of Bentham, Austin, Hart, Raz and their contemporary critics Rawls and Dworkin) which he considers somewhat puzzling, because one of the most persistent concerns of modern legal theorists has been about the nature of adjudication. Yet twentieth century Anglo-American jurisprudence has been extraordinarily court-centred, with many of the main debates focusing on the role of judges and reasoning about questions of law in hard cases. Given that *alternative* dispute resolution is mainly concerned with alternatives to civil adjudication, it seems to him strange that mainstream theories of adjudication do not feature prominently in discussions of ADR: Twining (1993).

[75] Fuller (1978), 363.

[76] *Ibid.*

[77] *Ibid*, 366.

[78] Galligan (1996); Jowell (2000).

[79] Lacey (1992). Lacey's notion of the 'legal paradigm' closely resembles Nonet and Selznick's 'autonomous law', which they identify as having four chief attributes: (a) law is separated from politics, drawing a sharp line between legislative and judicial functions; (b) the legal order espouses the 'model of rules' which helps ensure official accountability and limits the creativity of legal institutions and the risk of their intrusion into the political domain; (c) procedure is the heart of law—regularity and fairness (not substantive justice) are the first ends and main competence of the legal order; (d) fidelity to law is understood as strict obedience to the rules of positive law: Nonet and Selznick (1995), 54.

[80] According to Dicey, the rule of law meant: (i) action can be taken against a person only for a distinct breach of law established in the ordinary legal manner before the ordinary courts; (ii) the ordinary law applies to all and no one, including officials, is above it; and (iii) general principles of the constitution are the result of judicial decisions: Dicey (1961); Craig (1997).

governance by settled rules assists in defining and protecting the liberty of the person from the exercise of arbitrary state power.[81]

But there are a number of now familiar problems associated with using rules, such as their inability to control behaviour, which partly explains the movement away from strict command and control regulation.[82] These problems can be attributed to the inherent properties of rules themselves.[83] Rules are anticipatory, generalised abstractions which, when endowed with legal status, provide authoritative reasons for action.[84] Each of these elements is a source of difficulty. Rules will inevitably be under- or over-inclusive in relation to their overriding purpose, failing to catch situations which they should while catching situations which should be excluded, due to epistemological uncertainty and the inherent nature of generalisations.[85] Since rules are not self-executing, but require interpretation for their application, they are inevitably indeterminate, due to the inescapable indeterminacy of language and the subjective and contingent nature of the interpretation of the fact situations to which they are applied.[86] The problems associated with rule indeterminacy are particularly acute in relation to legal rules—for their authoritative status generates the possibility of sanction for breach so that knowing whether or not a particular action is covered by and in compliance with the rule is matter of considerable importance.[87]

(b) Bargaining and Negotiation

In contrast, the need for rules and settled standards seems largely alien to the process of bargaining and negotiation.[88] Rather, a critical feature of the bargaining and negotiation process is its reliance upon the consent of its participants, ideally given freely and on an informed basis.[89] Governance through rules relies upon coercion rather than consent—it is the application of rules that authoritatively determines the outcome of the parties' dispute.[90] In the regulatory context, one of the particular strengths of the negotiation process is its potential to overcome, or at least reduce, the problems associated with the

[81] Galligan (1995), 13; Jowell (2000), 14–15.

[82] Schauer (1991); Twining (1991); Black (1997); Baldwin (1990); Richardson *et al* (1984), 22–23. At an even more basic level, there may be some types of decisions for which determination by rules is simply inappropriate and where other types of decision-making procedures (such as decision-making by voting or agreement) are more suitable: Galligan (1996), ch 9.

[83] An illuminating critique of the way in which rules work in the sphere of financial regulation is provided in Black (1997).

[84] Black (1998), 89.

[85] *Ibid*, 89; Bardach and Kagan (1982),40–41.

[86] Black (1998), 89.

[87] *Ibid*, 90.

[88] Fuller (1971), 328 *cf* Eisenberg (1976).

[89] McEwan and Maiman (1984).

[90] This is not to say that parties cannot voluntarily consent to the determination of their adjudication, but by so doing they agree that the outcome of their dispute will be conclusively resolved by reference to the applicable standards to which they choose to submit.

inherent limits of rules.[91] This function is admirably illustrated by Black in her discussion of regulatory 'conversations', by which she refers to communications and discussions between a regulatory official and a regulated firm or individual as to the application of a generally applicable rule in their particular case.[92] Although she acknowledges a number of shortcomings associated with such conversations, Black argues that they fulfil an important and central function in regulation by providing a means by which the place of the individual in a generalised system of regulation is recognised. For the regulated, conversations can address uncertainty in the rule's application by seeking an assurance that if it takes a particular course of action the regulator will not proceed against it. For the regulator, this strategy enables the rule to be tailored to fit the particular circumstances of the regulated in a manner which conforms to the rule's underlying purpose, thus reducing the problems of over- or under inclusiveness and avoiding the problems associated with legalism in rule interpretation. Where conversations occur in relation to regulatory enforcement, negotiation and bargaining are consistent with the 'compliance strategy' of enforcement which, as I have already mentioned, is claimed by some commentators to provide an important means of stimulating compliance and avoiding a culture of resistance from the regulated parties.[93] In short, bargaining and negotiation can mediate the tensions between the desire for certainty on the one hand and flexibility on the other, alleviating some of the difficulties arising from the inherent limitations of rules.[94]

Black's analysis highlights the manner in which the process of negotiation and bargaining between the regulator and regulated can enhance the effectiveness of regulation. By reducing the scope for regulatory rules to be applied in a manner that fails to reflect their underlying 'spirit', thus promoting flexibility in interpretation and application, negotiation can enhance regulatory responsiveness. As a means of dispute-resolution and form of social ordering, negotiation and bargaining in general are often claimed by ADR advocates to generate a number of other practical benefits when contrasted with formal adjudication. ADR advocates seek to emphasise its informality (implying that it is less alienating and intimidating to ordinary citizens), low cost, width and ease of access, and speed of operation. But in addition to these practical claims, all of which can be regarded as various aspects of the negotiation process that may promote effectiveness in decision-making, lies a further ideological dimension. In particular, it is claimed that because the resolution of disputes through negotiation and bargaining relies primarily on the consent of its participants, who together arrive at a mutually satisfactory outcome, it is more consistent with individual autonomy and freedom than is formal adjudication.[95] Because the latter operates predom-

[91] Black (1998), 91; Baldwin (1990).
[92] Black (1998), 78.
[93] Bardach (1982), 105–07.
[94] Black (1998), 91.
[95] McEwan and Maiman (1984).

inantly on the basis of coercion rather than consent, it thus reflects a paternalistic and interventionist state. Modes of resolution that are primarily consent-based are thus claimed to be associated with images of accommodation, conciliation, inclusiveness and participation.[96] Court adjudication, on the other hand, is alleged to be associated with notions of combat, hostility, formality, resistance and exclusion.[97]

2. Bargaining and the Rule of Law

Enthusiasm for dispute processing by means that do not involve the formal process of law is, however, far from universal. Richard Abel, one of the staunchest critics of the movement to introduce large scale ADR mechanisms in North America, argues that processes of 'informal justice' involve techniques of subtle manipulation in which the state is able to expand its apparatus of control over citizens.[98] Informal processes simply disguise rather than eliminate coercion, providing the forum in which the 'velvet glove has largely hidden the iron fist.'[99] In a similar vein, Auerbach claims that ADR techniques have operated in practice to disempower and exclude the socially disadvantaged.[100] It is the weak and the poor who are denied the opportunity to avail themselves of their formal legal rights which remain the domain of the bourgeois elite who can afford to invoke the formal process and protections of the law. These largely political objections are essentially grounded in deep-seated scepticism of the ability of methods of alternative dispute resolution to live up to their promises when translated into a world fraught with distributional inequalities.[101]

Both Abel and Auderbach acknowledge, however, that the values to which ADR aspires are nevertheless worthy of allegiance.[102] In this respect, Fiss's arguments 'against settlement' reach further still.[103] To him, '[t]o settle for something means to accept less than some ideal.'[104] Fiss's objections to settlement rest on a particular view of the proper function of adjudication. In his view, the purpose of adjudication is not merely to resolve disputes, but to explicate and give force to the authority of legal rules, to interpret the values upon which they are grounded and to bring reality into accord with them. Thus, when legal

[96] Auerbach (1983), 145; Genn (1993), 394. Such images provide part of the foundation for claims that a compliance strategy is more likely to be effective than a deterrence approach: Hawkins (1984), 127–28.

[97] Abel (1982), 271.

[98] *Ibid*, 5.

[99] *Ibid*, 270.

[100] Auerbach (1983), 145.

[101] Genn (1987); Menkel-Meadow (1993).

[102] Abel (1982), 309; Auerbach (1983), 145.

[103] Fiss (1984).

[104] *Ibid*, 1086.

disputes are resolved outside the court, this purpose is left wanting. For Fiss, informal non-adjudicative justice is justice denied.[105] As Luban has stated:

> . . . we can see why Fiss finds nothing to celebrate in settlements. When a case settles, it does so on terms agreeable to its parties, but those terms are not necessarily illuminating to the law or to the public. Indeed, those terms may be harmful to the public. Instead of reasoned reconsideration of the law, we often find little more than a bare announcement of how much money changed hands (often accompanied by a disclaimer of actual liability)—unless the settlement is sealed, in which case we don't even find that out. . . . A world without adjudication would be a world without public conversation about the strains of commitment that the law imposes.

Fiss's objections point to an inherent tension between the use of negotiation and bargaining as a mechanism of decision-making and dispute-resolution and the rule of law, objections which resonate strongly in the critiques of the North American collaborative compliance approaches to regulatory policy implementation alluded to in the preceding section.

One can readily anticipate objections to the underlying assumptions upon which Fiss rests his claims. Lacey has, for example, lamented the tendency of lawyers and legal scholars to conceptualise disputes in terms of the legal paradigm in which disputes are seen as calling for the resolution on the basis of given rules and according to the standards of due process.[106] At the heart of the legal paradigm is the central place occupied by the rule of law in liberal legal ideology, for it involves the ideal of subjecting areas of legally relevant activity to general standards which emphasises formal justice and the importance of rationality in the liberal world-view.[107] Because the resolution of disputes through negotiation is shaped by the reciprocal needs and interests of the parties worked out through their bargain, rather than dictated by legal rules, it can be seen as contrary to the rule of law ideal. This is not to say, however, that legal rules have no part to play in the resolution of disputes by negotiation. Rather, participants are claimed to bargain 'in the shadow of the law' so that the outcome ultimately agreed upon will be shaped and constrained by the strict legal rights and duties of the parties.[108] But when legal disputes are settled by agreement rather than by adjudication, the resulting agreement need not reflect that which would have resulted from court adjudication through the application of legal rules.[109]

How then is resort to bargaining and negotiation in relation to legal disputes to be evaluated? To insist upon the court adjudication of all legal disputes would surely be impossible to achieve in practice, even if we thought that such an ideal

[105] Twining observes that Fiss's objections largely mirror those of Bentham. Both share a common view of the proper function of adjudication—that is, to achieve the full implementation of substantive laws. Because compromise involves a departure from this ideal, both view compromise with deep suspicion: Twining (1993), 382–85.

[106] Lacey (1992), 362.

[107] *Ibid*, 367; Nonet and Selznick (1995), ch 3.

[108] Mnookin and Kornhauser (1979) *cf* Jacob (1992).

[109] Shapiro (1979), 173.

was worth pursuing. To deny the value of bargaining and negotiation is to fall into the clutches of the legal paradigm, and to overlook the insights of social science in recognising the limitations of rules and the worth of negotiation in overcoming those limits. Not only can resort to negotiation assist in the effective resolution of disputes, but can also further the public interest in promoting the value of participation, encouraging relationships of trust, and resolving conflict in a flexible, responsive, inexpensive and timely manner. On the other hand, there is some cogency in the objection to ADR techniques such as bargaining on the basis that they may circumvent the standards of the law. This points us to the critical question: what is the public interest in having the law applied in accordance with legal standards rather than as agreed between the parties?[110] What, if anything, is lost when legal disputes are resolved privately between participants which inevitably implies, in some if not all situations, a departure from the general standards embodied in authoritative legal rules?[111]

My suspicion is that this question cannot be answered outside of the particular social context in which it arises and may depend heavily on the nature and purpose of the legal standards allegedly departed from. In revisiting Fiss's opposition to settlements, Luban suggests that the issue of settlements should be redefined. Rather than being, as the title to Fiss's well-known article suggests, 'against settlements', we should seek to position ourselves 'against the wrong settlements'.[112] Thus, for example, the resolution of allegations of serious criminal wrongdoing by resort to private bargaining and negotiation between a prosecutor and accused person in which an innocent-accused agrees to a lesser punishment than that which might ordinarily attach to the relevant crime seems unquestionably illegitimate. This is primarily because the punishment of the innocent represents a gross violation of the rule of law and an unjustified infringement of fundamental human rights, even if it could plausibly be said that the innocent person 'consented' to her punishment. But the illegitimacy also stems partly from the fact that the standards of the criminal law might be thought of as embodying minimum moral standards of behaviour demanded by the community, so that to depart from such standards, or a failure to apply them correctly, is seriously to undermine the moral and social fabric of the law and legal institutions.[113] In a similar, albeit less striking way, it could be argued that

[110] Galligan (1996), 285; Genn (1987), 169.

[111] The matter is posed by Galligan thus: 'For while agreements engender legitimacy, there is a public interest in upholding certain standards, whether in civil, criminal or administrative spheres, which are beyond bargaining. In other words, there are other values originating in deeper social principles and which place constraints on the way negotiations should be conducted and on the extent to which issues should be resolved by agreement. But, it is often not clear just how the relationship between the value in agreement and other values should be formulated': Galligan (1996), 41.

[112] Luban (1995), 2647.

[113] Fuller claims that, although a large majority of criminal disputes are resolved extra-curially through plea bargaining and other like practices, the emphasis placed in open court on the criminal act is an important kind of symbolic tribute to the principle of judging the deed and not the person which is of 'vital importance'. He claims that if we ever completely lost from view the principle of legality, the rule of law would become an empty sham: Fuller (1981a), 245.

the acceptance of an administrative settlement by an innocent firm alleged to have contravened regulatory law, may involve an unacceptable departure from the rule of law. On the other hand, the resolution of a contractual dispute between two well-resourced and well-informed commercial parties by reference to agreement does not appear to pose difficulties of a similar magnitude, and would seem to provide a socially desirable means of resolving the conflict between them. The importance of context strongly suggests that, in evaluating the use of administrative settlements as a means of enforcing regulatory law, we must consider the use of bargaining between the state and citizen.

3. Regulatory Bargaining Between State and Citizen

Now that we have briefly considered some of the implications of resolving legal disputes through bargaining and negotiation, we are in a position to refine our inquiry for the purposes of evaluating the use of administrative settlements in regulatory enforcement proceedings. For present purposes, our focus is on the use of negotiation between the regulator and regulated in response to observed or suspected non-compliance by the latter. In the following discussion, I identify two particular sets of concerns that may arise whenever the state negotiates with citizens, and which are not necessarily confined to bargaining in the regulatory context. The first set of concerns refers to the potential for coercion, and the second relates to their potential threat to constitutional values.

(a) Coercion and Consent

In ideal terms, the essence of agreement is one that results from negotiations between two equally resourced and well-informed participants. In other words, where the parties to the negotiations are positioned in situations of broad equality, we can have confidence that the agreement is reached on a truly consensual basis. But where there is a serious inequality in the bargaining positions of the parties, be it in terms of resources, knowledge, or expertise, then our faith in the resulting agreement is reduced. It may well be that their agreement cannot fairly be regarded as resting on a meaningful notion of consent or voluntariness. Where the state negotiates with a citizen, there appears to be an inherent institutional imbalance between their respective bargaining positions. This may be particularly true in circumstances where the subject matter of the negotiations is one in which the state possesses a monopoly.

There are at least two regulatory contexts in which the regulator may appear to possess a monopoly of the relevant form. First, when the regulated is seeking to secure some benefit or privilege from the regulator, such as the grant of a licence to carry out the regulated activity or an exemption from regulatory requirements.[114] Secondly, in the process of enforcement in which the regulated

[114] Anthony (1992).

negotiates with the regulator in relation to its response to suspected non-compliance. In both contexts, the regulator appears to have the upper hand, with the regulated firm or person seeming largely at the mercy of the regulator, in the hope that the regulator's discretion will be exercised in its favour.[115] The regulator's advantageous position opens up the possibility of what Noah refers to as 'arm-twisting': a threat by a regulator to impose a sanction or withhold a benefit in the hope of encouraging 'voluntary' compliance with a request that the regulator could not insist upon directly from the entity.[116] He observes that while North American regulatory policy initiatives may be applauded as refreshingly innovative alternatives to typically inflexible regulations and enforcement policies, no doubt preferred by the firms involved, the same flexibility carries opportunities for abuse.[117]

But the image of a mighty regulator twisting the arm of a hapless firm is too simplistic and thus apt to mislead. We must bear in mind that in the regulatory context, the regulated firms include well-resourced and sophisticated commercial parties not easily 'bullied' into agreement. Furthermore, throughout the process of negotiation, both regulator and regulated will be acutely aware of the relevant legal rules in the shadow of which their bargaining occurs. At any time, either of the parties could insist on the strict application of the law by invoking the formal court process in order to determine the matter. Thus, for example, if the regulatory statute identifies a number of conditions allowing the relevant rules to be waived, then the regulator is likely to be hard-pressed to deny a waiver if the relevant conditions appear to have been met, particularly when faced with the possibility that the applicant may threaten to bring court proceedings to determine its entitlement. Likewise, where the regulator alleges that the suspect has failed to comply with regulatory rules and seeks to resolve the matter by way of negotiated settlement, the suspect who denies that it has so acted is at liberty to refuse a settlement so that the regulator is forced to proceed to the formal adjudicative process to establish the validity of its allegations. The regulator may well want to avoid doing so, in light of the potentially extensive drain that it places on its resources, particularly when faced with a sophisticated and well-endowed opponent.

That said, even sophisticated commercial parties may not have the stomach for expensive, protracted litigation and may therefore be willing to submit to an agreement with the regulator which does not strictly represent its legal entitlements, leading Noah to observe that:

> When private parties settle, they bargain 'in the shadow of the law' but when agencies bargain with regulated firms, it is less clear that the operate in the shadow of the law, in particular the constraint of power delegated by Congress. Arm-twisting succeeds,

[115] Abel (1982), 271.
[116] Noah (1997), 874.
[117] *Ibid*, 912.

> and evades judicial or other scrutiny, in part because companies in pervasively regulated industries believe that they cannot afford to resist agency demands.[118]

In other words, the regulated firm may face significant pressure to agree to a settlement with the regulator rather than risk a more severe regulatory response. In such circumstances, it may be difficult to characterise the resulting settlement as one based on consent. Whilst for some this may not pose any real difficulties, it should be borne in mind that one of the benefits of negotiation as a means of resolving disputes is claimed to rest in the consensual and mutual nature of the outcome agreed to. In the absence of true consent, a key public interest in resolving the dispute by agreement is largely negated.

The risk of coercion arises not only in relation to negotiations between the state and citizen, but it also plagues any regulatory strategy which accords a central role to deliberation and dialogue between participants with a view to reaching consensus, including Ayres and Braithwaite's dynamic pyramid of enforcement strategy.[119] For Ayres and Braithwaite, regulators will elicit effective consensual solutions to suspected non-compliance by regulated firms by deploying the threat of punishment to secure their co-operation. In responding to criticisms that punishment and persuasion involve incompatible imperatives, Braithwaite has recently made explicit the centrality of coercion in a responsive regulatory strategy, claiming that 'the question seems not one of how to avoid coercion, but how to avoid the escalation of coercion and how to avoid threats.'[120] He attempts to disarm critics who claim that such a strategy relies upon the unacceptable use of threats and coercion which will undermine the trust necessary to make co-operative strategies work by arguing that such fears will not materialise if the 'spectre of punishment lies in the background but never threatening in the foreground'.[121] But Braithwaite's claim that trust may be elicited 'in the shadow of the axe'[122] seems unconvincing, failing to grapple with the intractable problem of identifying at what point regulatory attempts to persuade firms to co-operate oversteps the margins of legitimate pressure into the realm of unacceptable coercion.[123]

How then are we to assess the magnitude of the risk of coercion when the state negotiations with citizens concerning the latter's suspected violation of the law? Once again, reliable generalisations are unlikely to be readily forthcoming, and sensitivity to context remains vital. So, for example, the risk of coercion

[118] Noah (1997), 912.
[119] Black (2000), 609–10.
[120] Braithwaite (2002), 34.
[121] *Ibid*, 36.
[122] *Ibid*.
[123] To some extent, Braithwaite's unease is reflected in his claim that 'the greatest challenge facing regulatory institutions . . . is to have the Sword of Damocles always threatening in the background but never threatened in the foreground . . . the trick is for deterrence to be always threatening but never threatened. It is to enculturate trust in regulatory interactions while institutionalising distrust though an enforcement system.' Braithwaite (2002), 120.

may be minimal when the regulator seeks to negotiate an administrative settlement with a large, well-resourced commercial firm, yet may loom very large when negotiating with an individual business person whose very livelihood depends upon his or her ability to continue practising her profession, which might be jeopardised by a formal finding of violation and consequent penal sanctions. In short, a variety of factors are likely to be relevant in assessing the risk of coercion, focusing on the respective bargaining positions of the parties, and the consequences for each party of a failure to secure agreement.

(b) Regulatory Bargaining and Constitutional Values

The risk associated with undue pressure being brought to bear on one or other participant engaged in the process of negotiation is not a risk unique to negotiations between state and citizen, but can also arise in relation to entirely private negotiations. Another set of concerns, resting on constitutional values, are perhaps unique and largely confined to bargaining between the state and citizen. These concerns relate to the constitutional values of both procedural and substantive fairness, and the importance of openness, transparency and accountability in public decision-making.

It may be recalled that one of the strengths of court adjudication as a tool of regulatory enforcement is that the court process is strictly regulated, the trial is held in full public view and the court provides a written, reasoned judgment explaining its decision. In terms of due process, it is in the formal court procedures that we find the most stringent and rigorous procedural safeguards, particularly in criminal cases. But bargaining and negotiation between the regulator and the regulated occurring outside the court process is largely a closed affair, typically hidden from public view. It may well be that the general public is completely unaware that a bargain has been struck and even in situations where the outcome of negotiations may be made public, the underlying reasons upon which the settlement is based may remain undisclosed. As Farber has observed,

> much important policy is made through regulatory inaction, settlement of litigation and other techniques that operate outside full public view . . . they take place in the shadow of the law, not in the light of public deliberation.[124]

When contrasted with court adjudication, then, resolving regulatory matters by way of private agreement between regulator and the regulated can reduce openness and transparency in decision-making. Excessive or undue resort to bargaining and negotiation in regulatory enforcement, particularly where the matters in issue are contentious and may have wide-ranging effects, are likely to expose the regulator to claims that it is inadequately accountable for its decisions.

[124] Farber (1999), 324.

The secretive nature of such negotiations raises additional concerns of due process and participation. Typically, the process of negotiation is confined to the regulator and the regulated, so that others whose interests may be directly and perhaps significantly affected by the outcome of such negotiations may be excluded from participation in the decision-making process. Because third parties are generally excluded from participation in the largely bilateral process of regulatory bargaining which occurs in the context of enforcement negotiations, there is a real risk that their interests may not be given due consideration despite the effects of the agreement upon them. Furthermore, extensive reliance on negotiation and bargaining between the regulator and the regulated may suggest that their relationship is rather too cosy, generating allegations that the regulator has been subject to 'capture.'[125] Due process concerns arising from the bargaining process are not, however, limited to the exclusion of third party interests. There is also a real risk that, in the absence of the kinds of formal procedural safeguards accompanying court adjudication, the negotiation process may be conducted in an unfair manner providing too much scope for the regulated party to be harassed or unduly pressured into agreeing to a bargain. It should be acknowledged, however, that the bargaining process is not entirely unregulated. The administrative law requirements of procedural fairness that apply to the exercise of power by public authorities would doubtless apply to such negotiations. But it seems highly implausible that the individual or firm in question would bring a legal challenge on the basis of alleged procedural unfairness once an agreement had been made, particularly given that one of the strong incentives driving it to agreement is its desire to avoid formal legal processes.

Finally, negotiation and bargaining between the regulator and regulated parties may threaten the constitutional values required by substantive fairness, particularly those of proportionality and consistency or equal treatment.[126] As we have seen, one reason why negotiation may be usefully employed in the regulatory context is that it can assist in overcoming the inherent limitations of rules by allowing regulatory responses to be tailored to the individual circumstances in a manner conforming to the underlying purpose or spirit of regulatory rules. But there are risks of inconsistency and unequal treatment involved in providing individuated regulatory responses. Because the content of the agreement made between the regulator and regulated is largely a product of their respective bargaining strengths and skills, there is considerably greater scope for inconsistent outcomes when comparisons are made across multiple regulatory agreements. Inconsistency in decision-making may not only generate the appearance of unfair treatment between different parties, but is also contrary to the fundamental value of equality before the law. For similar reasons, there is also a risk that the content of the agreement ultimately concluded between the regulator and regulated may be substantively unfair. The regulated firm may

[125] Baldwin *et al* (1998), 10–11; Baldwin (1987), 9–10.
[126] Sellers (1984)

agree to terms that may be a disproportionate response to the circumstances, or may not be rationally related to the conduct in question. Nonetheless, the regulated firm might be willing to agree to terms that might otherwise be considered unfair in order to have done with the matter and avoid the risks and associated cost, expense and adverse publicity that would ensue if the regulator invoked the formal legal process if no agreement was forthcoming.

D. CONCLUSION

The vast majority of complaints concerning suspected competition law violations are dealt with by informal means rather than by formal punitive measures. While there may be a wide range of reasons why a regulator may properly decide not to pursue a suspected violation through the formal legal process, this chapter has sought to explore the use of administrative settlements in which the regulator has reasonable grounds for suspecting that a contravention has or may occur, but agrees not to pursue more severe enforcement action in return for the suspect's agreement to act (or to forbear from acting) in a specified manner. Conceived as a form of regulatory tool or sanction, administrative settlements display a number of functional characteristics that may readily explain the frequency of their use: they provide regulators with a flexible and responsive means for securing compliance efficiently and effectively, individually tailored to meet the particular context in which the suspected violation occurs.

Viewed in terms of Ayres and Braithwaite's pyramid of enforcement, administrative settlements may be seen as a form of 'intermediate' sanction, lacking the degree of legal coercion, formality, publicity or expense typically associated with the use of court-ordered remedies secured through litigation, yet are more formal, costly, and public than informal cautions or warnings. Ayres and Braithwaite's depiction of regulatory sanctions and techniques may be supplemented, however, by considering their purposive dimension. Because administrative settlements rest on the parties' consent, rather than the coercive force of law underpinning the decision of a formal court order, they may be used to implement a broader range of social purposes than those appropriately secured by court ordered remedies. So, for example, administrative settlements may be a suitable vehicle for establishing arrangements involving on-going supervision by the regulator or some other form of third party participation, encouraging regulatory innovation, or raising public awareness through broad-based education and compliance programmes. But the consensual basis of administrative settlements also implies a freedom to depart from the standards of the law, suggesting that they are ill-suited to securing punitive aims, due to the risk of punishing those who have not in fact violated the law.

While the growing body of scholarship concerned to prescribe the 'optimal' techniques or strategies that should be adopted by regulators in securing compliance, including Ayres and Braithwaite's pyramid of enforcement, provides valuable insights concerning the efficacy of various enforcement tools and techniques, much of this literature is essentially technocratic in orientation. Although rarely made explicit, the predominant if not exclusive goal informing these accounts is that of effective and efficient enforcement, with typically little more than vague references to some unexamined notion of 'political acceptability'.[127] But in so doing, this literature reveals a worrying tendency to marginalise, if not overlook, several constitutional values. The constitutional values placed under the most significant strain are those of proportionality, consistency, transparency and due process. For example, by exhorting regulators to adopt a 'tit for tat' strategy in which the degree of punitiveness characterising the regulator's response is contingent upon suspect's co-operation with the regulator, Ayres and Braithwaite's pyramid of enforcement strategy appears to overlook the need for proportionality in the exercise of state power. Their suggested approach could result in those suspected of very grave regulatory violations being given light-handed treatment because of their full co-operation with the regulator, while those suspected of minor infringements would be subject to more punitive measures due to their refusal to co-operate.

This penchant for 'pragmatism' reflected in the tendency to focus heavily on the values of effectiveness and efficiency, exhibited throughout much of the literature concerning regulatory tools and techniques, is not, however, so evident in academic scholarship concerned with exploring notions of regulatory legitimacy as part of a broader enterprise in seeking to understand, explain and structure the regulatory process. For example, there have been increasing calls for deliberative, 'co-operative' approaches to regulation, with scholars seeking to emphasise the values of participation, dialogue and consensus in promoting regulatory legitimacy. While some commentators attach particular weight to these values because they are seen as instrumental in securing effective regulation,[128] others see them as intrinsically valuable and worthy of independent allegiance.[129] Because administrative settlements rest on some form of consensual arrangement between the regulator and suspect, they arguably exemplify a regulatory compliance technique built upon a deliberative foundation. By drawing from academic reflection concerning regulatory legitimacy to inform and supplement what has tended to be more technically focused scholarship concerning regulatory tools and techniques, I have attempted to adopt a more integrated approach in seeking to understand administrative settlements as a regulatory compliance tool, demonstrating that questions of regulatory strategy, technique and sanction cannot be seen as purely technocratic and value-neutral.

[127] Eg Gunningham and Grabosky (1998), 26. Ayres and Braithwaite are more explicit about the political vision which they claim informs their policy presumptions, describing their analysis as 'grounded both normatively and instrumentally in the tradition of civic republicanism' (at p 112) but nevertheless claim that '[r]eaders need not buy our politics to buy our ideas': Braithwaite and Ayres (1992), 17.

[128] Caldart (1999); Elliot (1997); Gangully (1998).

[129] Freeman (1997); Seidenfeld (2000).

Support for deliberative, co-operative approaches to regulation in general, and the use of co-operative compliance techniques in regulatory implementation in particular, has not, however, been universal. While some commentators express scepticism about their ability to secure regulatory compliance more effectively and efficiently than more traditional mechanisms of control, others object to deliberative, consensual approaches to regulatory implementation on the basis that they undermine a number of constitutional values upon which the legitimacy of the regulatory process is claimed to rest. This debate can be more fully understood by examining the underlying social process upon which co-operative compliance techniques (including administrative settlements), on the one hand, and more formal command and control techniques, on the other, are secured. When pursued to formal conclusion, command and control enforcement processes entail impartial adjudication involving the authoritative application of rules. In contrast, administrative settlements are arrived at following a process of bargaining and negotiation between the regulator and party under investigation resulting in some form of agreed settlement. It is the consensual foundations of administrative settlements that enable them to overcome some of the inherent limitations of rules, allowing the regulator to tailor its enforcement response to the individual circumstances of the case and thereby promote responsive, flexible and efficient enforcement. In the process of negotiating such settlements, however, there may be a real risk, particularly if there is a significant imbalance in the respective bargaining positions of the regulator and citizen, that any agreement between them may lack a genuinely consensual base.

Furthermore, there is an inescapable tension between the resolution of legal disputes by informal negotiated settlement and the formal conception of the rule of law, and it is this tension that informs some of the more pessimistic critiques of collaborative compliance techniques. When enforcement matters are resolved by negotiation, this may involve a departure from the authoritative standards of the law. Whether this is a serious cause for concern may depend on the context (particularly the nature and content of the legal standards departed from) and the frequency with which such bargaining occurs. In addition, because the process of negotiation is largely a private matter between the regulator and the regulated firm, it also poses risks for constitutional values that constrain the pursuit of regulatory goals. In particular, there may be a resulting loss of transparency, openness, participation, due process, proportionality and equality of treatment when disputes are resolved by reference to private negotiation rather than by public court adjudication. While these risks are unlikely to be so grave as to justify excluding bargaining and negotiation from the regulatory process, given their significant benefits, they nonetheless suggest that administrative settlements in regulatory enforcement should be used with care.

In the present context, the remaining challenge is to consider how to manage the tension between the virtues of bargaining and negotiation in regulatory enforcement with the potential threats that they may pose to the constitutional values referred to above. In particular, it might be argued that the presence of the suspect's informed consent to a settlement agreement with the regulator to resolve incidents of suspected non-compliance should serve to override the constitutional values identified as under strain. So, for example, why should there be any objection if the parties resolve suspected non-compliance by way of an administrative settlement on terms which exceed the limits of the relevant regulatory legislation, or which involve terms which are disproportionately broad or intrusive in scope? If such settlements result in effective outcomes, and given that the purpose of constitutional values is ultimately to protect citizens from the exercise of arbitrary state power, then if the regulated firm consents to the settlement, why should such settlements be a cause for concern? In short, does the pursuit of effective compliance trump constitutional values where it is supplemented by the parties' consent? My own view is that a generalised answer to this question cannot be given: context is vital. Accordingly, the following chapter sets out to illustrate in more concrete terms how administrative settlements may be used to secure responsive, flexible, tailored solutions in the course of enforcing Australian competition law, while illuminating the antagonism which they may pose for constitutional values, suggesting how that tension might fairly be resolved.

7

*Administrative Undertakings in Australian Competition Law Enforcement**

A. INTRODUCTION

WHILE THE PREVIOUS chapter explored the strengths and limitations of administrative settlements in regulatory enforcement from a largely abstract and theoretical perspective, this chapter seeks to make that discussion more concrete by examining the Commission's experience of utilising administrative settlements as a regulatory compliance tool. Like its counterparts responsible for enforcing EU and US antitrust law, the Commission resolves the vast majority of complaints concerning suspected competition law violations administratively, rather than through formal adjudicative proceedings.[1] The Commission's disposal of complaints administratively may take one of two forms. Those which it describes as 'simple administrative resolutions', typically consist of an informal warning, caution or advice from the Commission and secondly, unilateral court enforceable undertakings given by the firm or person under investigation to the Commission pursuant to section 87B of the Act, undertaking to act, or to refrain from acting, in an agreed manner ('enforceable undertakings'). Breach of an enforceable undertaking entitles the Commission to bring proceedings in the Federal Court seeking, amongst other things, orders directing the person to comply with the undertaking.[2] The power to accept enforceable undertakings thus constitutes a means by which the administrative settlements described in the previous chapter have become formalised and institutionalised in the public enforcement of Australian competition law, providing the Commission with a tool not previously within its enforcement armoury.[3] This chapter therefore subjects the Commission's use of enforceable undertakings to critical scrutiny, drawing upon the theoretical groundwork laid in the preceding chapter as the basis for evaluation. In so doing, it seeks to illustrate in

* The primary data upon from which this analysis is documented in Yeung (2001), and has been subsequently developed and updated to reflect the position as at 31 December 2002.

1 Above, ch 6, n. 1.

2 Trade Practices Act 1974, s 87B(3)–(4).

3 Trade Practices Act 1974, s 87B(1).

more concrete terms how enforceable undertakings, and therefore administrative settlements more generally, may constitute a flexible and responsive compliance tool while drawing into sharper focus some of the potential constitutional difficulties generated by their use.

When the Bill inserting section 87B into the Act was introduced, the then Attorney-General explained its underlying purpose in his Second Reading speech thus:

> It has proved efficient in some cases for the Commission to avoid prolonged litigation by accepting undertakings from businesses to cease particular conduct or to take action which will lessen the otherwise undesirable effects of their conduct. This approach has been used in appropriate cases for several years and has avoided considerable cost to both the Commission and the businesses concerned. At the same time the outcomes have been demonstrably advantageous to affected third parties and to consumers generally.
>
> Recognising the importance and desirability of affording the Commission a flexible approach to the resolution of trade practices matters, the Government has decided to provide legislative recognition of this practice. This will promote a greater public awareness of the range of options available in the administration and enforcement of the Act. By providing for the enforceability of undertakings, the scheme will remove the need to rely on means outside the Act to enforce undertakings that people have given, should this prove necessary.[4]

The Australian Parliament's intention of creating a flexible and efficient enforcement tool appears to have borne considerable fruit. A review of the Commission's public register of enforceable undertakings reveals that, not only have such undertakings been accepted by the Commission with increasing frequency since their inception in January 1993, but also demonstrates the considerable breadth and diversity in the nature and content of the undertakings so given.[5] Although the section 87B power has been available for 10 years, judicial guidance concerning their lawful scope and use is only just beginning to emerge.[6] Because enforceable undertakings were, at the time of their introduction, a relatively novel compliance tool in the Australian regulatory context, the Commission has had to develop its own practices and procedures to govern their use and, to this end, has been at the forefront of developing new and innovative means of responding to regulatory violations.[7] Indeed, the Commission's

[4] Official Hansard, The Parliament of Australia, House of Representatives, 3 November 1992, 2407–8.

[5] See Yeung (2001); Parker (2003) and below, Part C (1).

[6] *ACCC v Woolworths (South Australia) Pty Ltd* [2003] FCA 530; *ACCC v Signature Security Group Pty Ltd* [2003] FCA 375: *Australian Petroleum Pty Ltd v ACCC* (1997) 143 ALR 381. Some doubt concerning the constitutional validity of s 87B was raised by Lockhart J presiding in the Australian Competition Tribunal in *Re Queensland Independent Wholesalers Ltd* (1995) ATPR ¶41–458, 40,390. The legal requirements applicable to enforceable undertakings are discussed below at Part B.

[7] Its current approach to enforceable undertakings is briefly outlined in a published administrative guideline: ACCC, *Section 87B of the Trade Practices Act*, Procedural Guide Series, August 1999, available via the ACCC's website www.accc.gov.au. The first guideline was published in August 1995 and subsequently revised in August 1999.

use of enforceable undertakings was perceived by the Commonwealth Parliament as so successful that in July 1998 it subsequently conferred a similar power on the Australian Securities and Investment Commission (ASIC), to deal with suspected violations of companies and securities legislation and other Australian regulators have expressed interest in introducing them.[8] One might, however, question the basis upon which such a perception was founded, given that administrative undertakings had not then been the subject of systematic review or research from either governmental or academic quarters.[9] This book therefore provides a valuable opportunity for critical reflection concerning their use.

In order to identify how enforceable undertakings have been used by the Commission, I reviewed its public register of undertakings, which contains the full text of all enforceable undertakings (other than those which the Commission accepted on the basis that their contents would be kept confidential) between their inception from 1 January 1993 up to and including 31 December 2002, focusing solely on undertakings concerned with competition law infringements.[10] Several other sources were also consulted, including the Commission's confidential operations manual, which includes brief guidance to Commission staff concerning the circumstances in which enforceable undertakings may be contemplated, the Commission's published guideline concerning enforceable undertakings ('the Policy Guideline'),[11] the Commission's bimonthly journal (containing information concerning its recent enforcement activities) and the Commission's archive of electronic media releases.[12] On the basis of this material, it is possible to obtain a reasonably clear impression of the different purposes and contexts in which enforceable undertakings have been used, the various types of obligations which the Commission has accepted by way of undertaking and the Commission's perception of the range of factors guiding and informing their use. One of the limitations of this methodological approach is that it offers little insight into the actual process of negotiation, that is, how enforcement officials succeed in eliciting undertakings from suspected offenders and how the precise text and content of undertakings is arrived at.

[8] ASIC was empowered to accept enforceable undertakings in relation to its functions and powers with the enactment of the Financial Sector Reform (Amendment and Transitional Provisions) Act 1998, Schedule 1, which inserted s 93AA into the Australian Securities and Investment Commission Act 1989. The text of s 93AA of the 1989 Act is identical to the text of s 87B of the Trade Practices Act 1974. The Australian Broadcasting Authority and the Civil Aviation Safety Authority have expressed interest in having recourse to powers similar to those available to the Commission pursuant to s 87B: ALRC (2003), 590. Enforceable undertakings have long been used, and given statutory recognition, in UK competition regulation, see n. 161 below.

[9] Since that time, critical analysis and reflection has begun to emerge: Yeung (2001), ch 5; ALRC (2002), 587–610; Parker (2004).

[10] In addition to Part IV of the Act, which contains the competition law rules, the Commission may also accept enforceable undertakings in relation in the enforcement of other regulatory provisions which it is responsible for enforcing, such as consumer protection (see above, ch 2, Part C (2) for a discussion of the Commission's other statutory duties).

[11] Above, n 7.

[12] The Commission's media releases are available via www.accc.gov.au.

Nonetheless, because my aim was to identify and illustrate the normative tensions arising from the use of administrative settlements as a compliance technique, rather than to explore the behavioural dynamic between the Commission and those under investigation, information of this nature was not required.

This examination identified two quite different and distinct contexts in which enforceable undertakings have been accepted by the Commission in seeking to secure compliance with Part IV of the Act, around which this chapter is structured. First, they have been used for remedial purposes in response to suspected past contraventions ('remedial undertakings'), and secondly, they have been used as a prophylactic in relation to proposed mergers, with the aim of preventing mergers that may lead to a 'substantial lessening of competition' and therefore contravene section 50 of the Act ('merger undertakings').[13] Although the principles and general framework of analysis set out in the previous chapter apply to both types of undertakings, we might expect to find differences in the extent to which particular issues and tensions arise in each context. As we shall see, the use of merger undertakings has been particularly controversial, partly due to the greater likelihood that mergers will impact upon third parties when compared with their use in a remedial setting. Hence, the constitutional values of participation, due process, accountability and substantive fairness are likely to be more sharply implicated in relation to merger undertakings. On the other hand, because merger undertakings are generally used prophylactically, to prevent an anticipated contravention, rather than remedially in response to a past suspected contravention, there is perhaps less risk than in the former case that the undertakings will lack a firm consensual foundation. In other words, the risk that firms and individuals may be unfairly pressured into offering administrative undertakings is somewhat higher in relation to remedial undertakings than in circumstances where merger undertakings are offered.

Despite these differences in emphasis, both contexts illustrate very clearly how resort to bargaining and negotiation in regulatory enforcement facilitates individuated regulatory responses, overcoming the limits of legalistic adherence to rules and thereby encouraging flexible, responsive and efficient enforcement. On the other hand, they also demonstrate the inescapable antagonism between this cluster of regulatory goals that together contribute to securing effective compliance, and the constitutional values of transparency, accountability, participation and substantive fairness. We are thus faced with the task of identifying how to strike the appropriate balance between these two sets of concerns, so that the primary benefits of informal, co-operative solutions may be reaped without unduly encroaching upon the constitutional values in circumstances where enforceable undertakings are contemplated or accepted.

[13] Trade Practices Act 1974, s 50 prohibits mergers and acquisitions which would be likely to have the effect of substantially lessening competition in a market.

B. ENFORCEABLE UNDERTAKINGS AND LEGAL CONSTRAINTS

Before examining the Commission's use of enforceable undertakings, it is important to set out the legal parameters of its powers under section 87B, in the shadow of which such undertakings are accepted. One of the constitutional values identified in chapter three as delimiting the boundaries of legitimate attempts to secure compliance was the requirement that any such action must be 'authorised by law'. I noted, however, that identifying the line between authorised and unauthorised action may be difficult, particularly when the action in question is rooted in discretionary powers conferred on governmental authorities that often possess a breathtakingly broad compass. The Commission's power to accept undertakings pursuant to section 87B of the Act is an example of such a power, so that identifying its lawful scope requires both careful statutory interpretation and an understanding of administrative law doctrine.[14] While this task involves rather dry technical analysis, we should bear in mind that not only are these the kinds of tasks facing courts called upon to adjudicate regulatory disputes, but such analysis is an inextricable and essential requirement in ensuring adherence to the rule of law. While enforceable undertakings may be 'voluntary' in nature, they nonetheless serve as a legal constraint on private commercial activity, generating significant legal consequences and potentially significant costs and it is therefore important that they conform to legal requirements. Although the following discussion is Australian-specific, the general principles of Australian administrative law applicable to the exercise of the Commission's power broadly reflect those which apply across Commonwealth legal systems.

The primary reference point for ascertaining the legal scope of the power to accept enforceable undertakings is the Act itself, with section 87B(1) providing that:

> The Commission may accept a written undertaking given by a person for the purposes of this section in connection with a matter in relation to which the Commission has a power or function under this Act (other than Part X).

It is clear from the text of section 87B that the Commission has no legal power to compel individuals or firms to provide enforceable undertakings. Rather, its power is limited to 'accepting' enforceable undertakings, underlining their consensual nature. In practice, however, those under investigation are only likely to offer undertakings if they fear that a failure to do so may result in a more severe (in terms of formality and consequences) response from the Commission, which

[14] *Council of Civil Service Unions v Minister for the Civil Service* [1985] AC 374, 410 per Lord Diplock. In Australian administrative law, the grounds of review set out in the Administrative Decisions (Judicial Review) Act 1977, s 5 largely constitute a codification of the common law grounds of review, but are intended to allow room for judicial development: *Kioa v West* (1985) 159 CLR 550.

they will, as rational actors, be keen to avoid.[15] Section 87B thus institutionalises the process of bargaining between the Commission and those under investigation so as to agree on the Commission's response to a suspected contravention. To that extent, it may appear that the source of the Commission's power to accept enforceable undertakings is derived from its prosecutorial discretion combined with its common law power to contract, in forgoing court action and accepting an enforceable undertaking by way of settlement.[16] But although the practical source of the Commission's bargaining power may be derived from its discretionary power to prosecute, this does not alter the fact that the legal source of the Commission's power to accept administrative undertakings is derived directly from the Act.[17] The Commission is therefore unconstrained by the contractual doctrine of consideration in accepting administrative undertakings and it is consequently not obliged to provide reciprocal commitments to the person offering undertakings to ensure their legal enforceability.

But while the Commission may be liberated from the private law of contract to ensure the legal enforceability of such undertakings, its status as a public authority deriving its powers from the Act and the executive power of the Commonwealth[18] requires it to exercise its powers in accordance with constitu-

[15] *ACCC v Signature Security Group Pty Ltd* [2003] FCA 375.

[16] *Re Toohey; ex parte Northern Land Council* (1981) 38 ALR 439; *Padfield v Minister of Agriculture, Fisheries and Food* [1968] AC 997. It is unlikely that the Commission could rely on its common law power to contract in order to achieve outcomes which could not lawfully be pursued by way of enforceable undertaking, because the inherent contractual powers of public authorities are not unlimited and ultra vires contracts may be declared unenforceable by a court: *Hazel v Hammersmith BC* [1992] 2 AC 1; *Credit Suisse v Allderdale BC* [1996] 4 All ER 129. It is also arguable that the Commission's power to accept non-statutory undertakings by deed has now been subsumed by s 87B and has fallen into abeyance: *Attorney-General v De Keyser's Royal Hotel Ltd* [1920] AC 508. In *ACCC v Woolworths (South Australia) Pty Ltd* [2003] FCA 530, Mansfield J stated at para 48 'of course, the proffering and acceptance of undertakings under s 87B of the Trade Practices Act may not properly be described as a contractual arrangement.' In *Australian Petroleum Pty Ltd v ACCC* (1997) 73 FLR 75 Lockhart J explained how an undertaking accepted under s 87B derives its force from the section itself and is an 'instrument' under the Act.

[17] *Australian Petroleum Pty Ltd v ACCC* (1997) 73 FCR 75. In any event, the Commission's discretionary power to institute proceedings to enforce the Act is also subject to judicial review. For example, in *Visy Board Pty Ltd v TPC* (1984) 53 ALR 283 the applicant sought judicial review of the Commission's decision not to institute court proceedings seeking an injunction to restrain a takeover bid of the applicant's principal competitor. The Full Federal Court held that the Commission had not exceeded its powers in deciding not to pursue court action against the bidder, noting that the Commission has a wide discretion as to whether it institutes proceedings or not, which inevitably involve consideration of a wide range of matters. Furthermore, the court has an inherent jurisdiction to review the exercise and non-exercise of prosecutorial discretion in order to guard against an abuse of process, so that an undertaking by a public authority not to prosecute may be struck down by a court, although the courts are very reluctant to interfere with the exercise of prosecutorial discretion. See for example *DPP v B* (1998) 155 ALR 539. *Grimwade v State of Victoria* (1997) 90 A Crim R 526; *R v Brown* (NSW Court of Criminal Appeal, 20 October 1989).

[18] Constitution of the Commonwealth of Australia, s 61; *Thompson v Trade Practices Commission* (1979) 27 ALR 55; *Allied Mills v TPC* (1981) 34 ALR 105, 116. Whether or not a Commonwealth statutory authority exercises the executive power of the Commonwealth is a matter of academic debate. See Renfree (1984), 324 cf *Australian Film Commission v Mabey* (1985) 59 ALR 25.

tional and administrative laws. While the Federal Court has acknowledged that the Commission has a wide discretion in carrying out its functions and duties, it has described the Commission as 'the guardian of the various public interests which the Act is intended to preserve and protect' and thus not free to act 'unlawfully, in bad faith, or otherwise beyond its powers'.[19] Although section 87B is drafted in exceptionally broad terms, it does not follow that the Commission's power to accept administrative undertakings is unlimited. As Mansfield J recently observed in *ACCC v Woolworths (South Australia) Pty Ltd*[20]

> . . . it may be expected that the circumstances where the terms of an undertaking are ex facie beyond the power of the ACCC to have accepted will be very rare. Nevertheless, the point to be made is that the Court should not sit idly by when it is apparent that an undertaking to engage in a proposed course of conduct, or an undertaking to refrain from a proposed course of conduct, does involve a commitment to the ACCC beyond that which its powers permit it to have accepted.

In democratic states, the power conferred on public authorities is subject to legal and constitutional constraints[21] which, if flouted, may lead to their decisions being impugned by the courts following an application for judicial review. Judicial review, and the principles of administrative law setting out the grounds for review, ensures that public authorities exercise their powers within their legal limits, facilitating accountability in the exercise of administrative power and ultimately serving to protect citizens from unlawful and excessive governmental action.[22]

In Australia, the availability of judicial review by the Federal Court arises either under the Administrative Decisions (Judicial Review) Act 1977 ('ADJR Act'), (which empowers the Court to review the legality of administrative decisions made under any Commonwealth enactment) or section 39B of the Judiciary Act 1903, enabling the Court to review the legality of action taken by an officer of the Commonwealth by means of the prerogative writs.[23] The Federal Court also has jurisdiction pursuant to section 163A of the Trade Practices Act 1974 to make a declaration or prerogative order in relation to the validity of any acts done or purported to be done under the Act on the application of a person in relation to a matter arising under the Act.[24] Administrative law principles thus circumscribe the proper limits of the Commission's power to accept enforceable undertakings, three of which are of particular relevance for

[19] *Visy Board Pty Ltd v TPC* (1984) 53 ALR 283.

[20] [2003] FCA 530, para 48.

[21] Public power is also subject to non-legal and political constraints, but this book is primarily concerned with the legal dimension of enforcement and thus focuses on constraints of a legal nature: Above ch 1 and ch 3, Part B.

[22] Administrative Review Council (1989), 5.

[23] Order 54A of the Federal Court Rules 1979 enables the applicant to seek relief under s 39B of the Judiciary Act and under the ADJR Act in the same application.

[24] For example, *Re Tooth & Co Ltd (No 2)* (1978) FLR 112.

this inquiry: the duty to act for proper purposes, the requirement of procedural fairness and the doctrine of proportionality.

First, the 'proper purposes' doctrine limits the exercise of administrative power to the pursuit of the purpose or purposes for which the power was conferred, the primary reference point being the statute from which the power is derived. Thus, although the Commission's power to accept administrative undertakings may appear unlimited, it is lawfully restricted to accept them only 'in connection with a matter in relation to which it has a power or function under the Act (other than Part X)'.[25] Because the Commission's primary function under the Act is to enforce and administer its provisions, this indicates that undertakings may only be accepted as part of the Commission's statutory function of securing compliance with the Act and therefore only in response to evidence of a specific contravention of the Act. The proper purposes doctrine, when read with the text of section 87B, indicates that enforceable undertakings are essentially 'negative' enforcement tools to be used primarily in response to specific violations rather than positively to encourage compliance in a proactive manner. In other words, such undertakings are more accurately characterised as 'sticks' rather than 'carrots'[26] to redress specific contraventions of the Act.

Furthermore, we saw in the previous chapter that different enforcement tools and instruments may be more suitable for securing particular social purposes but not others. In this respect, we also noted that although administrative settlements may be suited to achieving a broad range of social purposes, they were unsuited to achieving punitive ends. As a form of administrative settlement, this suggests that the use of enforceable undertakings to punish suspected offenders is unlikely to constitute a 'proper purpose', a conclusion reinforced by the constitutional doctrine of separation of powers. In interpreting the Australian Constitution, the Australian High Court has repeatedly affirmed that executive agencies are constitutionally procluded from using their power for punitive purposes because this involves an exercise of judicial power.[27] Accordingly, administrative undertakings cannot lawfully be used to punish suspects, either to secure general deterrence or as means of securing retribution.[28]

[25] Trade Practices Act 1974, s 87B(1).

[26] Brigham and Brown (1980).

[27] *NSW Bar Association v Evatt* (1968) 117 CLR 177; *Huntington v Atrrill* (1893) AC 150.

[28] In identifying the 'proper purposes' of enforceable undertakings, some assistance may be gleaned from the ALRC report on compliance with the Act, which specifically considered the role of administrative enforcement. The report acknowledged that while administrative action is often quicker and cheaper than judicial action, there are constitutional limits: ALRC (1993), 82. The ALRC therefore recommended that the Act should state clearly what the purposes of administrative action should be, and recommended that the Act should therefore be amended to make it clear that administrative action undertaken by the Commission should be taken to achieve one or more of the following purposes: (i) to compensate those who have suffered loss or damage as a result of the contravention; (ii) to undo the effects of the contravention, both immediately and in the longer term, and to promote and encourage community-wide compliance with the Act; and (iii) to prevent future contraventions of the Act. The ALRC's recommendations were concerned with administrative action taken in relation to suspected contraventions of Part V, which concerns consumer protection. Nonetheless, the ALRC's recommendations are equally applicable to administrative action taken in relation to Part IV of the Act.

Secondly, in Australian administrative law the doctrine of proportionality limits the exercise of constitutional or statutory power that is 'purposive' in nature.[29] Given that the section 87B power to accept enforceable undertakings may be regarded as purposive (in that its primary purpose is to respond to suspected contraventions of the Act) then the proportionality doctrine may therefore apply. As we have already noted, the test of proportionality is not a broad, freestanding test, but must be applied to the circumstances in which the question arises. Although administrative undertakings are given 'voluntarily', it would be somewhat misleading to describe them as entirely consensual in that no person would rationally offer such undertakings unless faced with a realistic threat of more severe action against them if they failed to do so.[30] In this respect, the proportionality doctrine circumscribes the scope and content of administrative undertakings which the Commission may fairly accept,[31] so that the obligations accepted should be reasonably proportionate to the seriousness of the suspected contravention and go no further than necessary to secure compliance with the Act.[32]

Thirdly, the administrative law doctrine of procedural fairness requires that decision-makers must not be biased in making decisions, and that those affected by the decision are given a fair opportunity to be heard.[33] An undertaking accepted in circumstances falling short of the requirements of procedural fairness may be impugned in judicial review proceedings.[34] In the present context, procedural fairness would seem to require that all those subject to its investigations are properly informed of the nature of the complaint being investigated, provided with reasons for the investigation, and given an opportunity to respond to any allegations against them. Following investigation and due consideration of any such submissions, if the Commission considers that it is appropriate to request enforceable undertakings, it ought first to ensure that the relevant party is informed of the purpose and legal consequences of such undertakings. Good administrative practice might also suggest that the Commission advise firms that they are not legally obliged to offer such undertakings, but failure to do so may result in further enforcement action (which may include

[29] The principle of proportionality does not provide a separate ground of review in Australian constitutional and administrative law, but applies only to constitutional and statutory powers that are purposive in nature: Selway (1996), 217; *South Australia v Tanner* (1989) 166 CLR 161, 164–65 and 174–79.

[30] Below, Part C (2) (b) (ii).

[31] *South Australia v Tanner* (1989) 166 CLR 161; *The Commonwealth v Tasmania (the Tasmanian Dam Case)* (1983) 158 CLR 1, 260.

[32] In *ACCC v Woolworths (South Australia) Pty Ltd* [2003] FCA 530 the Federal Court indicated that it would be inappropriate to take judicial notice of enforceable undertakings offered in settlement of litigation where it may be clear that the Commission has no power to accept them 'in connection with a matter in relation to which it has a power or function'. But, in interpreting this requirement, it stated that 'the extent of the requisite connection between the undertaking and the contravening conduct might be broader than that required by a Court when granting judicial orders' at para 53–58.

[33] Cane (1996); Craig (1999), chs 8–9.

[34] *The Hospital Benefit Fund of WA Inc v ACCC* (1997) ATPR ¶41–569.

the institution of court proceedings) if there are sufficient grounds to justify such action.

In addition to judicial review, legal constraints on the exercise of the Commission's power to accept enforceable undertakings arise directly from the Act itself. Although the Commission has exceptionally wide discretion in deciding whether to accept undertakings offered to it pursuant to section 87B, it cannot impose sanctions for violation of any undertakings so given. Rather, the Commission must approach the Court seeking an order directing compliance with the undertaking pursuant to section 87B(4) of the Act. Although there are only a handful of cases on record in which the Commission has commenced action seeking an order for compliance, the Federal Court has made it clear that it will not automatically defer to the Commission's judgement on the legality of the undertakings accepted, or whether the terms of the undertaking so given have been breached and/or should be subject to an order for compliance. Thus, in *ACCC v Woolworths (South Australia) Pty Ltd*[35] the Federal Court stated that it would refuse orders to enforce compliance with an undertaking if it was clearly beyond the power of the Commission to accept. However, it was willing to accord the Commission a very long leash in ascertaining the scope of its own power to accept enforceable undertakings, stating that it will take judicial notice of such undertakings provided that they do not 'clearly' fall outside the Commission's powers. Where uncertainty arises about the legal validity of enforceable undertakings, the Court will resolve the matter in the Commission's favour unless and until an order for compliance is sought.[36]

C. REMEDIAL UNDERTAKINGS

Now that we have a firmer understanding of the legal constraints circumscribing the proper deployment of enforceable undertakings, we are better placed to examine how they have been used in practice and assess whether that practice conforms with legal principles. The following discussion therefore proceeds by first, describing the different kinds of commitments accepted by the Commission when using enforceable undertakings as a remedial tool and secondly, sets out to assess whether the Commission's use of such undertakings falls within the proper legal and constitutional boundaries described above.

1. Types of Remedial Undertakings

A review of all the undertakings relating to Part IV of the Act published in the Commission's register during the relevant review period, indicated that remedial undertakings could be classified into seven broad categories:

[35] [2003] FCA 530.
[36] *Ibid*, para 42.

a) Cease and desist undertakings: enforceable undertakings often included commitments by the party issuing the undertaking to cease and forbear from engaging in specified conduct, in accordance with the Policy Guideline which states that '[t]he foundation of all undertakings accepted by the Commission must be a positive commitment to cease the particular conduct and not to recommence it.'[37] So for example, a vehicle repair firm gave undertakings to the Commission following an investigation into a suspected attempt to induce a competitor to engage in market rigging in breach of section 45 (prohibition on price fixing and anti-competitive agreements) requiring it to cease and desist from engaging in such conduct in the future.[38]

b) Compliance program undertakings: Remedial undertakings often require the firm under investigation to develop a comprehensive internal trade practices compliance programme, typically requiring it to review its operating procedures, to identify areas where risks of non-compliance arise and to develop and implement a comprehensive firm-wide compliance programme, including provision for regular review, internal accountability and independent audit of the effectiveness of the programme. The content of such trade practices compliance programmes is typically broad in scope, encompassing all the relevant provisions of the Act, not merely the statutory prohibition allegedly contravened.[39] During the course of the review period, Australian Standard AS3806 on Compliance Programs was developed and published, providing a benchmark standard for compliance programs generally.[40] The Commission's Policy Guideline was revised in 1999, refining the Commission's general approach to enforceable undertakings in several respects, including a statement that the Commission will 'normally expect the company concerned to use the Australian Standard on Compliance Programs AS3806 in the design and implementation of its compliance programs' as well as specifying the elements which the Commission would ordinarily require for inclusion in compliance programme undertakings.[41]

c) Compensation undertakings: If investigations reveal that a suspected breach has caused direct loss to third parties, the Commission has sometimes sought undertakings from the responsible firm requiring compensation to be paid to those so harmed. This is in keeping with the Policy Guideline, which states that in resolving any matter '[o]f paramount concern will be mechanisms for compensation, reimbursement or

[37] Policy Guideline, 6.

[38] S 87B undertaking accepted by the ACCC from Baldwin's Tractor and Truck Wreckers Pty Ltd, D00/3427 on 12 July 1999.

[39] For example, a local council gave enforceable undertakings to the Commission following in investigation into a suspected breach of s 47 (prohibition on third line forcing) alleged to consist of imposing contractual requirements on kerb-side collectors of recyclable materials to sell materials to nominated buyers. The Council admitted the contravention and undertook to implement a substantial compliance programme encompassing all its obligations under the Act, including an obligation to subject its compliance programme to an annual independent audit for a three year period: S 87B undertaking accepted from Canterbury City Council, D00/13685 on 24 May 2000.

[40] See Carroll and McGregor-Lowndes (2001).

[41] Policy Guideline, 7. Some compliance undertakings accepted by the Commission specifically state that the compliance programme must comply with AS3806, but others do not. For example, the sole distributor of Cartier Group products in Australia gave enforceable undertakings to the Commission following investigations into suspected resale price maintenance in breach of s 48, including an undertaking to provide a trade practices compliance programme for its employees at its own expense that will comply with AS3806: S 87B undertaking accepted from LMC Pacific Pty Ltd and Giles Haumont D00/42330 on 4 December 2000.

other appropriate forms of redress for parties adversely affected by the conduct.'[42] So for example, several obstetricians gave enforceable undertakings to the Commission following allegations that they had agreed not to provide private in-hospital obstetrics services on a 'no gap' billing basis to their privately insured patients, in breach of section 45 (prohibition on price fixing and anti-competitive agreements). These undertakings required them, amongst other things, to notify patients affected by the arrangement, reimbursing them for the gap payment that they were required to make as a result.[43]

d) Corrective undertakings: Some undertakings have sought to 'correct' the effects of an alleged contravention by seeking to reproduce the state of affairs that would have prevailed had the contravention not occurred. As the Commission notes in its Policy Guideline, 'forms of corrective action will be dictated by the circumstances of the breach'[44] such as publicly advertising that those with whom the suspected offender deals are not bound by any restrictive obligations previously imposed upon them. For example, an importer and distributor of archery products gave enforceable undertakings to the Commission following allegations that it had breached section 48 (prohibition on resale price maintenance), requiring it, amongst other things, to write to all its customers within 21 days, notifying them that it does not in any way seek to control the prices at which products supplied by it are sold to their customers, and that retailers were free to sell the product supplied at any price they wished.[45]

e) Community service undertakings: Several enforceable undertakings have sought not only to secure future compliance by the specific firm under investigation, but also to promote awareness of the Act by those in the industry in which the firm operates.[46] The Policy Guideline describes such undertakings as 'community service undertakings', containing 'novel requirements, in the nature of community service orders, which the courts have not usually ordered as the result of litigation'.[47] These undertakings typically require the suspect firm to develop, implement and fund industry wide education programmes so as to raise community awareness of the Act,[48] akin to those offered by a veterinary pharmaceuticals manufacturer in return for the Commission's agreement to discontinue seeking pecuniary penalties against it and agreeing to consent injunctions.[49] These undertakings included a commitment from the firm to produce and send to all veterinary surgeons in Australia a pocket Trade Practices Act checklist pamphlet and a letter advising them that they were free to decide for themselves the price at which the company's products were to be advertised and sold. The company also undertook to implement and fund an industry-wide program to promote a greater awareness of trade practices, including the provision of

[42] Policy Guideline, 6.
[43] S 87B undertaking accepted by the ACCC from Dr Mark Leyddon D0/58400 on 30 October 2002; S 87B undertaking accepted by the ACCC from Dr Paul Khoo and Paul P T Khoo Pty Ltd D02/53768 on 9 October 2002.
[44] Policy Guideline, 6.
[45] S 87B undertaking given to the ACCC by Archery Wizard Australia D01/23273, 13 July 2001.
[46] ACCC Annual Report 1995–6, 7; Policy Guideline, 8.
[47] Policy Guideline, 6.
[48] Policy Guideline, 8; Tamblyn (1993), 156.
[49] S 87B undertaking accepted by the ACCC from Rhone Merieux Australia Pty Ltd, 19 June 1996.

seminars and presentations.[50] More recent undertakings of this nature have required the firm under investigation to pay donations of a sum estimated to represent the size of the suspect's unlawful gain to a nominated charity, including a licensed club agreeing to donate $A 150,000 to an alcohol reduction, education and rehabilitation programme after it admitted engaging in unlawful price fixing in relation to the sale of alcohol, while also consenting to court injunctions and declarations to refrain from future unlawful conduct of this nature.[51]

f) Supply undertakings: Even outside the merger context, remedial undertakings have been used occasionally to oblige the firm under investigation to supply particular goods or services to other specified firms or classes of firms. For example, in response to the Commission's allegations that it had breached section 46 (misuse of market power) by refusing to supply data to a competitor, a telecommunications firm undertook to provide access to its commercial customer information database to interested third parties on certain specified terms (including price).[52] Similarly, a newspaper publisher gave enforceable undertakings to the Commission following allegations that it had breached section 46 (misuse of market power) by refusing to accept classified advertisements in its newspapers if they contained references to internet addresses or internet classified sites. The undertakings included obligations that the firm would establish a separate classified advertisement category for internet classified services and internet services and requiring the firm to accept any advertisement other than in the 'internet classified services' category provided that, if more than 15 per cent of the proposed advertisement consists of the advertiser's website or email address, the firm may elect to publish it in the general news or business pages of the newspapers on the advertising terms applicable to those newspaper sections.[53]

g) Investigation cost recovery undertakings: A significant number of the enforceable undertakings included an obligation to pay the Commission a sum of money to cover its investigation costs. In a large majority of these cases, the Commission accepted such undertakings in addition to pursuing the suspected contravention through the formal court enforcement process. In such cases, the obligation to pay costs typically formed part of the settlement package agreed between the Commission and the firm or individual offering the undertaking, resulting in both parties asking the Court to make consent orders agreed to by the parties in resolving the proceedings. In some cases, the specific sum payable is specified in the undertaking[54] while in others, the

[50] ACCC Annual Report 1996–7, 24. S 87B undertaking accepted by the ACCC from Rhone Merieux Australia Pty Ltd, 19 June 1996.

[51] S 87B undertaking accepted by the ACCC from Arnhem Club Incorporated, 8 May 2002. Judicial notice of these undertakings was given in *ACCC v Woolworths (South Australia) Pty Ltd* [2003] FCA 530.

[52] ACCC Digest, March 1998, para 10–1130.

[53] S 87B undertaking accepted by the ACCC from Queensland Newspapers Pty Ltd D02/64684 on 1 December 2002.

[54] For example, manufacturers and distributors of water supply equipment gave enforceable undertakings to the Commission as part of a broader settlement agreement relating to court proceedings brought against them by the Commission for alleged price fixing and bid rigging in which the firm undertook, amongst other things, to pay $10,000 towards the Commission's costs: S 87B undertaking accepted by the ACCC from Geoffrey Colin Clegg, Geoff Clegg Enterprises Pty Ltd (formerly Watergear Distributors Pty Ltd) D00/28491, 23 August 2000).

undertaking states that the sum payable will be determined between the parties as part of the settlement and resolution of the formal court proceedings.[55]

2. An Evaluation of Remedial Undertakings

The breadth and diversity of remedial undertakings evident from the range of undertakings accepted by the Commission in resolving suspected competition law violations clearly demonstrates the value of administrative settlements in providing a means by which regulatory officials can respond flexibly and creatively to suspected contraventions, tailoring them to suit the circumstances arising in individual cases. But while the potential benefits of enforceable undertakings are readily identifiable, further pause for reflection suggests that our endorsement of their value as a regulatory compliance tool should not be wholly unequivocal.

(a) Remedial Undertakings as Regulatory Sanctions

The categories of remedial undertakings accepted by the Commission and the contexts in which they have been accepted not only demonstrates their utility in the enforcement process, but also sheds light on the nature of administrative settlements as a regulatory compliance tool. When used as a substitute for litigation, enforceable undertakings may be characterised as a form of 'middle-ground' sanction, located half-way up Ayres and Braithwaite's pyramid of enforcement, involving less formality, coercive force, severity, time, expense, and publicity than court-ordered sanctions yet entail greater formality, cost and transparency than simple administrative resolutions.[56] But in the previous chapter we also observed that the enforcement pyramid imagery tends to overlook the distinct, although often overlapping, social purposes for which different enforcement tools may best be suited, because it takes its colour from the 'punishment versus persuasion' dialectic, characterising regulatory tools and sanctions in a largely hierarchical manner based largely on their punitive nature. Although some enforcement instruments may appropriately be used to secure the same or similar purposes, and may therefore be regarded as directly substitutable (albeit varying in the degrees of strength, severity, formality and expense associated with their use) this cannot fairly be said of all enforcement tools and sanctions. This is borne out by the different circumstances or contexts in which the Commission has accepted remedial undertakings.

[55] For example, the Commission instituted court proceedings against a natural gas supply firm seeking injunctions to restrain it from exercising pre-emptive rights arising under a gas purchase agreement, alleging that this would breach s 45 (prohibition on anti-competitive agreements). The firm agreed to settle the court proceedings by offering enforceable undertakings encompassing various obligations, including an undertaking to pay the Commission's costs 'as agreed': S 87B undertakings accepted by the ACCC from Gasgo Pty Ltd, DG99/1201 on 14 October 1999.

[56] Above, ch 6, Section B (2).

While the Commission has used them as a form of intermediate sanction, so that, for example, 'cease and desist' undertakings might be seen as more informal and less severe than a court injunction but may achieve the same objective in securing the termination of unlawful conduct,[57] it has also used enforceable undertakings more broadly and creatively. As we saw in the previous chapter, because courts are generally unwilling to grant orders which are likely to require on-going monitoring or supervision of the offender's behaviour, there are some social purposes which cannot be readily achieved by court order. In contrast, the flexibility and width of the power to accept enforceable undertakings has enabled the Commission to accept undertakings in conjunction with formal court enforcement proceedings to achieve outcomes, such as the recovery of investigation costs or the implementation of broadly-based community service programmes, that could not be secured by way of court order. In other words, enforceable undertakings have not only been used as a substitute for litigation, but also as a supplement to the formal court process and, less commonly, to settle litigation.

In particular, the Commission has often accepted enforceable undertakings in conjunction with litigation in which the offender undertakes to implement a comprehensive trade practices compliance programme of a standard regarded by the Commission as acceptable. So for example, in one price fixing case, the offenders admitted their unlawful conduct, submitted to consent injunctions and negotiated penalties, and also gave enforceable undertakings to the Commission to develop and implement comprehensive internal trade practices compliance programmes.[58] It is clear from *ACCC v Z Tek Computers Pty Ltd*[59] that a court would not have granted injunctions requiring the implementation of such extensive compliance programmes, on the basis that the nexus between the offender's contravention (which only concerned Part IV of the Act) and the scope of the compliance programme (which also encompassed the consumer protection provisions contained in Part V of the Act) was too remote. For similar reasons it is unlikely that a court would be prepared to grant court orders embodying the kinds of obligations encompassed in community service undertakings, particularly those involving the making of substantial donations by the firm alleged to be in contravention of the Act to nominated recipients who were not directly affected by the alleged contravention, a conclusion reinforced by Mansfield J's observations when asked to provide judicial notice of the

[57] ACCC Annual Report 1996–7, 3.

[58] For example, several NSW-based model agents gave enforceable undertakings to the Commission following court proceedings as part of a settlement with the Commission in which the model agents admitted to engaging in price fixing in relation to the price of service fees charged to clients. Undertakings accepted from Hirere Pty Ltd (trading as Vivien's Model and Theatrical Management), 14 November 1996; Gordon Charles Management Pty Ltd, 26 November 1996; Chadwicks Model Agency Pty Ltd, 14 November 1996; Priscilla's Model Management Pty Ltd, 27 November 1996 and Cameron's Model Management Pty Ltd, 29 April 1997; *ACCC v Chadwicks Model Agents Pty Ltd & Ors*, (Federal Court of Australia, 29 November 1996).

[59] (1997) FCR 197. Below, Section (2)(b).

undertakings offered by The Arnhem Club which was alleged to have engaged in unlawful price fixing in the Nhulunbuy take-away alcohol market in breach of section 45 of the Act.[60] The undertakings included an obligation to 'donate $150,000 to an alcohol harm reduction, prevention, education or rehabilitation program in Nhulumby and the surrounding communities, being a program identified as suitable by the applicant on advice from the Commonwealth Department of Health and Aged Care'.[61] In that case, Mansfield J observed that such obligations would probably be beyond the scope of the Court's power in section 86C(4)[62] to accept 'community service orders' since the requisite relationship between the obligation and the contravening conduct was not present.[63]

(b) Remedial Undertakings: Legal Principles and Constitutional Values

By considering the Commission's use of remedial undertakings, viewed in light of the Commission's Policy Guideline, it is possible to make a tentative assessment of the extent to which the Commission's general practice conforms with the legal requirements set out in section 2. This assessment is merely tentative, because a firmer evaluation would necessitate a thorough and comprehensive audit of all the Commission's enforcement files to evaluate whether the Commission had in fact complied with the law in every case, a task well beyond the limited purposes of this inquiry. The aim of the following discussion is more modest, setting out to illustrate in a more tangible fashion the strengths of bargaining and negotiation as a response to unlawful conduct and the strain they may place on several constitutional values.

(i) Proper Purposes

In section 2 we noted that the application of the proper purposes doctrine to the Commission's power under section 87B of the Act generates at least two conditions for its lawful exercise: first, it is to be used primarily in response to

[60] Above, n 51 and associated text.

[61] *ACCC v Woolworths (South Australia) Pty Ltd* [2003] FCA 530 referring to s 87B undertaking accepted by the ACCC from the Arnhem Club Incorporated, 8 May 2002.

[62] S 86C(4) of the Act provides that 'In this section: community service order, in relation to a person who has engaged in contravening conduct, means an order directing the person to perform a service that:

(a) is specified in the order; and
(b) relates to the conduct;

for the benefit of the community or a section of the community.
Example: The following are examples of community service orders:

(a) an order requiring a person who has made false representations to make available a training video which explains advertising obligations under this Act; and
(b) an order requiring a person who has engaged in misleading or deceptive conduct in relation to a product to carry out a community awareness program to address the needs of consumers when purchasing the product.'

[63] *ACCC v Woolworths (South Australia) Pty Ltd* [2003] FCA 530 para 54.

evidence of suspected contraventions of the Act and secondly, it may not be used to punish offenders. The Policy Guideline clearly reflects a firm commitment to viewing the purpose of administrative undertakings primarily as a means for responding to suspected contraventions of the Act, a view reinforced by the Commission's policy of refusing to accept such undertakings except where there is a breach of the Act that would otherwise justify litigation.[64] The various contexts in which administrative undertakings have been accepted, as a substitute for litigation, to supplement litigation or to settle litigation, appear largely consistent with this characterisation.

Not only has the width of section 87B enabled enforceable undertakings to be accepted in a variety of contexts, but it has also provided the Commission with scope to pursue a range of distinct social purposes in securing their acceptance. To this end, the Policy Guideline sets out four broad objectives that the Commission seeks to secure in negotiating them: cessation of the conduct leading to the alleged breach, redress for parties adversely affected by the conduct, implementation of compliance measures to help prevent future breaches by the business concerned, and by means of publicity, an educative and deterrent effect in the community at large and in particular in the industry concerned.[65] Apart from investigation cost recovery undertakings, each of the various types of remedial undertaking identified in my review seem to conform to these objectives, and, with the exception of the fourth objective, the Commission's stated objectives appear to fall clearly within its lawful authority.

Of the seven kinds of undertaking identified from my review, cease and desist undertakings, compensation undertakings, corrective undertakings, supply undertakings and compliance programme undertakings may all be seen as broadly restorative in nature, by bringing about the termination of conduct that may threaten to violate the Act and to place those affected by the suspected contravention in the position they would have been in had the contravention not occurred. While the restorative character of cease and desist undertakings, compensation undertakings and supply undertakings is readily apparent, this may not be so obvious in relation to compliance programme undertakings. These undertakings may also be seen as 'rehabilitative' as well as restorative, seeking to 'rehabilitate' the suspected contravenor, setting out to transform it from a non-compliant firm into a compliance-friendly firm, and they may thus be regarded as the administrative equivalent of court-imposed 'corporate probation or supervisory orders'.[66] While corporate probation orders may have

[64] Policy Guideline, 4.

[65] Policy Guideline, 3.

[66] Such orders were considered by the ALRC in its review of compliance with the Act. The ALRC identified the following advantages of corporate probation orders: their flexibility allows them to be individually tailored to the needs of the specific firm; they are likely to promote individual accountability of firm employees and management; they are likely to induce organisational change to avoid repetition; they can be more effective in inducing compliance by subsidiary corporations; and they avoid the 'deterrence trap' which may be associated with financial penalties: ALRC (1994), 72.

punitive effects if they are excessively wide in scope, their primary purpose might be more aptly classified as remedial rather than punitive[67] in setting out to transform the offender's unlawful commercial habits into 'good' trade practices compliant behaviour and so become a law-abiding corporate citizen.[68] What is perhaps more difficult to evaluate is whether the scope of the compliance undertakings typically accepted by the Commission is consistent with the principle of proportionality, an issue discussed more fully below.

We have also seen that due process concerns may exclude punishment from the range of social purposes for which administrative settlements may be suited, and this is reflected in rigid adherence to the separation of powers doctrine, forbidding Australian administrative agencies from using their powers to punish offenders. In this respect, there may be a risk that the Commission's acceptance of community service undertakings may go beyond restorative purposes and shade into the punitive. As the Commission notes in its Policy Guideline, community service undertakings are the administrative equivalent of court-sanctioned 'community service orders'.[69] Whether or not community service undertakings constitute a legally appropriate use of the section 87B power depends upon their proper characterisation, a matter largely dependent upon the specific circumstances of the suspected contravention and the content of the programme itself. In general terms, it would appear that community service programmes are, like judicially imposed community service orders, primarily punitive in nature insofar as they entail some form of hard treatment for the suspected offender in response to unlawful conduct with the aim of deterring others from engaging in similar kinds of unlawful activity.[70] But, as we saw in both chapters five and six, identifying the legal character and purpose of regulatory sanctions may be far from straightforward, and there might therefore be multiple, but equally plausible ways of characterising any given undertaking. So, for example, community service undertakings accepted by the Commission involving the provision of free playground equipment to local councils following suspected market-rigging in tendering to local councils[71] and the provision of

[67] ALRC (1993), 71–72.

[68] *Ibid.*, 68.

[69] Community service orders are now one of the criminal sentencing options under Parts IV and VC of the Act, introduced by Trade Practices Amendment Act (No 1) 2001 (Cth). The Explanatory Memorandum to the Bill noted that 'These proposed amendments would enable a Court to make an order directing a contravening party to inform the public of their unlawful conduct, correct the harm that they have inflicted on the community as a result of their contravention, or engage in activities that are aimed at altering the internal business operations of the contravening party. Orders of this nature would be regarded as putting in place mechanisms to foster an environment of legislative compliance by changing incorrect business practices and correcting the misallocation of resources brought about by and evident in the breach.' Explanatory Memorandum, Trade Practices Amendment Bill (No 1) 2001, Part 3. See ALRC (1987), para 302 for fuller discussion of community service orders for corporate offenders.

[70] ALRC (1994), 68.

[71] S 87B undertaking accepted by the ACCC from Quinsite Nominees Pty Ltd (Corporate Trustees for Moduplay) 98/24S on 30 October 1998; S 87B undertaking accepted by the ACCC from Megatoy Play Systems Pty Ltd 98/23S on 30 October 1998.

free ferry trips to old aged pensioners on a journey where suspected price fixing had occurred[72] could be regarded as punitive, but might alternatively be seen, as Parker suggests, as creative means for pursuing restorative rather than punitive aims.[73]

The category of undertaking that may also be at risk of falling foul of the 'proper purposes' doctrine are those which I have labelled 'investigation cost recovery undertakings', typically accepted by the Commission in settling formal court enforcement action. The Policy Guideline states that the Commission:

> will seek to ensure that section 87B undertakings and their development, implementation and monitoring are cost neutral to the Commission and may require cost recovery for the Commission as part of the undertaking.[74]

While it is beyond doubt that the Commission may properly and lawfully recover the costs associated with instituting and prosecuting enforcement proceedings through the courts, it is more doubtful whether the Commission may be entitled to accept payment to recover the costs of investigating suspected violations. In its recent submissions to the Dawson Inquiry, the Business Council of Australia claimed that 'undertakings which involve companies paying money . . . that are not direct recompense to those affected by the alleged breach of the [Act], raise the question whether the ACCC is using the threat of prosecution to extract 'fines' from companies', implying that enforceable undertakings may have been improperly used by the Commission to pursue punitive purposes.[75] As the ALRC recently observed, the introduction of a general right for regulators to recover the costs of investigating an alleged contravention raises public concerns that they might use such a right to make improper deals with those under investigation[76] and, for this reason, it recommended against introducing a general legislative right of this nature.[77] Whether or not such a right should be available raises deeper questions, beyond the scope of the present inquiry, concerning who should bear the costs of regulatory enforcement in general. Although the reasons why a regulator may wish to recover the costs of its investigation are readily identifiable, given the significant resources which such investigations may pose, there are real risks of impropriety associated with agreements of this nature suggesting that such undertakings may be beyond the scope of the Commission's power. That said, it is not clear whether the costs recovered by the Commission pursuant to enforceable undertakings are limited to the legal costs that might have been awarded by a court if the proceedings had continued (which a court would order as clearly recoverable) or whether they

[72] S 87B undertaking accepted by the ACCC from Quickcat Cruises (Qld) Pty Ltd D01/11657 on 18 April 2001.

[73] Parker (2003), 14.

[74] Policy Guideline, 13.

[75] Business Council of Australia submission to Dawson Inquiry at 56: http://tpareview.treasury.gov.au/content/subs/071_Submission_BCA.pdf

[76] ALRC (2003), para 33.26.

[77] ALRC (2003), Recommendation 33–1.

extended beyond the Commission's recoverable costs to encompass costs associated with the preceding investigation (which a court would not order as legally recoverable).[78]

Taken together, the range of remedial undertakings appear broadly consistent with the range of legal and social purposes identified as best suited to implementation by way of administrative settlement, although there may be a real risk that the Commission has, in a small minority of cases, sought to promote punitive goals or goals which extend beyond the overriding purpose of section 87B in securing compliance with the Act. This latter risk is most acute in relation to compliance programme undertakings, community service undertakings, and investigation cost recovery undertakings, depending upon their scope and content. Each of these categories of undertaking may be seen as creative and worthwhile mechanisms for pursuing social goals not readily achievable by court order (given that on-going monitoring is likely to be required for effective implementation), and may demonstrate the heightened flexibility associated with administrative settlements when compared with court-ordered sanctions. However, their potentially intrusive nature and scope for impropriety may also increase the risk that such undertakings may be seen as exceeding the purposes of securing compliance, underlining the importance of ensuring that scope and content of any such obligations are proportionate to achieving legitimate restorative goals, rather than seeking to promote social purposes beyond those contemplated by the regulatory scheme.

(ii) Procedural Fairness and Proportionality

The Policy Guideline states that 'the Commission is careful to ensure that obligations under the undertaking are reasonable, clearly expressed and have not been obtained unfairly.'[79] This seems to indicate that the Commission is, at least in principle, committed to complying with the administrative law requirements of procedural fairness and proportionality, although its concern that undertakings should be 'reasonable' in content may not be as rigorous and demanding as the principle of proportionality.[80] In respect of the latter principle, the

[78] In *ACCC v Woolworths (South Australia) Pty Ltd* [2003] FCA 530 Mansfield J expressed concern that the agreed costs submitted to the court as the basis for consent orders related to the Commission's investigation costs which 'are not clearly costs which the Court may order' (para 36). However, he accepted the Commission's assurances that the agreed costs were the costs of the proceedings, and not part of its costs incurred in its investigation of the suspected contravention, and the firm offering the undertakings did not dispute this assurance. On this basis, he was prepared to make the costs order requested by the parties.

[79] Policy Guideline, 6.

[80] Given that proportionality is not a formal requirement of the ADJR Act, the Commission's position might be defended on this basis. In the UK, there is considerable debate between academic commentators concerning the extent to which the administrative law test of Wednesbury 'unreasonableness' differs from the test of 'proportionality' which some argue is a more rigorous and demanding test which should be applied to the lawful exercise of administrative power: Jowell and Lester (1987); Wong (2000) and the literature cited therein. Although proportionality is not a separate and independent head of review in Australian administrative law, it has been held to apply to constitutional and statutory powers which are 'purposive' in nature: Selway (1996). Thus, if s 87B is

ALRC has recently noted concerns expressed by firms that such undertakings may be 'unduly onerous and disproportionate to the alleged contravention'.[81]

Although it is not possible fully to assess the extent to which the Commission has in practice adhered to the requirements of proportionality and procedural fairness in the absence of a thorough audit of the Commission's enforcement files, it is worth pausing to consider whether a departure from these two principles should be a cause for concern. It may be recalled from the previous chapter that how one evaluates the use of bargaining and negotiation to enforce regulatory law ultimately depended on how we view the public interest in having the law applied in accordance with legal standards, rather than as agreed between the parties. The 'public interest' in this context might extend not only to third parties directly affected by the agreement but who are excluded from participating in negotiations, but may also include the broader public interest in the open and publicised articulation of legal standards to particular disputes. I suggested that the answer to this question is likely to be heavily contingent on the particular social context in which the question arises, including the nature and purpose of the legal standard departed from. In the present context, then, the relevant question is whether anything is lost when suspected contraventions of the Act are resolved privately between the Commission and suspected offender in a manner that departs from the principles of proportionality and/or due process?

In attempting to find answers to this question, I shall focus on the proportionality principle as it applies to compliance programme undertakings, given that these undertakings may entail a significant risk that excessively onerous undertakings may be accepted. In *ACCC v Z Tek Computers Pty Ltd*[82] the Federal Court refused to grant consent injunctions requiring an offender to implement a comprehensive trade practices compliance programme which encompasses both Parts IV (competition law) and V (consumer protection law) of the Act, where the offence concerned only one of these parts. The Court regarded injunctions requiring the implementation of a comprehensive compliance program as unduly wide, displaying an insufficient nexus to the offence committed.[83] In reaching this conclusion, however, the Court seemed to suggest that such comprehensive compliance programmes might properly be the subject

regarded as a purposive power, as I have suggested, then the manner of its exercise should be subject to the proportionality principle.

[81] ALRC (2002) para 16.69.

[82] (1997) FCR 197.

[83] The ALRC expressed similar concerns, in recommending that court ordered corporate probation programs should be available in response to a contravention of the Act. It emphasised the need for safeguards to limit their scope to ensure that such programmes were not excessively intrusive nor excessively costly for the firm involved. Hence it suggested that any conditions should be 'reasonably related to the nature and circumstances of the contravention or the history and characteristics of the organisation and are necessary to achieve the purposes of deterrence and preventing future contraventions'. ALRC (1994), 110.

of voluntary undertakings offered to the Commission pursuant to section 87B.[84] One of the reasons why the Court was unwilling to order the implementation of broadly based compliance programmes, despite the defendant's willingness to consent to such an order, may be attributed to the serious consequences attaching to breach of a court order. Failure to comply with a court order constitutes a contempt of court, potentially resulting in criminal punishment. In other words, the seriousness of the consequences of non-compliance may override the significance attached to the defendant's willingness voluntarily to assume such obligations. While the court's refusal to endorse consent injunctions in these circumstances was couched in terms of a lack of jurisdiction, it might be attributed to deeper concerns that a court should not insist that a person abide by unduly onerous obligations, even where that person purports to consent to their imposition. In contrast, the Court might not demand such rigour when enforceable undertakings are employed, because contravention of an undertaking does not generate such serious consequences, merely empowering the Commission to seek court orders requiring that the undertakings be complied with. Thus, the claim that onerous obligations are entered into on a voluntary and consensual basis may have more persuasive force in relation to enforceable undertakings than court-ordered consent injunctions, and may perhaps explain why the courts may be more willing to tolerate them.

This is not to say, however, that those who provide enforceable undertakings in response to a Commission's allegations of a suspected contravention do not face significant burdens. The apparently consensual basis of enforceable undertakings should not allow us to lose sight of the fact that they represent a legal constraint on a firm's freedom of action, and impose potentially significant costs on it.[85] We should bear firmly in mind that in practice, firms and individuals assume these burdens on a 'voluntary' basis because they fear that, if they fail to do so, the Commission may respond more severely by instituting court proceedings against them.[86] Given the notorious costs, both in direct financial terms and in terms of management time, firms and individuals will generally be particularly keen to avoid becoming embroiled in litigation with the Commission. This factor may weigh even more heavily with small and medium-sized firms who lack the expertise and resources to mount a successful defence against

[84] Similarly, in *ACCC v Woolworths (South Australia) Pty Ltd* [2003] FCA 530, the Federal Court was prepared to take judicial notice of enforceable undertakings requiring the firm offering the undertaking to donate $150,000 to an alcohol harm reduction and rehabilitation programme in response to suspected price fixing in the take-away alcohol market in the relevant region even though such an order went beyond the power of the court to issue community service orders pursuant to s 86C(4) because the obligation entailed the performance of a service that did not 'relate to the conduct' contravening the Act, and nor were the payments and their purpose directly tied to the alleged contravention for there was nothing to indicate that the amount of the payment reflected the lost benefit to the community from the contravention, at para 54–57.

[85] Above, Part C (1).

[86] Above ch 6, Part C (3)(a).

Commission action.[87] In other words, those subject to Commission investigations may face considerable pressure to 'consent' to undertakings, agreeing to accept obligations that might otherwise appear unduly wide or disproportionately onerous in relation to the seriousness of their alleged contravention. It might even be suggested that, in circumstances where firms agree to disproportionately broad undertakings, this may provide an indication that their consent to these undertakings is unlikely to be 'genuine'. In other words, when a contravention of regulatory law is resolved by way of agreement between the regulator and regulated, we may have cause to doubt the authenticity of the consent upon which such an agreement is based.

But the matter does not end there. Not only does a departure from the principle of proportionality suggest that the consensual basis of administrative undertakings may be more apparent than real, we lose something further. To regard as legitimate the acceptance by the Commission of disproportionately harsh or burdensome undertakings from suspected offenders is to fail to respect the deeper constitutional values of substantive fairness upon which the principle of proportionality rests. If we are to take seriously our commitment to these constitutional values, then we ought to insist that administrative power is exercised in a manner that conforms to them. In other words, these constitutional values cannot simply be overridden by the consent of the individuals involved, particularly given that such consent is unlikely to be freely and fully given. On the other hand, to adopt such an uncompromising approach may be thought unduly paternalistic, failing to accord due respect to individual autonomy. Why, it may be asked, should a firm or person not be free to accept disproportionately burdensome obligations by way of administrative undertaking if it genuinely considers this burden preferable to the burdens associated with the vagaries of litigation and its associated costs and potentially adverse publicity? [88] Perhaps the seeds of our discomfort lie not so much in the quality of the consent so given, but in the failure of our court processes to operate on an inexpensive, swift and accessible basis so that suspects may in practice prefer to accept disproportionately onerous restrictions on their conduct rather than to become involved in the formal legal process. In an ideal world, the use of the court process would not

[87] Parker's interviews with Commission staff involved in the negotiation of enforceable undertakings document their concern that some smaller businesses had 'agreed to everything the ACCC wanted without seeking legal advice and without fully understanding the commitments they were making', Parker (2004), 11.

[88] A number of submissions to the Dawson Inquiry which may be expected to be sympathetic to the needs and interests of business expressed serious concerns about excessively onerous or intrusive undertakings. For example, the Business Council of Australia has also raised concerns that some undertakings appear to:(i) bear no relationship to the contravention of the Act; (ii) be disproportionate to the contravention; (iii) go beyond the scope of the Act; (iv) go beyond the scope of what a court could or would order; (v) be designed to achieve social objectives other than creating a competitive environment (where the undertaking relates to competition as opposed to a consumer protection issue; (vi) be used as a means of cost recovery for the ACCC's other activities; and (vii) single out one class of consumers over another; See Business Council of Australia, *Submissions to the Review of the Trade Practices Act 1974*, [<*ww.tpareview.treasury.gov.au/content/subs/071_Submission_BCA.pdf*> 11 July 2002.

be synonymous with the delay and expense with which it is now typically associated. But, given that we do not live in such an ideal world, there appears to be no simple way out of this dilemma. My own view is that we should insist on adherence to constitutional principle. In this respect, I am heartened by the ALRC's recent recommendation that a Regulatory Contraventions Statute should be enacted, to include a provision that:

> in the absence of any clear, express statutory statement to the contrary, where legislation provides a regulator with authority to accept an enforceable undertaking, the terms of an enforceable undertaking must:
>
> (a) bear a clear or direct relationship with the alleged breach;
> (b) be proportionate to the breach;
> (c) not require the payment of money to the regulator other than in recompense to those affected by the alleged breach or in payment of the regulator's costs (if these are otherwise recoverable at law); and
> (d) stipulate a time period within which compliance with undertakings is required and not be otherwise open-ended.[89]

I accept, however, that for others my view may be thought naïve and unduly restrictive of the freedom of commercial enterprise to order their affairs as they so wish, even if this involves accepting obligations that might, in the absence of consent, be regarded as unduly severe.[90]

D. MERGER UNDERTAKINGS

Although enforceable undertakings have provided the Commission with a flexible and responsive tool to deal with suspected contraventions, they have been a particularly valuable means for enabling the Commission to anticipate and prevent contraventions, at least in relation to mergers that risk exceeding the market power thresholds established in section 50 of the Act.[91] Yet despite their popularity with the merging parties, the Commission's use of merger undertakings has generated a considerable level of public anxiety, thrice being the subject of critical scrutiny and adverse comment by a Committee of the Commonwealth Parliament in three successive reviews of the Commission's Annual Reports.[92] Accordingly, the following discussion sets out to probe more

[89] ALRC (2003), Recommendation 16–2.

[90] Even Bardach and Kagan, enthusiastic advocates of the use of bargaining between the regulator and regulated to secure compliance, express serious reservations about the regulator's use of bargaining to extract, as a *quid pro quo* for refraining from formal enforcement action, actions not specifically required by law but which would help prevent serious violations in future: Bardach and Kagan (1982), 141. Contrast Parker, who argues that there is some connection between the suspected violation and community service undertakings, and they are not therefore 'truly punitive': Parker (2003).

[91] Above, n 13.

[92] House of Representatives Standing Committee on Financial Institutions and Public Administration (1997); House of Representatives Standing Committee on Financial Institutions and Public Administration (1998); House of Representatives Standing Committee on Economics, Finance and Public Administration (2001); Industry Commission (1996); Zumbo (1997).

deeply into these concerns in order to evaluate both the benefits and risks associated with using merger undertakings.

1. The History of Merger Undertakings

Although the power to accept undertakings pursuant to section 87B has only been available since January 1993, undertakings (albeit of a contractual rather than statutory nature) were accepted by the Commission in relation to mergers prior to that time. During the high level of merger activity prevailing in the 1980s, a practice developed whereby firms proposing to merge or make acquisitions in marginal cases sought clearance from the Commission on an informal basis.[93] Occasionally, the Commission would agree to a 'deal' in which the parties proposing to merge agreed to partial divestiture of some of the assets of the merged entity, or some voluntary restraint on conduct by the merged entity post-completion, in order to reduce the market power of the merged entity to what the Commission considered to be acceptable limits, thereby avoid contravening section 50 of the Act.[94] It was, however, doubtful whether such deals were legally enforceable, particularly once a merger had proceeded[95] and the Commission was also criticised for doing back-room deals in relation to proposals that had not been subjected to the rigours of public scrutiny required by the formal merger authorisation process.[96] In response to these criticisms, the Commission thereafter ceased to entertain such arrangements[97] until Parliament enacted section 87B, following the recommendations of the Griffiths and Cooney Committees that the Commission be given statutory power to accept undertakings in respect of divestiture or other conduct pursuant to the authorisation or informal clearance of a proposed merger.[98] The legislative history to section 87B thus indicates that the Australian Parliament specifically contemplated that enforceable undertakings would empower the Commission to accept them in relation to proposed mergers. Since the introduction of section 87B, the Commission has accepted enforceable undertakings in relation to at least 40 mergers to the end of December 2002 prior to their completion.[99] In order to understand how the Commission has used merger undertakings, it is

[93] Tonking and Castle (1993).

[94] Walker and Woodward (1996), 36; Tonking and Castle (1993).

[95] Walker and Woodward (1996), 36; Tonking and Castle (1993), 38; TPC Annual Report 1988/89, 16.

[96] Tonking and Castle (1993), 38

[97] *Ibid*, 39.

[98] House of Representatives Committee on Legal and Constitutional Affairs (1991), Recommendation 19; House of Representatives Committee on Legal and Constitutional Affairs (1989), Recommendation 9.

[99] ACCC's Public Register of Undertakings from 1 Jan 1993 to 31 Dec 2002. For mergers up to the end of 1996/7 financial year, see ACCC (1998), 12–13. The acceptance of s 87B undertakings in relation to the proposed acquisition of QDL Ltd by FH Faulding Wholesale Pty Ltd appears to have been omitted from the ACCC publication.

necessary to locate their use within the broader context of the scheme of merger regulation established and administered under the Act, to which we now turn.

2. How Have Merger Undertakings Been Used?

(a) Informal Clearance

One distinguishing feature of Australian merger regulation is that, unlike the EU and US regulatory regimes, it does not include a scheme of mandatory pre-merger notification.[100] The Act does not establish a formal process through which the Commission is routinely given an opportunity to assess the competitive impact of a proposed merger or acquisition, except in the small minority of cases where the parties apply to the Commission for formal 'authorisation' of their proposed transaction pursuant to Part VII of the Act, which empowers the Commission to grant authorisation to mergers that generate sufficient relevant public benefits that they are considered to outweigh any anti-competitive effects likely to arise.[101] The formal merger authorisation process is subject to a series of time limits and other strict procedural requirements set out in the Act, including a specified consultation period, during which the Commission considers the parties' application.[102]

Rather than seek formal authorisation, parties to a proposed merger or acquisition have approached the Commission on an informal basis, seeking its view on whether it is likely to oppose the merger.[103] These informal clearances have been actively encouraged by the Commission and have become commonplace in recent years, particularly where parties proposing to merge are concerned that their transaction is at risk of contravening section 50 of the Act.[104] In its Merger Guideline, the Commission states that if, following an informal assessment, it concludes that a proposed acquisition would (or would be likely to) have the effect of substantially lessening competition, the parties will be so advised and it will then be for the parties to decide which of the following options it wishes to pursue:

—abandon the proposal;
—modify the proposal to address any of the likely anti-competitive consequences, either informally or formally by way of s 87B undertakings;
—apply for authorisation if the acquirer considers that it may be able to establish that the proposal would result in a net public benefit;

[100] Drauz (1996); Kolasky and Lowe (1997).
[101] Trade Practices Act 1974, s 88.
[102] Trade Practices Act 1974, s 90A.
[103] ACCC (1999), para 4.4. See Dawson Report (2003), ch 2 for a discussion of the shortcomings of the current merger authorisation process.
[104] ACCC (1998), 22.

—take their own risk and seek to complete the acquisition; or
—seek a court declaration that the proposed acquisition does not contravene the Act.[105]

As a practical matter, enforceable undertakings are typically only considered if the Commission has formed the view, on the basis of an informal assessment, that the merger proposal is likely to contravene section 50, although it has also accepted them before completing its informal merger assessment seeking to ensure that an acquisition is not completed until after it has completed appropriate market inquiries ('hold separate' undertakings).[106] The Merger Guideline states that, if the Commission takes the view that a proposed acquisition is likely to lessen competition substantially (and thus contravene section 50), it will seek either an informal undertaking or an enforceable undertaking from the parties not to proceed,[107] and if no such undertakings are forthcoming, then it will seek to stop the acquisition by pursuing court action rather allowing the acquisition to proceed and later seek to unwind it by divestiture.[108]

(b) *The Nature and Content of Merger Undertakings*

If the parties decide to offer enforceable undertakings, rather than pursuing any of the alternative options, then the decision to accept them lies wholly within the Commission's discretion. While the Commission cannot impose or demand undertakings from the parties, it can refuse to accept undertakings that it considers inappropriate or otherwise incapable of alleviating its concerns. The Merger Guidelines states that the Commission's primary concern in evaluating merger undertakings is the potentially anti-competitive impact of a proposed merger,[109] so that the aim of such undertakings is to ensure that the resulting merger will not have the effect (or likely effect) of substantially lessening competition in breach of section 50. In making this assessment, the Commission has indicated that it is likely to favour undertakings that address structural issues in the relevant market rather than behavioural undertakings.[110] A classic example of the former might involve one of the merging parties agreeing to divest certain assets or businesses of the merged entity prior to completion, while an example of the latter would include a commitment by the merged entity to supply particular services on an on-going basis at or below a specified price. The Commission justifies its preference for structural rather than behavioural undertakings (the latter are not defined in the *Merger Guidelines* but examples are cited to include undertakings by which the acquirer agrees to certain price,

[105] ACCC (1999), para 4.16.
[106] ACCC (1999) para 7.3; Walker and Woodward (1996), 36. The use of such 'hold separate' undertakings has been relatively uncontroversial and will therefore not be the focus of this evaluation.
[107] ACCC (1999), para 4.15.
[108] *Ibid,* para 4.16.
[109] *Ibid,* para 7.2 and 7.17.
[110] *Ibid,* paras 7.6–7.14.

product/output or quality constraints[111]) on the basis that 'structural solutions provide an ongoing basis for the operation of competitive markets. The regulatory costs are one-off rather than a permanent burden.'[112] In contrast, the Commission claims that behavioural undertakings 'may well interfere with the ongoing competitive process through their inflexibility and unresponsiveness to market changes', as well as giving rise to 'substantial regulatory difficulties'—requiring on-going monitoring (and associated costs) and substantial complexity in determining their scope, terms, administration and enforcement.[113] One influential industry body has, however, questioned the Commission's adherence to its stated policy, observing that an analysis of the mergers allowed subject to enforceable undertakings in the 18 months to July 2002 reveals that 80 per cent of the undertakings included behavioural undertakings.[114]

3. The Benefits of Merger Undertakings

Merger undertakings rest on a simple core idea. They enable parties to a proposed merger that might otherwise contravene section 50, to provide the Commission with legally binding commitments to alter their proposals with the aim of reducing the merger's anticipated anti-competitive impact and so bring it within the section 50 market power threshold. The availability and use of enforceable undertakings in the merger context is considerably advantageous for both the parties to a proposed merger and for the Commission as competition regulator. From the merging parties' perspective, the availability of enforceable undertakings extends the range of strategic options available to them in seeking to implement their proposal. Prior to the introduction of section 87B, parties to a merger proposal that risked falling foul of section 50 faced a more limited and somewhat stark set of choices concerning how to proceed. They could abandon their proposal altogether, proceed with the proposal and thus risk court proceedings by the Commission to block the merger which might expose them to hefty pecuniary penalties, or seek authorisation (which is granted only on proof by the parties that the public benefits of the merger outweigh its anti-competitive effects). The introduction of section 87B has injected greater flexibility into the merger regulation process, while removing a significant source of uncertainty and commercial risk, since parties now have an opportunity to modify their merger proposals and proceed without contravening section 50. Although in strict legal terms, the acceptance of enforceable undertakings by the Commission does not confer statutory immunity from breach of section 50 (unlike authorisation) so that the merger remains at risk of

[111] ACCC (1999), para 7.9; Walker and Woodward (1996), 36.
[112] ACCC (1999), para 7.6.
[113] *Ibid*, para 7.10; Walker (1996), 36. TPC Annual Report 1994/5, 37.
[114] Business Council of Australia submissions to Dawson Inquiry at 59: http://tpareview.treasury.gov.au/content/subs/071_Submission_BCA.pdf

proceedings being instituted by either private litigants [115] or the Commission,[116] in practice, however, once the Commission has granted informal clearance to a merger following the acceptance of enforceable undertakings, this drastically reduces the risks of subsequent court proceedings.[117] The Commission would be unlikely to challenge a merger which it had informally cleared, for to do so would signal a lack of good faith by the Commission in the absence of compelling reasons for taking such action.[118] Private parties would also be significantly discouraged from issuing proceedings against a transaction that had been cleared by the Commission in advance, with clearance providing cogent (albeit not conclusive) evidence that the merger is unlikely to contravene section 50. By allowing the parties to proceed with their merger without engaging in litigation and/or the need to resort to the more formal and more costly authorisation process, the availability of enforceable undertakings may thereby substantially reduce the commercial risk arising from legal uncertainty and its associated compliance costs.

But the commercial parties are not the only beneficiaries of the power to accept merger undertakings, for they also benefit the Commission in several distinct albeit related ways. They provide the Commission with an enforcement tool not previously available, allowing it to respond in more sensitive, flexible and creative ways to individual merger proposals rather than rely on the bluntness of court action, which can only be invoked to prevent a merger entirely or to unwind it, post-completion, by way of divestiture. Nor is the function of merger undertakings identical to that of the merger authorisation process: authorisation requires the Commission (and on appeal, the Australian Competition Tribunal) to evaluate whether the public benefits flowing from a merger outweigh its anti-competitive detriments. In essence, authorisations are intended to deal with problems of 'market failure', that is, circumstances in which allowing anti-competitive conduct is likely to yield more efficient outcomes than those likely to prevail in the absence of such conduct.[119] Merger undertakings have been used for a different purpose: their concern is to ameliorate the potential anti-competitive effects of a merger, rather than to ensure that mergers whose benefits are likely to outweigh the anti-competitive effects are allowed to proceed.[120] By comparison with both the court and authorisation processes, the process of negotiating merger undertakings is also likely to

[115] Private litigants are not, however, entitled to seek injunctions to restrain a threatened contravention of Trade Practices Act 1974, s 50.

[116] Walker and Woodward (1996), 41.

[117] But see n 160 and associated text.

[118] Informal clearance by the Commission may, however, give rise to a 'legitimate expectation' on the part of the merging parties which the Commission may have difficulty resiling from as a matter of administrative law: Allars (1997), ch 11.

[119] Smith (1997), 352–54.

[120] The Commission states in its Merger Guideline that s 87B undertakings provide a flexible alternative rather than simply opposing an acquisition where it believes that the acquisition is likely to have the effect of substantially lessening competition: ACCC (1999), para 7.2.

be considerably swifter and cheaper, thereby generating cost savings for the Commission so that it can respond more efficiently to potentially anti-competitive conduct.

By enhancing the flexibility associated with the merger regulation process, enforceable undertakings may encourage commercial parties to approach the Commission on an informal basis if their proposal risks contravening section 50, opening up a more co-operative dialogue between industry and the Commission. This may be desirable for several reasons. First, it may be recalled from chapter three that ethnographic studies of regulatory agency behaviour suggest that the use of suasion and co-operation to secure regulatory outcomes may be more effective in securing compliance than deterrent-based strategies.[121] Secondly, by fostering 'regulatory conversations'[122] between the Commission and industry, the risk of 'over-deterrence', which may be a product of legalistic adherence to rules, may be reduced. In the absence of section 87B, the lengthy and expensive nature of court proceedings (including the possibility of corporate penalties of up to $10 mil) may well deter mergers that do not in fact breach section 50 because commercial parties are unwilling to run the risk of proceeding.[123] Thirdly, by encouraging a co-operative dialogue between the Commission and commercial parties, the availability of merger undertakings may facilitate greater voluntary pre-merger notification. It is generally accepted that it is more effective and efficient to prevent anti-competitive mergers before they are consummated, rather than unwind them after the event by forced divestiture.[124] But in order to do this, the Commission must have information concerning mergers prior to their occurrence. Yet because pre-merger notification is not mandated by the Act, the Commission must be pro-active in acquiring information concerning proposed mergers and is thus heavily reliant on industry to provide information concerning mergers before they occur. Thus, to the extent that parties are encouraged voluntarily to notify the Commission of their merger proposals in advance, the availability of enforceable undertakings may facilitate more timely responses from the Commission and reduce the monitoring costs that it might otherwise incur if voluntary pre-merger notification was not forthcoming.[125] Finally, this co-operative dialogue might provide the stimulus for commercial parties to take action exceeding that which is necessary to secure compliance with legal standards, enabling the

[121] Above, ch 5, Part B (3).

[122] Black (1998).

[123] Industry Commission (1996), 13.

[124] House of Representatives Committee on Legal and Constitutional Affairs (1991), ch 4 considered the benefits and draw-backs of compulsory pre-merger notification and concluded that only mergers of a 'substantial' nature should be subject to obligatory pre-merger notification (recommendation 5). Legislative recognition of pre-merger notification was also considered by the House of Representatives Standing Committee on Legal and Constitutional Affairs (1989).

[125] As the Industry Commission points out, however, the greater the number of merger investigations undertaken by the Commission, the greater the regulatory cost involved: Industry Commission (1996), 11.

Commission to secure outcomes 'beyond compliance' by seeking to improve the competitive functioning of the industry in which the merger is proposed by using the undertakings to effect industry restructuring.[126]

It is clear that there are considerable benefits for both the Commission and commercial parties accompanying the use of merger undertakings, which may fairly be regarded as public benefits. Because merger undertakings are arrived at following a process of negotiation and bargaining between the Commission and commercial parties, they clearly demonstrate how a co-operative dialogue (or, to use Black's terminology 'regulatory conversations') may serve to overcome, or at least reduce, the inherent limitations of rules. This dialogue reduces the difficulties associated with the indeterminacy, inclusiveness and formality of rules by enabling the Commission to fashion individuated responses to the particular circumstances presented to it by the parties. In other words, co-operation between the regulator and the regulated encourages flexibility and responsiveness but also provides additional certainty and stability by reducing the level of regulatory risk faced by the commercial parties. It enhances regulatory efficiency, by reducing the Commission's enforcement and monitoring costs as well as reducing the commercial parties' compliance costs. Yet despite these benefits, support for merger undertakings has by no means been unqualified, and they have been subject to considerable criticism, to which we now turn.

4. Criticisms of Merger Undertakings

A number of distinct but related and sometimes far-reaching criticisms have been directed towards the use of merger undertakings, resting upon claims that they are ineffective in achieving desired market outcomes, unfair, and confer excessive discretionary power on the Commission for which it is inadequately accountable. Each of these claims is explored more fully below.

(a) Ineffective

Many criticisms focus on the use of merger undertakings to 'restructure industries', referring to the commitments typically found in merger undertakings obliging the merged entity to divest itself of certain specified assets or aspects of its business, to conduct particular business activities in a manner intended to encourage market access to competitors or to guarantee the continued provision of specified services to consumers or acquirers. The effect of these undertakings is, to a greater or lesser extent, to alter the structure of the particular industry in which the merged entity operates, so that the Commission is sometimes

[126] Anderson *et al* (1996); The Ampol/Caltex merger is one such example of the Commission seeking positively to improve the competitive structure of industry by accepting merger undertakings: Walker (1996). But see criticisms of the Commission's attempts at 'industry restructuring' by way of merger undertaking, below at Part D (4) (a).

described as accepting merger undertakings in order to achieve 'industry restructuring'.[127] Scepticism concerning the effectiveness of merger undertakings to achieve industry restructuring that will enhance its competitive functioning has been either ideological or practical in nature.

Ideological objections to industry restructuring are rooted in a particular view of the state, the market and the relationship between them. Opposition to the use of merger undertaking to achieve industry restructuring may ultimately rest on fundamental objections to the very notion of state intervention in the operation of markets, either due to faith in the superiority of the market mechanism and/or scepticism about the ability of the state to correct market imperfections.[128] Criticisms of this nature echo the concerns often expressed by advocates of private-interest theories of regulation, who claim that any attempt by the state to intervene in the operation of markets is doomed to failure, because the regulatory process operates in favour of a 'rent-seeking' bureaucratic elite who seek to further their own status and influence rather than promote the broader public interest.[129] While this is a perfectly plausible view of regulation, it need not concern us because I have assumed, for the purposes of this book, that state regulation to preserve the integrity and competitive functioning of markets is a worthwhile endeavour.[130]

Others may have no ideological opposition to state intervention in malfunctioning markets, but may regard merger undertakings as an impractical and inappropriate vehicle for seeking to correct market distortions, questioning the mode of implementation rather than the underlying goals of industry restructuring. While it is not possible to offer more than a tentative evaluation of this claim because it can only be meaningfully tested against reliable, objective and comprehensive data that may be very difficult (if not impossible) to obtain, we can nevertheless identify the logical premises underlying it. Even well meaning attempts to improve the competitive functioning of markets may have unforeseen and undesirable effects, reducing (or indeed exacerbating) the competitive functioning of the industry in question: the more extensive and ambitious the undertakings, the greater the scope for unintended effects. Although these risks may arise whenever the state intervenes in markets, whether by enforceable undertaking or by some other mechanism, they are particularly acute when implemented through enforceable undertakings for two reasons. First, the information upon which such decisions are based is likely to be incomplete, largely due to the informal and largely bilateral process of negotiating such

[127] Shell Ltd submissions to the Dawson Inquiry: http://tpareview.treasury.gov.au/content/subs/015_Submission_Shell.pdf; Minter Ellison Legal Group submissions to Dawson Inquiry:http://tpareview.treasury.gov.au/content/subs/048_Submission_ME.pdf.

[128] In a less emphatic form, it may be argued that, however well-intentioned the state's plans in seeking to improve the operation of markets, 'regulatory failure' is more harmful to the welfare of the community than market failure, so that social policy should err on the side of non-intervention.

[129] Baldwin *et al* (1998), 10–11. Above, ch 1, Part B (1) (b).

[130] Above, ch 1, Part B (1) (b).

undertakings. While the informality and timeliness associated with using undertakings is one of its strengths, it may also be a source of weakness. The kind of in-depth, comprehensive and wide-ranging data likely to be required for careful and effective industry restructuring may simply not be available to the Commission, given the limited nature of the inquiries which it conducts in clearing a proposed merger subject to enforceable undertakings.[131] Secondly, merger undertakings may fail to bring about the desired alterations to industry structure because such intervention is inevitably sporadic and piecemeal. Even assuming that industry restructuring is a laudable objective for the Commission to pursue, it can only respond to merger proposals as and when they arise. It cannot use enforceable undertakings strategically and systematically in relation to the major industry participants because firms not party to the proposed merger would not rationally offer them, and the Commission has no legal power to compel them to do so.[132] Strategic, wholesale restructuring of malfunctioning industries is therefore unlikely to be successfully implemented via enforceable undertakings.

(b) Unfairness

In a somewhat different vein, it has been argued that the use of merger undertakings may be unfair for several reasons. Although the Commission cannot compel parties to offer undertakings, it might be argued that merger undertakings are coercive in practice because the Commission's status as a regulator places it in an inherently superior bargaining position, so that parties proposing

[131] In contrast, in the UK the Enterprise Act 2002 empowers the Office of Fair Trading to refer a merger to the Competition Commission (formerly the MMC) to conduct an investigation into whether a proposed merger may be expected to substantially lessen competition. The Competition Commission describes the major stages of its merger investigations as involving information gathering (including the issue of questionnaires), hearing witnesses, verifying information, providing a statement of issues, considering responses to the statement of issues, notifying parties of and publishing provisional findings, notifying and considering possible remedies, considering exclusions from disclosure and publishing reports. Whish (2003) 897–98.

[132] This argument against the use of enforceable undertakings as an instrument for securing industry restructuring does not necessarily entail rejection of the view that 'partial-industry regulation' may be superior to industry-wide regulation. Ayres and Braithwaite advocate 'partial industry regulation' in which the regulator seeks to regulate a section of the participants an industry rather than all of its participants. The purpose of partial intervention is based on the view that by seeking to regulate certain key players within an industry, the non-regulated firms will be faced with incentives to behave in a manner which maximises the competitive nature of the industry as a whole. However, the partial industry regulation advocated by Ayres and Braithwaite is critically dependent on strategic regulation, based on identifiable areas where intervention may be used to generate competitive outcomes: Braithwaite (1992), ch 5. Identifying the need for strategic intervention may involve regulating only one firm where that firm is dominant but may also require the regulation or targeting of several firms in order to generate the desired outcome, depending on the structure of the particular market (either by way of 'fringe firm intervention' or by 'oligopolistic firm intervention'). By contrast, enforceable undertakings are ill-equipped to facilitate partial industry regulation of the strategic kind so advocated because they can only be used in response to specific merger proposals on an ad hoc basis as and when they are notified to the Commission for informal clearance. But see n 134 below.

to merge have no practical choice but to accede to the latter's request for undertakings if they wish to proceed.[133] This argument overlooks the fact, however, that enforceable undertakings are only likely to be requested in relation to proposed transactions that are likely to result in the merged entity possessing such a significant degree of market power that it is at risk of contravening section 50. Commercial parties in this position are invariably sophisticated, well-resourced and expertly advised and are therefore unlikely to succumb to pressure from the Commission unless the Commission's position is firmly supported by a legitimate interpretation of the law as it applies to the parties' circumstances. Perhaps more importantly, because merger undertakings are used prophylactically, the merging parties are not subject to the same degree of pressure that may arise when enforceable undertakings are used in a remedial sense. The parties to a merger have a genuine choice: if they do not wish to offer undertakings of the sort requested by the Commission, then they may walk away from the deal altogether without fear of adverse regulatory consequences from the Commission.

Another slightly different variant of the argument from unfairness is based on the principle of equality. By accepting legal restraints from the merged entity that do not apply to incumbent firms in the industry, who may be in a similar competitive position to that of the merged entity (assessed in terms of its market power), there is an apparent violation of the principle that 'like should be treated alike'. This apparent disparity in treatment arises because enforceable undertakings can only be used sporadically in an ad hoc fashion in response to particular merger proposals, rather than on a strategic industry-wide basis.[134] In response, it might be claimed that the merged entity and incumbent firm referred to in this example are not similarly situated, because the former is seeking to engage in a transaction that is proscribed by law, while the latter is not. Furthermore, by consenting to the restrictions set out in the undertakings provided to the Commission, it might be argued that any perceived unfair treatment

[133] Business Council of Australia submissions to the Dawson Inquiry: http://tpareview.treasury.gov.au/content/subs/071_Submission_BCA.pdf; W Pengilley submissions to Dawson Inquiry: http://tpareview.treasury.gov.au/content/subs/008_Submission_Pengilley.pdf; Franchise Council of Australia Ltd submissions to the Dawson Inquiry: http://tpareview.treasury.gov.au/content/subs/044_Submission_Franchise.pdf.

[134] Ayres and Braithwaite acknowledge the 'important equitable difficulty inherent in partial industry regulation' and therefore suggest two possible responses to the problem. First, they suggest that the government could use specific regulation as a threat so as to single out the firm which has behaved least competitively in the past so as to provide incentives for firms trying to avoid regulation to avoid regulatory constraints by behaving more competitively. Secondly, they suggest that the government might randomly choose the firm that it is to be subject to regulation for a finite period, and different firms could be chosen in each successive period. However, neither of these suggestions are capable of implementation by enforcement undertakings for the very reason why the first variant of the unfairness argument has no force: the Commission cannot unilaterally compel firms to provide undertakings—they can only be provided voluntarily by firms which are at risk of contravening the Act. Moreover, the two suggestions put forward by Ayres and Braithwaite, which are effectively based on lottery and turn-taking, do not fully or adequately overcome the problem of discriminatory treatment which is inherent in selective regulation: Braithwaite and Ayres (1992), ch 5.

is effectively 'cured', although whether consent is adequate to override values of substantive fairness is a thorny question, explored more fully below.

While the above claims concern potential unfairness to the parties providing merger undertakings, other criticisms focus on unfairness to third parties who may be significantly affected by the undertakings, yet are largely excluded from participating in the negotiations leading to their acceptance.[135] At present, the Act does not prescribe any procedural requirements applicable to the acceptance of enforceable undertakings in either the remedial or merger context. Third parties may, however, be entitled to limited participation rights arising from general administrative law. In particular, the doctrine of procedural fairness requires that those whose rights, interests or legitimate expectations are likely to be affected by the decision of an administrative body (such as the Commission) are entitled to procedural protections, the extent and scope of which varies in accordance with the circumstances of the case and, in particular, the extent of the individual's interest in the matter.[136] For example, those who are likely to have their livelihood or property rights encroached upon enjoy more extensive participation rights than those who have a mere hope or expectation that executive discretion may be exercised in their favour. These participation rights may range from a simple right to be notified of decisions through to a right to a full-blown oral hearing by an independent tribunal. Thus, the nature and extent of third party rights to participate in the negotiation of merger undertakings will vary with the individual circumstances of the case, although they are likely to be fairly limited in scope.

In response to concerns about the lack of third party participation in the informal merger clearance process, the Commission states in its Policy Guideline that:

> in most, if not all, cases the Commission will want to consult with relevant market participants before accepting a substantive s 87B undertaking. While the Commission will usually already have undertaken extensive consultation through the market inquiries process, this consultation may not be sufficient to address all issues relevant to a decision to accept a proposed undertaking or not. Once having formed the view that an acquisition would be or is likely to be anti-competitive, and having received the offer of undertakings, the Commission will need to undertake a separate assessment of the impact of the proposed undertakings. This will almost always require further consultation with marketplace participants.[137]

While there is doubtless merit in the Commission's approach, one might question whether a general administrative policy favouring consultation provides adequate protection to third parties likely to be affected, sometimes significantly, by merger undertakings. Even buttressed by the general law requirements of procedural fairness, the variable and contingent nature and

[135] Black (1998), 93.
[136] Above, ch 3, Part B (2) (d).
[137] Policy Guideline, 10.

content of third party rights to consultation may be too vague and uncertain to provide a sufficient level of protection to third party interests. Because the impact of mergers and merger undertakings on third parties may be very significant, stronger institutional mechanisms may be desirable in order adequately to ensure that third parties are provided with an opportunity to participate in the decision-making processes affecting them.

(c) Excessive Discretion

A similar but distinct set of objections to merger undertakings assert that they confer excessive discretionary power on the Commission for which it is insufficiently accountable.[138] Like the preceding criticisms, this claim has several different but related facets. First, it may be claimed that the Commission's legal and administrative accountability is relatively weak, given that there is no mechanism of appeal or review against the Commission's refusal to accept merger undertakings.[139] Although Commission decisions are subject to a degree of political scrutiny, notably in the form of parliamentary scrutiny of the Commission's annual reports, this does not amount to an institutional mechanism for review of the legality and merits of individual Commission decisions on a systematic basis. Because the form and content of enforceable undertakings are arrived at by a process of negotiation between the Commission and the parties to the proposed merger, there is no formal opportunity for third parties to participate in the discussions, nor for independent scrutiny by either a court or the Tribunal to assess whether the content of the undertakings is appropriate.[140] As a result, the Commission commands considerable discretionary power in determining the nature and scope of the legal restraints that it accepts by way of enforceable undertakings, in practice constrained only by the bargaining power of the merging parties.[141] Because the impact of decisions to allow mergers

[138] House of Representatives Standing Committee on Financial Institutions and Public Administration (1997), ch 3; Anderson *et al* (1996).

[139] In *Australian Petroleum Pty Ltd v ACCC* (1997) 73 FCR 75 the Federal Court held that the Commission's decision to refuse to negotiate a variation or withdrawal of an enforceable undertaking was reviewable under the ADJR Act, but it did not specifically address whether the initial decision to accept an undertaking was reviewable. In *Virgin Blue Airlines Pty Ltd v ACCC* (2002) 186 ALR 377 the applicant sought to challenge the Commission's decision to accept an undertaking from a rival firm. The Court reserved its decision on the question of standing for hearing, but the applicant announced that it had settled the proceedings with the Commission on 23 November 2001.

[140] *Ibid.*

[141] One commentator has even suggested that s 87B of the Act provides a means by which the Commission can avoid the procedural safeguards which are built into the authorisation process (which requires third party consultation and the publication of a draft determination prior to final decision) thereby conferring unacceptable discretionary power on the Commission: Zumbo (1997) *cf* Tonking and Castle (1997). The ALRC noted concerns that the Commission might use the s 87B undertaking power oppressively and the calls for greater scrutiny of the way in which the s 87B undertaking power is used. It concluded, however, that in the absence of any evidence that parties need additional protection or that the power had been abused, the ALRC was not satisfied that such scrutiny was necessary: ALRC (1994), 131.

between powerful enterprises may be far-reaching, review by an independent tribunal might be thought to be a vital and important safeguard, particularly for parties to the proposed merger and affected third parties.[142]

That said, the desirability of merits review by an independent body may be linked to claims that the task of regulation requires specialised knowledge, expertise and professional judgement. One reason why merits review may be considered inappropriate in relation to administrative decisions is that the tasks involved require difficult professional judgements[143] so that to require an independent tribunal, even if it possesses the appropriate expertise, to second-guess these judgements would add little to the quality of decisions so made. While this claim has some merit, it does not seem sufficiently weighty to justify denying those adversely affected by the Commission's decision to accept merger undertakings an opportunity to have that decision subject to independent scrutiny.[144] A rather more powerful objection to the availability of independent review of such decisions is grounded in concerns that this would lead to excessive formalisation, delay and juridification of the merger clearance process. In other words, independent review of merger undertakings would threaten to eliminate the very benefits of flexibility, responsiveness, certainty, stability and efficiency associated with the existing informal process in which merger undertakings are accepted. In a related vein, there are also fears that the review mechanism may be used for strategic purposes by competitors of the merging parties that are directly antagonistic to the entire rationale of competition regulation, being used to thwart transactions that may well be efficiency-enhancing.[145] On balance, these risks seem to have sufficient force to justify the absence of a mechanism by which the content of merger undertakings may be subject to independent merits review, provided that there are other safeguards in place which ensure that the process is as open, transparent and as sensitive to third party interests as realistically feasible.[146]

Secondly, complaints concerning the adequacy of the Commission's accountability in accepting merger undertakings are exacerbated by the absence of any general legal obligations on the Commission to publish clear and comprehensive

[142] Zumbo (1997).

[143] Baldwin (1987), 4; Galligan (1996), 26.

[144] *cf* The Dawson Inquiry concluded that dissatisfaction with the formal authorisation process could be attributed to concerns about the time which was taken by the Commission to reach a formal decision, and the risk of third party intervention by way of appeal to the Australian Competition Tribunal, rendering the authorisation process commercially unrealistic for many merger proposals: Dawson Report (2003), 4.

[145] In recommending the introduction of a formal clearance process, the Dawson Inquiry proposed that only the applicants should be entitled to seek a review of the Commission's clearance decision, recommending against conferring such a right on third parties, but it did not set out the reasons for excluding a third party right to review: Dawson Report (2003), Recommendation 2.2.4.

[146] The Commission is required to prepare and publish an Annual Report which is laid before Commonwealth Parliament. Its Annual Reports are typically scrutinised by the House of Representatives, Standing Committee on Legal and Constitutional Affairs.

reasons for its acceptance of enforceable undertakings,[147] rendering scrutiny of Commission's actions even more difficult.[148] While the Commission has sought to enhance the transparency of enforceable undertakings by voluntarily establishing a public register of undertakings, publishing an administrative guideline concerning their use, and issuing media releases broadly outlining the content of enforceable undertakings at the time of their acceptance, such measures may be a rather inferior substitute for a legal obligation to publish comprehensive reasons for its decisions.[149] Once again, however, the flexibility and fluidity of the informal merger clearance process whilst in one sense a source of strength, is also a source of weakness. There have been occasions when the Commission has had a very short period of time to consider merger proposals with a view to informal clearance, particularly in the context of hostile take-overs. As a result of these circumstantial pressures, the Commission may be called upon to make rapid judgements based on the limited information available to it at that time. In such circumstances, it may not be realistic to expect the Commission to draft and publish detailed reasons for its decision prior to the acceptance of merger undertakings.[150] But the occasional urgency of Commission decisions does not of itself appear to justify dispensing with a general requirement to give reasons in ordinary cases. It therefore seems that considerable scope exists for improving the general level of transparency associated with the acceptance of merger undertakings, but without unduly impeding the fluidity and flexibility of the informal clearance process.[151] To this end, the Dawson Inquiry's recommenda-

[147] Third parties are only entitled to obtain a written statement of reasons for a decision by a Commonwealth agency (including the Commission) under the ADJR Act, s 3(1) if they fall within the statutory test for standing, which refers to a 'person aggrieved' by a decision: ADJR Act, s 5(1).

[148] Shell Australia Ltd submissions to Dawson Inquiry: http://tpareview.treasury.gov.au/content/subs/015_Submission_Shell.pdf;

United Energy Submissions to Dawson Inquiry: http://tpareview.treasury.gov.au/content/subs/025_Submission_United_E.pdf; SFE Corporation Limited Submissions to Dawson Inquiry: http://tpareview.treasury.gov.au/content/subs/092_Submission_SFE.pdf.

[149] See n 198 and associated text.

[150] SFC Corporation's submissions to the Dawson Inquiry stated that 'The fact that informal clearance does not require the regulator to publish detailed reasons is both a blessing and a curse for the ACCC. On the one hand, the fact that staff papers are not required to be published or made available to the parties assists the ACCC in providing a relatively swift indicative view. On the other hand, the lack of 'precedent' means the ACCC is open to public and often unfair criticism in relation to the basis of its decisions. Much of that criticism has manifested itself in emotional criticism of the ACCC itself without reference to the procedural background against which the Commission must operate' (para 5.13): http://tpareview.treasury.gov.au/content/subs/092_Submission_SFE.pdf

[151] Concerns about the transparency of merger undertakings may also be partly attributable to the Commission's willingness to accede to requests by the merging parties that the content of the undertakings so given be kept confidential. Although transparency is inevitably diminished by the grant of confidentiality, there are circumstances in which the disclosure of the content of such undertakings may have material adverse effects on the parties, the avoidance of which may justify preserving confidentiality while that information remains commercially sensitive. For example, when parties undertake to divest themselves of certain assets, the parties may request that the time limits within which the undertakings are to be completed may be kept confidential in order to avoid forcing the parties to a 'fire sale'. In applying EU competition law, the European Commission has in practice kept confidential the time limits applicable to divestiture undertakings so as to avoid

tion that the Commission should be required to provide adequate reasons for its decisions when requested to by the parties and in cases where it has rejected a merger or accepted undertakings is to be warmly welcomed.[152]

Thirdly, the lack of transparency associated with the Commission's decisions to accept merger undertakings becomes a source of uncertainty for commercial parties seeking to understand how the Commission interprets, and seeks to enforce, the section 50 prohibition on anti-competitive mergers. The absence of detailed reasons attaching to Commission decisions to accept or decline merger undertakings in individual cases may not only serve to conceal inconsistency in the treatment of commercial parties, but it also fails to provide adequate guidance to firms concerning how the Commission decides whether to accept undertakings.[153] While merger undertakings may be beneficial to the merging parties and the Commission by enabling competition concerns to be resolved in advance of the transaction without the need for costly and protracted litigation, these informal settlements have resulted in a dearth of court judgments elucidating the scope and meaning of the Act's legal prohibitions. Although litigation is costly and time-consuming for the parties concerned, the resolution of disputes by judicial adjudication generates a 'public good' through the provision of binding legal precedent, giving courts an opportunity to make authoritative statement on novel questions of law and thereby allow the substantive law to keep pace with developments in the commercial environment and advances in academic reflection.[154] Court judgments thereby provide authoritative guidance both to regulated firms and the regulator by reducing uncertainty concerning the scope and content of substantive regulatory laws.[155] The scarcity of authoritative judicial statements on the requirements of section 50 has meant that settlements concluded between the Commission and merging parties have in practice attained the status of 'soft law', providing a source of guidance to those seeking to interpret the meaning of substantive law and how it is likely to be applied.[156] But because the nature and content of merger are arrived at through an essentially private process of bargaining and negotiation between the Commission

forcing a fire sale on the parties. In contrast, the US antitrust authorities have published the time limits, and the necessity of a fire sale is regarded in the US as a cost of doing business. Eg Drauz (1996), 234.

[152] Dawson Report (2003), Recommendation 2.1.

[153] For example, SFE Corporation's Submission to the Dawson Inquiry stated at para 5.10 that 'because Australian companies have made extensive use of the informal [merger clearance] process and largely avoided seeking authorisation, the informal clearance decision has attained a practical stature that may not have been initially anticipated by the ACCC or the legislature. In the limited time available for commercial deals to proceed, a negative informal clearance response from the ACCC may sound the death knell for a proposed acquisition. Given the often substantial funds at stake, it seems incongruous for such a crucial decision to proceed using a process that remains relatively shrouded in mystery.' http://tpareview.treasury.gov.au/content/subs/092_Submission_SFE.pdf.

[154] Luban (1995).

[155] Above, ch 6, Part C (1).

[156] Since s 50 was amended from a test of 'dominance' to one of 'substantially lessening competition' there has not been a single court judgment elucidating the meaning of the reformed s 50.

and the merging parties, the undertakings ultimately agreed upon may result from a compromise reached with the parties and may not accurately reflect the requirements of substantive law.[157] As a consequence, the content of the undertakings concluded with the Commission may not provide reliable guidance on the content of substantive regulatory rules and their application, particularly when the reasons underlying the Commission's decision to accept such undertakings are not fully and publicly stated.

Fourthly, it may be argued that the accountability deficit relating to the Commission's acceptance of merger undertakings applies to the extent of its political accountability, and not merely its administrative accountability. In particular, it has been claimed that the power to accept enforceable undertakings confers an unacceptably wide discretion on the Commission to interfere with the operation of markets. Because the regulation of mergers, particularly where it involves attempts to restructure industries, may impact upon a wide range of persons and interests in a differential way, such a task is inherently political. To entrust this task to an independent statutory agency, such as the Commission, may be thought inappropriate, given that the Commission lacks any direct democratic mandate to make political decisions. This objection echoes familiar concerns that arise occasionally in debates concerning the regulation of social and economic activity by independent agencies. These concerns are grounded in an intrinsic tension between two claims. On the one hand, the task of regulation may be seen as a matter requiring particular 'expertise' and professional judgement (for present purposes, economic expertise) but on the other, such tasks often involve the evaluation of competing claims to resources by diverse and sometimes hostile social interests which call for political judgement.[158] The regulation of mergers is one area of economic regulation where the tension between these two claims is thrown into high relief, in Australia and elsewhere. Although it is unlikely that this tension can ever be satisfactorily resolved or eliminated, it might to some extent be reduced to the extent that the regulator's decisions and decision-making procedures are open and transparent.

Finally, it may be argued that the Commission's power to accept merger undertakings is excessively wide in practice, by enabling the Commission to accept commitments that are unacceptably broad and intrusive in scope, particularly when used to effect wide-scale industry restructuring, thereby violating the principle of proportionality.[159] In response, it might be argued that the consensual nature of these undertakings overcomes this and other concerns rooted in the alleged substantive unfairness inherent in their use. How are we to evaluate this claim: does the fact that merger undertakings are given voluntarily by the parties, reduce or even override the seriousness of these objections of substantive unfairness? It may be recalled that, in relation to remedial undertakings,

[157] Waller (1997).

[158] Above ch 3, Part B (2) (c).

[159] Shell Australia Ltd submissions to Dawson Inquiry: http://tpareview.treasury.gov.au/content/subs/015_Submission_Shell.pdf.

I considered whether anything was lost if firms and individuals were permitted to provide remedial undertakings to the Commission that were otherwise unduly burdensome and disproportionate in scope. I suggested that, particularly in situations where the Commission is in a significantly superior bargaining position, it was doubtful whether such undertakings could be regarded as genuinely voluntary, given that in practice the parties would fear that failure to consent might result in the Commission taking more severe regulatory action, including instituting court proceedings seeking pecuniary penalties against them. In addition, I suggested that something further might be lost—that is, by regarding a departure from the principle of proportionality as legitimated by consent, we may fail to take seriously the constitutional values of fairness upon which the proportionality principle rests. Might not the same be said of disproportionately wide or onerous merger undertakings?

Although we may have reason to doubt the genuineness of consent upon which remedial undertakings are based, we may have more faith in the consensual basis of merger undertakings because parties to a merger proposal have a genuine choice to proceed with their proposal or not. Accordingly, there may be greater justification for deferring to the parties' agreement and therefore respecting their freedom to accept what might otherwise be regarded as particularly onerous obligations in the form of merger undertakings. But, this would nevertheless entail a departure from the proportionality principle and hence the deeper constitutional values of substantive fairness upon which it rests. As a matter of logical consistency, it would seem to follow that, in denying the legitimacy of disproportionately wide remedial undertakings, I must also deny the legitimacy of disproportionately wide or burdensome merger undertakings. But my view of remedial undertakings was based on my concern to protect citizens from giving their consent to burdensome obligations arising from their desire to avoid the notorious costs and delays associated with the formal and coercive processes of law. By contrast, the desire to avoid litigation in the merger context may not be so pervasive. If, due to market pressures, commercial parties are so committed to the implementation of their merger proposal that they are willing to take on what might otherwise appear to be unduly burdensome obligations, then my inclination is to respect their freedom to adjust their plans accordingly. In other words, where undertakings are used in a prophylactic sense, then the argument from consent holds considerably more force than in the remedial context, and it is thus tentatively suggested that consent may be sufficient to override the principle of proportionality.

5. An Evaluation of Merger Undertakings

It is not difficult to discern why the use of merger undertakings has stimulated considerable public disquiet. While there are undeniable benefits associated with the use of enforceable undertakings in the regulation of mergers, they have also been the subject of some powerful criticisms which, as we have just seen, are not entirely without foundation. Merger undertakings encourage a co-operative dialogue between industry and the Commission in the application of section 50 of the Act, allowing the Commission to tailor and individualise its response to the particular anti-competitive concerns raised by a merger in a sensitive, timely and cost-effective manner. The process of negotiation and bargaining, upon which enforceable undertakings rely serves to overcome the indeterminacy and over- and under-inclusiveness of rules, and also provides a mechanism by which the Commission and commercial parties can co-operate together to develop innovative solutions which enable the parties to proceed with their business proposals whilst avoiding a contravention of the law. In short, merger undertakings offer considerable potential for enhancing regulatory effectiveness by promoting flexibility, responsiveness, stability and certainty, and efficiency in the enforcement of the Act.

But our assessment of merger undertakings is far from unqualified. The process of negotiation and bargaining upon which merger undertakings rely appears to display double-edged qualities, being at once a source of strength and weakness. Because merger undertakings are arrived at following a largely private process of negotiation between the Commission and commercial parties, this has generated complaints that the process lacks transparency, confers an unacceptably wide discretion on the Commission for which it is inadequately accountable, and denies third parties an opportunity to participate fully in decisions affecting them. In other words, the use of merger undertakings threatens the constitutional values of accountability, procedural fairness and proportionality.

The informality characterising the current Australian approach to regulating mergers may be viewed as a double-edged sword, injecting the process with flexibility and speed but, in so doing, tends to reduce the transparency, certainty and overall accountability of the decision-making process. In assessing the current arrangements under which many mergers may receive informal clearance, the Dawson Review concluded that:

> The strengths of the current informal clearance process stem from its informal nature, as do its weaknesses. The speed and efficiency of the process are generally regarded as being its greatest strengths. The voluntary nature of the process minimises the possibility of unduly delaying mergers that are unlikely to be in breach of section 50.
>
> The weaknesses of the system are inherent in its informality. There can be no review of the ACCC's decision to refuse clearance and the ACCC cannot be required to give reasons for its decision. Where the ACCC forms the view that a merger would substantially lessen competition, the parties proposing the merger must either seek authorisation or proceed with the transaction and risk proceedings in court for penalties and divestiture. If neither option is attractive, as is likely, the parties must either withdraw their proposal or negotiate section 87B undertakings with the ACCC. The absence of an effective appeal mechanism may place the ACCC in a position to extract undertakings which go beyond competition concerns arising from a merger. The absence of reasons for the ACCC's decisions hinders the development of a body of precedent to assist in the making of consistent and predictable determinations.

The proposals for change to the informal merger process would require it to be formalised to some extent with the risk that there would be a reduction in speed and efficiency.[160]

This tension, between the desire for informality and flexibility in public decision-making processes, on the one hand, and the desire for transparent and accountable processes that will ensure consistency and fair treatment, on the other, is common throughout merger clearance regimes across a range of jurisdictions. While the current Australian regime appears to lean more heavily in favour of the former, the institutional framework within which mergers are assessed in both EU and US competition regulation appears to place greater emphasis on the latter, by establishing formal procedures in which transparency and third party participation are emphasised. In order to evaluate the Australian regime, and suggest possible avenues for reform, it is therefore worth pausing to consider how the EU and US have attempted to resolve this tension in their approach to merger regulation.[161]

(a) USA Antitrust Law

One commentator has observed that the USA has the most 'extensive and allegedly most intrusive' pre-merger review in the world.[162] If the effect of a merger may substantially lessen competition or tend to create a monopoly, then US antitrust law establishes several avenues by which the merger can be challenged and prohibited.[163] Although a number of public bodies are entrusted with responsibility for antitrust enforcement in the USA, the primary responsibility for regulating mergers falls to the US Department of Justice Antitrust Division ('DoJ') and the Federal Trade Commission ('FTC') which have concurrent jurisdiction over mergers and acquisitions.[164] The Hart-Scott-Rodino Antitrust Improvement Act 1976 ('HSR Act') mandates that both the FTC and

160 Dawson Report, ch 2, 9.

161 Enforceable undertakings negotiated between the regulatory authority and parties to a proposed merger that raises competition concerns have long been used, and given legislative recognition, in UK competition regulation: See Whish (2001), 373–81; 815–34. Recent reforms to UK merger regulation introduced under the Enterprise Act 2002 also formalises the use of enforceable undertakings, thereby continuing the 'fix it first' approach to merger regulation: See Office of Fair Trading (2003), ch 7 for information on OFT procedures in accepting undertakings under the merger control regime set out under the Enterprise Act 2002 available at www.oft.gov.uk and Whish (2003) 901–6.

162 Halverson (1998), 6.

163 There are also several different antitrust statutes which may apply to mergers, but the principal provisions are section 7 of the Clayton Act which prohibits any transaction 'where in any line of commerce or in any activity affecting commerce in any section of the country, the effect of such acquisition may be substantially to lessen competition, or to tend to create a monopoly', and section 5 of the Federal Trade Commission Act, which prohibits 'unfair methods of competition' and allows the Federal Trade Commission to challenge a merger.

164 As a practical matter, the FTC tends to apply the same standards developed under s 7 of the Clayton Act in applying s 5 of the Federal Trade Commission Act: Halverson (1998).

DoJ must be notified of mergers which exceed a certain threshold size,[165] and prohibits such mergers from being consummated until after a specified time period[166] during which the agencies have an opportunity to review the proposed merger and to issue a 'second request' for further detailed information concerning the proposal. If such a request is made, then this prolongs the period which must elapse before the transaction may be completed. If a second request is made, and the agency continues to believe that the transaction will be anti-competitive, costly court enforcement proceedings can still be avoided by negotiating a settlement, which often includes the acquiring firm's agreement to divest certain portions of its business.[167]

If the FTC handled the investigation, then the agreement would take the form of a consent order and it would be enforced, if necessary by action by the FTC in a federal court. If the DoJ handled the investigation, then the agreement would be embodied in a consent decree, which is an agreement between the DoJ and the parties to antitrust litigation to settle the litigation on the terms set out in the consent decree, and which is regulated by the Antitrust Procedures and Penalties Act 1974 (the 'Tunney Act').[168] The Tunney Act was passed in order to address the three major criticisms of the negotiation and approval of consent decrees in antitrust cases: (a) interested third parties had little opportunity to participate in the process and little consideration was given to their views; (b) the DoJ conducted negotiations in secret so that the justifications for settlements were not made public; and (c) judicial scrutiny was perfunctory and judges merely 'rubber stamped' proposed consent decrees.[169] The Tunney Act

[165] Where one party has at least $US 10 mil and the other at least $US 100 mil in sales or assets, and the acquired stock or assets are worth at least $US 15 mil or result in control of an acquired party with at least $US 25 mil in sales or assets. There are several exceptions to the HSR Act, such as the acquisition of goods and realty in the ordinary course of business, the acquisition of voting securities solely for investment purposes where the acquirer will not hold more than 10% of the voting securities, intracorporate transactions and complex exceptions regarding stock or assets of foreign entities. For details on the application and administration of the HSR Act, see the FTC Premerger Notification Sourcebook: www.ftc.gov/bc/hsr/hsrbook.htm.

[166] The initial waiting period is generally 30 days, but if the transaction is a cash tender offer or bankruptcy sale, the initial waiting period is 15 days.

[167] One FTC official has claimed that the principal purpose of such settlements is 'to identify the competitive concern and ensure that the negotiated settlement will resolve the problem': Parker (1998). Thus, the FTC prefers structural remedies in the case of horizontal mergers, because in the FTC's view such remedies provide the greatest assurance of an effective cure without the need for continuous monitoring. The FTC will, however, consider non-structural remedies in relation to vertical mergers.

[168] The Tunney Act was introduced following revelations in which it was discovered that the Nixon administration had directed that court proceedings under the Clayton Act aimed at opposing the ITT/Hartford Fire Insurance merger be dropped in return for ITT's offer to help finance the 1972 Republican National Convention. It was also subsequently discovered that one of the reasons for the government's settlement was a concern that divestiture would lead to the plummeting of ITT's share price resulting in hardship to ITT shareholders. One consumer advocate unsuccessfully sought to have the case re-opened on the basis that investor hardship was not a legitimate reason for settlement. Prior to that, AT&T had successfully lobbied the Eisenhower Administration to drop divestiture proceedings against IT&T which had been commenced under the previous Truman Administration.

[169] Anderson (1996a).

imposes procedural and substantive requirements on the consent decree process aimed at ensuring that a proposed consent decree is 'in the public interest'.[170] It provides that a proposed consent decree together with a 'competitive impact statement' must be published in the Federal Register at least 60 days before the date on which the settlement would become effective. The government must file with the district court material the government considered 'determinative' in formulating the decree, and within this 60 day period, any person may file written comments on the proposed decree with the district court which must also be published in the Register. Summaries of the determinative materials, competitive impact statements and written comments must also be published in appropriate newspapers. The government is required to take into account the written comments and file and publish its response to those comments. It is then for the district court to approve the decree, but only if it first determines that the decree is 'in the public interest'. The factors which the court may consider in assessing the public interest are specified in the Act and include the competitive impact of the decree, the extent to which it requires termination of the alleged antitrust violations, provisions for enforcement and modification of the decree, how long the decree will remain effective, the anticipated effects of alternative remedies, any other considerations bearing upon the 'adequacy of such judgment', the impact of the decree 'upon the public generally' and upon individuals alleged to have been injured by the antitrust violations set forth in the government's complaint, and 'any public benefit that would be derived from a determination of the issues at trial'.[171]

The degree of formality, transparency and scope for third party participation associated with the process of negotiating administrative settlements concerning proposed mergers in the US appears to contrast rather starkly with the informal, closed and opaque nature of the informal merger clearance process adopted in Australia. But the formality and transparency mandated by the Tunney Act may not be an accurate reflection of reality. For example, Waller observes that, because the defendant may have been under strong pressure to settle, both government and private lawyers admit that consent decrees often contain 'window-dressing' provisions which in form look more significant than they are in business fact.[172] Furthermore, it is debatable whether judicial approval of consent decrees under the Tunney Act serves adequately to protect the public interest, with commentators differing in their assessment of whether the courts have engaged in the appropriate level of scrutiny of consent decrees. Some claim that courts have been appropriately deferential towards the exercise of prosecutorial discretion so as to prevent the settlement process from being turned into a virtual trial on the merits and thereby preserving consent decrees

[170] For a more detailed discussion of the Tunney Act procedure, see Von Kalinowski (1985) and Waller (1997).

[171] S 55 (e), Clayton Act.

[172] Waller (1997), para 13.9.

as a useful tool of settlement,[173] while others advocate more intense and independent judicial scrutiny.[174]

(b) EU Merger Regulation

Like its US counterpart, the scheme of merger regulation established in the EU mandates pre-merger notification of mergers of a certain size.[175] Once notified, the European Commission is required by the EC Merger Regulation[176] to assess whether or not a transaction would 'create or strengthen a dominant position as a result of which effective competition would be significantly impeded in the common market or a substantial part of it.'[177] Once a merger has been notified, a two stage procedure follows, consisting of a short initial phase (one month) during which the Commission undertakes a preliminary examination and must decide whether to initiate proceedings and, where the Commission so decides, a second contentious phase that in a majority of cases is closed by a decision on the operation's compatibility with the common market.[178] Although the majority of cases are cleared unconditionally within the first phase of the procedure because they do not raise competition concerns, one leading commentator observes that there is a 'very important group of cases' where the Commission grants clearance subject to commitments by the parties to modify their proposals in order to overcome the problems identified by it.[179] During both the first

[173] Anderson (1996a), 38. In the recent Microsoft Consent Decree, the US Court of Appeal took the view that in applying the public interest test, the court may a) insist upon correction of ambiguous provisions; b) require adequate implementation provisions; c) consider injury to third parties, and d) reject decrees that 'make a mockery of judicial power'. Academic commentators have variously advocated that judicial scrutiny should be stronger or weaker in its intensity: Boyder (1983); Savin (1997).

[174] Savin (1997).

[175] A concentration has a Community dimension where: (a) the combined aggregate worldwide turnover of all the undertakings concerned is more than EUR 5000 million; and (b) the aggregate Community-wide turnover of each of at least two of the undertakings concerned is more than EUR 250 million, unless (a) the combined aggregate worldwide turnover of all the undertakings concerned is more than EUR 2500 million; and (b) in each of at least three Member States, the combined aggregate turnover of all the undertakings concerned is more than EUR 100 million; (c) in each of the three Member states included for the purposes of (b), the aggregate turnover of each of at least two of the undertakings concerned is more than EUR 25 million; and (d) the aggregate community-wide turnover of each of at least two of the undertakings concerned is more than EUR 100 million; unless each of the undertakings concerned achieves more than two-thirds of its aggregate Community-wide turnover within one and the same Member State: Council Regulation (EEC) No 4064/89 of 21 December 1989 on the Control of Concentrations Between Undertakings O.J. L/257/14 (1990) (hereafter 'EC Merger Regulation'), Art 1(2). The EC Merger Regulation was amended in important respects by Regulation 1310/97 OJ [1997] L 180/1, Corrigendum OJ [1998] L 40/70 with effect from 1 March 1998.

[176] *Ibid*. For a new institutionalist perspective on EU merger control, see Bulmer (1994).

[177] EC Merger Regulation, Art 2.

[178] The EC Commission introduced a fast-track procedure for concentrations that can be expected not to give rise to competition concerns, which became operative on 1 September 2000 OJ [2000] C 217/32, 5 CMLR 774. On the operation of the EC Merger Regulation, see Whish (2003) ch 21 and the literature cited there.

[179] Whish (2001), 783B.

and second phases of the procedure, the European Commission is empowered under the EC Merger Regulation to attach conditions and obligations to a decision of compatibility which are intended to ensure that firms comply with the commitments they have entered into with the Commission, with a view to modifying their original merger proposal.[180]

Very tight timetables are prescribed in the Merger Regulation for the negotiation of commitments. In Phase I cases, commitments must be submitted to the EC Commission within three weeks of the date of receipt of the notification,[181] and this period cannot be extended. In Phase II cases, commitments must be submitted within three months of the date on which the Phase II proceedings were initiated, which may be extended in exceptional circumstances.[182] Commitments will be 'market tested' by the EC Commission, reflecting Regulation 1310/97's concern that 'transparency and effective consultation of Member States and interested third parties should be ensured in both phases of the procedure.'[183] If commitments are offered during Phase I, it is Commission practice to consult the competition authorities of Member States and affected third parties seeking their views on the effectiveness of the commitments offered.[184] If commitments are offered during Phase II, the EC Merger Regulation requires the Commission to consult the competition authorities of Member States, the Advisory Committee (consisting of representatives of the competition authorities of Member States[185]) and any third parties with a 'sufficient interest' for their views prior to making any formal decision.[186]

The legal effect of undertakings so given depends primarily on the terms of the undertakings themselves, and secondly on the type of commitment accepted. A distinction is made between conditions and obligations.[187] Where an obligation is breached, the Commission may revoke the clearance decision (whether offered during Phase I or Phase II), and the parties may be subject to fines and periodic penalties.[188] But if a condition is breached, then the clearance decision becomes

[180] EC Merger Regulation, Art 6(2) and Art 8(2). For examples of the types of commitments accepted by the EC Commission modifying merger proposals, see the Commission's *Notice on Remedies* OJ [2001] C 68/3. Prior to Reg 1310/97 there had been no legal basis for the acceptance of commitments during Phase I, a significant omission remedied by that legislation. Phase I commitments will be acceptable to the commission in fairly straightforward cases, 'where the competition problem is readily identifiable and can easily be remedied' (per Recital 8 of Regulation 1310/97). More complex cases will usually require a Phase II investigation before the Commission will consider a settlement. Whish observes that there is an increasing number of cases in which Phase I commitments are given, providing a useful table of statistics concerning conditional clearances: Whish (2001), 783B and 791–92.

[181] Regulation 447/98, Art 18(1).

[182] *Ibid,* Art 18(2).

[183] Regulation 1310/97, Recital 8.

[184] Commission Notice on Remedies Acceptable under Council Regulation No 4064/89 and Commission Regulation No 447/98 [2001] OJ C 68/3 paras 34–35.

[185] EC Merger Regulation, Art 19(4).

[186] EC Merger Regulation, Arts 19(1), 19(3) and 18(4).

[187] Commission Notice on Remedies Acceptable under Council Regulation No 4064/89 and Commission Regulation No 447/98 [2001] OJ C 68/3 para 12.

[188] *Ibid.*

void, and the Commission may order any appropriate action to restore the conditions of effective competition,[189] as well as subjecting the parties to fines.[190]

The above outline may suggest that there is a reasonably high degree of transparency and consultation built into the EC Commission's practice and procedure under the EC Merger Regulation, but it may not in fact present an entirely accurate impression.[191] In particular, the very tight time frames established under the EC Merger Regulation often result in commitments being offered at the eleventh hour, with the result that there is insufficient time for consultation with Member States, interested third parties and for a full analysis to be presented to the Advisory Committee in advance of its consideration of the commitments so offered.[192] In order to avoid this difficulty, a great many cases are thus dealt with by 'prenotification' meetings in which the EC Commission may provide guidance to notifying parties regarding its major competition concerns, thereby providing them with a framework to modify their proposals *before* formally notifying them under the EC Merger Regulation procedure.[193] Indeed, the European Competition Lawyer's Forum has, following discussions with the EC Commission's Merger Task Force, produced 'Best Practice Guidelines' which suggest that, even in the simplest cases, there should be 'prenotification' contact with the Merger Task Force prior to actual notification.[194] Commentators have expressed trenchant criticism at the lack of transparency and the absence of procedural restraints applicable to the negotiation of settlements in EU competition regulation,[195] and, partly in response to these criticisms and following extensive consultation, the EC Commission has recently accepted far-reaching reforms to the EC Merger Regulation which include automatically extending the period for negotiating commitments to seven weeks during Phase I, to provide parties with the opportunity to extend the time for negotiating commitments during complex Phase II cases, as well as automatically extending the Phase II deadline by 15 working days to allow for better consultation with Member States.[196] These reforms cannot, however, take effect unless and until approved by EU ministers.

[189] EC Merger Regulation Art 8(4).

[190] EC Merger Regulation Art 14(2)(c).

[191] Phase I decisions are not published in the Official Journal, other than a brief statement of outcome. However, Phase I decisions can be obtained via the home page of the Director General for Competition: http://europa.eu.int/comm/competition/index_html although they are only available in the language in which the parties notified. A press release summarising the Commission's finding in each case will usually be published in English, French, German and in the language of the notification, and a press release issued on the day following adoption of the decision. Phase II decisions are published in the 'L' series of the Official Journal: Whish (2001), 742.

[192] Green Paper on the Review of Council Regulation No 4064/89, 11 December 2001, COM(2001) 745, para 208.

[193] Drauz (1996), 233.

[194] The Best Practice Guidelines are available on the Commission's website: http://europa.eu.int/comm/competition/mergers/en/best_practice_gl.html

[195] Bourgeois (1993); Reynolds (1996); Van Bael (1986); Waelbroeck (1986).

[196] Proposal for a Council Regulation on the Control of Concentration Between Undertakings, [2003] OJ C 20/4, paras 75–77.

(c) Evaluation and Reform

The brief overview of USA and EU merger regulation, when considered in the light of Australian merger regulation, not only demonstrates the value and importance of administrative settlements as a technique for responding to mergers that may threaten to contravene competition law by providing a mechanism by which merger proposals may be modified in a manner which avoids contravening the law before they are consummated, but also illuminates the difficulties in devising procedural mechanisms that will enable the regulator to respond swiftly and creatively, while maintaining an acceptable level of transparency, accountability and third party participation. In contrast to the Australian approach to merger regulation, the formal procedures for regulating mergers established in both the US and EU appear to provide a considerably more structured, transparent and public framework in which third parties are given ample opportunity to participate. Yet one of the salutary and rather sobering lessons emerging from both sides of the Atlantic is the failure of formal procedural mechanisms to secure the levels of transparency, openness and accountability that formed the basis of their establishment, masking the actual informal negotiation process occurring between the parties that takes place behind a whitewash of procedural formality. In other words, the impulse to achieve flexible, individuated responses in regulatory enforcement, particularly when regulatory scrutiny occurs in advance of a contravention, may be so strong that attempts to introduce greater formality and rigour in the decision-making process may be circumvented in practice. The paradoxical result is that formal procedures designed to increase openness and participation may have directly contrary practical results, providing a veneer of respectability disguising the basis of the parties' true settlement.

In attempting to enhance the openness and accountability of the administrative settlements in the merger context, care is therefore required to avoid destroying the very flexibility and responsiveness that comprise its greatest strengths. It is clear that the existing process of informal clearance, which provides the backdrop within which merger undertakings are utilised, fails to provide an adequate degree of transparency, accountability and certainty in merger law and its administration. Yet attempts to remedy these weaknesses will inevitably entail the introduction of more formal, and consequently more cumbersome, procedures. The US and EU experience seems to indicate that laudable attempts to enhance the transparency, accountability and degree of third party participation in the merger process may well have counter-productive effects, rendering the merger negotiation and clearance process even more opaque in practice, closing off rather than opening up, avenues for review and participation. In this respect, there is much to be said for the recent recommendations of the Dawson Inquiry, which recognised the intractable difficulties associated with subjecting the current informal decisions taken by the Commission to review without formalising them in a manner that would increase the regulatory burden both on firms proposing to merge and the Commission.[197] Thus, rather than recommending a radical overhaul of the Commission's current informal clearance process, it recommended first, that the Commission should be required to provide adequate reasons for its decisions where it has rejected or accepted merger undertakings, and secondly, that a voluntary formal clearance process should be introduced, parallel to the existing informal clearance process. This formal clearance process would enable the Commission to grant binding clearances, thereby conferring formal immunity on the transaction while ensuring the legal enforceability of any conditions attached to the clearance, would be subject to strict time limits, and would be subject to merits review by the Australian Competition Tribunal at the suit of the applicants.[198]

E. CONCLUSION

This chapter has examined the Commission's use of enforceable undertakings, drawing upon the theoretical groundwork set out in the preceding chapter, in order to explore in more concrete terms the use of administrative settlements in the public enforcement process. Although enforceable undertakings are, in one sense, a relatively novel and unusual type of enforcement instrument, in another sense they may be seen as a form of administrative settlement, which is a well-established legal technique in dispute resolution generally, and for responding to regulatory violations in particular. What might be thought of as unique about enforceable undertakings is that they represent a means by which the process of administrative bargaining and negotiation in enforcement is institutionalised and given formal statutory recognition and endorsement. By examining the Commission's use of enforceable undertakings, we have seen how enforceable undertakings (and hence administrative settlements more generally) may provide a flexible, responsive enforcement tool, while drawing into sharper focus some of the constitutional difficulties which their use may generate.

It is beyond doubt that enforceable undertakings provide the Commission with an extremely useful and powerful enforcement tool, both as a remedial tool for responding to suspected contraventions of the Act and, in relation to proposed mergers, as a prophylactic that is intended to prevent anticipated contraventions of section 50. In both these contexts, we have seen how the use of bargaining and negotiation in regulatory enforcement may facilitate individuated regulatory responses that may help to overcome the limits of legalistic adherence to rules, encouraging flexibility, responsiveness, stability and efficiency in enforcement. In the remedial context, the legal force and flexibility of enforceable undertakings has meant that they have been more versatile than litigation or simple administrative resolution as regulatory enforcement tools,

[197] Dawson Report (2003), 9.
[198] Dawson Report (2003), Recommendations 2.1–2.2.

used not merely as an alternative to litigation, but also to settle or supplement litigation, so as to achieve outcomes and to pursue social purposes which could not readily be secured by way of court order. In the merger context, the availability of enforceable undertakings has encouraged a co-operative dialogue between the regulator and regulated and provided them with opportunities to develop creative and innovative responses enabling commercial parties to proceed with their proposals whilst complying with regulatory requirements. Competition concerns arising from a proposed merger may thus be identified prior to its consummation, avoiding the need to resort to costly and cumbersome litigation which is a particularly blunt instrument for regulating mergers, and may not always provide effective remedies post-completion.

On the other hand, the use of enforceable undertakings in both contexts also demonstrates the inherent tensions arising between the regulatory goals of flexibility, responsiveness and efficiency which together contribute to effective regulation, and several constitutional values. Although the same general framework of analysis and principles set out in the previous chapter apply to both remedial and merger undertakings, there are differences in the extent to which particular regulatory issues or tensions arise in each context. In particular, enforceable undertakings have generated considerable controversy in the merger context, partly due to the greater likelihood that mergers will impact upon third parties when compared with their use in a remedial setting, so that issues of participation, due process, accountability and substantive fairness arise much more acutely in relation to merger undertakings. On the other hand, because merger undertakings are generally used prophylactically, in order to prevent an anticipated contravention, rather than remedially in response to a past suspected contravention, there appears to be less of a risk that in the former case the undertakings will lack a genuinely consensual foundation. In other words, the risk that firms and individuals may be unfairly pressured into offering enforceable undertakings is somewhat higher in relation to remedial undertakings than in circumstances where merger undertakings are offered. I have thus suggested that it may not be legitimate for parties to provide remedial undertakings that are unduly burdensome or disproportionate in scope, but we may be more tolerant of excessively wide merger undertakings given that in the latter case the parties are willingly consenting to these obligations. I accept, however, that this issue generates considerable room for disagreement.

In sum, enforceable undertakings have considerable potential for promoting effective compliance, largely arising from the value of the bargaining and negotiation process upon which they are founded. Suspected and anticipated contraventions may be dealt with swiftly, while allowing the content and scope of the undertakings to be tailored to suit the individual circumstances and context in which the contravention allegedly arises. This sensitivity to context may serve to ameliorate some of the limits of legalistic adherence to rules while avoiding the formality, expense and hostility that may accompany the use of more formal adjudicative mechanisms for enforcement. Not only does bargaining and negotiation between the suspect and regulator open up the possibility for crafting creative, co-operative solutions that may promote effective compliance, but it may also be seen as fostering values, such as deliberation and participation, considered worthy of allegiance in a democratic state. On the other hand, because the bargaining and negotiation process is largely a closed and private one, the use of enforceable undertakings may tend to thwart, rather than nurture, the constitutional values of transparency, accountability, participation and substantive fairness. The dialogic process upon which enforceable undertakings rely appears to generate an inescapable conundrum, in that attempts to bolster these values is likely to necessitate greater formality, yet the qualities of informality and flexibility are essential to their effectiveness in securing creative, responsive, tailored solutions. In other words, we confront what is largely an inherent conflict between the virtues of informality that may be vital for securing effective compliance, and some of the constitutional values that underpin a flourishing liberal democracy. We cannot realistically expect to devise procedures that will enable all of the benefits of informal, co-operative enforcement approaches to be reaped without placing certain constitutional values under strain. Rather, the challenge is to identify whether or not the appropriate balance has been struck between these competing concerns. It is the resolution of conflicts of this kind, and the source of that conflict, to which we now turn in the closing chapter.

Part III

8

Conclusion

A. INTRODUCTION

IN THE PREVIOUS chapter, our examination of the Commission's use of enforceable undertakings demonstrated in more concrete and practical terms how the technique of bargaining and negotiation can enhance flexibility, responsiveness and timeliness in regulatory enforcement. But while resort to consensual decision-making processes between the regulator and regulated firm may promote regulatory effectiveness, it may tend to pull against several constitutional values. This tension, between the promotion of regulatory effectiveness and the deeper constitutional values that circumscribe the extent to which that endeavour may be uncompromisingly pursued, recurs throuhout our analysis of each aspect of enforcement examined in this book. In this concluding chapter, I wish to draw together some of the common threads which have been woven throughout the preceding pages, by excavating beneath the dissonance that may arise between the pursuit of regulatory goals and the need to take seriously the constitutional values limiting regulation's instrumentalist enterprise. But in seeking to highlight the principal issues lying at the heart of this inquiry, my aim is not solely to retrace my steps, for I shall also look ahead to the future, by briefly consider the potential implications of this research for the theory and practice of regulatory enforcement and for regulatory scholarship more generally.

B. RECURRING THEMES

In my examination of public competition law enforcement, I have chosen not to undertake a broad and generalised review of all the activities that might conceivably be considered as constituting public enforcement activity. Instead, I have focused on three activities that have real practical and theoretical importance and which often occur in regulatory enforcement: determining the quantum of penalties payable for regulatory violations, the use of 'plea bargains' or negotiated settlements to determine liability and/or the quantum of such penalties, and the resolution of suspected violations by administrative settlements. By adopting a public law perspective, drawing upon the principled framework of regulatory goals and constitutional values developed in chapter three as the lens through which these activities have been analysed, my aim has been three-fold.

First, I have sought to understand why rumblings of discontent have arisen in relation to each of these activities. Secondly, I have sought to assess the 'legality' of these activities, both in a 'thin' sense, in determining whether they conform with the standards of the law, and also in a 'thicker', deeper sense, by evaluating whether, and to what extent, they give expression to constitutional values. Thirdly, by viewing these activities contiguously, I have sought to illuminate deeper normative questions that pervade and animate regulatory enforcement practice more generally. It is these deeper issues which I wish to reflect upon in the closing pages of this book.

1. Regulatory Goals and Constitutional Values

Although friction arises between regulatory goals and constitutional values throughout each of the enforcement activities discussed in the preceding chapters, the particular configuration of regulatory goals and constitutional values around which this dissonance coalesces differs with each activity. So, for example, in chapter four we saw an inherent tension between two claims in seeking to identify the principles that should inform the quantification of regulatory penalties. On the one hand, it may be argued that penalties should be an effective deterrent, and thus set at a level that ought to deter those who might otherwise be tempted to contravene the law. But, on the other hand, if penal severity is determined wholly and exclusively by reference to the instrumentalist goal of deterrence, this may generate penalties that fall foul of the proportionality principle. The latter constitutional principle, which is grounded in the right to fair treatment, serves as an important delimitation on the extent to which the coercive power of the state may fairly be used to inflict the hardship of penal deprivation upon its citizens. In contrast, it is the potentially competing demands of efficiency in regulatory enforcement, and the importance of ensuring that due process values are adequately respected, that generates the primary site of tension between regulatory goals and constitutional values in the analysis of negotiated penalty settlements provided in chapter five. On the one hand, resort to negotiation and bargaining between the regulator and suspect to determine liability and quantum of penalties may promote efficiency and timeliness in regulatory enforcement, due to the significant savings in time and expense arising from the avoidance of formal adjudicative proceedings. But, on the other hand, such settlements not only lack transparency but may also generate a risk that the suspect may be unfairly pressured into accepting a settlement, thereby falling short of the demands of due process. A similar tension is apparent when suspected violations are resolved even more informally, via administrative settlement, rather than through the imposition of punitive sanctions. While resort to administrative settlements may promote the regulatory goals of flexibility, responsiveness and efficiency and thus contribute to effective regulation, there is a real risk that the values of due process, transparency, accountability and substantive fairness may be overlooked in the quest to secure agreement.

By drawing upon the normative framework of regulatory goals and constitutional values as the basis for examination, the source of the disquiet associated with these three enforcement activities can readily be identified. It seems attributable to a sense of unease concerning how the resolution of conflict between regulatory goals and constitutional values is reflected in current enforcement practice. While the pursuit of effectiveness is regulation's first and primary goal, it may be that insufficient attention has been paid to ensuring that the deeper constitutional values that should temper that endeavour are given adequate expression. In the context of Australian competition law enforcement, this may account for much of the anxiety concerning the transparency, accountability and fairness of some aspects of the Commission's enforcement practices. Although the aspects of Australian enforcement activity discussed throughout this book largely satisfy the strict requirements of legality, it is more doubtful whether they give adequate expression to the thicker concept of legality embodied in constitutional values. How, then, should antagonism between regulatory goals and constitutional values be resolved in regulatory enforcement practice? Finding principled answers to this question is a fraught and contestable task. One immediate source of difficulty stems from the enormous diversity of the commercial actors subject to regulation, ranging from massive multi-national corporations commanding vast resources through to individual tradespeople and professionals for whom the freedom to trade is critical to their livelihood. Accordingly, it may be difficult to identify general principles that may be simply and readily applied to any factual situation. But even if we look beyond the plurality of commercial actors who make up the regulated community, it is possible to attribute a weighty portion of the difficulty in finding clear, sharp-edged principles for resolving conflict to the uncertain moral and legal character of regulatory wrongs. But before we consider the problem of characterisation, it is worth pausing to reflect upon the context in which regulatory wrongs are enforced, for the way in which that context is understood will bear directly upon our understanding of the wrongs themselves.

2. Discretionary Power and Regulatory Enforcement

A common feature of regulatory regimes is the extent to which the regulator, as public enforcement authority, is typically invested with extraordinarily broad discretionary powers of enforcement yet is provided with very little statutory guidance concerning how that power should be exercised. In such circumstances, the regulator is largely left to exercise its own judgement, albeit guided to some extent by administrative law norms and practical realities (particularly resource constraints), in deciding how best to fulfil its enforcement role. As a rich and varied range of ethnographic studies have demonstrated, the way in which this discretionary power is exercised by regulatory officials may have a profound impact not only on specific cases, but on regulatory outcomes more generally. For example, we have seen how that broad discretion provides the foundation for 'regulatory bargaining', both in the form of negotiated penalty settlements and in the acceptance administrative settlements between the regulator and those suspected of violating regulatory standards. The use of bargaining and negotiation enables suspected violations to be resolved informally (to a greater or lesser extent), rather than by formal adjudication, and may thus promote several regulatory goals. By encouraging flexibility and responsiveness in enforcement, negotiation can help to overcome the inherent limitations of rules through sensitive, purposive, application and thus avoid formalism in interpretation and the shortcomings associated with 'creative compliance'. This may be particularly true of administrative settlements, for they allow the regulator to tailor its enforcement response to individual circumstances and to secure outcomes and achieve social purposes that might not be readily attainable by formal adjudication. Negotiated solutions may also be expected to promote efficiency in enforcement, particularly to the extent that they enable compliance to be secured without resorting to resource-intensive contested adjudicative proceedings. For all of these reasons, it is not surprising that empirical studies of regulatory behaviour reveal that a large number of regulatory agencies exhibit a strong preference for a 'compliance approach' involving the use of persuasion and co-operation to elicit compliance, in which the use of formal, punitive techniques is used only as a last resort, when more informal, negotiated approaches have failed.

Likewise, it is this broad enforcement discretion that provides the 'regulatory space' in which normative scholarship has blossomed, with academics setting out to construct models prescribing the 'optimal' techniques and strategies that should be used to secure compliance with regulatory goals. Perhaps the best-known of these strategies is the 'pyramid of compliance' approach advocated by Ayres and Braithwaite, resting on the idea that regulators should trade on the goodwill of the regulated community, encouraging compliance by persuasion and negotiation in the first instance, resorting to more intrusive, punitive strategies only if co-operation is not forthcoming. These ideas have been developed and refined further by other scholars, seeking to identify a set of 'regulatory design principles', intended to provide guidance to policy-makers in setting out to design regulatory regimes that will secure its collective goals effectively.

But while these prescriptive strategies might be of considerable assistance in promoting effective regulatory compliance, they may tend to detract from the fulfilment of several constitutional values. While regulatory compliance scholars may view broad discretionary powers as an opportunity for creative, innovative regulatory solutions, public lawyers within the Anglian tradition tend to see such power as opening up opportunities for abuse. Suspicion of discretionary power held by public officials remains an enduring and firmly entrenched legacy of the Diceyan tradition of constitutionalism. The essence of

Dicey's objection to discretionary power lay in the absence of clear, stable and relatively certain rules which could be relied upon by individuals to plan their lives and so avoid the suffering of punishment that would follow from a breach of the law. Although, as we have seen, there are many valuable reasons for investing public authorities with broad discretionary power, such power carries with it the risk that the coercive power of the state will be exercised arbitrarily or unfairly. So, for example, criminal lawyers have repeatedly warned of the risks associated with investing prosecutors with discretionary power to resolve criminal charges against suspected offenders by negotiation, fearing that innocent persons may be unfairly pressured into accepting a settlement which involves an acknowledgement of guilt. The risk of these and other similar threats to the liberty of the individual may be exacerbated in circumstances where the institutional framework within which the public authority operates lacks mechanisms for ensuring that discretionary power is exercised in a transparent and accountable manner. Within a democratic system, accountability requires that public officials to whom powers have been delegated must account for their actions to the community. The demands of accountability have their foundation in an assumption that all government powers are held on behalf of the community and therefore account must be made to it. Yet, when regulatory decisions are arrived at by a largely private process of negotiation, with perhaps only the end result open to public scrutiny, the transparency of regulatory enforcement decisions is diminished, at least when contrasted with contested court proceedings which are exposed to full public view. A lack of transparency in the regulatory process may not only diminish the accountability of the regulator but, in turn, may erode public confidence in the regulatory process. The challenge is to develop a framework of norms that may structure, inform and constrain the exercise of discretionary power in order to allow its benefits to be reaped, whilst alleviating, or at least reducing, these constitutional anxieties to a tolerable level. But in rising to this challenge, we have encountered a number of difficulties, ultimately attributable to difficulties in identifying the legal character of regulatory contraventions. Resolving the problem of characterisation provides the key to unlocking this challenge, and thus warrants further reflection.

3. Characterising Regulatory Wrongs

Throughout the preceding chapters, we have encountered a series of difficulties associated with identifying the substantive character of regulatory contraventions within the civil and criminal law paradigms that lie deeply embedded within the western legal tradition. At a formal level, the characterisation of unlawful conduct as civil or criminal is simply a matter of legislative choice. But our concern is with the substantive character of legal wrongdoing, and not merely its formal labelling, and this requires a more probing, context-sensitive examination of the nature of the wrong, the social purpose of the law in sanctioning the wrong, and the severity of the consequences of the sanction associated with its commission.[1]

The distinction drawn in western legal systems between civil and criminal liability, although to some extent a product of historical contingency, serves both to generate and to encapsulate a set of normative standards or ideals typically associated with the commission of legal wrongdoing. These norms or standards have both a substantive and procedural dimension, which may be illuminated by constructing and contrasting the criminal and civil law paradigms. According to the criminal law paradigm, the prohibited activity is thought to be morally blameworthy, the sanction for wrongdoing may entail serious consequences for the wrongdoer (including restrictions upon, or the deprivation of, individual liberty) and may carry a significant degree of moral stigma. Because a finding of criminal liability has serious consequences for the individual, the so-called 'responsibility principle' is of particular importance. Thus, from the perspective of the criminal law academic, the standard of liability for criminal wrongdoing paradigmatically requires proof of culpability, whether in the form of intent or recklessness. In addition, the suspected wrongdoer is entitled to a full range of procedural rights in the process of determining criminal liability, so as to guard against the grave injustice arising from the wrongful criminal conviction of the innocent.

By contrast, the civil law paradigm is not primarily concerned with censuring the wrongdoer for morally blameworthy conduct. Its principal social function is typically to impose 'obligations of repair' on the wrongdoer, thus encompassing an obligation to pay compensation or restitution to the victim harmed by the wrongdoing. Although remedies within the civil paradigm may impose significant financial burdens on the wrongdoer, they are payable to the victim, not to the state, primarily to repair damage done, not to condemn the wrongdoer. Accordingly, they do not paradigmatically involve the punishment of the wrongdoer, nor are they associated with the degree of moral stigma typically accompanying a finding of criminal liability. Because the consequences of civil liability for the wrongdoer are considerably less serious than those associated with criminal wrongdoing, proof of culpability need not be insisted upon in defining the relevant standards of liability, and the procedural rights of the suspected wrongdoer are considerably weaker than those available to the criminal defendant.

These contrasting paradigms illustrate how the characterisation of unlawful conduct as civil or criminal both reflects and informs the legal standards associated with wrongdoing. The characterisation of regulatory wrongs as more closely akin to civil or criminal wrongdoing has often been invoked by legislators and legal scholars to argue in favour of less or more stringent normative standards of liability and sanction. For example, if regulatory wrongs are seen

[1] Above, ch 5, Part C (2).

as largely analogous to civil wrongs, then this may suggest that the constitutional limits that circumscribe the imposition of criminal liability and punishment need not be adhered to. And, conversely, if regulatory wrongs are seen as more analogous to criminal wrongs, then this suggests that any such relaxation of constitutional limits cannot be justified. One of the distinctive and problematic features of regulatory wrongs is that the character of liability and sanction for such wrongs may be located in the shadowy twilight between the civil and criminal divide. In particular, the sanctions imposed for regulatory wrongs may be punitive in nature—in that the wrongdoer is subject to some state-imposed form of hard treatment for violating legal standards, rather than subject to a private obligation to repair the harm caused to the victim. Because the legal characterisation of regulatory wrongs is slippery and elusive, identifying the appropriate substantive and procedural norms that should attach to the imposition and sanctioning of regulatory wrongs is inevitably complex and contestable.

It is the use of sanctions to secure compliance with regulatory law, combined with its instrumental purpose, that create difficulties in locating regulatory contraventions within the civil and criminal paradigms, rendering the task of identifying the substantive norms applicable to regulatory wrongdoing problematic. These two features may tend to pull in opposite directions in our endeavour to locate the character of regulatory wrongdoing along the civil/criminal divide. Although theoretical models of paradigm civil and criminal law wrongs may be readily constructed, they may create the impression that qualitative, binary distinctions may easily be made. In the social practice of modern western legal systems, identifying the character of legal wrongs as civil or criminal is a considerably more indeterminate and equivocal task. In particular, the location of regulatory wrongs in the obscure middle-ground between civil and criminal wrongdoing may suggest that we may be a need to develop a distinctive 'middle-ground jurisprudence' reflecting a set of norms that are capable of facilitating the pursuit of regulation's collectivist goals, yet ensuring that constitutional values that limit the exercise of state power are given adequate expression. In the following discussion, I shall point to some of the difficulties associated with characterising regulatory law along the traditional civil/criminal divide which have emerged throughout the preceding chapters, and briefly outline how this middle-ground jurisprudence might be fashioned.

(a) *Substantive Norms and Regulatory Wrongs*

It may be useful to adopt a functionalist approach as a starting point in seeking to characterise the nature of regulatory wrongs as civil or criminal. Throughout this book, I have emphasised that regulatory law has a primarily instrumentalist function, seeking to induce a modification of behaviour in order to secure the attainment of the collective goals underpinning a regulatory scheme. To the extent that the targeted conduct lacks the moral reprehensibility typically associated with traditional crimes, regulatory wrongs may appear to bear a stronger resemblance to civil rather than criminal wrongs. The perceived moral ambivalence associated with regulatory wrongdoing has often been invoked by legislators as a justification for dispensing with constitutional principles that typically circumscribe the imposition of criminal liability and punishment. This argument has been asserted both in relation to the standards of liability, and in the principles that should inform the content and severity of punishment for regulatory wrongdoing.

At the level of liability, the moral ambivalence of regulatory offences is often claimed to justify the use of strict liability in proscribing the regulated conduct. Because regulatory offences are claimed to be less 'serious', typically lacking the degree of moral opprobrium associated with more traditional crimes, and the sanctions for regulatory wrongdoing are typically less severe than those associated with punishment for traditional crimes, the suspension of proof of fault may appear justified. In a similar fashion, it might be argued that the absence of a strong degree of moral antipathy associated with regulatory wrongdoing implies that constitutional principles limiting punishment need not be adhered to in sanctioning regulatory conduct.

On the other hand, some commentators reject the legitimacy of a qualitative distinction between traditional and regulatory crimes on the basis of moral repugnance, claiming that traditional crimes arouse moral disgust partly because they have been labelled as criminal for so long.[2] Such commentators emphasise the influence of historical conditioning and social convention in shaping moral convictions. Others seek to rely upon the reflexive quality of legal characterisation in advocating that regulatory offences ought to be labelled as criminal, and that this may, in turn, lead to a perception that regulatory offences are equally as serious and morally repugnant as more 'traditional' crimes.[3]

The contestable character of regulatory wrongs demonstrates both the dynamic nature of a community's moral values, and the absence of a sharp and rigid distinction marking the boundary between civil and criminal wrongdoing. But although social conditioning and convention may have a significant role in shaping one's moral beliefs, it is nonetheless possible to appeal to the critical morality of society to lend support to the validity of a distinction between the *degree* of wrongdoing associated with traditional crimes when compared with regulatory offences. This is not to suggest, however, that failure to comply with all laws that seek primarily to regulate economic and social activity is trivial, at least not in terms of the extent to which non-compliance may wreak harm on individuals and/or the community. Nor is it to deny the existence of a broad band of overlap in which some types of legal wrongdoing may display a mix of characteristics, some of which are typically associated with civil wrongs, but others bearing a stronger resemblance to criminal wrongdoing. It is in this

[2] Above, ch 4, Part B, (2) (a).
[3] *Ibid.*

elusive middle ground that regulatory wrongs might fairly be located. By conceptualising legal wrongs along a continuum, crimes involving deliberate and brutalising violations of physical integrity might lie at one end, with minor and often unintentional offences, such as parking infringements, traffic fines and other similarly trivial offences lying at the other end. Yet situating regulatory wrongs along this continuum is itself a contestable matter, for not all regulatory wrongs display the same level of seriousness: the careless release of toxic emissions into a public water supply may be thought qualitatively different to the inadvertent removal of a statutory tag from a mattress.[4]

But while there may be grounds for accepting the validity of a distinction between traditional crimes and regulatory wrongs, there is good reason to be suspicious of claims that the existence of such a distinction necessarily implies that we need not adhere to constitutional principles in sanctioning regulatory wrongdoing. Such claims, which seek to emphasise the instrumentalist function of regulatory law, tend to overlook the important fact that the sanctioning of regulatory wrongs involves bringing the coercive power of the state to bear against the citizen for violating the law—that is, it constitutes a form of punishment. Because regulatory law has an important public and punitive dimension, constitutional principles and values cannot simply be dispensed with in the absence of a strong censuring function. Thus, for example, the fact that regulatory contraventions are often associated with moral ambivalence may not be sufficient to justify dispensing with the responsibility principle by adopting a strict liability standard in proscribing regulatory wrongs. Given that the responsibility principle has its foundation in the Kantian injunction that individuals should be not be treated merely as disposable pawns in the pursuit of the collective interest, but as morally valuable and autonomous agents, it is doubtful whether the arguments for strict liability, even in the context of regulatory violations, may withstand critical scrutiny. Likewise, although the primary purpose of regulatory law is to modify the behaviour of the regulated community in order to achieve certain collectivist goals, this does not alter the punitive effect of regulatory sanctions. In a liberal democratic society, state-imposed penal deprivation not only requires particularly strong justification, but the scope of punishment must itself be clearly and narrowly circumscribed. Accordingly, the proportionality principle should not be dispensed with in determining the appropriate sanctions for regulatory wrongdoing. It serves as a general constitutional delimitation on the intrusive powers of the state, providing a ceiling on the extent to which regulation's instrumentalist goals may properly be pursued.

[4] Green (1997).

(b) Procedural Norms and Regulatory Wrongs

The significance of legal characterisation of regulatory wrongs upon the normative standards with which such wrongs are associated also resonates at the level of procedure and not only in shaping the appropriate substantive norms of liability and sanction. At its thinnest, the characterisation of regulatory wrongs as civil or criminal may assist in identifying the range of procedural rights capable of invocation by those 'charged' with regulatory wrongdoing. Although I have emphasised the importance of substance over form in characterising regulatory wrongs, the formal labels ascribed by the legislature to legal wrongs and the sanctions for legal wrongdoing are not without significance, for they have tended to dictate the procedural setting in which liability is determined. So, if a wrong (and its associated sanction) is labelled as criminal by the legislature in Anglian legal systems, a much greater range of procedural protections is accorded to the defendant in the determination of liability: it is for the prosecutor to establish the guilt of the accused beyond reasonable doubt, the innocence of the defendant is presumed and other procedural rights such as the right to silence and the right to privilege against self-incrimination also apply. By contrast, where wrongs and sanctions are labelled as civil in nature, then the procedural rights accorded to the defendant are considerably less rigorous: liability need only be established on the balance of probabilities, and the defendant has fewer procedural grounds for resisting demands to disclose relevant but potentially incriminating evidence.

Yet the practice of modern western legal systems has shown an increasing tendency towards the hybridisation of sanctions displaying a mixture of features, some characteristic of criminal sanctions, but others more reminiscent of civil sanctions. This tendency is particularly prominent in the regulatory sphere. Some commentators have observed the growing popularity of the 'punitive civil sanction'—its primary purpose is punitive in nature, seeking to deter conduct thought to impede the collective goals underpinning the regulatory scheme. But liability is formally characterised as civil rather than criminal, and it is imposed in the context of civil rather than criminal proceedings. The growing popularity of the so-called 'administrative offence', in which the label 'criminal' traditionally attached to the legal notion of an offence is replaced with the label 'administrative', might be seen as one example of this trend. These administrative offences refer to legal sanctions which impose some form of hard treatment on the offender (usually a monetary penalty) in response to legal violations for which the element of clear moral disapproval connoted by the use of a criminal sanction is absent, or only weakly expressed.[5] Indeed, one of the reasons why the use of these and other similar forms of 'hybrid' sanction may be popular with legislatures lies in enabling the state to penalise wrongdoers without

[5] Harding (1993), 133–35.

having to satisfy the more onerous procedural requirements associated with the criminal process.[6]

The use of such hybrid sanctions has also been accompanied by a shift away from conceptualising legal procedures, and the scope and content of procedural rights with which they are typically associated, in binary terms. Both courts and legal scholars are beginning to recognise that the level of procedural protections applicable in any given case should not be determined solely by reference to the formal label prescribed by the legislature. Rather, the range and rigour of procedural protections to be applied in any given case should not be seen as importing the entire range of extensive procedural guarantees which accompany the criminal process, or the correspondingly weaker protections typically associated with the civil process. Thus, for example, the seriousness of the consequences attached to a civil penalty may be such that greater procedural protections than those typically associated with civil proceedings may be warranted, while falling short of the extensive range of procedural protections which apply in criminal proceedings.

The characterisation of regulatory wrongs along the civil/criminal divide may also shed light upon the application of the 'thicker', deeper constitutional value of due process in the regulatory context. The procedural rights typically associated with the civil and criminal process referred to above presuppose that the process for determining whether or not a regulatory contravention has occurred falls to be determined by judicial adjudication. Indeed, the legal doctrine of procedural fairness may be seen as rooted in an assumption that the paradigm of fair process is that of a full-blown criminal trial, where the accused is accorded an array of procedural protections and a finding of guilt is determined by the application of clearly defined and publicly known rules by a neutral and impartial adjudicator. But it does not follow that decisions arrived at by non-adjudicative procedures necessarily fail to give adequate expression to the requirements of procedural fairness when viewed in its deeper constitutional sense, rather than as a doctrine of Anglian administrative law.

One of the reasons why a full-blown criminal trial is often thought of as the paradigm of fair process is the centrality of adjudication in determining the liability and punishment of the accused. The essence of adjudication as a decision-making process lies in its institutional commitment to a decision based on 'principle'. It depends critically on governance through rules authoritatively applied by a neutral and independent arbitrator. This adherence to rules, which involves the ideal of subjecting areas of legally relevant activity to general standards and which emphasises formal justice and the importance of rationality, is central to the Diceyan vision of the rule of law. Because the resolution of disputes through negotiation is shaped by the reciprocal needs and interests of the parties worked out through their bargain, rather than dictated by legal rules, it might be seen as contrary to the rule of law ideal. Although legal rules may

[6] Charney (1974).

cast a long shadow over the bargaining process, the resulting agreement need not reflect that which would have resulted from court adjudication through the application of legal rules.

Throughout the preceding chapters, I have emphasised that the constitutional importance of due process is rooted in both instrumental and non-instrumental values. In other words, the extent to which procedures may be regarded as fair depends, at least in part, on the extent to which they ensure accuracy in outcome, and partly on the extent to which they give expression to non-outcome based values, including the values of fairness and rationality implicit in the structure of the legal process. If we accept that fairness of legal procedures depends, to some extent, on securing accurate outcomes and on the seriousness of the outcome of the decision in question and its associated consequences, then we need to clarify what, in the regulatory enforcement context, constitutes an accurate outcome. To some extent, this depends on the social purpose of the law in seeking to impose sanctions on those who fail to abide by the law's commands. If the primary purpose of the law in the regulatory enforcement context is to secure agreement between the parties, then the bargaining process may be regarded as fair if the resulting settlement is genuinely consensual. But if the social purpose of the law lies in the accurate application of legal standards, then it may not be sufficient that the resulting bargain is genuinely consensual. Rather, we must inquire further into the content of the settlement agreement itself, before we can have confidence in its fairness.

Identifying the social purpose of the law is likely to be heavily dependent upon the context in which the issue arises. To that end, the distinction between civil and criminal wrongdoing may again be of assistance. Thus, for example, the resolution of allegations of serious criminal wrongdoing by resort to private bargaining and negotiation between a prosecutor and an innocent defendant in which the latter agrees to a lesser punishment than that which might ordinarily attach to the relevant crime seems unquestionably illegitimate. This is primarily because the punishment of the innocent represents a gross violation of the rule of law, even if it could plausibly be said that the innocent defendant genuinely 'consented' to her punishment. But the illegitimacy also stems partly from the fact that the standards of the criminal law might be thought of as embodying important minimum standards of behaviour demanded by the community, so that to depart from such standards, or to fail to apply them correctly, is seriously to undermine the moral and social fabric of the law. By contrast, the resolution of a contractual dispute between two well-resourced and well-informed commercial parties by agreement may appear to provide a socially desirable means of resolving the conflict between them. Contract law may be seen as essentially private and 'facilitative' in nature[7] so that departure from legal rules does not generate any cause for serious concern, unlike public law (including regulatory law) which cannot be overreached by private agreement.

[7] Collins (1999), ch 4.

Even within the sphere of regulatory enforcement, identifying the social purpose of the law is also likely to be context-specific. So, for example, the characterisation of pecuniary penalties imposed pursuant to section 76 of the Act as a form of punitive civil sanction suggests that the social purpose associated with the accurate application of standards is of importance in determining the fairness of the process by which liability and quantum are determined. Because the rule of law requires that only those who have acted unlawfully in contravention of the Act should be liable for a penalty, we cannot claim that a negotiated penalty settlement is fair simply because it represents a genuine and consensual agreement. We must also have confidence in the accuracy of the outcome so agreed, and that the terms of the bargain accurately reflect the true facts giving rise to the alleged contravention. Fair treatment requires, in this context, primarily that the individual is not exposed to an undue risk of being wrongfully penalised and, secondly, that those proved to have engaged in wrongdoing are not excessively penalised. Thus the process for determining liability and quantum of penalty payable for contraventions should seek to ensure that innocent persons are not wrongfully penalised, and that penalties imposed on an offender are not unfairly disproportionate or oppressive. By contrast, when considering the fairness of merger undertakings pursuant to an administrative settlement between the regulator and regulated firms, there may be grounds for adopting a less restrictive approach to the adherence to rules and principles, and to accord greater respect for the commercial autonomy of the parties involved, given that there is less risk of wrongful and excessive penalisation. No question of punishment arises—those involved in the merger negotiations have complete freedom to reject any proposal put to them by the regulator without thereby rendering themselves liable to the coercive threat of the law.

4. Finding the Right Balance?

Our brief reflection upon the broad discretionary powers that shapes the regulatory space in which enforcement occurs, and the difficulties of characterising regulatory contraventions in terms of the orthodox distinction between civil and criminal wrongdoing, illuminates the potential scope for antagonism between regulatory goals and constitutional values. One of the virtues associated with the conferral of broad discretionary power on public officials is that it enables them to resolve conflict between competing social values in a responsive, flexible and context-sensitive manner. Similar claims may also be made of the resolution of suspected regulatory violations by resort to informal decision-making processes that rely on bargaining and negotiation, rather than resort to the formal, time-consuming and costly process of judicial adjudication.

But the informal resolution of suspected contraventions of regulatory law may threaten a number of important constitutional values. There may be a real risk that the values of due process, transparency, accountability and substantive fairness may be marginalised or overlooked. Assessing the seriousness of these risks is a complex and contentious matter, partly due to the difficulties associated with characterising regulatory wrongdoing as civil or criminal in nature. If regulatory violations are considered to be largely analogous to civil wrongdoings, then resolution by the regulator by resort to the informal process of bargaining and negotiation may appear to generate few difficulties. But, because regulatory law constitutes a form of 'public law', seeking to facilitate the achievement of collective goals by seeking to modify the behaviour of the regulated community, and which cannot be overreached by private agreement, the analogy with civil law wrongs is not entirely apposite. Yet nor can regulatory wrongs be readily characterised as akin to criminal wrongdoing of the traditional kind, for they are only weakly associated (if at all) with the moral opprobrium with which the latter are typically associated.

The 'public' quality of regulatory wrongdoing, combined with the absence of strong moral antipathy, renders the task of characterisation both slippery and elusive. Even within a command and control scheme involving the imposition of very significant sanctions for regulatory wrongdoing, there is apparent resistance to viewing regulation as forming part of a society's system of justice. Regulatory wrongs tend to be thought of as avoidable by-products of otherwise laudable economic and social activity, to be discouraged but not condemned. They therefore tend to be viewed as constituting part of society's social-harm reduction system, rather than as a distinctive component of a society's system of justice. Yet regulatory programmes that utilise legal sanctions appear to sit uncomfortably on the periphery of both systems. Although they are not central to the community's system of justice (unlike the criminal justice system), nor can they be accurately characterised as solely and exclusively concerned with social–harm reduction (unlike, for example, infant immunisation programmes aimed at community-wide disease prevention). So, for example, competition regulation may be primarily conceived as a system of social-harm reduction: its primary goal being to eliminate anti-competitive conduct that might otherwise threaten the efficient functioning of markets. However, the use of significant punitive sanctions as a means for enforcing competition law rules indicates that competition regulation is directly related to a community's system of justice, despite the absence of a strong retributive flavour.

Difficulties in identifying which values ought to inform regulatory processes, and how to resolve tensions between competing values in situations of conflict, may be directly attributed to the ambiguous character of regulatory wrongs. To the extent that they resemble traditional crimes, the greater the emphasis that may appropriately be placed on constitutional values. But to the extent that they resemble private or 'civil' wrongs, the greater the emphasis that may appropriately be placed on regulatory goals in securing effective outcomes. Because there is a substantial margin for reasoned disagreement about the appropriate characterisation of regulatory violations, disputes are only to be expected in specifying the values that ought to shape and constrain regulatory processes.

In this book, I have developed a structured framework of normative standards, drawing from the rule of law within a liberal democracy, that may be used to resolve conflict that may arise between regulatory goals and constitutional values in a principled manner. By using this normative framework as a basis for evaluating several significant enforcement activities arising in the course of publicly enforcing competition law, I have also sought to demonstrate how such conflicts and tensions may arise, and to suggest how they might fairly be resolved. Throughout the preceding chapters, I have drawn upon the Australian experience of public competition law enforcement to give my discussion a more concrete focus. That experience highlights the extent to which the pursuit of effectiveness has shaped and influenced the exercise of the Commission's enforcement discretion, but has also attracted considerable criticism, including claims that it wields excessive discretionary power for which it is not sufficiently accountable. As we have seen, striking an appropriate balance between the pursuit of regulatory goals, and ensuring that the constitutional values, constraining that endeavour, are given adequate expression, forces us to confront a set of challenging and contestable questions. Thus, before concluding, it is worth pausing to consider, albeit briefly, the potential implications of these findings.

C. IMPLICATIONS FOR THE FUTURE

The normative framework of principles that I have developed in embarking upon a public law analysis of the three aspects of competition law enforcement focused upon in this book has been central to my evaluation. Accordingly, this book has demonstrated how these three activities may be understood, and may be in need of reform and refinement in order to meet the normative standards that I have identified. For the purposes of these concluding remarks, rather than repeat the concerns identified in the preceding chapters, I will seek briefly to identify the broader potential implications of my approach for the theory and practice of securing regulatory compliance, and of regulatory scholarship more generally.

One of my principal motives for developing and drawing upon the above framework of principles as the basis for examining the three enforcement activities focused upon in this book, is to stimulate reflection and debate concerning the *values* that ought to inform and shape regulatory processes. As we have seen, the study of regulatory enforcement and compliance has captured the attention of a number of scholars and forms the focus of a growing and increasingly sophisticated literature. Although there are some stirrings within recent scholarship that are beginning to consider which values should shape regulatory processes,[8] nonetheless most such scholarship tends implicitly to assume that

[8] Vincent-Jones (2002); Black (2000); Braithwaite (2002).

regulatory implementation is a technocratic process, concerned exclusively with identifying 'what works'. Given the instrumentalist nature of the regulatory enterprise, the effective achievement of the collective goals underpinning a regulatory regime is appropriately given prominence. But there are other values of importance besides effectiveness and efficiency. The particular set of values which ought to be reflected in regulatory implementation will depend, ultimately, on how regulation is understood, and on some chosen background political theory. Disagreement about those values is thus only to be expected. One of the distinctive features characterising a significant body of regulatory compliance scholarship is the absence of any debate about what these values should be, and it is this kind of debate and reflection that I hope to stimulate and encourage.

By adopting a public law approach, I have sought to underline the importance of constitutional values in tempering the pursuit of effectiveness, pointing to deeper questions of fairness (or justice) which regulatory enforcement may throw up, yet which have tended to be overlooked or ignored in the existing literature. In so doing, I have cast significant doubt on the constitutional legitimacy of prescriptive models of regulatory enforcement advocated by scholars who draw heavily from game theory as the basis for their analysis, including the well-known pyramid of compliance approach advocated by Ayres and Braithwaite.[9] Even if such models are correct in identifying the most 'successful' enforcement strategies, defined in terms of their ability to bring about regulatory compliance in the most cost-effective manner, the legitimacy of regulatory implementation must also be evaluated in terms of the extent to which it gives expression to the richer and deeper constitutional values that shape and inform the exercise of public power.

Although my normative framework of regulatory goals and constitutional values has been used throughout this book to examine various aspects of regulatory enforcement activity, it might also be profitably used as a basis for evaluating the legitimacy of other aspects of regulatory implementation, including institutional design, standard setting, and even for full programme evaluation. For example, at the level of institutional design, one of the predominant concerns infusing a considerable body of literature on regulation refers to the so-called 'crisis' of regulatory accountability.[10] While this notion may be seen as encapsulating a number of different but related concerns, these concerns coalesce around the somewhat anomalous constitutional position of independent regulatory agencies. These agencies are independent in the sense that they are designed to operate in a largely autonomous manner and are not subject to day to day ministerial direction. One of the difficulties associated with these agencies is that they are, like the Australian Competition and Consumer Commission, often invested with very broad discretionary powers yet provided

[9] Braithwaite and Ayres (1992).
[10] Graham (1998).

with very little legislative guidance in the exercise of that power. Thus, academic critiques have often referred, not only to the enormity and complexity of the regulator's task in seeking to reconcile multiple and often conflicting legislative objectives in administering the regulatory scheme, but the constitutional difficulties associated with conferring the task of making what are effectively political decisions on an unelected and therefore politically unaccountable body. The normative framework set out in this book may provide a fruitful approach for those involved in the practical design of regulatory institutions, by providing a basis for constructing an institutional framework which allows for such conflict and tensions to be both openly identified, and resolved in a principled and consistent manner, and also for theorists seeking to evaluate regulatory programme design and implementation.

From a legal perspective, this book also serves to highlight the intersection of two bodies of law, criminal law and administrative law, which tend to be viewed in a largely independent and autonomous fashion. Yet these two bodies of law share a common foundation, being rooted in constitutional values which are themselves more deeply anchored in philosophical and political theories of democracy. This commonality is often overlooked, at least in the Anglian context, by both criminal and administrative lawyers alike. While administrative lawyers have paid close attention to analysing the discretionary power of public officials, a vast swathe of existing literature adopts an essentially abstract and doctrinal approach, attempting to flesh out the appropriate scope and content of the principles of judicial review. Relatively few scholars have been concerned to adopt a more context-sensitive approach, which seeks to evaluate the extent to which the demands of administrative law are borne out in the practice of real-world decision-making. Criminal lawyers, by contrast, have been much more alive to the importance and pervasiveness of enforcement discretion in the criminal process. But in warning of the dangers associated with the informal resolution of criminal proceedings, criminal lawyers tend to view the conventional list of common law rights of the criminal defendant in a relatively 'thin' fashion. By this I refer to the tendency of academics from within the criminal law tradition to take as given the existence of various procedural rights of the criminal defendant (such as the right to trial, the right to privilege against self-incrimination and so forth) rather than probing more deeply into the thicker, richer constitutional value of due process upon which the procedural rights of the accused are anchored, in order to define their nature and scope.[11]

By examining the exercise of discretion by public enforcement officials in the context of competition law enforcement, this book illuminates the common wellspring of constitutional values from which the critiques of both the criminal and administrative law traditions are drawn. The normative approach adopted in this book may also point to an important and fruitful agenda for future research. It has, I hope, highlighted the value of adopting what might be

[11] For example, Ashworth (1998); Greenawalt (1978); Wadham (1994).

termed 'applied public law' scholarship. Administrative lawyers may have more in common with criminal lawyers than traditional Anglian administrative law scholarship, with its focus on judicial review, may suggest. By adopting a context-sensitive analysis, which seeks to evaluate the extent to which the constitutional values around which judicial review is constructed are reflected in the practice of public decision-making, it may not only assist in shaping the practice of public decision-making in the regulatory context, but in enriching legal scholarship more generally.

Bibliography

ABEL R, (1982) *The Politics of Informal Justice* (Los Angeles, Academic Press)

ACCC, (1999) *Merger Guidelines* (Canberra, Australian Competition and Consumer Commission)

—— (1998) *Mergers—A Statistical Summary* (Canberra, ACCC)

Administrative Review Council, (1989) *Review of the Administrative Decisions (Judicial Review) Act: The Ambit of the Act*, Report No 32 (Canberra)

ALLARS M, (1997) *Australian Administrative Law: Cases and Materials* (Sydney, Butterworths)

ALRC, (1994) *Compliance with the Trade Practices Act 1974*, Report No 68 (Sydney, Australian Law Reform Commission)

—— (2002) *Principled Regulation*, Report No 95 (Sydney, Australian Law Reform Commission)

—— (1988) *Sentencing*, Report No 44 (Canberra, Australian Law Reform Commission)

—— (1980) *Sentencing of Federal Offenders*, Report No 15 (Canberra, Australian Law Reform Commission)

—— (1987) *Sentencing: Penalties*, Interim Report No 30 (Sydney, Australian Law Reform Commission)

AMATO G, (1997) *Antitrust and the Bounds of Power* (Oxford, Hart Publishing)

ANDERSON L, (1996a) '*United States v Microsoft*, Antitrust Consent Decrees, and the Need for a Proper Scope of Judicial Review' 65 *Antitrust Law Journal* 1

ANDERSON W, et al (1996) 'Merger Misconceptions: the Industry Commission's Paper on the ACCC's Draft Merger Guidelines' 4 *Competition & Consumer Law Journal* 128

ANTHONY R, (1992) ' "Well, You Want the Permit Don't You?" Agency Efforts to Make Nonlegislative Documents Bind the Public' 44 *Administrative Law Review* 31

ARP DJ and SWAAK C, (2003) 'A Tempting Offer: Immunity from Fines for Cartel Conduct under the European Commission's New Leniency Notice' 24 *European Competition Law Review* 9

ASHWORTH, A (1995) *Principles of Criminal Law*, 2nd edn (Oxford, Clarendon Press)

—— (1998) *The Criminal Process: An Evaluative Study*, 2nd edn (Oxford, Oxford University Press)

—— (2000) *Sentencing and Criminal Justice*, 3rd edn (London, George Weidenfeld and Nicholson Ltd)

—— (2000a) 'Is the Criminal Law a Lost Cause?' 116 *Law Quarterly Review* 225

AUBERT V, (1952) 'White-Collar Crime and Social Structure' 58 *American Journal of Sociology* 263

AUERBACH J, (1983) *Justice Without Law?* (New York, Oxford University Press)

BALDWIN R, (1997) 'Regulation: After "Command and Control" ' in K Hawkins (ed) *The Human Face of Law: Essays in Honour of Donald Harris* (Oxford, Oxford University Press)

BALDWIN R, (1996) *Rules and Government* (Oxford, Clarendon Press)

—— (1990) 'Why Rules Don't Work' 53 *Modern Law Review* 321

BALDWIN R and Cave M, (1999) *Understanding Regulation* (Oxford, Oxford University Press)

BALDWIN R and MCCRUDDEN C, (eds) (1987) *Regulation and Public Law* (London, George Weidenfeld and Nicholson Ltd)

BALDWIN R, SCOTT C and HOOD C, (eds) (1998) *A Reader on Regulation* (Oxford, Oxford University Press)

BARDACH E and KAGAN R, (1982) *Going by the Book: The Problem of Regulatory Unreasonableness* (Philadelphia, Temple University Press)

BATOR F, (1958) 'The Anatomy of Market Failure', *Quarterly Journal of Economics* 351

BAUMOL WJ, (1982) 'Contestable Markets: An Uprising in the Theory of Industry Structure' 72 *American Economic Review* 1

BAYNE P, (1988) 'Administrative Law and the New Managerialism in Public Administration' 62 *Australian Law Journal* 1040

BECKER G, (1968) 'Crime and Punishment: An Economic Approach' 76 *Journal of Political Economy* 169

BELLONI F and HODGESON F, (2000) *Criminal Injustice* (Basingstoke, MacMillan Press Ltd)

BENTHAM J, (1789) *An Introduction to the Principles of Morals and Legislation*

BENTHAM J, (1838-1843) 'The Principles of Penal Law' in J Bowring (ed) *The Works of Jeremy Bentham*

BEYLEVELD D, (1979) 'Deterrence Research as a Basis for Deterrence Policies' 18 *Howard Journal of Criminal Justice* 135

BILMES J and WOODBURY J, (1991) 'Deterrence and Justice: Setting Civil Penalties in the Federal Trade Commission' 14 *Research in Law and Economics* 191

BLACK D, (1993) *Sociological Justice* (New York, Oxford University Press)

BLACK J, (1997) *Rules and Regulators* (Oxford, Oxford University Press)

—— (1998) 'Talking About Regulation' *Public Law* 77

—— (2000) 'Proceduralising Regulation' 20 *Oxford Journal of Legal Studies* 597

—— (2001) 'Managing Discretion" Paper presented at the 'Penalties: Policy, Principles and Practice in Government Regulation Conference', Sydney, 7 June 2001

—— (2003) 'Enrolling Actors in Regulatory Systems: Examples from the UK Financial Services Regulation' *Public Law* 63

BLACK J, MUCHLINSKI P and WALKER P, (eds) (1998) *Commercial Regulation & Judicial Review* (Oxford, Hart Publishing)

BLECKMANN A and BOTHE M, (1986) 'General Report on the Theory of Limitations on Human Rights' in A de Mestral, (eds), *The Limitation of Human Rights in Comparative Constitutional Law* (Quebec, Les Editions Yvon Blais Inc)

BLOCK M and SIDAK J, (1980) 'The Cost of Antitrust Deterrence: Why Not Hang a Price Fixer Now and Then?' 68 *The Georgetown Law Journal* 1131

BORK RH, (1978) *The Antitrust Paradox* (New York, Basic Books)

BOS P, STUYCK J and WYTINCK P, (1992) *Concentration Control in the European Economic Community* (London, Graham & Trotman Ltd)

BOTTOMS A, BURNEY E, VON HIRSCH A and WIKSTROM P-O, (1999) *Criminal Deterrence and Sentence Severity* (Oxford, University of Cambridge Institute of Criminology)

BOURGEOIS JHJ, (1993) 'Undertakings in EC Competition Law' in PJ Slot and A McDonnell (eds), *Procedure and Enforcement in EC and US Competition Law* (Leiden, Sweet & Maxwell)

BOYDER A, (1983) 'Form as Substance: A Comparison of Antitrust Regulation by Consent Decrees in the USA, Reports of the MMC in the UK, and Grants of Clearance by the European Commission' 32 *International and Comparative Law Quarterly* 904

BRAITHWAITE J, (1993) 'Responsive Regulation for Australia' in P Grabosky and J Braithwaite (eds), *Business Regulation and Australia's Future* (Canberra, Australian Institute of Criminology)

—— (2002) *Restorative Justice and Responsive Regulation* (New York, Oxford University Press)

BRAITHWAITE J and AYRES I, (1992) *Responsive Regulation: Transcending the Deregulation Debate* (New York, Oxford University Press)

BRENT R, (1995) 'The Binding of Leviathan?—The Changing Role of the European Commission in Competition Cases' 44 *International and Comparative Law Quarterly* 255

BREYER S, (1982) 'Alternatives to Classical Regulation' in S Breyer (ed) *Regulation and its Reform* (Cambridge, MA, Harvard University Press)

BRIGHAM J and BROWN D, (1980) 'Distinguishing Penalties and Incentives' 2 *Law & Policy Quarterly* 5

BRUNT M, (1994) 'The Australian Antitrust Law after 20 Years—a Stocktake' in D Round (ed) *Review of Industrial Organisation* (Netherlands, Kluwer Academic Publishers)

BULMER S, (1994) 'Institutions and Policy Change in the European Communities: The Case of Merger Control' 72 *Public Administration* 423

CALDART C and ASHFORD N, (1999) 'Negotiation as a Means of Developing and Implementing Environmental and Occupational Health and Safety Policy' 23 *Harvard Environmental Law Review* 180

CANE P, (2002) *Responsibility in Law and Morality* (Oxford, Hart Publishing)

—— (1996) *An Introduction to Administrative Law* (Oxford, Clarendon Press)

CARROLL P and MCGREGOR-LOWNDES M, (2001) 'A Standard for Regulatory Compliance? Industry Self-Regulation, the Courts and AS3806-1998' 60 *Australian Journal of Public Administration* 80

CATO C, (1998) *The Law and Practice of Criminal Litigation* (North Ryde, LBC Information Services)

CHARNEY JI, (1974) 'The Need for Constitutional Protections for Defendants in Civil Penalty Cases' 59 *Cornell Law Review* 478

CINI T and MCGOWAN L, (1999) 'Politicisation and Discretion in EU Competition Policy: The Case of Merger Control' 12 *Governance* 175

CLARK P, (1986) 'The Public Prosecutor and Plea Bargaining' 60 *The Australian Law Journal* 199

COFFEE JJ, (1991) 'Does "Unlawful" Mean "Criminal"?: Reflections on the Disappearing Tort/Crime Distinction in American Law' 71 *Boston University Law Review* 193

—— (1992) 'Paradigms Lost: The Blurring of the Criminal and Civil Law Models—And What Can Be Done About It' 1992 *Yale Law Journal* 1875

COLLINS H, (1999) *Regulating Contracts* (Oxford, Oxford University Press)

COOTER R, (1984) 'Prices and Sanctions' 84 *Columbia Law Review* 1523

COOTER R and ULEN T, (1997) *Law and Economics*, 2nd edn (USA, Addison-Wesley Educational Publishers Inc)

CORRY D, (1995) 'Approaches to Accountability' in D Corry (ed) *Profiting from the Utilities* (London, Centre for Regulated Industries)

COTTERRELL R, (1992) *The Sociology of Law—An Introduction*, 2nd edn (London, Butterworths)

CRAIG E, (1998) 'Professional Ethics' *Routledge Encyclopaedia of Philosophy* (London, Routledge)

CRAIG P, (1997) 'Formal and Substantive Conceptions of the Rule of Law: An Analytical Framework' *Public Law* 467

—— (1999) *Administrative Law*, 4th edn (London, Sweet & Maxwell)

CRASWELL R, (1999) 'Deterrence and Damages: The Mutliplier Principle and its Alternatives' 97 *Michigan Law Review* 2185

CRISPIN K, (1995) 'Prosecutorial Ethics' in S Parker and C Sampford (eds), *Legal Ethics and Legal Practice* (Oxford, Clarendon Press)

CURRAN P, (1991) 'Discussions in the Judge's Private Room' *The Criminal Law Review* 79

DAINTITH T, (1994) 'The Techniques of Government' in J Jowell and D Oliver (eds), *The Changing Constitution* (Oxford, Oxford University Press)

—— (1998) 'Legal Measures and Their Analysis' in R Baldwin, C Hood and C Scott (eds), *A Reader on Regulation* (Oxford, Oxford University Press)

DANA D, (2000) 'The Emerging Regulatory Contract Paradigm in Environmental Regulation' *University of Illinois Law Rev* 35

DAU-SCHMIDT K, (1990) 'An Economic Analysis of the Criminal Law as a Preference Shaping Policy' *Duke Law Journal* 1

DAVIES A, (2001) *Accountability: A Public Law Analysis of Government by Contract* (Oxford, Oxford University Press)

DAVIS K, (1969) *Discretionary Justice* (Baton Rouge, Louisiana State University Press)

DE BURCA G, (1993) 'The Principle of Proportionality and its Application in EC Law' 13 *Yearbook of European Law* 105

Department of Trade and Industry, (1998) *A Fair Deal for Consumers—Modernising the Framework for Utility Regulation* (London)

DICEY AV, (1961) *The Law of the Constitution* (London, Macmillan)

DIVER CS, (1999) 'The Optimal Precision of Adminstrative Rules' in R Baldwin, C Hood and C Scott (eds), *A Reader on Regulation* (Oxford, Oxford University Press)

DRAUZ G, (1996) 'Remedies Under the Merger Regulation' in B Hawk (ed) *Fordham University School of Law: US and Common Market Antitrust Policies* (New York, Sweet & Maxwell, Juris)

DUFF RA, (1999) 'Punishment, Communication and Community' in M Matravers (ed), *Punishment and Legal Theory* (Oxford, Hart Publishing)

DUFF RA and GARLAND D, (eds) (1994) *A Reader on Punishment* (Oxford, Oxford University Press)

DUMONT M, (eds) (1825) *Works—A Treatise on Judicial Evidence extracted from the Manuscripts of Jeremy Bentham*, translated into English (London, Baldwin, Cradock and Joy)

—— (eds) (1827) Bentham's Works—*Rationale of Judicial Evidence, Specially Applied to English Practice* (London, Hunt and Clarke)

—— (eds) (1837) *Works—Bentham's Principles of Judicial Procedure* (London)

DUNNING MN and DEAN MR, (1995) 'Negotiated Penalties—A New Zealand Perspective' Paper presented at the 'The Business Law Section, Law Council of Australia, Trade Practices Workshop', Fremantle, Western Australia, 15 July

DWORKIN R, (1978) *Taking Rights Seriously* (London, Duckworth)

—— (1985) *A Matter of Principle* (Cambridge, MA, Harvard University Press)

EASTERBROOK F, (1987) 'Allocating Antitrust Decision Making Tasks' 76 *The Georgetown Law Journal* 305

—— (1985) 'Detrebling Antitrust Damages' 28 *Journal of Law & Economics* 445

—— (1992) 'Plea Bargaining as Compromise' 101 *Yale Law Journal* 1969

EEKELAAR J, (1991) *Regulating Divorce* (Oxford, Clarendon Press)

EISENBERG M, (1976) 'Private Ordering Through Negotiation: Dispute-Settlement and Rulemaking' 89 *Harvard Law Review* 637

ELLIOT D, (1997) 'Towards Ecological Law & Policy' in Marian Chertow and Daniel Esty (eds), *Thinking Ecologically: The Next Generation of Environmental Policy* (New Haven, Yale University Press)

ELZINGA K and BREIT W, (1985) 'Private Antitrust Enforcement: The New Learning' 28 *Journal of Law and Economics* 405

EMMERSON B and ASHWORTH A, (2001) *Human Rights and Criminal Justice* (London, Sweet & Maxwell)

FARBER D, (1999) 'Taking Slippage Seriously' 23 *Harvard Environmental Law Review* 297

FEATHERSTON R, (1995) 'Negotiated Penalties—Trick or Treat?' Paper presented at the 'The Business Law Section, Law Council of Australia, Trade Practices Workshop', Fremantle, Western Australia, 15 July

—— (1997) 'Negotiating Penalties with the ACCC' Paper presented at the 'Law Council of Australia, 30th Australian Legal Convention', Melbourne, 18-21 September

FEINBERG J, (1970) 'The Expressive Function of Punishment' in J Feinberg *Doing and Deserving: Essays in the Theory of Responsibility* (Princeton, Princeton University Press) 95

FELDMAN D, (1996) 'The Privilege Against Self-Incrimination and Conflicting Interests' in D Feldman and F Meisel (eds), *Corporate and Commercial Law: Modern Developments* (London, Lloyd's of London Press)

FELS A, (1982) 'The Political Economy of Regulation' 5 *UNSW Law Journal* 29

—— (1998) 'Address to the National Press Club' 16 *ACCC Journal* 2

FINNIS J, (1980) *Natural Law and Natural Rights* (Oxford, Oxford University Press)

FISS O, (1984) 'Against Settlement' 93 *Yale Law Journal* 1073

FISSE B and Braithwaite J, (1984) 'Sanctions Against Corporations: Dissolving the Monopoly of Fines' in R Tomasic (ed) *Business Regulation in Australia* (Sydney, CCH)

FISSE B and BRAITHWAITE J, (1993) *Corporations, Crime and Accountability* (Cambridge, Cambridge University Press)

FOSTER CD, (1992) *Privatization, Public Ownership and the Regulation of Natural Monopoly* (Oxford, Blackwell)

FOX EM, (1981) 'The New American Competition Policy—From Anti-Trust to Pro-Efficiency' 2 *European Competition Law Review* 439

FOX RG and FRIEBERG A, (1999) *Sentencing—State and Federal Law in Victoria*, 2nd edn (Melbourne, Oxford University Press)

FREEDLAND M, (1994) 'Government by Contract and Public Law' *Public Law* 86

FREEMAN J, (1997) 'Collaborative Governance in the Administrative State' 40 *University of California Law Review* 1

—— (2000) 'The Private Role in Public Governance' 75 *New York University Law Review* 543

—— (2000a) 'The Contracting State' 28 *Florida State University Law Review* 155

FREIBERG A, (1983) 'Monetary Penalties Under the Trade Practices Act 1974 (Cth)' 12 *Australian Business Law Review* 4

FREIBERG A and O'MALLEY P, (1984) 'State Intervention and the Civil Offense' 18 *Law and Society Review* 373

FRIEDMAN LM, (1993) *Crime and Punishment in American History* (New York, Basic Books)
FULLER L, (1971) 'Mediation' 44 *Southern California Law Review* 305
—— (1978) 'The Forms and Limits of Adjudication' 92 *Harvard Law Review* 353
—— (1981) 'Two Principles of Human Association' in K Winston (ed) *The Principles of Social Order* (Durham, North Carolina, Duke University Press)
—— (1981a) 'Human Interaction and the Law' in K Winston (ed) *The Principles of Social Order* (Durham, Duke University Press)
GAEBLER T and OSBORNE D, (1992) *Reinventing Government* (New York, Addison Wesley)
GALLIGAN DJ, (1986) *Discretionary Powers in the Legal Order* (Oxford, Oxford University Press)
—— (1981) 'The Return to Retribution in Penal Theory' in C Tapper (ed) *Crime, Proof & Punishment* (London, Butterworths)
—— (1994) 'Regulating Pre-Trial Decisions' in N Lacey (ed) *A Reader on Criminal Justice* (Oxford, Oxford University Press)
—— (1996) *Due Process and Fair Procedures* (Oxford, Oxford University Press)
GANGULLY J, (1998) 'Environmental Remediation Through Supplemental Environmental Projects and Creative Negotiation: Renewed Community Involvement in Federal Enforcement' 26 *Boston College Environmental Affairs Law Review* 189
GENN H, (1987) *Hard Bargaining* (Oxford, Clarendon Press)
—— (1993) 'Business Responses to the Regulation of Health and Safety in England' 15 *Law and Policy* 219
—— (1993) 'Tribunals and Informal Justice' 56 *Modern Law Review* 393
GILLOOLY M and WALLACE-BRUCE NL, (1994) 'Civil Penalties in Australian Legislation' 13 *University of Tasmania Law Review* 269
GOLDSTEIN AS, (1992) 'White-Collar Crime and Civil Sanctions' 101 *Yale Law Journal* 1895
GOYDER D, (1998) *EC Competition Law*, 3rd edn (Oxford, Clarendon Press)
GRABOSKY P, (1993) 'Australian Regulatory Enforcement in Comparative Perspective' in Peter Grabosky P and Braithwaite J, (eds), *Business Regulation and Australia's Future* (Canberra, Australian Institute of Criminology)
GRABOSKY P and BRAITHWAITE J, (1985) *Of Manners Gentle—Enforcement Strategies of Australian Business Regulatory Agencies* (Melbourne, Oxford University Press)
GRAHAM C, (1998) 'Is There a Crisis in Regulatory Accountability?' in Robert Baldwin, Colin Scott and Christopher Hood (eds), *A Reader on Regulation* (Oxford, Oxford University Press)
GRANT J, (1984) 'The Economic Costs and Benefits of the Australian Trade Practices Legislation' in R Tomasic (ed) *Business Regulation in Australia* (Sydney, CCH)
GREEN S, (1997) 'Why It's a Crime to Tear the Tag off a Mattress: Overcriminalization and the Moral Content of Regulatory Offences' 46 *Emory Law Journal* 1533
GREENAWALT K, (1978) 'Perspectives on the Right to Silence' in J Baldwin and AK Bottomley (eds), *Criminal Justice Selected Readings* (London, Martin Robertson)
GUNNINGHAM N, (1987) 'Negotiated Non-Compliance: A Case Study of Regulatory Failure' (1987) 9 *Law & Policy* 67
GUNNINGHAM N and GRABOSKY P, (1998) *Smart Regulation* (Oxford, Clarendon Press)
GUNNINGHAM N and JOHNSTONE R, (1999) *Regulating Workplace Safety: Systems & Sanctions* (Oxford, Oxford University Press)

HADDEN T, (1970) 'Strict Liability and the Enforcement of Regulatory Legislation' *Criminal Law Review* 496

HAINES F, (1997) *Corporate Regulation—Beyond 'Punish or Persuade'* (Oxford, Clarendon Press)

HALVERSON JT, (1998) 'US Merger Policy: Economics and Efficiencies' A Global Competition Special Report *The United States Antitrust Review* 6

HAMMOND A and PENROSE R, (2001) *Proposed Criminalisation of Cartels in the UK* (London, Office of Fair Trading)

HANKS F and WILLIAMS P, (1990) 'The Treatment of Vertical Restraints under the Australian Trade Practices Act 1974' 17 *Melbourne University Law Review* 437

HARDING C, (1996) 'Diversity and Convergence in Enforcement' in C Harding and B Swart (eds), *Enforcing European Community Rules* (Aldershot, Dartmouth)

HARDING C, (1993) *European Community Investigations and Sanctions* (Leicester, Leicester University Press)

HARDING C and JOSHUA J, (2002) 'Breaking Up the Hard Core: the Prospects for the Proposed Cartel Offence' *Criminal Law Review* 931

HARLOW C and RAWLINGS R, (1999) *Law and Administration*, 2nd edn (London, Butterworths)

HART HLA, (1961) *The Concept of Law* (Oxford, Oxford University Press)

—— (1962) *Law, Liberty and Morality* (Oxford, Oxford University Press)

—— (1968) *Punishment and Responsibility* (Oxford, Clarendon Press)

HAWKINS K, (1984) *Environment and Enforcement* (Oxford, Clarendon Press)

—— (2002) *Law as Last Resort* (Oxford, Oxford University Press)

HAY D, (1989) 'The Assessment: Competition Policy' 9 *Oxford Review of Economic Policy* 1

HAY DA and MORRIS DJ, (1991) *Industrial Economics and Organization* (Oxford, Oxford University Press)

HAZARD G and ORTS E, (2001) 'Environmental Contracts in the United States' in Eric W Orts and Kurt Deketelaere (eds), *Environmental Contracts—Comparative Approaches to Regulatory Innovation in the United States and Europe* (London, Kluwer Law International Ltd)

HETHERINGTON ST, (1989) *Prosecution and the Public Interest* (London, Waterlow Publishers)

HIRSCH D, (2001) 'Understanding Project XL: A Comparative Legal and Policy Analysis' in Eric W Orts and Kurt Deketelaere (eds), *Environmental Contracts—Comparative Approaches to Regulatory Innovation in the United States and Europe* (London, Kluwer Law International Ltd)

HONDERICH T, (1969) *Punishment* (London, Penguin)

HOOD C, (1990) 'A Public Management for All Seasons' 69 *Public Administration* 3

HOOD C and SCOTT C, (1996) *Bureaucratic Regulation and New Public Management in the UK: Mirror-Image Developments?* , No 2 (London, London Schoool of Economics)

HOPKINS A, (1983) 'Marxist Theory and Australian Monopoly Law' in E Wheelwright and K Buckley (eds), *Essays in the Political Economy of Australian Capitalism* (Sydney, ANZ Books)

HORDER J, (2002) 'Strict Liability, Statutory Construction, and the Spirit of Liberty' 118 *Law Quarterly Review* 458

House of Representatives Committee on Legal and Constitutional Affairs, (1991) *Mergers, Monopolies & Acquisitions—Adequacy of Existing Legislative Controls* (Canberra, Parliament of Australia)

House of Representatives Committee on Legal and Constitutional Affairs, (1989) *Mergers, Takeovers and Monopolies: Profiting from Competition?* (Canberra, Parliament of Australia)

House of Representatives Standing Committee on Economics Finance and Public Administration, (2001) *Review of the ACCC 1999–2000 Annual Report* (Canberra, Parliament of Australia)

House of Representatives Standing Committee on Financial Institutions and Public Administration, (1997) *Review of the ACCC 1995–6 Annual Report* (Canberra, Parliament of Australia)

House of Representatives Standing Committee on Financial Institutions and Public Administration, (1998) *Review of the ACCC Annual Report 1996–7* (Canberra, Parliament of Australia)

HUNT M, (1997) 'Constitutionalism and the Contractualisation of Government' in M Taggart (ed) *The Province of Administrative Law Determined* (Oxford, Hart Publishing)

HUTTER B, (1988) *The Reasonable Arm of the Law?* (Oxford, Oxford University Press)

—— (1997) *Compliance: Regulation and Environment* (Oxford, Oxford University Press)

Industry Commission, (1995) *Work, Health and Safety: Inquiry into Occupational Health and Safety*, 47 (Canberra, Australian Government Publishing Service)

—— (1995a) *Regulation and its Review: 1995—96* (Canberra, Industry Commission)

—— (1996) *Merger Regulation: A Review of the Draft Merger Guidelines Administered by the ACCC* Industry Commission)

JACOB H, (1992) 'The Elusive Shadow of the Law' 26 *Law & Society Review* 565

JACONELLI J, (2002) *Open Justice: A Critique of the Public Trial* (Oxford, Oxford University Press)

JONES P, (1994) *Rights* (London, Macmillan)

JOWELL J, (2000) 'The Rule of Law Today' in D Oliver and J Jowell (eds), *The Changing Constitution* (Oxford, Oxford University Press)

JOWELL J and LESTER A, (1987) 'Beyond Wednesbury: Substantive Principles of Administrative Law' *Public Law* 368

JUSTICE, (1993) *Negotiated Justice : A Closer Look at the Implications of Plea Bargains* (London, Justice)

KADISH S, (1963) 'Some Observations on the Use of Criminal Sanctions in Enforcing Economic Regulations' 30 *The University of Chicago Law Review* 423

KAGAN R, (1994) 'Regulatory Enforcement' in RD Schwartz and DH Rosenbloom (eds), *Handbook of Regulation and Administrative Law* (New York, Marcel Dekker)

KAUPER TE, (1993) 'The Use of Consent Decrees in American Antitrust Cases' in PJ Slot and A McDonnell (eds), *Procedure and Enforcement in EC and US Competition Law* (Leiden, Sweet & Maxwell)

KELL D, (1997) 'Immunity From Prosecution for Prospective Illegal Conduct' 71 *Australian Law Journal* 553

KENCH J, (1998) 'Economics of Negotiated Penalties' 10 *ACCC Journal* 8

KIRZNER IM, (1973) *Competition and Entrepreneurship* (Chicago, Chicago University Press)

KLAIWITER DC, (2001) 'After the Deluge: The Powerful Effect of Substantial Criminal Fines, Imprisonment, and Other Penalties in the Age of International Cartel Enforcement' 69 *George Washington Law Review* 745

KLEIN S, (1999) 'Redrawing the Civil-Criminal Boundary' 2 *Buffalo Criminal Law Review* 679

KLEINIG J, (1978) 'Human Rights, Legal Rights and Social Change' in E Kamenka and A Erh-Soon Tah (eds), *Human Rights* (London, Edward Arnold)

KOBAYASHI BH, (2001) 'Antitrust, Agency, and Amnesty: An Economic Analysis of the Criminal Enforcement of the Antitrust Laws Against Corporations' 69 *George Washington Law Review* 715

KOLASKY W and LOWE JM, (1997) 'The Merger Review Process at the Federal Trade Commission: Administrative Efficiency and the Rule of Law' 49 *Administrative Law Review* 889

LACEY N, (1992) 'The Jurisprudence of Discretion: Escpaing the Legal Paradigm' in K Hawkins (ed) *The Uses of Discretion* (Oxford, Clarendon Press)

—— (1998) 'Punishment and Community' in A Ashworth and A von Hirsch (eds), *Principled Sentencing* (Oxford, Hart)

—— (2001) 'In Search of the Responsible Subject: History, Philosophy and Social Sciences in Criminal Law Theory' 64 *Modern Law Review* 350

LANDES W, (1983) 'Optimal Sanctions for Antitrust Violations' 50 *University of Chicago Law Review* 652

LANDES W and POSNER R, (1975) 'The Private Enforcement of Law' 4 *Journal of Legal Studies* 1

LANGBEIN J, (1978) 'Torture and Plea Bargaining' 46 *University of Chicago Law Review* 3

Law Reform Commission of Canada, (1989) *Plea Discussions and Agreements*, Working Paper 60 (Ottawa)

Law Reform Commission of Canada, (1992) *Immunity from Prosecution*, Working Paper 64 (Ottawa)

LEIGH L, (1982) *Strict and Vicarious Liability* (London, Sweet & Maxwell)

LENAERTS K and VANHAMME J, (1997) 'Procedural Rights of Private Parties in the Community Administrative Process' 34 *Common Market Law Review* 531

LEVITT M, (1997) 'Access to the File: The Commission's Administrative Procedures in Cases Under Articles 85 and 86' 34 *Common Market Law Review* 1413

LEWIS N, (1993) 'Reviewing Change in Government: New Public Management and Next Steps' *Public Law* 105

LITTLECHILD SC, (eds) (1990) *Austrian Economics* (Aldershot, Edward Elgar)

LOUGHLIN M, (2000) *Sword & Scales* (Oxford, Hart Publishing)

LUBAN D, (1994) *The Ethics of Lawyers* (Aldershot, Dartmouth Publishing)

—— (1995) 'Settlements and the Erosion of the Public Realm' 83 *Georgetown Law Journal* 2619

MACK K and ANLEU S, (1995) *Pleading Guilty: Issues and Practices* (Carlton South, Vic, Australian Institute of Judicial Administration)

MACK K, (1996) 'Guilty Pleas: Discussions and Agreements' 6 *Journal of Judicial Administration* 8

MAJONE G, (eds) (1992) *Deregulation or Re-regulation? Regulatory Reform in Europe and the United States* (London, Pinter Publishers)

—— (1996) *Regulating Europe* (London, Routledge)

MANN K, (1992) 'Punitive Civil Sanctions: The Middleground Between Criminal and Civil Law' 101 *Yale Law Journal* 1795

MARTIN J, (1993) 'Making the Giant Competitive Rather than Crushing—Industry Perspectives on Regulation Enforcement' in P Grabosky and J Braithwaite (eds), *Business Regulation and Australia's Future* (Canberra, Australian Institute for Criminology)

MASHAW J, (1983) *Bureaucratic Justice* (New Haven, Yale University Press)

MATRAVERS M, (1999) 'What to Say?': The Communicative Element in Punishment and Moral Theory' in M Matravers (ed) *Punishment and Political Theory* (Oxford, Hart Publishing)

MCEWEN CA and MAIMAN RJ, (1984) 'Mediation in Small Claims Court: Achieving Compliance Through Consent' 18 *Law & Society Review* 1

MCBARNET D and WHELAN C, (1991) 'The Elusive Spirit of the Law: Formalism and the Struggle for Legal Control' 54 *Modern Law Review* 848

MCCORMICK N, (1973) 'Rights in Legislation' in A W B Simpson (ed) *Oxford Essays in Jurisprudence* (Oxford, Clarendon Press)

MCDONALD W, (1985) *Plea Bargaining: Critical Issues and Common Practices* (Washington DC, US Department of Justice, National Institute of Justice)

MCELDOWNEY JF, (2000) 'The Control of Public Expenditure' in D Oliver and J Jowell (eds), *The Changing Constitution* (Oxford, Oxford University Press)

MCKAY I, (1998) 'Penalties, Remedies and Court Processes Under the Commerce Act 1986: A Commentary on the Ministry of Commerce Discussion Document' Paper presented at the 'Ninth Annual Workshop of the Competition Law and Policy', Wellington, 31 July

MENKEL-MEADOW C, (1993) 'Lawyer Negotiations: Theories and Realities—What We Learn From Mediation' 56 *Modern Law Review* 361

MNOOKIN R and KORNHAUSER L, (1979) 'Bargaining in the Shadow of the Law: The Case of Divorce' 88 *Yale Law Journal* 950

MONTAG F, (1996) 'The Case for a Reform of Regulation 17/62: Problems and Possible Solutions from a Practitioner's Point of View' 17 *European Competition Law Review* 428

MOORE M, (1998) 'The Moral Worth of Retribution' in A Ashworth and A von Hirsch (eds), *Principled Sentencing* (Oxford, Hart Publishing)

MORAN M, (2002) 'Understanding the Regulatory State' 32 *British Journal of Political Science* 391

MORGAN B, (2003) *Social Citizenship in the Shadow of Competition* (Dartmouth, Ashgate)

MORRIS N, (1998) 'Desert as a Limiting Principle' in A Ashworth and A von Hirsch (eds), *Principled Sentencing* (Oxford, Hart Publishing)

New Zealand Ministry of Commerce, (1988) *Penalties, Remedies and Court Processes Under The Commerce Act 1986—A Discussion Document* (Wellington, Commerce and Enterprise Branch)

NOAH L, (1997) 'Administrative Arm-Twisting In the Shadow of Congressional Delegations of Authority' *Wisconsin Law Review* 873

NONET P and SELZNICK A, (1995) *Law and Society in Transition* (Berkeley, University of California Press)

NORMAN N, (1993) 'Economists in the [Trade Practices] Act' 1 *Competition and Consumer Law Journal* 49

OECD, (2002) *Report on the Nature and Impact of Hard Core Cartels and Sanctions Against Cartels Under National Competition Laws*, DAFFE/COMP(2002)7 (Paris, OECD)

Office of Regulation Review, *Guide to Regulation* (2nd edn) Productivity Commission, 1998. Available from www.pc.gov.au/orr/reguide2/index.html.

Officer R and Williams P, (1995) 'The Public Benefit Test in an Authorisation Decision' in P Williamson and M Richardson (eds), *The Law and the Market* (Sydney, The Federation Press)

OGUS A, (1992) 'Regulatory Law: Some Lessons from the Past' 12 *Legal Studies* 1

—— (1994) *Regulation—Legal Form and Economic Theory* (Oxford, Oxford University Press)

O'KELLY C, (1979) 'The Constitutional Rights of Corporations Revisited: Social and Political Expression after *First National Bank v Belotti*' 69 *Georgetown Law Journal* 1347

OLIVER D, (1994) 'Law, Politics and Public Accountability: The Search for a New Equilibrium' *Public Law* 238

OLIVER D and DREWRY G, (1996) *Public Service Reform: Issues of Accountability and Public Law* (London, Pinter Publishing Ltd)

PARKER C, (2004) 'Restorative Justice in Business Regulation? The Australian Competition and Consumer Commission's Use of Enforceable Undertakings', *Modern Law Review*, forthcoming

—— (1999) *Summary of Scholarly Literature on Regulatory Compliance* (Paris, OECD)

—— (1999a) *The State of Regulatory Compliance: Issues, Trends and Challenges*, Report No PUMA/REG(99)3 (Paris, OECD)

PARKER RG, (1998) 'Trends in Enforcement and Litigation', *Address to the Annual Briefing for Corporate Counsel*, Washington DC, 16 September

PEARCE F and TOMBS S, (1990) 'Ideology, Hegemony, and Empiricism' 30 *British Journal of Criminology* 423

—— (1991) 'Policing Corporate "Skid Rows"' 31 *British Journal of Criminology* 415

PENGILLEY W, (1984) 'Competition Policy and Law Enforcement: Ramblings on Rhetoric and Reality' 2 *Australian Journal of Law & Society* 1

PILDES RH and SUNSTEIN CR, (1995) 'Reinventing the Regulatory State' 62 *University of Chicago Law Review* 1

POSNER RA, (1976) *Antitrust Law—An Economic Perspective* (Chicago, The University of Chicago Press)

—— (1977) *Economic Analysis of Law*, 2nd edn (Boston, Little, Brown & Co)

—— (1979a) 'The Chicago School of Antitrust Analysis' *University of Pennsylvania Law Review* 925

—— (1979) 'Utilitarianism, Economics & Legal Theory' 8 *Journal of Legal Studies* 103

—— (1985) 'An Economic Theory of Criminal Law' 85 *Columbia Law Review* 1193

POTAS I, (1984) *Prosecutorial Discretion* (Canberra, Australian Institute of Criminology)

POWER M, (1997) *The Audit Society* (Oxford, Oxford University Press)

PROSSER T, (1997) *Law and the Regulators* (Oxford, Clarendon Press)

RAZ J, (1977) 'The Rule of Law and its Virtue' 93 *Law Quarterly Review* 195

—— (1986) *The Morality of Freedom* (Oxford, Clarendon Press)

REISS A, (1984) 'Selecting Strategies of Social Control over Organisational Life' in K Hawkins and J Thomas (eds), *Enforcing Regulation* (Boston, Kluwer-Nijhoff)

RENFREE HE, (1984) *The Executive Power of the Commonwealth of Australia* (Sydney, Legal Books Pty Ltd)

Report by the Independent Committee of Inquiry, (1993) *National Competition Policy*, Australian Government Publishing Service (Canberra)

REYNOLDS SP, (1996) 'International Antitrust Compliance for a Company with Multinational Operations' 8 *International Quarterly* 76

RICHARDSON G, (1993) *Law, Process and Custody: Prisoners and Patients* (London, Butterworths)

—— (1994) 'The Legal Regulation of Process' in G Richardson and H Genn (eds), *Administrative Law & Government Action: The Courts and Alternative Mechanisms of Review* (Oxford, Blackwells)

RICHARDSON G, OGUS A and BURROWS P, (1984) *Policing Pollution* (Oxford, Clarendon Press)

RICHARDSON R, (1999) 'Guidance Without Guidance—A European Revolution in Fining Policy? The Commission's New Guidelines on Fines' 20 *European Competition Law Review* 360

ROUND DK, SIEGFRIED JJ and BAILLIE AJ, (1996) 'Collusive Markets in Australia: an Assessment of their Economic Characteristics and Judicial Penalties' 24 *Australian Business Law Review* 292

ROWAN-ROBINSON J, Watchman P and Barker C, (1990) *Crime and Regulation: A Study of the Enforcement of Regulatory Codes* (Edinburgh, T&T Clarke)

SAJO A, (1999) *Limiting Government—An Introduction to Constitutionalism* (Budapest, Central European University Press)

SALLMANN P, (1984) *Report on Criminal Trials* (Melbourne, Australian Institute for Judicial Administration)

SAVIN J, (1997) 'Tunney Act '96: Two Decades of Judicial Misapplication' 46 *Emory Law Journal* 363

SCHAEUR F, (1989) 'Formalism' 97 *Yale Law Journal* 509

—— (1991) *Playing by the Rules* (Oxford, Clarendon Press)

SCHERER F and ROSS D, (1990) *Industrial Market Structure and Economic Performance*, 3rd edn (Boston, Houghton Mifflin)

SCHULHOFER S, (1992) 'Plea Bargaining as Disaster' 101 *Yale Law Journal* 1979

SCHWARTZ LB, (1979) '"Justice" and Other Non-economic Goals of Antitrust' 127 *University of Pennsylvania Law Review* 1076

SCHWARTZ W, (1980) 'An Overview of the Economics of Antitrust Enforcement' 68 *Georgetown Law Journal* 1075

SCOTT C, (2000) 'Accountability in the Regulatory State' 27 *Journal of Law and Society* 38

SCOTT R and STUNTZ W, (1992) 'A Reply: Imperfect Bargains, Imperfect Trials and Innocent Defendants' 101 *Yale Law Journal* 2011

SEIDENFIELD M, (2000) 'An Apology for Administrative Law in the Contracting State' 28 *Florida State University Law Review* 215

—— (2000) 'Empowering Stakeholders: Limits on Collaboration as a Basis for Flexible Regulation' 72 *William & Mary Law Review* 411

SELLERS JM, (1984) 'Regulatory Values and the Exceptions process' 93 *Yale Law Journal* 938

SELWAY B, (1996) 'The Rise and Rise of the Reasonable Proportionality Test in Public Law' 7 *Public Law Review* 212

SELZINICK P, (1985) 'Focusing Organizational Research on Regulation' in R Noll (ed) *Regulatory Policy and the Social Sciences* (California, Berkeley)
SHAPIRO M, (1979) 'Compromise and Litigation' in J R Pennock and J W Chapman (eds), *Compromise in Ethics, Law and Politics* (New York, New York University Press)
SHARKEY WW, (1982) *The Theory of Natural Monopoly* (Cambridge, Cambridge University Press)
SHAVELL S, (1993) 'The Optimal Structure of Law Enforcement' *Journal of Law and Economics* 270
SHEARING C, (1993) 'A Constitutive Conception of Regulation' in P Grabosky and J Braithwaite (eds), *Business Regulation and Australia's Future* (Canberra, Australian Institute of Criminology)
SINCLAIR D, (1997) 'Self-Regulation Versus Command and Control? Beyond False Dichotomies' 19 *Law & Policy* 529
SMITH AM, (1999) 'SEC Cease-And-Desist Orders' 51 *Administrative Law Review* 1197
SMITH J, (1996) *Smith & Hogan Criminal Law*, 8th edn (London, Butterworths)
SMITH R and GRIMWADE T, (1997) 'Authorisation: Some Issues' 25 *Australian Business Law Review* 351
SPARROW M, (2000) *The Regulatory Craft* (Washington, Brookings Institution Press)
STEINER A and ALSTON P, (2000) *International Human Rights in Context—Law, Politics, Morals*, 2nd edn (Oxford, Oxford University Press)
TAGGART M, (1991) 'Corporatisation, Privatisation and Public Law' 2 *Public Law Review* 77
TAMBLYN J, (1993) 'Progress Towards a More Responsive Trade Practices Strategy' in P Grabosky and J Braithwaite (eds), *Business Regulation and Australia's Future* (Canberra, Australian Institute of Criminology)
TEMBY I, (1985) 'Immunity from Prosecution and the Provision of Witness Indemnities' 59 *Australian Law Journal* 501
THORPE J, (1996) 'Determining the Appropriate Role for Charge Bargaining in Part IV of the Trade Practices Act' 4 *Competition & Consumer Law Journal* 9
TOMBS J, (1984) "Prosecution—In the Public Interest?" Paper presented at the 'Prosecutorial Discretion Conference', Melbourne, 7–9 November
TONKING A and CASTLE L, (1993) 'Mergers: The Use and Utility of Undertakings' 1 *Trade Practices Law Journal* 37
TONKING AI, (1997) 'Letter to the Editor' *Trade Practices Law Journal* 274
Trade Practices Review Committee, (2003) *Review of the Competition Provisions of the Trade Practices Act* (Canberra, Commonwealth of Australia)
TRIBE L, (1978) *American Constitutional Law* (New York, Foundation Press)
TWINING W, (1993) 'Alternative to What? Theories of Litigation, Procedure and Dispute Settlement in Anglo-American Jurisprudence: Some Neglected Classics' 56 *Modern Law Review* 380
TWINING W and MIERS D, (1991) *How To Do Things With Rules*, 3rd edn (London, Weidenfeld)
VAN BAEL I, (1986) 'The Antitrust Settlement Practice of the EC Commission' 23 *Common Market Law Review* 61
—— (1995) 'Fining a la Carte: the Lottery of EU Competition Law' 16 *European Competition Law Review* 237
VINCENT-JONES P, (2002) 'Values and Purposes in Government: Central-local Relations in Regulatory Perspective' 29 *Journal of Law and Society* 27

VOGEL D, (1980) *National Styles of Regulation—Environmental Policy in Greater Britain and the United States* (New York, Cornell University Press)

VON HIRSCH A, (1981) 'Doing Justice: The Principle of Commensurate Deserts' in H Gross and A von Hirsch (eds), *Sentencing* (New York, Oxford University Press)

—— (1993) *Censure and Sanctions* (Oxford, Clarendon Press)

—— (1998) 'Desert and Previous Convictions' in A Ashworth and A von Hirsch (eds), *Principled Sentencing* (Oxford, Hart Publishing)

—— (1999) 'Punishment, Penance, and the State' in M Matravers (ed) *Punishment and Political Theory* (Oxford, Hart Publishing)

VON HIRSCH A and JAREBOURG N, (1991) 'Gauging Criminal Harm: A Living Standard Analysis' 11 *Oxford Journal of Legal Studies* 1

VON HIRSCH A and WASIK M, (1997) 'Civil Disqualifications Attending Conviction: A Suggested Conceptual Framework' 56 *Cambridge Law Journal* 599

VON KALINOWSKI JO, (1985) 'Consent Decrees' in JO Von Kalinowski (ed) *Antitrust Laws and Trade Regulation* (New York, Matthew Bender)

VORENBERG J, (1981) 'Decent Restraint of Prosecutorial Power' 94 *Harvard Law Review* 1521

WADHAM J, (1994) 'Miscarriages of Justice: Pre-trial and Trial Stages' in M McConville and L Bridges (eds), *Criminal Justice in Crisis* (Aldershot, Edward Elgar Publishing)

WAELBROECK D, (1986) 'New Forms of Settlement of Antitrust Cases and Procedural Safeguards: Is Regulation 17 Falling into Abeyance?' 11 *European Law Review* 263

—— (2002) 'Twelve Feet All Dangling Down and Six Necks Exceeding Long'. The EU Network of Competition Authorities and the ECHR' in C Ehrelerman and I Atanasiu (eds), *European Competition Law Annual* (Oxford, Hart Publishing)

WAELBROECK D and FOSSELLARD D, (1994) 'Should the Decision-Making Power in EC Antitrust Procedures be left to an Independent Judge?—The Impact of the ECHR on EC Antitrust Procedure' 14 *Yearbook of European Law* 111

WALKER J and WOODWARD L, (1996) 'The Ampol/Caltex Australia Merger: Trade Practices Issues' 4 *Trade Practices Law Journal* 21

WALKER N, (1980) *Punishment, Danger and Stigma* (Oxford, Blackwell)

WALLER SW, (1997) *AntiTrust & American Business Abroad*, 3rd edn (Clark, Boardman Callaghan)

WARNER P and TREBILCOCK M, (1993) 'Rethinking Price Fixing Law' 38 *McGill Law Journal* 679

WEBER M, (1954) *Law in Economy and Society* (Cambridge MA, Harvard University Press)

WELLMAN C, (1978) 'A New Conception of Human Rights' in E Kamenka and A Ehr-Soon Tay (eds), *Human Rights* (London, Edward Arnold)

WELLS C, (1993) *Corporations and Criminal Responsibility* (Oxford, Clarendon Press)

WERHAN K, (1996) 'Delegalizing Administrative Law' *University of Illinois Law Rev* 423

WESSELING R, (2001) 'The Draft-Regulation Modernising the Competition Rules: The Commission is Married to One Idea' 26 *European Law Review* 357

WHISH R, (2003) *Competition Law*, 5th edn (London, Lexis Nexis UK)

—— (2001) *Competition Law*, 3rd edn (London, Butterworths)

WILKS S and MCGOWAN L, (1995) 'Disarming the Commission: The Debate over a European Cartel Office' 32 *Journal of Common Market Studies* 259

WILLIAMS M, (1993) 'The Effectiveness of Competition Policy in the United Kingdom' 9 *Oxford Review of Economic Policy* 94

WILS W, (2003) 'Does the Effective Enforcement of Articles 81 and 82 EC Require Not Only Fines on Undertakings but Also Individual Penalties, in Particular Imprisonment?' in C Ehlermann and I Atanasiu (eds), *European Competition Law Annual 2001* (Oxford, Hart Publishing)

WILS W, (2002) 'EC Competition Fines: To Deter or Not to Deter' in Wouter Wils (ed) *The Optimal Enforcement of EC Antitrust Law* (The Hague, Kluwer Law International)

WONG G, (2000) 'Towards the Nutcracker Principle: Reconsidering Objections to Proportionality' *Public Law* 92

WOOD D, (2002) 'Retribution, Crime Reduction & Justification' 22 *Oxford Journal of Legal Studies* 301

YEUNG K, (1998) 'Privatising Competition Regulation' 18 *Oxford Journal of Legal Studies* 581

—— (1999) 'Quantifying Regulatory Penalties: Australian Competition Law Penalties in Perspective' 23 *Melbourne University Law Review* 440

—— (2001) *The Public Enforcement of Australian Competition Law* (Canberra, ACCC Publishing Unit)

ZEDNER L, (1994) 'Reparation and Retribution: Are They Reconcilable?' 57 *Modern Law Review* 228

ZIMRING FE, (1992) 'The Multiple Middlegrounds Between Civil and Criminal Law' 101 *Yale Law Journal* 1901

ZUCKERMAN A, (1989) 'Trial by Unfair Means—The Report of the Working Group on the Right to Silence' *Criminal Law Review* 855

ZUMBO F, (1997) 'Section 87B Undertakings: There's No Accounting for Such Conduct!' 5 *Trade Practices Law Journal* 121

Index

www.ingramcontent.com/pod-product-compliance
Ingram Content Group UK Ltd.
Pitfield, Milton Keynes, MK11 3LW, UK
UKHW020243290926
15470UKWH00002B/713

9 781841 133775